THE SOCIALIST REGISTER 1994

For Joe

May be
Transplant
a new heart
in The Left.

Leo

BETWEEN GLOBALISM AND NATIONALISM

SOCIALIST REGISTER 1994

Edited by RALPH MILIBAND and LEO PANITCH

THE MERLIN PRESS
LONDON

First published in 1994
by The Merlin Press Ltd
10 Malden Road
London NW5 3HR

British Library Cataloguing in Publication Data

The Socialist Register. — 1994
  1. Socialism — 1994
  I. Miliband, Ralph   II. Panitch, Leo
355'.005

ISBN 0-85036-441-8
ISBN 0-85036-440-X Pbk

Typesetting by
Computerset, Harmondsworth, Middlesex
Printed in Finland by WSOY

TABLE OF CONTENTS

PREFACE

This thirtieth issue of the *Socialist Register* opens with a survey of its direction, policy and output since its first appearance; and this is followed by John Saville's recollections of his work with Edward Thompson in 1956. Like countless people in Britain, America and elsewhere, we mourn Edward's death. He was a friend of the *Register* and we were privileged to publish some outstanding essays by him, notably *The Peculiarities of the English* (1965) and *An Open Letter to Leszek Kolakowski* (1973). Rather than add to the many obituaries which appeared when he died, we thought it would be of interest to our readers to have an account by John Saville, who worked closely with Edward at the time, of the events which led to their break with the Communist Party.

The essay by Norman Geras challenges Richard Rorty's anti-universalism by examining the motives of the 'righteous' in saving the lives of Jews in Nazi-occupied Europe.

The main theme of this year's *Register* – 'Between Globalism and Nationalism' – deals with the ever-greater global reach of capital and its impact on the policies of nation-states. The conventional wisdom on the Left has been that the internationalization of capital means that there is now very little space for national governments to adopt policies which run counter to the logic of international capital. We think that the *Register* is performing an important service in probing and challenging this assumption. This is the burden of the essays by Leo Panitch, Manfred Bienefeld, Arthur MacEwan and Gregory Albo. They demonstrate the dangers and limits of the practice of 'competitive austerity' into which even social democratic governments in the developed capitalist world are drawn by virtue of their acceptance of the logic of global competitiveness; and their essays advance the case for left strategies based on more inwardly-oriented and democratic economic alternatives, while avoiding the pitfalls of parochial and undemocratic nationalist reactions to globalism.

Although the rhetoric of 'free markets and democracy' infuses the ideology of globalism, the strategic dilemmas facing the Left in one country after another invariably centre on the incompatibility between progressive advances and global markets. This is the central theme of John Saul's essay on the dilemmas facing the African National Congress as it moves towards power in South Africa; and Gerard Greenfield's account of the development of capitalism in Vietnam under the auspices of the Communist Party demonstrates how dismal are the results of market fetishism. This is followed by a survey of the state of the Left in South East Asia by Kevin Hewison and Garry Rodan; and an essay by Poul Funder Larsen and David Mandel discusses the state of the Left in post-Communist Russia. Patty Lee Parmelee discusses the position of workers and intellectuals in the former German Democratic Republic under the Socialist Unity Party; and Eric Canepa analyses the nature and significance of the transformation of that party into Germany's Party of Democratic Socialism today.

Among our contributors, John Saville, who was for many years a co-editor of the *Register*, is Emeritus Professor of Economic and Social History at Hull University. Norman Geras teaches politics in the Department of Government, Manchester University. Manfred Bienefeld is in the School of Public Administration at Carleton University, Ottawa, and Arthur MacEwan teaches economics at the University of Massachusetts, Boston. Gregory Albo teaches in the Department of Political Science at York University, Toronto, as does John Saul, who is also Professor of Social Sciences at Atkinson College, which is part of York University. Gerard Greenfield is a doctoral candidate at the School of Humanities, Murdoch University, Western Australia. Garry Rodan is Senior Lecturer in Politics, also at Murdoch University, and Kevin Hewison is Professor of Asian Languages and Societies at the University of New England, New South Wales. Poul Funder Larsen is a Danish journalist and film-maker presently living in Moscow and David Mandel teaches politics at the Université du Québec, Montreal. Patty Lee Parmalee, an independent scholar and writer, and Eric Canepa, a harpsicordist and musicologist who is also editorial associate of the journal *Socialism and Democracy*, are both organizers at the New York Marxist School

We are very grateful to all our contributors, but we must once again note that neither they nor the editors necessarily agree with everything that appears in the following pages. We are also very grateful to Martin Eve and Julie Millard, of Merlin Press, for their indispensable help in the speedy production of this volume.

March 1994   R.M.
                                                                      L.P.

THIRTY YEARS OF *THE SOCIALIST REGISTER*

Ralph Miliband

1

Early in 1963, *New Left Review* was reorganised, minus most of its editorial board. NLR had been the product of a merger in 1959 between *Universities and Left Review* and *The New Reasoner*, a move to which I, as a member of the editorial board of the latter publication, was strongly opposed, on the ground that the two journals represented two very different currents of thought and experience, whose amalgamation would not produce happy results. *New Left Review*, under the editorship of Stuart Hall, led a rather chequered existence from 1959 to 1963, when it was taken over by Perry Anderson. The political path which NLR would follow under its new editors was not clear; and John Saville and I decided that a different publication was needed, which would embody the spirit which had informed *The New Reasoner*. Neither of us had the resources or the time to edit a quarterly or bi-monthly periodical; but we thought we might be able to manage an annual publication.

In a memorandum dated 7th April 1963, I proposed that Edward Thompson, John Saville and myself should publish a socialist annual between 300 and 400 pages in length, which would include articles on socialist theory and practice, labour history and contemporary events; book reviews and reviews of socialist classics; a calendar of events of interest to socialists; and a review of the year in relation to labour and socialist movements around the world; plus a review of important events of the year, analysed, like all else, in a socialist perspective.

Edward Thompson expressed strong support for the idea of an annual publication, but declined to be a co-editor, and he warned that to publish an annual that would serve as a record would be a formidable editorial task. He was obviously right, and we very soon scaled down our ambitions to the publication of an annual volume of essays that would constitute 'a survey of movements and ideas', which was the sub-title we gave to what became *The Socialist Register*. We owed the title itself to Martin Eve, who ran Merlin Press, and who agreed to publish the annual, which he has done from 1964 to the present. It is unlikely that it would have seen the light of day without his support, or that it would have gone on for all these years without his unfailing help. We were also fortunate in having *Monthly Review Press* of New York as our American publisher for the first two issues, and again, after an interval of some years, for all subsequent issues.

Both John Saville and I had no doubt that a socialist annual that was not an annual of record was a rather unusual type of publication on the Left, and that it would not make possible the kind of prompt response to events which could more easily be managed in a monthly, bi-monthly or quarterly journal. On the other hand, we hoped that an annual would allow a more reflective and measured type of essay. Also, an annual would provide the space for articles of a length that journals could not normally accept.

In retrospect, it is perhaps remarkable that at no time did John Saville and I devote any time to the discussion of the ideological and political orientation of the prospective publication. This was, I suppose, due to the fact that he and I had been discussing questions of socialist theory and practice for some years previously and had found ourselves in rough (sometimes very rough) agreement; and there was also a largely unspoken agreement between us that we would mainly publish work that would fall within the broad Marxist tradition to which, with rather different political histories, we both belonged – he had for many years until 1956 been a member of the Communist Party, I had always viewed myself as an independent socialist, who had joined the Labour Party in the early fifties as a way of working with Labour Left people whose leader (in so far as he was willing to lead at all) was then Aneurin Bevan; and I had left the Labour Party around 1960, when this no longer seemed worth doing.

Before discussing the *Register* further, something should be said about its editorship. From 1964 to 1983, it was edited by John Saville and myself, with the exception of the 1982 volume, when we took a 'sabbatical' and the *Register* was edited by Martin Eve and David Musson, who worked with him at Merlin Press – an unusual case of a publisher turning editor. In 1984, Marcel Liebman became a third co-editor; and with the double volume of 1985/6, Leo Panitch became a fourth one. To our deep sorrow, Marcel Liebman died soon after the publication of that volume. In 1990, John Saville decided that the time had come for him to cease being a co-editor (a move which I had resisted for a good many years), and the editorship has since then remained with Leo and me. With the 1984 volume, we decided that each volume should henceforth be devoted to one broad theme, and so it has been until now.

2

I do not propose to present here a comprehensive catalogue of the articles which the *Register* has published over the years, an enterprise that would be as tiresome for the reader as for the writer; but it may nevertheless be useful to go into some detail about the contents of the first two issues, 1964 and 1965, since what appeared then reflects accurately the themes which constantly recurred in subsequent issues.

The 1964 volume opened with an essay on Maoism by Isaac Deutscher, who had strongly encouraged us to proceed with an annual, and who was then at the height of his renown as an analyst of Communist affairs and as the biographer of Stalin and Trotsky. That volume also included articles by Ernest Mandel on neo-capitalism, André Gorz (writing under the pseudonym Michel Bosquet) on Italian Communism, Anouar Abdel Malek on Nasserism, an essay by Jean-Marie Vincent on West Germany, and one by Hamza Alavi on 'Imperialism Old and New'. John Saville contributed an acerbic essay on *Encounter*, then a major influence in the dissemination of Cold War liberalism. An essay by Marcel Liebman discussed the significance of 1914 for labour and socialist movements; and another by Royden Harrison discussed the relationship of the British labour movement to the First International; and there were also articles by the co-editors on 'Labour Policy and the Labour Left'; by Victor Kiernan on imperialism; by Vic Allen and Jim Mortimer on trade unionism; by Michael Barratt Brown on 'Nationalization in Britain'; and so on.

The 1965 volume was equally remarkable for the exceptional quality of the material it presented. Under the rubric of Contemporary Politics, the volume included another essay by Isaac Deutscher, this time on 'The Failure of Khrushchevism' (Khrushchev had been deposed in 1963); an essay by K.S. Karol on 'The People's Democracies'; and another essay by Jean-Marie Vincent on East Germany. The same section also had essays by Francis Jeanson and Richard Fletcher on Algeria, and an essay by D.A. Nicholas Jones on 'Arabia – the British Sphere'.

A second section, on Britain, had a prescient essay by Dorothy Wedderburn on 'Facts and Theories of the Welfare State' which concluded that 'welfare state legislation in capitalist society is a battleground not only for the short-term solution of immediate social problems but also for the longer-term battle of ideas'; 'the former, she noted, 'has received much attention from the Left; the latter all too little'; an article by John Saville on 'Labour and Income Redistribution' assailed the 'utter wrongheadedness of the Labour intellectuals after 1950' who proclaimed how great had been the redistribution of income in the previous years; and two articles, by Tony Topham and Ken Coates, on income policy, then a very live issue in the labour movement.

The third section, on Theory and History, included an essay by Georg Lukács on 'Solzhenitsyn and the New Realism', an essay by Hamza Alavi on Peasants and Revolution, an essay by me on 'Marx and the State', a subject which, remarkably enough, had attracted little attention on the Left after Lenin's *The State and Revolution* of 1917; and last, but very much not least, Edward Thompson's 'The Peculiarities of the English', a stringently critical discussion of the work which Perry Anderson and Tom

Nairn had published in *New Left Review* on English history, notably Perry Anderson's 'The Origins of the Present Crisis'.

3

As noted, it was these and related topics which were explored in subsequent years. Again and again, the *Register* came back to the changes that were occurring in contemporary capitalism; to the critique of Western, notably American, imperialism, and this was linked to reports on independence struggles in the 'third world', particularly in Africa; to the analysis and critique of social democratic and Communist parties in various countries, notably Western Europe; to the analysis and critique of Communist regimes, particularly the Soviet Union; and successive issues also discussed various questions of Marxist theory, questions of socialist strategy, and aspects of labour and socialist history.

Perhaps the most notable feature of the *Register*'s output is how consistent was its perspective over the years. Consistency is not necessarily the most admirable of virtues, since it may well indicate a stubborn blindness to changes that are occurring in the world. On the other hand, it may also indicate a refusal to indulge in passing fads and fashions. We avoided this; and while the *Register*, for instance, took account of such episodes as the 1968 'May events' in France, and similar eruptions elsewhere, the article by Lucio Magri in the 1969 issue, 'The May Events and Revolution in the West', was a careful appreciation of the fact that for revolutionary change to occur, 'there must be forces which are capable and determined enough to make good use of the chances offered by history', and that 'from this point of view, the May experience tells us that this is no simple matter'. The same volume also included some sober reflections by Victor Kiernan on the role of the intelligentsia and by John Cowley on the likely impact of student protest on the university. In a different context but in the same vein, and in a period when guerilla struggles in Latin America, with peasants as the main actors in these struggles, were widely thought on the revolutionary Left to be the key to revolutionary advance, the 1970 issue of the *Register* included an article by Victor Kiernan which warned of the limitations of 'voluntarism', and argued that 'further expansion of socialism in either the advanced or the undeveloped regions seems to depend on the emergence of a combination of forces. . . . It does not seem likely to be brought about by the peasantry alone, any more than by the working class alone, to say nothing of the lesser forces that have been hopefully thought of, like the intelligentsia or the student movement'. For his part, Eric Hobsbawm, in an essay on 'Guerillas in Latin America' in the same issue, presented a remarkable survey of guerilla struggles in a number of countries, and concluded that 'revolution in Latin America . . . is likely to combine social forces – peasants, workers, the marginal urban poor, students, sectors of the middle strata . . .'; also that 'when a prolonged struggle is envisaged (as in the classical theory of revolutionary guerillas) organisation is more crucial than ever and political analysis is indispensable'. Even these cautious and thoughtful remarks reflect a degree of optimism about the possibilities of revolutionary change which is now out of fashion – for how long it is impossible to say. At least, what we published was free from a naive belief that revolution was five, or at the most ten minutes, away. In 1978, we published an essay by Tariq Ali, 'Revolutionary Politics: Ten Years after 1968', which suggested that 'the central political lessons of the last ten years can be summed up in a sentence: a socialist revolution in the West will either be made with the consent of the working masses or it will not be made at all'.

The character which the *Register* assumed was obviously due in large part to our choice of contributors: from the start, it was understood between the co-editors that we would mostly call on people who occupied a place on the political spectrum well on the left of social democracy, but who were not the prisoners of sectarianism and dogma. The key term (one greatly favoured by Marx) was 'critique'. The weakness of that approach was that it did not dispose us to explore in depth the tremendous problems which the construction of the new social order in which we and our contributors believed was bound to present. This is a weakness which was shared by the socialist Left as a whole. Whereas social democrats have tended to be obsessed by the problems, and paralysed by their acuity, socialists to the left of them have tended to ignore the problems, or to belittle them, or to rely on sloganeering as a substitute for serious engagement with them. This is the weakness which Leszek Kolakowski, in his rejoinder in the 1974 *Register*, to Edward Thompson's splendid 'Open Letter to Leszek Kolakowski' in the 1973 *Register*, accurately and bitterly pinpointed. Thompson's essay was, as well as much else, an eloquent and moving defence of an open, critical Marxism – critical not least of the Marxist canon itself. The essay exemplified the kind of theoretical work which is an essential preface to programmatic work, but which is no more than a preface to that work.

To say that the *Register* ignored the problems of socialist construction is perhaps a little unfair. The 1964 volume did have an article by John Saville and myself on the Labour Left and what it ought to press for. Also in 1964, Michael Barratt Brown was suggesting how nationalisation might be improved. In 1968, we published a major essay by André Gorz on 'Reform and Revolution', in which he formulated his influential thesis of socialist advance by way of structural reforms; and the 1969 volume, as noted, also had an essay by Lucio Magri which explored the same question. The 1973 volume had an essay by me on what lessons socialists should draw from the overthrow of Salvador Allende in Chile about the difficulties of socialist advance. The 1974 volume included a critical review by Richard Hyman of the publications issued by the Institute of Workers' Control; and the 1975 volume had a reply to that essay by Michael Barratt Brown, Ken Coates and Tony Topham. In 1981, we published a searching essay by Raymond Williams on 'An Alternative Politics'; and subsequent volumes also did address various questions relevant to socialist construction.

Even when all this is taken into account, however, the point seems to me to remain valid that we did not address the question of socialist construction with anything like the rigorous and detailed concern which it requires. To people who might, honestly and not rhetorically, have asked, 'what would *you* do?', the *Register* did not return a sufficiently plausible answer. There are people on the Left who would say that the answer should be 'nothing much can be done until the revolution, save preparing for it'; but even if this were to be taken as realistic, 'preparing for it' would still involve a series of struggles over specific issues, with a clear indication of what was being struggled for, and without resort to incantation. We were far from the worst culprits in not being more specific about what socialist construction entailed; but we should have tried harder to present material on the subject.

4

The *Register* began in its early days to carry articles on a subject which was to grow in importance as the years went on, namely the internationalisation of capital and what this meant for the Left. In 1966, we published an article by Michael Barratt Brown on 'European Capitalism and World Trade', and in 1967 one by Ernest Mandel on 'International Capitalism and "Supra-Nationality"'; and the 1974 issue had a remarkably prescient article by Walter Goldstein with the significant title 'The Multinational Corporation: A Challenge to Contemporary Socialism'. I thought then that he was exaggerating the constraints which multinational corporations imposed on national states, and I indicated my disagreement with him in the Preface I wrote for the volume; he obviously had a far better grasp of what the prospects were in this respect than I had. Somewhat distant from 'globalisation', yet related to it, an essay by Peter Worsley in the 1980 *Register* was critical of Immanuel Wallerstein's world system theory; and in 1981, an essay by William Graf was sharply critical of the Brandt Report on the North-South divide.

It was only in 1990 that we again picked up the transnational theme with an essay by Stephen Gill on 'Intellectuals and Transnational Capital'; and the 1992 volume, whose title was 'The New World Order?' included, apart from an introduction from the editors on 'The New World Order and the Socialist Agenda', a number of major essays by Robert Cox, Harry Magdoff, Andrew Glyn and Bob Sutcliffe, Immanuel Wallerstein, John

Palmer and Stephen Gill, which dealt in one way or another with the internationalisation of capital and its significance for the Left.

5

Given our critique of social democracy, one issue which did keep popping up in the *Register* was that of *agencies*. On this, in relation to Britain, there were three distinct positions. On the one hand, there were those who believed that socialists had no alternative but to work inside the Labour Party, and to try and push it in more radical directions. On the other hand, there were those who thought that what was needed was a new socialist party, which would not supplant the Labour Party, but which would establish a socialist presence which neither that party, nor any other – certainly not the Communist Party – was able to achieve; and there were also those who, in the later years, thought that new social movements and grassroots organisations were far more important than parties.

The first position was very cogently represented in the 1973 volume by Ken Coates with an essay on 'Socialists and the Labour Party'. This essay, I should add, was in reply to a Postscript of 1969 to a second edition of my *Parliamentary Socialism*, in which I had suggested that the notion of turning the Labour Party into a socialist party was illusory. In the 1976 issue, I argued for 'the formation of a socialist party free from the manifold shortcomings of existing organisations' so as 'to provide a credible and effective rallying point to help in the struggle against the marked and accelerating drift to the right in Britain'. This produced not a ripple – not that I had really expected that it would. The argument continued in the 1977 *Register* with an article by Duncan Hallas which said that 'moving on' (the title of my article) was 'only possible on a revolutionary basis' and that the Socialist Workers Party had 'made some modest progress on that basis'. For his part, Leo Panitch, in an essay in the 1979 volume entitled 'Socialists and the Labour Party: A Reappraisal', concluded, after a closely-argued analysis of recent experience, that, while the Labour Party would not 'conveniently fall apart', it was 'by no means inappropriate to ask' whether socialists should not come together to begin building a party 'that would be free from all the burdens that come with the Labour Party tradition'.

Ken Coates came back to the issue after the Labour Party's defeat in the general election of 1983, with an essay on 'The Labour Party and the Future of the Left' in the volume of that year. He noted the dramatic extent of Labour's loss of support and was scathing about the Labour leaders' attempts 'to pull the Party's political commitments back to levels accept-able to the editor of *The Sun* and to their own well-established identifica-tion with the logic of private capital accumulation and US imperialism' – strictures which have remained remarkably apposite ever since. The question, he concluded, was whether 'the Labour Party can be persuaded quickly to make a sharp break with its own past', or whether, 'as seems more likely, the politics of fudge predominate again', in which case 'socialists will have to leave the Party and take on the undeniably more difficult task of consolidating a new Left that has no official Labour Party presence within it at all'. In the 1988 volume, devoted to the theme 'Problems of Socialist Renewal: East and West', Leo Panitch, in an essay on 'Socialist Renewal and the Labour Party', noted that while socialists had recently been concerned 'with associating the struggle for socialism with the struggles of new social movements', what had been missing from even the most creative currents was 'a much more serious analysis of what kind of political organisation could embody a renewed socialist project'. Most of the essay was concerned with both the strengths and the limitations of the upsurge of the Labour Left in the early eighties, and with its defeat at the hands of the Labour leadership, and concluded that socialist renewal 'will have to concentrate less on reforming the Labour Party and more on building a long-term independent campaign for a democratic socialism that transcends the limits of parliamentary paternalism'. This represented an acknowledgement of the importance of grassroots movements, and the *Register* did carry in the eighties material on the green and feminist movements, but we did not explore in any systematic way the relationship which these movements might have to the political parties which we believed socialist advance required.

The 1985/6 *Register* had as its theme 'Social Democracy and After', and continued the earlier critique of social democracy but greatly widened the scope of the analysis. A number of authors discussed what George Ross and Jane Jenson called 'the crisis of left politics' and Leo Panitch called 'the impasse of social democratic politics'. These and other articles in the volume discussed in depth the economic, social, political and cultural factors which had led to the crisis of left politics in France, Germany, Australia, Greece, and an essay by Frank Webster dealt with 'The Politics of the New Technology'. A number of other essays also offered more general reflections on the same theme; and most of them called for a new left politics that would not be mired either in the politics of accommodation of social democracy, or in the self-ghettoisation of the sectarian left. There were in the volume useful hints as to what such a new left politics would require; but these were no more than hints. The same volume also carried essays by John Saville and Richard Hyman on the miners' strike of 1984-85, essays by Andrew Gamble on the Austrian critique of socialism, by Mario Nuti on economic planning in market economies, a review by Roland Lew of Alec Nove's *The Economics of Feasible Socialism*, an essay by Ernest Mandel on 'Marx, the Present Crisis and the Future of Labour', and one by Mateo Alaluf on 'Work and the Working Class'.

The crisis of left politics of course also encompassed Communist parties, and the *Register* devoted a good deal of attention to their evolution. Rather belatedly, it had an article in 1969 by Rex Mortimer on the obliteration of the Indonesian Communist Party in 1965 and the massacre of hundreds of thousands of Communists and alleged Communists. In 1971, an article by Daniel Singer on 'The French Left since 1968' included some critical reflections on the PCF and the Communist-led CGT. The volume for 1976 had a section marking the twentieth anniversary of Khrushchev's 'secret' speech at the 20th Congress of the CPSU and the Soviet invasion of Hungary. Articles by John Saville, Malcolm MacEwen, and Margot Heinemann discussed the impact of Khrushchev's speech on the British Communist Party, and articles by Jean Pronteau, Maurice Kriegel-Valrimont and Rossana Rossanda dealt with its impact on the French and Italian parties. For their part, Mervyn Jones and Bill Lomax wrote about Hungary and Soviet intervention. In 1977, the *Register* included an essay by George Ross on 'The New Popular Front in France', which was mainly devoted to the PCF; and another essay in 1978 by him discussed 'The Crisis in Eurocommunism: the French Case'. A third essay by him and Jane Jenson on 'Conflicting Currents in the PCF' in the 1981 volume brought the analysis forward to the eve of the Left's presidential and legislative victories of that year. The 1988 volume, entitled 'Problems of Socialist Renewal' included another essay by George Ross on 'Organization and Strategy in the Decline of French Communism', and an essay by Stephen Hellman on 'The Crisis of Italian Communism'. The titles indicate the point of view which inspired these pieces.

The *Register* also paid some attention to the question of agencies as it related to the United States. In 1967, we published an essay by Ronald Aronson and John Cowley on 'The New Left in the United States', and in 1968 an essay by Franklin Adler on 'Black Power', which analysed the development of black consciousness in the sixties. In 1979, Jerome Karabel took up the age-old question 'Why is There No Socialism in the United States?'; and in 1980, Stanley Aronowitz discussed 'The Labour Movement and the Left in the United States'. In the 1985/6 volume, Vincente Navarro analysed 'The 1980 and 1984 US Elections and the New Deal', and showed how brittle and limited in terms of electoral support had been Reagan's electoral victories in the presidential elections of those years – very much like Thatcher's electoral victories. In 1987, Kim Moody had an essay on 'Reagan, the Business Agenda and the Collapse of Labour'; and a number of essays on the United States appeared in that 1987 volume and will be noted presently in a different context. In 1988, Joshua Cohen and Joel Rogers discussed '"Reaganism" After Reagan'; and Vincente Navarro analysed 'Social Movements and Class Politics in the United States'. In 1992, Joel Kovel wrote on post-Communist anti-communism, and Scott Forsyth gave us an article on Hollywood, 'Hollywood's War on the World: The New World Order as Movie'.

6

As I noted at the beginning, a notable feature of the *Register* was the amount of space it devoted to Western imperialism and liberation struggles in the 'third world'. We were extremely fortunate in being able to enlist the help of Basil Davidson, with his deep insights into the African experience, and were happy to publish a number of articles by him. Another of our most valuable contributors on African struggles was John Saul. He first appeared in the *Register* in 1969 with an essay (jointly with Giovanni Arrighi) on 'Nationalism and Revolution in Sub-Saharan Africa'; in 1973 with an essay on 'Neo-Colonialism versus Liberation Struggle'; in 1974 with an essay on 'The State in Post-Colonial Societies: Tanzania'; in 1980 on Zimbabwe; in 1989 on 'The Southern African Revolution'; and in 1993 with an essay on 'Rethinking the Frelimo State'. We also published essays on Africa by a good many other people – Jules Gérard-Libois in 1966 on 'The New Class and Rebellion in the Congo' and Jitendra Mohan on 'Varieties of African Socialism', Conor Cruise O'Brien on Arthur Lewis's *Politics in West Africa*, Robin Cohen on class in Africa, Ben Turok on South Africa, Jo Slovo in 1973 on 'Problems of Armed Struggle', Colin Leys on Kenya, Suzanne Muller on Tanzania. There is in this instance, for most of Africa, a sad trajectory, from the high hopes of the sixties to the disappointments of later years, encapsulated in the title of Basil Davidson's essay of 1992, 'Africa: The Politics of Failure'.

A fair amount of work published in the *Register* also dealt with other parts of the 'third world'. In 1966, we published a wide-ranging essay by Malcolm Caldwell, whose murder in Cambodia was a grievous loss to the Left. In the same issue, we also published some reflections by Victor Kiernan on 'India and Pakistan: Twenty Years Later'. By 1967, the war in Vietnam was raging with ever more ferocious intensity, and the *Register* published an article by me noting the fact 'brought home every day by the constant stream of news and images from Vietnam, that the United States has over what is now a period of years been engaged there in the wholesale slaughter of men, women and children, the maiming of many more, the obliteration of numberless villages and the forcible transplantation of whole populations into virtual concentration camps, the use of gas and chemical warfare, the devastation of large areas of cultivation, and much else which forms part of a catalogue of horrors which has by now been abundantly, sickeningly documentated'. However, the article, entitled 'Vietnam and the Western Left', was not only concerned to condemn the war which the United States was waging in Vietnam; its main purpose was to suggest how grave and bitter had been the default of the Left in Britain in failing to mount far greater opposition to the Wilson Government's 'consistent defence of American actions in Vietnam', which I described as 'the most shameful chapter in the history' of the Labour Party.

Articles already mentioned dealt with different facets of imperialism, and in 1971 and in 1974, we also published essays by Victor Kiernan, 'Imperialism, American and European' and 'American Hegemony under Revision', which placed imperialism in an historical perspective. In 1983, we published an essay by Paul Joseph on 'Nuclear Strategies and American Foreign Policy'; and most of the articles we published in 1984 in a volume on 'The Uses of Anti-Communism' also dealt with general reflections on imperialism and with its manifestations in different countries – Philip Brenner on U.S. policy in Central America, James Petras and Morris Morley on 'Anti-Communism in Guatemala: Washington's Alliance with Generals and Death Squads', and Alan Wolfe on 'Ideology and Interest in Postwar American Foreign Policy'. The 1987 volume also had an article by Larry Pratt on 'The Reagan Doctrine and the Third World', and another article by Scott Forsyth on Hollywood's contribution to the ideology of American interventionism.

In 1988 and 1989, the *Register* carried articles by Carlos Vilas, the one on 'War and Revolution in Nicaragua', and the other on 'Revolution and Democracy in Latin America'; and in 1991, Carlos Vilas helped us again with an essay on the shortcomings of the Sandinista regime. The same volume also had articles by Val Mogadham on Iran and by Saul Landau on Cuba, which allied warm support for the revolution with sharp criticism of the regime's failings.

7

There were not many years after the first two issues in which the *Register* did not include articles on the Soviet Union or other Communist regimes. In 1968 and 1969, we published two posthumous essays by Isaac Deutscher (he had died in 1967 at the tragically early age of 60), one of them entitled 'Ideological Trends in the USSR', the other 'Roots of Bureaucracy'. The 1968 volume also included an essay by Michael Ellman on 'Soviet Economic Reforms' and one by K.S. Karol on 'Two Years of the Cultural Revolution'. In 1973, an article of mine, 'Stalin and After', reviewed two books by the Soviet historian Roy Medvedev, one on Stalinism, *Let History Judge*, the other on socialist democracy. In the 1974 issue, Rossana Rossanda discussed 'Revolutionary Intellectuals and the Soviet Union', and Jean-Marie Chauvier analysed the work of Solzhenitsyn. In 1977, Wlodzimierz Brus recalled 'The Polish October – Twenty Years Later'. In 1978, we carried a self-interview by Rudolph Bahro, and an essay by Tamara Deutscher on 'Voices of Dissent' in the USSR. The 1981 issue had an essay by Mario Nuti on 'The Polish Crisis: Economic Factors and Constraints', and also included an essay by Isaac Deutscher which had first appeared in *Les Temps Modernes* on 'The Tragedy of the Polish Communist Party'. The same issue reprinted Christa Wolf's speech on receiving the

Buchner Prize in October 1980; and it also had an essay by Ernest Mandel
on the Chinese economy. In 1983, we had an essay by Roy Medvedev on
'The Soviet Union at the Beginning of a New Era'. This referred to the
demise of Leonid Brezhnev and the hope which it engendered that 'in the
next few years there will be a serious renewal in all the leading departments
of government, and that younger, more intelligent, more highly qualified
and bolder persons will be promoted to the leading posts'. This anticipated
by three years the coming to power of Mikhail Gorbachev. What no one
anticipated was the catastrophic results which the incoherent nature of the
reforms which Gorbachev set in train would ultimately produce. In 1988,
the *Register* published articles by K.S. Karol, R.W. Davis, Patrick
Flaherty and David Mandel on different aspects of the Gorbachev revolution, and on China by Roland Lew, but it was only in 1991, when the
Register was devoted to the theme of 'Communist Regimes: the Aftermath', that a series of articles did analyse in depth the failings of *perestroika*, again with the help of David Mandel and Patrick Flaherty, and
also Justin Schwarz, Robert Cox, Ernest Mandel, Daniel Singer and two
Soviet authors, Alexander Buzgalin and Andrei Kalganov, who boldly
entitled their essay 'For a Socialist Rebirth: A Soviet View'. The same
issue also carried an essay by Peter Bihari on post-Communist Hungary,
and one by Susan Woodward on Yugoslavia. Taken as a whole, it seems
fair to say that the material we published on the Soviet Union and the
Communist regimes over the years was balanced and well-reasoned, terms
which hardly apply to so much else that was written on the Soviet Union.
On the other hand, it may be said in retrospect that the essays which were
published in the *Register* on Maoism, though critical of some of its aspects,
did not sufficiently emphasise how disastrously destructive was much of its
practice. But I do not recollect the editors themselves making that point at
the time.

8

As I look back on the volumes of the *Register*, one of its strongest features
seems to me to be the work we published on Marxist theory, and socialist
theory in general. Here too, it would be tedious to catalogue all that we
published, but some of the items which appeared over the years should be
noted. An article by Peter Sedgwick in the 1966 volume reflected well the
critical spirit in which we wanted articles on these topics to be written.
Sedgwick's article was a scholarly and sharply critical review of Herbert
Marcuse's *One-Dimensional Man*, which was then much acclaimed, and
which Sedgwick contrasted very unfavourably with earlier work of Marcuse, notably his *Reason and Revolution*: 'the work of critical philosophy,
rooted in Hegel and Marx, that Marcuse pioneered in *Reason and Revolution*', Sedgwick wrote, 'now has been almost entirely abandoned in favour

of a grandiose journalism of doom', and he gave ample evidence for this negative verdict. In 1967, the *Register* carried a notable essay by Maurice Godelier on 'System, Structure and Contradiction in *Capital*'. Victor Kiernan gave us an essay on 'Marx and India', and in 1968 another essay entitled 'Notes on Marxism in 1968' (the 150th anniversary of Marx's birth), which suggested that 'the time has come, or rather has long since been coming, when Marxism needs a thorough spring-cleaning, or a throwing overboard of mouldy stores'. Also in 1968, we published an essay by John Merrington on 'Theory and Practice in Gramsci's Marxism', an essay which still had then something of a pioneer quality. The 1970 *Register* carried a number of articles on Marxism and questions of socialism – Rossana Rossanda on 'Class and Party', Jean-Paul Sartre on 'Masses, Spontaneity, Party', Harold Wolpe on 'Some Problems Concerning Revolutionary Consciousness', Hal Draper on 'The Death of the State in Marx and Engels', and myself on 'Lenin's *The State and Revolution*'. The 1971 issue had a similarly generous spread of articles on these themes. Apart from Rossana Rossanda' essay on Mao's Marxism, it carried an essay by Hal Draper on 'The Principle of Self-Emancipation in Marx and Engels', and a thorough demolition of Althusser's scientific pretensions by Leszek Kolakowski, this at a time when Althusser was being hailed by many Marxists as the thinker who had at long last established Marxism on a solid scientific foundation. The same issue of the *Register* also had an essay by István Mészáros on 'Alienation and Social Control', and one by Jeff Coulter on 'Marx and the Engels Paradox'. In 1972, we published another essay on Gramsci and Marxism, this time by Victor Kiernan, and two other theoretical essays, one by István Mészáros on 'Ideology and Social Science', the other by Anthony Arblaster on 'Liberal Values and Socialist Values'. Still in the same issue, Peter Worsley had an essay which discussed in depth the work of Frantz Fanon.

I have already noted the appearance in the 1973 *Register* of Edward Thompson's 'Open Letter to Leszek Kolakowski', which was a hundred pages long: whatever the shortcomings of an annual, we felt that it at least made it possible to carry an essay of that length. As also noted earlier, the 1974 volume had a reply by Kolakowski, 'My Correct Views on Everything'; and it was also in that issue that Hal Draper published another essay on Marx, this time on 'Marx on Democratic Forms of Government'; and this essay was accompanied by an essay written by Alastair Davidson on 'Gramsci and Lenin; 1917–1922'. Still in that issue, George Ross had a highly critical review of Daniel Bell's *The Coming of Post–Industrial Society*. In 1976, we published an essay by Ben Fine and Laurence Harris on 'Controversial Issues in Marxist Economic Theory'; and feminism at last made its appearance in that year's *Register* in the form of an essay by Hal Draper and Anne Lipow, 'Marxist Women versus Bourgeois Feminism', in which the authors sought 'to revive acquaintance with a revolutionary women's movement which was undoubtedly the most important one of the kind that has yet been seen', namely the women's movement in pre-1914 Germany, deeply inspired by Marxism. In that article, Draper and Lipow presented work by August Bebel, Clara Zetkin, Rosa Luxemburg, Louise Kautsky and Eleanor Marx, which showed how seriously the 'women's question' had been taken by men and women steeped in classical Marxism. A year later, a section of the *Register*, was devoted to Marxist economic theory, with an essay by Geoff Hodgson, 'Papering Over the Cracks', which consisted of strongly critical comments on the essay by Fine and Harris in the previous year's volume, and a response to Hodgson from them. That issue also had an essay by Marion Sawyer on 'The Genesis of *State and Revolution*', and a searching essay by Edward Thompson on Christopher Caudwell, who was killed in Spain in 1937 at the age of 29, and whose books, such as *Illusion and Reality*, *Studies in a Dying Culture*, and *Further Studies*, all published posthumously, played, in Thompson's words, 'a significant part in the intellectual biography of my own generation'.

In 1978, we published a strong critique of the work of Barry Hindess and Paul Hirst, then leading exponents of Althusserian thinking; and the same volume included a critical essay by Ellen Meiksins Wood on 'C.B. Macpherson: Liberalism and the Task of Socialist Theory'. This provoked a response from Leo Panitch in 1981, 'Liberal Democracy and Socialist Democracy: The Antinomies of C.B. Macpherson', in which Panitch took a rather more positive view than Wood had done of Macpherson's relation to Marxism; and she in turn responded to Panitch in the same issue with an article on 'Liberal Democracy and Capitalist Hegemony'. Still in the same issue, David Beetham, in an article entitled 'Beyond Liberal Democracy', sought to deal 'with objections raised by liberal democrats to the possibility of a socialist democracy'. In 1982, Stuart Hall wrote on 'The Battle for Socialist Ideas in the 1980s', and Peter Sedgwick gave another review to the *Register*, this time on Alasdair MacIntyre's *After Virtue: A Study in Moral Theory*, which had appeared in 1981. The review was an elegant, informed and critical appraisal not only of the book, but of MacIntyre's 'journey through polemic'. Sedgwick's death not long after deprived the Left of one of its most incisive writers.

The concern with Marxist and socialist theory inspired many of the other articles which we published in the late seventies and beyond, and a lot more room was now given to various aspects of feminism. Also, the *Register* devoted a good deal of attention in those years to the ideological shifts that were occurring on the Right, and to the deepening intellectual and political crisis that was gripping the Left. In 1979, the year in which Mrs Thatcher, as she was then, first came to power, we had published an essay by Andrew Gamble, 'The Free Economy and the Strong State', in which he noted, all too accurately, that 'the slow-down in the pace of accumulation has provided the opportunity for a widespread rejection of

Keynesian political economy and an onslaught on the policies, values and organizations of social democracy'. The same issue also had an essay by Mario Nuti on 'The Contradictions of Socialist Economies', and another one by Elmar Altvater and Otto Kallscheuer on 'Socialist Politics and the "Crisis of Marxism"'. In 1980, we published an essay by Laurence Harris on 'The State and the Economy', which sought to provide an explanation in Marxist terms of the developing attack on the welfare state; that issue also has an essay by Jane Jenson on 'The French Communist Party and Feminism'. In 1982, an article by David Ruben discussed 'Marxism and the Jewish Question'; and John Saville had an essay on recent Labour historiography. Two articles in the 1983 *Register* dealt with feminist themes, the one by Dorothy Smith on 'Women, Class and Family', the other by Varda Burstyn on 'Masculine Dominance and the State'. Also in 1983, the *Register* had an article by Ellen Meiksins Wood, 'Marxism Without Class Struggle', in which she argued against 'a substantial transformation of Marxist theory', which, she said, had displaced 'class struggle and the self-emancipation of the working class . . . from the centre of Marxism'. Still in the same volume, Richard Hyman presented a critique of André Gorz's *Farewell to the Working Class: An Essay on Post-Industrial Socialism*, which had been published in 1982; and Monty Johnstone reviewed the attitude of Marx and Engels to majority rule in 'Marx, Blanqui and Majority Rule'. The theme of the 1987 volume was 'Conservatism in Britain and America', and included a range of essays on Reaganism and Thatcherism, with such essays as Reg Whitaker's 'Neo-Conservatism and the State', Bill Schwarz's 'The Thatcher Years', Joel Krieger's 'Social Policy in the Age of Reagan and Thatcher', Elizabeth Wilson's 'Thatcherism and Women', and Zillah Eisenstein 'Liberalism, Feminism and the Reagan State'. It was also in that volume that we published essays by James Cronin and Terry Radtke on 'The Old and the New Politics of Taxation', Ian Taylor's 'Law and Order, Moral Order: The Changing Rhetorics of the Thatcher Government', Harvey Kaye's 'The New Right and the Crisis of History', Laurence Harris and Ben Fine on 'Ideology and Markets: Economic Theory and the New Right', Simon Clarke on 'Capitalist Crisis and the Rise of Monetarism', and Leo Panitch and myself on 'Socialists and the "New Conservatism"'. For good measure, we also had an essay by Joel Kovel on 'The Theocracy of John Paul II', an essay by John Saville on American bases in Britain, and one by Larry Pratt on 'The Reagan Doctrine and the Third World'.

The 1984 volume had included articles tracing the ways in which conservative forces had exploited the 'Soviet threat' and anti-communism in general as a bludgeon against the Left. The volume had an introductory essay by Marcel Liebman and myself, an essay by Reg Whitaker on 'Fighting the Cold War on the Home Front: America, Britain, Australia and Canada', an essay by John Saville which threw much-needed light on

'Ernest Bevin and the Cold War', one by William Graf on anti-
communism in the Federal Republic of Germany, an essay by Martin Eve
on 'Anti-Communism and American Intervention in Greece', and further
essays on various aspects of anti-communism, including one by François
Houtart on anti-communism and the Catholic Church. As noted earlier, a
number of essays in that volume also dealt with American foreign policy
and intervention in Central America.

The 1989 *Register* celebrated the bi-centenary of the French Revolution
by devoting the volume to the theme 'Revolution Today. Aspirations and
Reality'. The first article, by Leo Panitch, sought to answer the question:
'What meaning can we give to the notion of socialist revolution in the
advanced capitalist countries today?'; and a number of essays in the
volume, which will be noted later, asked the same question in different
contexts. That issue of the *Register* also carried an essay by Tony Benn,
drawing on his experience as a Cabinet minister for eleven years, on
'Obstacles to Reform in Britain'; Victor Kiernan's 'Reflections on Revolution in an Age of Reaction'; an essay by Ernest Mandel on 'The Marxist
Case for Revolution Today', and a rigorously argued essay by Norman
Geras on the crucial topic of 'Our Morals: The Ethics of Revolution'.
Other essays in the volume highlighted other aspects of the topic of
revolution – Michael Löwy on nationalism and internationalism, Frieder
Otto Wolf on the need to rethink the idea of revolution, Joanna Brenner on
'Feminism's Revolutionary Promise', Lawrence Letwin on religion and
revolution, and Saul Landau on the Cuban revolution.

9

In the volumes that we published from 1984 onwards, the word 'crisis'
insistently recurs; and these volumes do indeed chart the defeats and
disappointments which the Left sustained in those years, and the
hegemony, in thought and deed, which the Right had established in the
eighties. On the other hand, the *Register* never shared the pessimism which
was so prevalent on the Left. We acknowledged the crisis, and sought to
analyse its deeper roots. But we were also very critical of the ideological
and political retreat which the pessimism both nurtured and reinforced;
and the 1990 volume, entitled 'The Retreat of the Intellectuals', was
largely concerned with various aspects of the retreat and also with the
affirmation of socialist perspectives. It is in this vein that Norman Geras
discussed 'Seven Types of Obloquy. Travesties of Marxism', and John
Saville dissected the positions of a main organ of retreat, *Marxism Today*.
Ellen Meiksins Wood had an essay on the uses and abuses of the notion of
civil society, and noted 'two contradictory impulses' in the use of the term:
'the new concept of civil society', she noted, 'signals that the left has learnt
the lessons of liberalism about the dangers of state oppression', but, she

also noted, 'we seem to be forgetting the lessons we once learned from the socialist tradition about the oppressions of civil society'. For his part, Terry Eagleton directed a sharp satire at Richard Rorty's anti-universalism; Fredric Jameson had an essay on Postmodernism and the Market; and Bryan Palmer gave us a well-documented essay on the retreat from Marxism in the writing on social history in the eighties. Paul Cammack wrote on 'Statism, New Institutionalism, and Marxism'; and Linda Gordon had an essay on 'The Welfare State: Towards a Socialist-Feminist Perspective' in which she analysed the weaknesses in the Left's necessary defence of the welfare state. There were also essays by George Ross on 'Intellectuals against the Left' in France, a critical essay on Jacques Derrida by Eleanor MacDonald, and an essay on Marx and Rights by Amy Bartholomew. John Bellamy Foster, in an essay on 'Liberal Practicality and the U.S. Left', analysed 'the contradictions of the dominant liberal democratic ideology'. Stephen Gill had an essay on 'Intellectuals and Transnational Capital'; Arthur MacEwan explained 'Why We Are Still Socialists and Marxists After All This'; and Richard Levins offered reflections on the future of socialism. Finally, I argued for the importance of 'counter-hegemonic struggles' against the corrosive notion that there was no plausible alternative to the prevailing social order.

Many of the articles in the 1993 *Register*, entitled 'Real Problems, False Solutions', pursued the theme of intellectual retreat in the eighties. David Harvey discussed the different – and often misguided – approaches to the 'environmental issue', and sought to 'establish a theoretical position from which to try and make sense' of that issue; and Christopher Norris gave us a caustic critique of commentators who 'queued up to renounce any lingering attachment to such old-hat notions as truth, reason, critique, ideology, or false consciousness', and linked this 'realignment of theoretical positions on the left' with 'a widespread tactical retreat from socialist principles among Labour Party politicians, policy-makers, and (more or less) well-disposed media and academic pundits'. Marsha Hewitt wrote on 'the regressive implications of post-modernism'; Lynne Segal discussed 'anti-pornography feminism', and John Griffith argued, in an essay entitled 'The Rights Stuff', that 'proposed changes to the constitution [by such organisations as Charter 88] and the incorporation of a Bill of Rights, will enable private interests, of individuals and of corporations, to override measures designed to promote the general welfare'.

In the Preface to the volume, we said that we conceived the volume 'as addressing a broad range of "dead-end" or "morbid symptom" responses to various aspects of the current global disorder, offering analyses why they arise as well as a critique and corrective to them'. This could well be taken to describe the spirit of much that appeared in the *Register*.

10

There are some important topics which did not get the attention they deserved. One of them was Northern Ireland. We published an article by Anders Boserup in 1972 on 'Contradictions and Struggles in Northern Ireland'; and the 1977 *Register* had a section on the topic, with articles by Anthony Arblaster, Michael Farrell and Peter Gibbons. But we should no doubt have done more. The same applies to Israel and Palestine. On this topic, we published two essays with very different perspectives in the 1970 *Register*, one of them by Mervyn Jones on 'Israel, Palestine and Socialism', the other by Marcel Liebman on 'Israel, Palestine and Zionism'; and it was only in 1992 that another essay, by Avishai Ehrlich, on 'The Gulf War and the New World Order', made reference to the place of Israel in the Middle East.

Nor did we do any better with matters related to science, a field which the post-1945 Left, unlike the Left of the inter-war years, has tended to neglect. We published an essay by Steven and Hilary Rose in 1972 on 'The Radicalisation of Science', which discussed what they saw as 'a clear shift in consciousness of many scientists – especially science students – of the role of science and technology in contemporary capitalism'. Another essay in 1973, by Steven Rose, John Hambley and Jeff Haywood, on 'Science, Racism and Ideology', dealt with the re-emergence of what they called 'scientific racism', that is to say the argument that 'certain groups, notably Blacks and working class, are less intelligent than others, notably White middle class, and that this difference is genetic'; but neither this, nor any other topic related to science was pursued further in subsequent issues of the *Register*.

We did a little better with the ever-expanding field of mass communications. In 1973, we published an essay by Graham Murdoch and Peter Golding, 'For a Political Economy of Mass Communications'. This was followed in 1979 with an essay by Kevin Robins and Frank Webster on 'Mass Communications and Information Technology'; and they gave us another essay in 1981 on 'Information Technology: Futurism, Corporations and the State'.

However, the most notable gap in the *Register*'s output lay in a different area altogether, namely in the paucity of articles devoted to the discussion of literature and the arts in general. It is not that we were unaware of their importance, but rather that the more directly 'political' subjects tended to crowd out all else, which is no great excuse.

To say that we should have done more on various topics is in some ways a bit hard on ourselves, given the circumstances in which we were producing the volumes. For one thing, as I noted at the beginning, there was for many years only John Saville and I to edit the *Register*, and both of us were very busy full-time teachers. We could no doubt have brought together an editorial board, but we had decided at the start, rightly or wrongly, that this would present problems of organisation and require too great an expenditure of time and energy. Later, there was also, for all too short a time, Marcel Liebman; and, from 1985/6 onwards, there has been Leo Panitch, whose co-editorship has been truly invaluable. But there was never enough time; and this was particularly true in one critical respect, namely finding authors whose work would reflect the independent socialist and critical spirit which we wanted to inform all that we published. The point is not that such people were particularly rare, but that finding them, and getting them to agree to write for us (of course free of charge) *and* getting them to deliver their essays on time, or at all, was often a very demanding business. All the more am I deeply grateful to all the people who, over the years, have made the *Register* possible; and I present my apologies to those contributors whose essays I have not mentioned. Thanks are also due to Brian Pearce, Mike Gonzalez and David Macey for the excellent translations they have done for us.

I have always thought that the *Register* was doing useful socialist work, and its survival for thirty years, in a period which has not been good for the Left, may be reckoned to be a matter of some satisfaction, not least because the *Register* has consistently been ignored by the journals in which it might have been reviewed. Save for the occasional review here and there, we have had to do without any such attention, even though the single-theme volumes we published from 1984 onwards easily lent themselves to review. Yet we know that the *Register*, without the benefit of much reviewing, has had a keen readership, not only in Britain and North America, but in many other parts of the world as well; and many articles which appeared in the *Register* have been reprinted elsewhere, in English and in other languages. All in all, I think the publication deserves the mention 'has done well, could do better'; and over the next thirty years, it will.

EDWARD THOMPSON, THE COMMUNIST PARTY AND 1956*

John Saville

The death of Edward Thompson on 28th August 1993 has inevitably pushed memories back to the early beginnings of the New Left, and it may be helpful at this stage to survey the documentation and suggest some of the problems that require further political discussion. The account that I wrote for the *Socialist Register* in 1976 set down the chronology that led to the publication of *The Reasoner* July–October 1956 and the general crisis in the Communist movement in Britain that produced its three issues. This 1976 article provides a useful account that is still acceptable but it had some omissions of emphasis and gaps in fact that require to be remedied. Edward Thompson was not able to make it a joint article, as originally had been hoped, because he was teaching in the United States, and my draft was sent to the printer without his comments because I was already beyond my promised deadline.

Some preliminary observations are necessary. There are two main sources of information for the events in Britain within the Communist Party for the year 1956. The first is the correspondence between Edward Thompson and myself, together with a considerable volume of letters from our friends and correspondents, the latter after the first number of *The Reasoner* had appeared. The second major collection of directly relevant material will be the Communist Party archives, at present (winter 1994) being catalogued and soon to be deposited in the National Museum of Labour History in Manchester. There are problems with the large amount of correspondence between Edward and myself. On several occasions, over the years, Edward and I discussed the deposit of our material but always in a somewhat indecisive manner. This was not because we had any objections in principle, but because we both knew the amount of work that would be involved to get our correspondence etc. in reasonable order. We had both kept carbon copies of most letters we had written to each other,

---

*I am grateful to Dorothy Thompson for her permission to reprint extracts from Edward's letters

20

but the greater part of his correspondence to me was not dated; and on either side therefore we cannot be certain that every item is correctly placed. My papers are going into the Labour Archive of the Brynmore Jones Library, University of Hull, and in his last years Edward seemed to think that the Bodleian might be his depository: but the decision is for his executors.

*   *   *

It will be useful to recapitulate, briefly, the main sequence of events in 1956 which brought about the very considerable ferment within the CPGB, and, of course, elsewhere in the Communist world. The story begins with the 20th Congress of the CPSU in late February 1956. The speeches of Khrushchev and Mikoyan in open session both emphasised the 'negative' aspects of the cult of the individual, and the absence of collective leadership in the Soviet Communist Party – 'for approximately twenty years' said Mikoyan; and these comments were naturally picked up and widely discussed in the world press. On the last day of the Congress, the 25th February, Russian delegates went into secret session; foreign delegates were excluded and for them a programme of visits to factories and various other activities had been arranged. It was in this secret session that Khrushchev pronounced his shattering speech about the infamies of the Stalinist regime. Some of the senior international leaders, Togliatti and Thorez among them, knew the main contents of the secret speech before they returned home; and it later became evident that what may have been an edited version of Khrushchev's speech was made available to foreign Communist parties within a month or six weeks after they had left Moscow.

The main points of the secret speech soon became known, at least to those who read beyond the London *Daily Worker*. On 4th March Walter Ulbricht, then vice-premier of East Germany, said in a speech that Stalin had done 'severe damage to the Soviet State and the Soviet Communist Party'; and a fortnight later he expanded his statement to include the comment that the 'myth' of Stalin as a military leader had been developed by Stalin himself: a repetition of what Khrushchev had also said. On March 16th the text of the secret speech was available in Bonn, and on the following day the Hungarian Government announced the rehabilitation of Lazslo Rajk, the former general secretary of the CP who had been executed after the usual 'trial'. The *Daily Worker* had begun to receive letters on the published statements of the 20th Congress in late February and there was great difficulty in getting them published. On the 12th March publication ended, with the editor, J. R. Campbell, explaining to readers that he was gratified that most letters had not indulged in 'exaggerated denigration of Stalin' but that now the space for correspondence must be given over to a discussion of the forthcoming Congress of the British Party, to be held at the end of March. The flood of letters continued; the question of Stalin and the 20th Congress was debated in secret session at the British Party Congress and the resolution that emerged made the now familiar points that mistakes had been corrected and the further advance of Communism in the Soviet Union could now go ahead unimpeded. Throughout April and May comment and criticism continued to swell, and in reluctant and very piece-meal fashion, the Party leadership responded in cautious and wholly conservative ways, ignoring the central problems at issue. Much of the story of these middle months of the year, when serious debate was being refused by the Communist leadership in Britain, was told in the 1976 *Socialist Register* by Malcolm McEwan and myself; but a re-reading of the correspondences requires further comment and a note of the omissions in my own original article.

* * *

Before I began corresponding with other Communist party members I had written privately to Harry Pollitt on March 19th, 1956. I wrote because I was incensed by the leader in that day's *Daily Worker* which I said in my letter 'appears to accept as uncritically as was done in the past the present line of the Russian Party'. It was a longish letter and the quotation that follows is included to indicate what certainly was not an isolated opinion concerning the attitudes that we had to take towards the revelations of the secret speech. Page two of my letter:

> A University colleague, supporter of the Labour Party, and personally friendly to me, said the other day: 'I feel less like working with Communists than ever before; how can I ever seriously believe your political line again?' I understand only too well why he says these things, and it seems clear to me, if ever a matter was clear, that we shall only convince people like my colleague if we are frank, open and honest in our criticisms of ourselves. My answer, which I shall give in public and private, runs like this:
>
> There is no question of our not admitting our mistakes as a Party. Neither do I seek to exonerate myself as an individual party member. It is true that I was much more critical of certain aspects of Soviet society than the official party line (i.e. in private I always admitted the existence of labour camps, disliked the Stalin cult, and was appalled at the way people 'disappeared') but I never made these criticisms, except in milder form, public. I believe now, as I have always believed, that these were transitory phenomena, and I have, as I have always had, confidence in the long term development of socialism in Russia. But it is now abundantly plain to me that while I thought I was curbing my criticisms in the general interests of working class internationalism, I was wrong. I believe now that had the Communist Parties outside Russia been more critical, the forces inside Russia working for greater democracy would have been strengthened, not weakened as in fact they were; and the whole world movement would today have been stronger, because it would have been based upon honest opinion, and not double think. I hold fast to the Communist answer to the world's problems, and I value more than I can say in a few words my membership of the British party; but never again shall I accept any political line without question. I feel humiliated by what I have let pass in the name of the Party and the extension of inner party democracy means for me a much more personal responsibility for the work of the Party.

My letter ended with fraternal greetings. Pollitt had just resigned from the position of General Secretary because of poor health, and my letter was acknowledged formally from King St. I have included it here because it illustrates several important themes that were to dominate the political discussions in the weeks and months that followed. It also exhibits how far along the road I had travelled in less than a month since the Russian Congress, as well as how far there was still to go.

I was late in contacting Edward Thompson over these impassioned matters. As I noted in the 1976 article I had been friendly with Edward and Dorothy for half a dozen years but we were not close. Edward did not take an active part in the work of the Historians' Group although Dorothy did in the years immediately preceding 1956. Indeed, in spite of the great volume on William Morris, which I very much admired, I thought of Edward not primarily as an historian but rather as a literary historian who because of his extra-mural teaching in the West Riding was becoming increasingly interested in the radical movements before 1850; at the same time as he was working on his *William Morris* and the revival of socialism in the 1880s. The more one examines Edward's career the more impressive becomes his capacity for research and his ability to express himself in vivid and exciting language. He published his *William Morris*, a volume of just over 900 pages, when he was thirty years old; then through the convulsions of the *Reasoner* years he produced *The Making of the English Working Class* before he was forty years old. It is an astonishing record.

Edward's reply to my first letter to him on the secret speech and its repercussions was dated 4th April, and it began:

> Thank God for your letter. Never have I known such a wet flatfish slapped on the face as our 24th [Party Congress]. It is the biggest Confidence Trick in our Party's history. Not one bloody concession as yet to our feelings and integrity: no apology to the rank and file, no self-criticism, no apology to the British people, no indication of the points of Marxist theory which now demand revaluation, no admission that our Party has undervalued intellectual and ideological work, no promise of a loosening of inner party democracy, and of the formation of even a discussion journal so that this can be fought out within our ranks, not one of the inner ring of the Executive felt that he might have to resign, if even temporarily. The whole old gang back, who bayed after Haldane, threw Zhdanov down the throats of musicians and writers, alienated thousands, acted as apologists for the 'people's democracies' whenever our doubts rose; not even the concession of putting one or two men, like Bernal or Hill, on the E.C. who would retain the confidence of the intellectuals.

This was only the beginning. It was a long, full-blooded letter which attacked the 'pitiful and fatuous' approach towards the Labour Party of Gaitskell; called for a 'sharpening of differences within the Party'; complained bitterly of the 'complaisance' of most members of the Yorkshire District Committee (of which he was a member); and towards the end of this highly charged epistle, much of which was to become the centre of a great deal of our personal debates and discussions in the months that followed:

> If necessary we shall have to leave the Party and found a small Marxist educational league. I hope this will never have to take place, but it is more important that we should remain loyal to our intellectual integrity as Marxists than to the Party under all circumstances. Our

duty to the British working class as honest intellectuals is more important than blind loyalty to a Party which has become distorted and warped by a series of historical accidents. But this is the extreme position which I hope we shall not reach.

At the time of writing this letter, Dorothy Thompson was in the London area with her children, and she was planning to attend the Communist Party Historians' annual general meeting on 8th April. Nineteen out of a total of thirty-four members attended, and there was a vigorous debate around the failure of the 24th Congress to address seriously the historical problems thrown up by the Russian 20th Congress. A perceptive account and analysis of the Historians Group was published by Eric Hobsbawm in the symposium in honour of A. L. Morton (*Rebels and their Causes* 1978). In the present context, the main point to be emphasised is that of all the various groups within the National Cultural Committee of the British CP the historians were 'the most consistently active and flourishing group of communist intellectuals'; and inevitably, as Hobsbawm further notes, they were drawn into the debates precisely because historical analysis is at the centre of Marxist politics. Most of the full-time historians who were members of the Communist Historians Group left within a year or so of the Khrushchev speech. Their ten years of working together when the war ended had been conducted in a spirit of serious critical enquiry without personal difficulties or the translation of opposing views into recrimination. It was these characteristics that made the Historians Group such a lively and pleasant experience and it was the comradeship and friendship of its members that continued through the *Reasoner* years and their aftermath.

A month after the Historians annual meeting the National University Staffs Committee issued a long Resolution dated May 5/6th 1956 which was concerned entirely with the political problems that had arisen following the secret speech. It was a sober statement which both emphasised the crisis within the Communist Party and assumed that however difficult the political and intellectual analysis might be, it was within the Communist Party – as an essential component of the British labour movement – that the questions had to be resolved. By contrast, the national student committee produced an edition of their Newsletter (No. 7, May 1956) which summarised a two-day meeting of the national committee and which had nothing to say about the 20th Congress and Khrushchev's speech except that it was 'epoch-making in its announcement of the rapid advances in human freedom'.

To return to Edward's letter of 4th April, and the quotation taken from the end of his letter which expressed firmly the hope that the open discussion we were asking for would not be done outside the Party. It was a hope, and an argument, that went right through the debates that we had between ourselves and with a wide section of those who were in general agreement with the political stand that we were going to take; and it is necessary to appreciate the background and political history of those who were to become dissidents. My own career was not untypical although I was eight years older than Edward and I belonged therefore to the generation of the nineteen thirties whereas his initiation into left wing politics was mostly an affair of the war years and their aftermath. What it is first necessary to appreciate is our complete rejection of the Labour-Socialism of the Labour Party. The record of the Labour leadership in the thirties was appalling. One would not expect them to support the four national hunger marches of the decade – 1930, 1932, 1934 and 1936 – since the National Unemployed Workers Movement was, mostly, Communist led, although in those days there was an active Left Wing in many areas which disregarded the bans that came from Transport House; and Clement Attlee, alone among the top Labour leadership, spoke at the 1936 rally in Hyde Park (Attlee was similarly alone among Labour's political leaders who actually went to Spain during the Civil War). But what exhibited the nature and character of the Labour Party of the thirties or rather its leadership through the National Council of Labour (on which right-wing trade unionists were in a majority) was the denial of support for the Jarrow March of the autumn of 1936. Ellen Wilkinson, who was M.P. for the Jarrow constituency, was refused the support of the Labour Party Executive at the Edinburgh conference of the Labour Party; and when the march was under way, with the unanimous support of Jarrow Town Council, and led on the road by a Conservative councillor as well as one from the majority Labour Party, the TUC circularised Trades Councils advising them against giving support. Chesterfield was one of the towns whose Trades and Labour Council obeyed the circular, and the local Conservative Party gave the marchers hot meals and accommodation for the night.

Almost all of my generation, and of Edward's, of course, served in the armed forces during the war. Many had a 'political' war, by which I mean that in quite a large number of situations in which one found oneself, it was possible to engage in political activity of some kind or another. About two years before his death Edward, who had been a junior officer in a tank regiment and saw service in North Africa and Italy, told me of the time when it was strongly rumoured that the regiment would be sent to Greece to reinforce the military intervention of December 1944; and of the serious discussions he had as to the political morality of being used in the suppression of a national liberation movement. In the event the regiment remained where it was. The Labour leaders' support of the Greek intervention was the beginning of the openly reactionary foreign policy which Ernest Bevin, when he became Foreign Secretary after the Labour victory of July 1945, was to develop and extend from the first days of taking office. Within a month the Labour government had begun its military intervention on behalf of the French in what was soon to be called Vietnam; at the same time it was sending troops to support the Dutch in Indonesia. A Party that further provided troops for the American war in Korea and supported

German rearmament and did not officially oppose imperialist repression in Malaya, Kenya and Cyprus was not a politically comfortable home for those who tried to be principled; and by the middle nineteen fifties Labour -Socialism was a wholly tainted practice. By contrast, a re-reading of the correspondence of 1956 from members of the Communist Party who were increasingly critical of the way the Communist leadership was reacting to the Russian 20th Congress underlines the extraordinary power of the idea of a disciplined organisation which was assumed to be incorruptible, intellectually as well as in more earthy matters. There was an interesting difference in certain matters between Edward and myself: at least that is how I now see ourselves. I remember a meeting of the Artists International in London – sometime in the winter of 1946–7 – when the speaker, Francis Klingender, was bitterly attacked from different parts of the room where distinctive groupings had assembled themselves; and it used to be accepted that there were various literary and writers' groups much in dissent one with the other. Writing of the early 1950s, in his essay on Christopher Caudwell in *Socialist Register* for 1977, Edward Thompson commented (note 15): 'There were a good many frustrated proto-revisionists in the Communist Party in those days; in my own circles we designated the enemy as 'King Street' and as 'Jungle Marxism', of which we increasingly came to see *The Modern Quarterly* as the leading intellectual organ'. And Edward, who was a leading figure in the Yorkshire Peace movement in the first half of the nineteen fifties, and by 1956 a member of the Yorkshire District Committee (at a time when the majority were industrial militants) had a number of expressed disagreements with the full-time officials of the Yorkshire District.

My own experience of Party life after I was demobilised and had moved to an academic job at the then University College of Hull, was different. It was a friendly town branch and I accepted the usual chores, such as delivering Saturday copies of the *Daily Worker* round a housing estate. I had a special relationship with the North-East district and would tutor two or three times a year Party weekend schools, mostly of miners from the coalfields of Durham and Northumberland. But the most exhilarating intellectual times of my life were those with the Historians' Group, mostly in London. This first post-war decade of life in the Communist Party was, of course, the very difficult period of the Cold War, much more difficult than is often appreciated. No years were more fraught than those of the Korean War and to speak publicly against the war was to meet great hostility.

Our somewhat different personal histories during these years made no difference to the outlook of Edward and myself in respect of our general understanding and appreciation of the world we found ourselves in. Our rejection of the Labour Party at the national level – as well as our recognition of the nepotism and corruption of too many local Labour and trade union bureaucrats – continued unchanged, and our belief in the political importance of the Communist Party comes through again and again in the correspondence between us during the spring and summer of 1956. As in Edward's letter of the 4th of April, quoted above, we were fully aware of the problems of ensuring open and free discussion and debate within the Communist Party, and of the consequences of failure; but we began and continued in the belief, and hope, that change would come about. The Labour Party was not an alternative, and what Edward described as the 'extreme position' of a small marxist educational league outside the Communist Party, was emphatically not a future prospect that could be welcomed. From April until late June when the decision to publish was taken we argued and debated, and changed our minds on this or that argument almost daily, yet never did we really believe that we should have to move outside the Communist Party. That came later, and from around the beginning of September – it is difficult to be precise about the timing – we both began to appreciate that we were confronted with a bureaucratised Party that could not accept the transformation for which we were working.

In the first number of *The Reasoner* (mid July 1956) our first editorial, under the title 'Why We Are Publishing' explained to our readers that it was a journal which in the main was written by and addressed to members of the Communist Party; and we went on to insist that it was above all a discussion journal concerned with fundamental questions which included issues such as the need for a Communist Party in Britain and what should its relationship be with the Labour Party. We stressed that in the existing crisis full and open debate was a necessity, and that, we emphasised, was not so far available through the existing journals of the Party. We continued:

> The first need of our movement is a re-birth of Socialist principle, ensuring that dogmatic attitudes and theoretical inertia do not return.

> We accept the need, as do all members of the Communist Party, for a degree of self-imposed discipline in action, based upon discussion and collective decisions. It may be that this concept of discipline has been interpreted too rigidly in the past; and it is certain that the democratic processes within the party are in need of attention. But we must state emphatically that we have no desire to see the party degenerate into a number of quarrelling sects and self-opinionated individuals. It is no part of the aim of this journal to encourage the formation of political factions.

> It is now, however, abundantly clear to us that the forms of discipline necessary and valuable in a revolutionary party of action cannot and never should have been extended so far into the processes of discussion, of creative writing, and of theoretical polemic. The power which will shatter the capitalist system and create Socialism is that of the free human reason and conscience expressed with the full force of the organised working-class. Only a party of free men and women, accepting a discipline arising from truly democratic discussion and decision, alert in mind and conscience, will develop the clarity, the initiative, and the élan, necessary to arouse the dormant energies of our people. Everything which tends to cramp the intellect and dull their feelings, weakens the party, disarms the working class, and makes the assault upon Capitalism – with its deep defences of fraud and force – more difficult.

Neither the reason nor the conscience of man can be confined within the discipline and procedures appropriate to decisions of action; nor can great theoretical issues be solved by a simple majority vote.

We take our stand as Marxists. Nothing in the events of past months has shaken our conviction that the methods and outlook of historical materialism, developed by the work of Marx and Engels, provide the key to our theoretical advance and, therefore, to the understanding of these events themselves; although it should be said that much that has gone under the name of 'Marxism' or 'Marxism-Leninism' is itself in need of re-examination.

History has provided a chance for this re-examination to take place; and for the scientific methods of Marxism to be integrated with the finest traditions of the human reason and spirit which we may best describe as Humanism.

This opportunity may be of short duration. Once passed it may not soon return. It would be treason to our cause, and a betrayal of the strivings, past and present, for a class-less society, to let it pass in silence.

★ ★ ★

Throughout the months which followed our first contact, we not only debated every day between ourselves, by correspondence or the telephone or in quite frequent personal meetings, but we listened to our friends and the comrades around us. The absence of any reference to others with whom we worked closely was an unfortunate and regrettable omission from my 1976 article. First, our wives. Dorothy worked actively and closely alongside Edward, and I often addressed my letters to both of them. My own wife did not hold a Party card, having been sceptical of the change of line in 1939, and retaining her scepticism in the years that followed. But she was active in many aspects of Party life, and during the time of *The Reasoner* she was an invaluable critic. There was the draft of an editorial in our second number that she dismissed as patronisingly *de haut en bas* and that we should think again; which is what we did. Of those outside our families, Ken Alexander was our constant support, in corre-spondence and in meetings. He was a lecturer in the department of economics at the University of Sheffield, then moved to Aberdeen and ended his academic career as Vice-Chancellor of Stirling University. He was involved with us from the beginning of our collaboration and he read all or nearly all of our joint editorials. After we had published the first issue of *The Reasoner* we were called to a meeting with the Yorkshire District Committee on 10th August. It was a meeting I could not attend and I exchanged several drafts of a statement I was going to submit. In the end, I left the matter of the final draft to Edward. An extract is published in the 1976 article (pp. 9–10). Before this was sent, Edward had written a long, handwritten letter to Ken Alexander (with a copy to me) which, although an interim view (his words) set down very well the questionings that were developing in our minds. The date of the letter was July 25th. He began by listing the kind of theoretical questions that must be discussed: a frank examination of the history of the British Party and of its international connections; the delineation of party democracy, and so on. He continued by insisting that discussion must be in written expression as against 'soul-searching collective discussions' which could be useful but could also lead to nothing; and further, that we were agreed that 'eventually' changes would have to come in the leadership of the Party and probably in its organisational structure. If we could not get these changes, then two things would follow: first the British Party would probably not get anywhere or might even do damage, and second, that without change, and especially the acceptance of open discussion, we ourselves would be better outside.

Edward then followed these comments with an insistence upon the current role of *The Reasoner* as a *necessary* (his emphasis) instrument in doing the job that must be done; and arguing therefore the case for the continuation of further issues of *The Reasoner* since it had now become the symbol of the whole case for unfettered discussion within the Party's organisation. We could not, therefore, agree to any suspension of the journal until we had clear and precise guarantees that free discussion would become an integral part of the Party's general approach. He concluded on an interesting note which underlines once again that we were both continuing to work for serious change within the Party. It should, of course, be repeated that this letter I am summarising was not a public statement, yet it was, as the contemporary documentation makes plain, a fair summary of what our general position was at this time. 'Perhaps' he wrote 'we should modify somewhat the tone of *The Reasoner* – to develop possibly a more conciliatory tone' in order to encourage full-time officials such as Howard Hill, the Sheffield District secretary, who was much troubled by the developing crisis within the Party and who was far from being a bureaucratic hatchet. Conciliatory, Edward wrote, 'as is compatible with principle'. It was an interesting letter and as remarked above, it was followed within a few days by an exchange of drafts between Edward and myself that was to represent my/our views before the Yorkshire District Committee. The Yorkshire meeting was followed by one with the Political Committee of the Communist Party on Friday 31st August. Harry Pollitt was in the chair. It was not, in any respect, a meeting of minds. The members of the Political Committee took a wholly constitutional line on our independent publication outside the Party press and the violation of rules and regulations that was involved. On the central questions of the political fall-out consequent on the secret speech at the 20th Congress, there was no response. Towards the end of the day we made it clear that we were not prepared to cease publication without the guarantees we had stipulated, and later we both wrote, as requested, to Pollitt confirming our position. We managed to produce the second number of *The Reasoner* twenty four hours before the September Central Committee instructed us to cease publication, which meant that if we published again we should certainly be disciplined. We had a further meeting during September with John Gollan, now the General Secretary, and George Matthews, the

Assistant General Secretary. I think it was these meetings at King Street with the leading officials of the Communist Party that made me begin to recognise what I did not want to acknowledge: that we would never make a serious impact upon the leadership and that the Party hierarchy was imperishably bureaucratic. We were also becoming aware of the hostility that was growing against us among party members of long standing. That, of course, was to be expected but we were increasingly conscious that the personalities question was beginning to obscure the basic principles we were endeavouring to establish. In a letter written to Edward and Dorothy on 22nd September I included the comment: 'Whatever view we may have of the leadership I take the line, and I believe Edward does too, that in the Party there are thousands of honest socialists. True that only hundreds are active; but the others would become alive, as we are always arguing.'

By the beginning of October we had agreed our policy: to publish the third issue of *The Reasoner* while stating that we were stopping future publication for reasons that we thought were in the best interests of the Party. We expected of course that we would be disciplined but I think we assumed we should be suspended rather than expelled. So we wrote and published the third and last *Reasoner* and our long main editorial was dated 31st October 1956. Then came the first Soviet intervention in Hungary, and Edward's article 'Through the Smoke of Budapest' was dated November 1st. Our final editorial, which we agreed over the telephone, was November 4th, and printed as the first two pages. It demanded that the executive Committee of the British Party dissociate itself publicly from the Soviet intervention; the withdrawal of Soviet troops; that it proclaim solidarity with the Polish Workers Party: and that District and National Congresses should be summoned early in the New Year.

We were suspended, and immediately resigned, along with a total of about 7,000 other members including, contrary to myth, large numbers of industrial workers and trade union officials.

* * *

It is interesting to speculate what would have happened if the Hungarian crisis and Soviet intervention had not occurred. I doubt whether Edward and I would have remained members, although for me it might have been a very difficult decision at least until the Easter 1957 Congress of the British Party. That Congress showed two things of quite central significance. The first was that the Party leadership were not prepared to confront in any way the political problems that flowed from Khrushchev's speech; and the second was that the leadership could count upon a majority of its membership to follow its lead. The Party was now incapable of encouraging a theoretical and political debate; its leadership had been too long in place and were dominated in their thinking by the past; and too many of the rank and file were burdened with the weight of encrusted beliefs, unchallenged by the creative thinking that Marxism ought to provide and which Stalinism had degraded.

* * *

Statement in Response to Suspension

The Executive Committee of the Committee of the Communist Party has informed us of its decision – taken last weekend – to suspend us from membership of the party for three months, and to 'review' our position at the end of this period, as a result of our action in publishing the unofficial Communist journal *The Reasoner*. The Executive Committee's statement makes it clear that a decisive factor in their action was our editorial condemning Soviet intervention in Hungary.

The meaning of the Executive's decision is this: despite our own attempt to find some way for compromise, the leadership of the British Communist Party is determined not to permit discussion to develop in the party free from their control, since they fear that such discussion might lead on to the 'de-Stalinisation' of the British party – the ridding of the party of authoritarian methods and attitudes, and of political subservience to the Soviet leadership.

The response to our journal has shown that a very large number of British Communists – including many of the most active members – want to see sweeping changes in methods and policies, but are prevented from breaking through by the Executive's command over the party's publications and the loyalty of most of the full-time workers.

We do not intend to appeal against the Executive's decision, and we have both decided to resign from the party at once. The alternative would be for us to remain silent during the three months of our suspension, and then to hope for re-admission next February upon a promise of good behaviour in the future, and perhaps a confession of past mistakes. This is quite unacceptable to us on three grounds. 1. We believe that in our attempt to promote a serious discussion of Communist theory, we – and not the Executive Committee – have been defending Communist principle. 2. We cannot remain silent while the official organs of the Communist Party attempt, day by day, to justify Soviet actions in Hungary. 3. While we sympathise with those who are remaining in the party in the hope of effecting major changes in policy and leadership at the emergency Congress next Easter, we do not believe that they can shift the full-time machine without a real rebirth of Socialist principle throughout the movement. This cannot be effected within the restrictions and controls imposed by the present leadership, nor in an atmosphere of faction.

We are also much concerned about the hundreds of Communists, many with years of active service, who have left the party during the past few months, especially over the question of Hungary. We ourselves have no intention of promoting a breakaway party: nor do we want to see Communists and ex-Communists wasting energy in mutual recriminations. The times call above all for a new movement of ideas, reaching out beyond party barriers and bringing socialists together on the basis of principle rather than of opportunism. Organisational questions will become clearer later. To this end, we ourselves will promote the publication of discussion pamphlets and we are in touch with others who are hoping to initiate a new socialist journal, on non-party lines, early in the New Year. In our view ex-Communists should keep together, and should take the initiative in forming local socialist groups, open to all irrespective of party affiliations, in order to keep alive in every locality centres for Socialist propaganda and for the discussion of theory and policy, alongside the practical activity of the members within the organised labour movement. If this is done, regional and national conferences of such groups might later be held. The question of future relations with the Communist Party can be reconsidered in the light of any changes effected at its emergency Congress next Easter.

John Saville
152 Westbourne Avenue, Hull
E. P. Thompson
Holly Bank, Whitegate, Halifax
Joint Editors of *The Reasoner*
November 1956

RICHARD RORTY AND THE RIGHTEOUS
AMONG THE NATIONS

Norman Geras

In the early hours of 2nd February 1945, several hundred Russian prisoners escaped from Mauthausen. Apart from the killing centres in Poland, Mauthausen, not far from Linz in Upper Austria, was the most brutal of camps in the Nazi concentrationary system, those forced to labour in its stone quarry having a life expectancy of one to three months. The escapees were from the remnant (by then a mere 570) of some 4,700 Soviet officers sent to Mauthausen less than a year before, who were being subjected to a regime even harsher than the norm there and aimed specifically at destroying them all. They were dying at a rate of between twenty and thirty every day. Some of these men, once they had got beyond the outer wall, were too weak to go further, and more than half of them were caught and summarily killed during the same day. In the end only a dozen are known to have made good their escape and survived.

In anticipation of the advance of the Red Army, these Russian prisoners had placed their hopes in finding succour among the civilian population, but in vain. Their recapture was widely witnessed, in fright and sympathetic horror or with ghoulish curiosity, and the SS and local Nazi party encouraged citizen participation in the manhunt. It was forthcoming: the fugitives, many of them begging for their lives, were simply slaughtered.

In general, residents of the area who were approached by the fleeing men to shelter them, declined under public threat of lethal reprisals. Maria and Johann Langthaler, however – with four of their children living with them – did not. Taking in one man who came to their door, she persuaded her husband, at first alarmed at the awful risk, that they should harbour him. They then also took in a second man. Both of these hid there at the Langthalers for three months until the end of the war. We have Maria Langthaler's explanation of why she acted as she did. She was obligated as a Christian, she said, to help when someone was in need: 'The Lord God is for the whole world, not only for the Germans. It is a community and there one must help. I did not ask them to which party they belong, I asked nothing at all; that made no difference to me. Only because they were human beings.'[1]

32

Only because they were human beings. Although the men she took into her home were in fact Russian prisoners of war, I let this story symbolize a continent-wide phenomenon of that era: against a background of the persecution and massacre of the Jews of Europe, in which very many Europeans were complicit as participants whilst very many more stood by in fearful or indifferent passivity, some – not nearly as many, but still, more than just a handful – were yet willing to take risks, often terrible risks, in their efforts to harbour and rescue those in danger. I want to address here the question of how common amongst these rescuers was the sort of reason voiced by Maria Langthaler.

I

I start from the contrary hypothesis: that it was not very common. This is the view of Richard Rorty, which I shall report first at some length. Rorty begins his essay, 'Solidarity', as follows:

> If you were a Jew in the period when the trains were running to Auschwitz, your chances of being hidden by your gentile neighbours were greater if you lived in Denmark or Italy than if you lived in Belgium. A common way of describing this difference is by saying that many Danes and Italians showed a sense of human solidarity which many Belgians lacked.

Asserting that the basic explanatory notion in this connection is that of being 'one of us', Rorty goes on to argue that this notion carries less force when its sense is 'one of us human beings' than it does when referring to some narrower grouping, such as 'a comrade in the movement' or a 'fellow Catholic'. Typically, he claims, 'it contrasts with a "they" which is also made up of human beings – the wrong sort of human beings.'

> Consider . . . those Danes and those Italians. Did they say, about their Jewish neighbours, that they deserved to be saved because they were fellow human beings? Perhaps sometimes they did, but surely they would usually, if queried, have used more parochial terms to explain why they were taking risks to protect a given Jew – for example, that this particular Jew was a fellow Milanese, or a fellow Jutlander, or a fellow member of the same union or profession, or a fellow bocce player, or a fellow parent of small children. . . . [Or] Consider . . . the attitude of contemporary American liberals to the unending hopelessness and misery of the young blacks in American cities. Do we say that these people must be helped because they are our fellow human beings? We may, but it is much more persuasive, morally as well as politically, to describe them as our fellow *Americans* – to insist that it is outrageous that an *American* should live without hope.

Our sense of solidarity, Rorty then says again, is strongest with collectivities 'smaller and more local than the human race' and 'imaginative identification' easier; whereas '"because she is a human being" is a weak, unconvincing explanation of a generous action.'[2]

I address myself elsewhere to some general philosophical issues raised by Rorty's argument. My concern here is only with the hypothesis about the rescuers' explanations of their actions.[3] I shall take it as he presents it. I shall focus, that is to say, on the question of their motives. But I need to guard, then, against one possible misunderstanding, as I now briefly do.

Let us extend Rorty's comparison to cover the Netherlands. Where only 56 per cent of the Jews in Belgium survived the 'Final Solution', as compared with 99 per cent and 83 per cent, respectively, of the Jews of Denmark and Italy, the greatest catastrophe outside eastern Europe was actually that visited on the Dutch Jews. More than 70 per cent of them perished. This comparison now secretes a fact of some apparent relevance to the question to be pursued. No more than 10 per cent of the Jews living in Belgium at the start of the war were Belgian citizens. The rest were recent immigrants or refugees. In the Netherlands, on the other hand, these proportions were almost exactly reversed, only 10 per cent of the Jews there being refugees. A considerably smaller proportion of the Dutch than of the Belgian Jews was saved, in other words, notwithstanding any advantage the former might be thought to have had on account of longer established citizenship and social integration.

This fact however, though certainly relevant to Rorty's reflections, is not by itself decisive – and not only because of some further hypothesis we might venture as to modes of 'imaginative identification' by Belgians which reached across the divide of citizenship. The point is that such comparisons simplify a very complex historical issue. Identification with, and effective aid and support, to the Jews on the part of any given national population in Europe was only one of the factors governing their fate. Some others were the type and degree, if any, of German political and administrative control in each country; the time at which the Nazis moved decisively to deport its Jews to the death sites and the military prospect then – how soon a German defeat in the war might be anticipated; the response also of the Jews themselves in each country; the accessibility or otherwise of a secure haven (as the Danes had in nearby Sweden); and still other things beside. There is by now a large analytical literature on all this.[4] To focus on the reasons of individual rescuers is to abstract only one feature from a much larger picture. With that clarification made, I shall myself adopt the same focus nonetheless. If the rescuers' solidarity and their motives for it constituted only one factor in the outcome, they were an important factor. And there are reasons I shall come to presently for caring about what their motives were.

The striking thing, however, is how abstract, even within that partial focus, how obviously speculative, Rorty's thesis about the rescuers is. 'Perhaps', he suggests, they occasionally said something like this; but 'surely' they more often said something like that. These rescuers were real people and there is a body of writing about them, though in-depth study is mostly quite recent. An early piece is worth mentioning. In 1955, Philip Friedman, a pioneer of what is now called Holocaust research, published a short essay in which, after referring to rescuers who were activated by love, friendship, association through work or politics, he went on to speak also of the many whose motives were 'purely humanitarian' and who 'extended their help indiscriminately to all Jews in danger.' As a prime example of this latter kind of rescue, Friedman detailed some of the efforts made in different countries to save thousands of Jewish children.[5] He was writing,it is true, at a time when it was rarer than it is now for scholars of progressive outlook to put in question the viability of a 'universalistic attitude',[6] and his talk of purely humanitarian motives could be thought to be mere imputation, the construction of a pre-'post-modern' mind. But Friedman's example of the rescue of children may give one pause on this score.

Rescued children did not generally fall into such categories as 'comrade in the movement', 'fellow member of the same union or profession' or 'fellow bocce player'. They may, of course, have been fellow Milanese, Jutlanders, Belgians and the like, or even the children *of* fellow members of one parochial category or another. But it seems a nice point whether risking your life to save a child – or, as it was frequently, children – requires a more difficult act of sympathetic identification than does taking that risk for a fellow Milanese, bocce player or whatever. In a book he published two years later, *Their Brothers' Keepers*, Philip Friedman told the story of another Maria, a Mother Maria. A Russian woman (born Elizabeth Pilenko) who had settled in France and become a nun in the Russian Orthodox church, during the Nazi occupation she was at the centre of a clandestine organization rescuing Jews, amongst them many children. She was eventually captured and interrogated by the Gestapo. Her interrogator at one point put it to Mother Maria's mother, who was with her, that she had educated her daughter stupidly; the daughter only helped Jews. 'This is not true,' the old woman is said to have responded. 'She is a Christian who helps those in need. She would even help *you*, if you were in trouble.' Mother Maria died at Ravensbruck.[7]

I have no way of knowing, naturally, how well Mother Maria's mother understood her daughter's heart. But the story as told may suggest a counter-hypothesis to Rorty's. Children are only young humans. They are for a greater or lesser time dependent on adults, often vulnerable, a repository of hope and of much else. Can they not stand as a token in this context of the other routes to protective empathy there may be within the shared experience of human beings than just belonging to some smaller, exclusive community, whether concretized by locale and language, or functionally, or by political or religious belief? If the route may go via a child's vulnerability or its hope, or via the hope on its behalf, then so, surely, may it go via any person's anguish or desperate need; via any qualities indeed that transcend particular communities by being just common modes, so to say, of the human condition. But I may seem, now, to speculate in my own turn.

In neither his essay nor his book did Friedman give much in the way of direct quotation from rescuers themselves as to why they acted as they did. But his judgements were clearly based on a wide familiarity with actual cases throughout Europe and the sources of this familiarity were documented by him. On the other hand, what Rorty says on the subject gives every appearance of being only a casual example. There are reasons all the same, of both a general and a historically more specific kind, why his thesis may be seen by many as a plausible one. Generally, the theme of limited human altruism has a long pedigree already and there is enough evidence, goodness knows, of the realities which have inspired it. It has not just been confected out of thin air. Then, too, the taking of risks and making of sacrifices on behalf of other people plainly is often based on bonds of emotional or social contiguity. More specific to the cultural context in which we presently move is the fact that universalist viewpoints now sometimes get rather short shrift. Rorty demurs at having his ideas identified lock, stock and barrel with post-modernist thought,[8] but there is no doubt that what he has to say on this matter chimes in with anti-universalist philosophical attitudes which post-modernism has lately made fashionable. These seem to me to be good enough grounds for looking at his hypothesis in a serious way, mere casual example or not.

There is another reason for doing so. It concerns just what it was the rescuers did, what they are an example of. Although they tend in their own explanations to make little of what they did, treating it as the most obvious or natural thing, a simple duty and so on, the fact is that all around them others were acting otherwise. The rescuers present an example of uncommon generosity and moral courage in a murderous time, and it is not surprising if they assume for many writers the figure of heroes, a source of some redeeming optimism in a context yielding not very much of that.

Something should be said, as well, about the specific quality of their heroism, given the word's close association with military and, as it were, dragon-slaying exploits. While the stories of Jewish rescue do certainly include much that was extraordinary and dramatic, they also attest to a more mundane, resilient kind of heroism: drawn out and trying, burdened with the minutiae and costs of domestic life, a caring-for heroism, though not any less dangerous for that. It involved, over long periods, the getting and preparing of additional food, coping with extra laundry, having to carry away waste buckets from the hiding places to which those being sheltered were sometimes confined. And it involved just being, daily, at close quarters with them, attempting to maintain harmony under pressure. While strong affective ties between rescuers and rescued were often nurtured through the experiences they shared, people hidden could, like anybody else, turn out to be difficult or worse than difficult. In the words of one rescuer, 'Just because you have risked your life for somebody doesn't mean that that person is decent.'[9] For well-known reasons, and as male rescuers themselves emphasize, these burdens tended to fall more heavily on women, with men away from the house at work or otherwise out in the public domain, sometimes engaged in rescue and resistance activity elsewhere. They were burdens carried by individuals and families within an existence, as one Dutch scholar has put it, 'that was threatened every day, every hour, every minute.'[10] The penalties for sheltering Jews were extreme, often final. In Poland even the children of people caught doing so might not be spared.[11]

It seems at least incautious to draw advantage from this sort of moral example on the basis of no more than a 'surely'. Co-opting it willy-nilly to the side of one's argument is the less important aspect of the thing. The more important aspect is what that argument might then suggest about those who endured such risks on behalf of others. I don't want to get too heavy about this, but directly preceding Rorty's thesis on the rescuers and their reasons, a distinction is explicated by him (between 'us' and 'them') in terms of a notion of 'the wrong sort of human beings'. There are, of course, contexts where notions like that – 'another class of people', 'not my kind of folk' and so on – can be uttered more or less harmlessly or in a humanly understandable way. But Rorty's immediate context has to do with what reasons rescuers might have had for feeling that people in danger 'deserved to be saved'. If it is indeed true that most rescuers were moved by anti-universalist impulses, then this is something we need properly to register. The real sources of their behaviour are certainly worth trying to under-stand, unobstructed by myth or mere phrases. On the other hand, *unless* it is true that they were moved by such impulses, Rorty's suggestion may unintentionally dishonour them.

II

Yad Vashem in Jerusalem, the Holocaust Martyrs' and Heroes' Re-membrance Authority, has sought for more than three decades now, by a law of 1953 of the Israeli parliament, to identify and give due recognition to these people – under the honorific, 'Righteous Among the Nations'. This title is awarded on the basis of survivor testimony and other documenta-tion, and each of those so recognized may plant a tree bearing his or her name on an avenue commemorating them all at Yad Vashem. The criteria which have evolved to cover the award are that it is for the carrying out of, or extending of aid in, an act of rescue; which was at personal risk; and without monetary reward.[12] To date more than nine thousand people have been recognized as 'Righteous Among the Nations', that figure not includ-ing the honour bestowed, exceptionally, on the Danish nation as a whole for its collective rescue of the Jews of Denmark.[13] Scholarly and more general interest in the recipients and in others like them (some of whom have declined to be honoured, disavowing any special virtue) has been slower to emerge. But there is now something of a literature on the subject. On several issues this literature – or such of it as I am familiar with, anyway

– is inconclusive or not very illuminating. It can be reviewed, nevertheless, for what it does reveal.

There has been an interest in how far, if at all, rescuer behaviour can be related to differences of social position, gender, religious and political affiliation, family background, personal character and moral belief. To start with a local point, of the eleven hundred or so Jews who survived the war in hiding in Berlin, most, according to Yehuda Bauer, found refuge in the working class sections of the city. Moshe Bejski, who was a member of the Commission for the Designation of the Righteous, formed the more general impression from his years of work on it that, though rescuers came from all sectors of the population, the majority of them were from 'the lower classes'.[14] But there are also studies, on the other hand, including the two most thorough of recent works on this subject, that indicate a fairly even spread in terms of class and professional status. From her research on Polish rescuers, reported in her book *When Light Pierced the Darkness*, the sociologist Nechama Tec concluded that class was 'a weak predictor of Jewish rescue'. She found the numbers of both middle class and working class rescuers to be approximately par for the proportions of these two categories in the overall population; whilst, relative to their numbers, intellectuals were somewhat more, and peasants somewhat less, apt to give Jews shelter. Similarly, in *The Altruistic Personality*, a study of rescuers from several European countries, S. P. and P. M. Oliner report a quite even distribution in terms of occupational status. They suggest in this connection that 'economic resources . . . were not a critical factor influencing the decision to rescue.'[15]

In the essay I have already cited, Philip Friedman says that women, more easily moved emotionally than men, played an important role in rescue activity; and another author tells us that '[i]t was often women who were faced with the initial all-important decisions as to whether or not to take a stranger into their kitchens and into their homes . . .' The story of Maria Langthaler may come back to mind here. However, there are also studies of aid to German Jews from which it seems that fewer women than men may have been involved in it. In general there appears not to have been, as yet, enough detailed investigation of the gender aspects of this issue to enable any firm conclusions to be drawn.[16]

So it continues. According to Yehuda Bauer again, left-wing groups were on the whole inclined to help Jewish victims of Nazism. This is confirmed in some sort by Tec for the case of Polish rescuers: amongst those who were politically involved, most of the rescuers in her study were communists and socialists. On the other hand, the politically involved were themselves a minority relative to rescuers of no political affiliation – a pattern reported also by the Oliners from their wider study. And Tec records non-leftists as well, albeit a minority, amongst her politically affiliated rescuers. The Oliners' categorization is different here but implies a smaller proportion (amongst the 'political' rescuers) specifically of the left: of the minority of rescuers in their study who were politically affiliated (21 per cent), the majority belonged to democratic parties, not distinguished as between left and other, but only a minority of them to parties described as of the 'economic left'.[17]

As for religion, the research all points towards the same broad picture. Many rescuers were religious, and many rescuers were not. They were devout Christians of all denominations, people of a more general, less attached kind of faith, humanists, atheists. Because of long-standing traditions of anti-semitism within it, Christianity could dispose its adherents against helping Jews – though a few anti-semites did help, their prejudices notwithstanding – and, through its ethical teachings, it could also dispose them towards helping Jews. There is some consensus, in fact, amongst researchers that it was the moral content of religious teaching that was primary with most of the rescuers who do cite their religion as a central motivating impulse.[18]

An interim observation may perhaps be made before we proceed further. The findings so far summarized confirm an impression gained from more general, popular accounts of rescue activity. In one sense, obviously, there were too few rescuers. They made up a very small proportion of the European populations to which they belonged. However, there were enough of them in each of the categories we have been considering – enough women and men, enough workers, peasants, middle-class people and intellectuals, enough believers and non-believers, enough communists and liberals – and there were, *a fortiori*, enough non-rescuers as well within the same categories, for the question under discussion here to be pertinent across all the categories. What were the reasons of those (men, women, intellectuals, Christians, etc.) who risked their lives?[19]

The existing research has also concerned itself with other, broadly characterological, kinds of indicator. It has sought to discover if there might be clues to the rescuers' conduct in the temperaments, types of personality or childhood influences discernible amongst them. An early study, not completed owing to lack of funds, has been influential in directing subsequent researchers towards certain questions. In an essay published in 1970, Perry London reported three impressions derived from his unfinished study: a significant sense amongst the rescuers interviewed of being socially marginal, of standing at odds with or apart from the surrounding community in some way; then, a spirit of adventurousness, evident from the lives of many of them even prior to their rescue activity; finally, an intense identification with a parental model of moral conduct – with no apparent pattern, here, relating to gender.[20] Later work, by Douglas Huneke, and by Samuel Oliner (as relayed by him in articles preceding the *Altruistic Personality* study aforementioned), supported

London on the finding of social marginality; as did Nechama Tec's book, though under the description she preferred of 'separateness' or 'individuality', in which she merged London's categories of social marginality and adventurousness.[21] Others too (Huneke, Samuel Oliner, Coopersmith) have fallen in with London's impressions on adventurousness – or at any rate 'confidence' – as they have on the strong parental moral influence as well.[22]

However, there are contrary indications once again, most strongly with regard to social marginality. In a study of Dutch rescuers, Lawrence Baron did not find a high proportion of socially marginal individuals; and this result is repeated across several countries by the latest and most comprehensive Oliner study, which thereby contradicts his own earlier suggestions on the point. The finding of *The Altruistic Personality* is that 'the overwhelming majority of rescuers (80 percent) had a sense of belonging to their community', a proportion which was almost identical to that found in the comparative sample of non-rescuers.[23]

As to London's other two tentative impressions, although there is no precise or detailed data to set against them so far as I am aware, there are certainly counter-impressions – and from writers as well placed in terms of their knowledge of actual cases. Tec, whose other findings, as we have seen, agree with London's, demurs over just how general among rescuers was the identification with parental values. The family could, but also need not, be the reference point. Rescuers' values sometimes originated independently, from religious or political sources. And Mordecai Paldiel at Yad Vashem, who is sceptical of these correlations in their entirety, puts in question both the generalization about parental identification and that about adventurousness and the like. For each generalization, as for most such, he argues, there are counter-examples aplenty to go with the many examples.[24] With respect to these two generalizations, in any case, it seems appropriate to ask what we would have discovered even were they to be confirmed. It could hardly be surprising if people who took great risks on behalf of others did score higher on 'adventurousness' or 'confidence' than people at large. (It should be registered though, at the same time, that most rescuers do not present themselves as fearless or inordinately bold. From what they say, they had just the sort of feelings you and I can imagine having in a situation of grave risk.) Equally, since one important source of moral education clearly is parental influence, it should not be too startling if a fair to good proportion of the Righteous do profess something like the identification reported by Perry London. The same, I think, goes for the finding of Douglas Huneke that rescuers in his study came out well on 'hospitality'.[25]

How common was it for rescuers to be acquainted – as friends, lovers, neighbours, colleagues – with the Jews they helped? I have not found a precise answer to this question and it is unlikely anybody knows it.

Because people do often go out of their way for those they like or love, cherish, and so on, one would expect there to have been such cases in significant number, and there were. They are emphasized in some of this literature. In his earlier articles, Samuel Oliner focuses on them, both in summarizing Coopersmith's uncompleted work and on his own behalf. He estimates that perhaps as many as 75 per cent of those rescued were previously known to their rescuers or belonged to the same social network as they did. Reporting this estimate Lawrence Baron, too, encourages the inference that prior relationship may have been the more typical case. But Baron himself cites a study (by Wolfson) according to which, in a group of Germans who helped Jews between 1938 and 1945, only a few had been friends with those they saved.[26] And in general the notion that prior relationship was the most frequent case seems to have been formed impressionistically. Where there are specific data – and from studies involving hundreds of both rescuers and rescued – the picture comes out different.

In Nechama Tec's Polish study, a minority of the Jews rescued reported having been helped by friends. More than half were protected by strangers: 51 per cent, as compared with 19 and 30 per cent, respectively, by friends and acquaintances. Similarly, a minority of her rescuers helped only friends; an 'overwhelming majority' helped total strangers or mere acquaintances, the distribution strongly tilted towards the former. The Oliners' *Altruistic Personality* project reveals the same thing: 'More than half had no pre-war acquaintance with any of the Jews they helped. Almost 90 per cent helped at least one Jewish stranger.'[27] Even in terms of more general familiarity and contact, these two studies indicate large numbers of rescuers without previous ties with Jews. According to the Oliners, more than 40 per cent of their rescuers had no Jewish friends, and more than 65 per cent no Jewish co-workers. Of Tec's rescuers 20 per cent had no ties of any kind with Jews.[28] It is not perhaps surprising in the light of all this that Tec should say about the attitude prevailing amongst them, 'Anyone in need qualified for help.'[29]

Or is it surprising? For we are brought back by this to the hypothesis with which we began. Richard Rorty, we saw, reckons on the likelihood of parochial identifications and commitments having been more typical than universalist ones amongst people who risked their lives on behalf of Jews. Others may well reckon otherwise. They may reckon that universalist commitments are exactly what you would expect to find amongst them. However this may be, here finally we do come upon something on which there is near unanimity in the literature under review. In an area of research where, as I have tried to show, the findings are very various, at odds with one another, inconclusive; or else are just indicative of a diversity of rescuer belief, as on religion – in this area the commentators speak with respect to one point in practically one voice. It is a universalist voice.

Moshe Bejski believes 'the humanitarian motivation which dictates a charitable attitude toward one's fellow man' to have been dominant amongst the numerous considerations that moved rescuers. André Stein concludes his book about Dutch rescuers, 'what [they] seem to have in common is a direct link with their fellow humans, regardless of who those humans are. They see the suffering, and . . . they take action.' From a study of French Catholics who aided Jews, Eva Fleischner could isolate no single common motive other than 'the conviction, shared by all, that Jews must be helped because they were victims – fellow human beings in need'. Kristen Monroe and her co-authors found amongst the rescuers they interviewed a 'perception of themselves as one with all humankind', 'part of a shared humanity'. In connection with parental models of moral conduct, Douglas Huneke refers to the religious teachings and 'humanistic perspectives' imparted to the rescuers he interviewed. 'They had been taught,' he says, 'to value other human beings.' Or they knew, as he also says, how to contain their prejudices, and he gives a sort of limit case of this, of a rescuer who believed that the Jews may have brought their suffering upon themselves: by declining to forsake Judaism for Christianity; because they had crucified the Christ; and so forth. Shocked by the suggestion that her views might be seen as a justification for Nazi aims, this woman went on to say, 'But the Jews are human beings. No one has the right to kill people because of what they believe.'[33]

Samuel Oliner, even in the earlier articles highlighting cases of people with a prior social link to those they helped, does not neglect to pick out as one of several key motives amongst rescuers, 'their love of humanity'. He speaks of them, also, as having been reared in an environment emphasizing 'a universal sense of justice'. Subsequently, he and Pearl Oliner report the finding of their *Altruistic Personality* study, that a large majority of rescuers emphasized the ethical meaning for them of the help they gave: some of these in terms of the value of equity or fairness; more of them in terms of the value of care; but in any case with a sense of responsibility common amongst them that was 'broadly inclusive in character, extending to all human beings.' In fact, the Oliners' figures give half of all rescuers as owning to 'a universalistic view of their ethical obligations' – this as compared with 15 per cent moved by a desire to assist friends. Nechama Tec, for her part, gives as many as 95 per cent of rescuers from her study as ascribing their decision to help to simple 'compassion for Jewish suffering' (against 36 per cent to bonds of friendship and 27 per cent to religious convictions). They displayed, she says, a 'universalistic perception of the needy'. And Mordecai Paldiel postulates an innate human altruism which, weakened by societal influences of one kind and another, can be suddenly activated 'in order to uphold the principle of the sanctity of life'.[31]

I now propose two more – although competing – hypotheses. I shall call them the 'naive' hypothesis and the 'sceptical' hypothesis. Each responds differently to the question of what one is to make of the broad consensus just documented. The naive hypothesis, which is mine, is this. If so many who are familiar with actual rescuers concur on this one point regarding the motives prevalent amongst them, it is likely to be because a 'universalistic attitude' was indeed general, contrary to Rorty's speculation. The commentators' judgements, so to say, mirror the explanations of the people about whom those judgements are made. The sceptical hypothesis, on the other hand, I construct merely by anticipation, and it is as follows. Well, of course, this is just what the commentators *would* say – in an intellectual culture saturated by universalist grand narratives, essentialist concepts of 'human nature' and the like.[32]

We need perhaps, then, to give some attention to the voice of the rescuers themselves. That is what I next undertake.

III

I have not, it should at once be said, interviewed any of the people about to make an appearance here. I have only read of them. Nevertheless, if from the literature I have managed to consult one leaves aside a certain volume of quotation not attributed to specific individuals, a sample of several dozen rescuers can be assembled, all of them identified by name, who tell something of their stories and something of their reasons.[33] Obviously, this assembly is not governed by any scientific sampling method. I tread, possibly, on thin ice. But I venture to say all the same that, unless by a freak chance an altogether odd collection of rescuers has been thrown before me, the naive hypothesis looks pretty good. I will go further. It is not very easy to find people – from some eighty of them – who say the sort of thing, or at any rate just the sort of thing, that Rorty surmises rescuers usually said.

Here are Arnold Douwes and Seine Otten, two close friends interviewed together. They were part of a network of people in the town of Nieuwlande in the Netherlands, who provided shelter to hundreds of Jews. Otten recalls his wife's saying, 'we should try to save as many as we can.' In fact, she and he hid fifty Jews in all during the period of the Nazi occupation. Douwes, though not himself Jewish, was arrested early on for wearing the yellow star. His role in rescue activity came to include attending to the many needs of Jews in hiding – for food, money, false papers and so on – and searching the countryside to find people willing to take them in. 'It wasn't a question', he says, 'of why we acted. The question is why things weren't done by others. You could do nothing else; it's as simple as that. It was obvious. When you see injustice done you do something against it. When you see people being persecuted, and I didn't care whether they were Jews or Eskimos or Catholics or whatever, they were persecuted people and you had to help them.'[34]

Here is John Weidner. A Dutch businessman working in France during the war, he helped escort hundreds of Jews to safety in Switzerland, travelling on skis across the mountains. Involved in the same rescue organization, his sister was caught and killed by the Nazis. Weidner himself was tortured, suffering a permanent impairment of his speech. On one occasion, at the station in Lyon, he witnessed an SS officer crushing the head of a Jewish infant under his boot. Weidner says that what the Nazis did went against everything he was taught to believe; they 'had no respect for [the] human dignity' of the Jews. A Seventh-Day Adventist, he speaks of 'his concept of love and compassion', of the need 'to have a heart open to the suffering of others.' He says: 'I hope God will know I did the best I could to help people.'[35]

Such sentiments are not unusual in my quasi-sample of rescuers, they are typical. Eva Anielska, a Polish woman, a socialist and member of Zegota – the underground Council of Aid to Jews that was active in Poland from late 1942 on – helped save many people, most of them strangers. 'One saw the Jew,' she says, 'not as a Jew, but as a persecuted human being, desperately struggling for life and in need of help . . . a persecuted, humiliated human being . . .' Jorgen Kieler was a member of the Danish Resistance Movement. Ascribing to the Danish people 'a traditional humanistic attitude to life', he says: 'National independence and democracy were our common goals, but the persecution of the Jews added a new and overwhelming dimension to the fight against Hitler: human rights. Our responsibility toward and our respect for the individual human being became the primary goals of the struggle.' Kieler mentions also the German official, Georg Duckwitz. Duckwitz was at the time shipping attache at the German legation in Copenhagen. He warned his Danish contacts when the deportation of the Jews was about to begin, so making a decisive contribution to the collective rescue that followed. When the risk he had taken was later pointed out to him, he responded, 'Everyone should see himself in the situation in which he, too, like his fellow man, might find himself.'[36]

Bill and Margaret Bouwma sheltered on their farm in turn a woman, a teenage girl who was murdered by Dutch Nazis when she was out one day on her own, and then another girl. Induced by a question from the woman to ponder just why he was doing what he was, Bill Bouwma answered: because he was brought up always to help the weak; because he knew what it felt like to be the underdog; because his faith taught him to open his door to the homeless, the refugee – and, more simply, because a voice inside him said he had to do it, otherwise he would no longer be himself. Margaret Bouwma told one of the girls, 'It's not that we are friends of the Jews or their enemies. It is our human duty to open our home . . . and our hearts to anyone who suffers.' Another Dutch couple, Rudy and Betty de Vries, hid a family of three not previously known to them and then others as well in the home above their butcher shop; and Rudy was involved more generally in underground and rescue activity. Betty felt at times over-whelmed by the extra work, but convinced herself 'that it was a very small price to pay for saving three lives.' Rudy reports a sympathetic encounter with a German soldier in the shop. He says that many 'failed to see the man in their enemy', but 'Jews or Germans – it made no difference to me, as long as I could see them as human beings.' When first approached to shelter people, he hesitated only a moment; he had been taught as a child to distinguish between justice and injustice. 'My faith', he says, 'commands . . . me to love my fellow man, without exclusions.'[37]

One repeatedly comes across instances, in fact, of Perry London's sort of rescuer: people who cite a strong parental influence in speaking about the help they gave. A German engineer, Hermann Graebe – known also for some terrible, heart-breaking testimony concerning an episode he witnessed during the mass shooting of the Jews of Dubno – saved the lives of dozens of Jews working under his management in eastern Poland. 'I believe that my mother's influence on me when I was a child has a lot to do with it. . . . She told me . . . that I should not take advantage of other people's vulnerability. . . . She said, "Take people as they come – not by profession, not by religion, but by what they are as persons."' Mihael Mihaelov, a Bulgarian, tells that both his parents were of very generous disposition. Mihaelov hid property for many Jews and brought food to them in the labour camps. He had seen Germans beating Jews and breaking their bones. 'I don't know exactly why I helped. It's just the kind of person I am. When I see someone who needs help I help them, and my whole family is like that.' In the town of Topusko on the Bosnian border in Yugoslavia, Ivan Vranetic helped and hid many Jews fleeing from the Nazis. The first of them was a man who approached him in desperate straits: 'He had no shoes, nothing, and when he started to tell me his story I had to help him. I think it must be in my upbringing. . . .' Vranetic says that his father 'liked people no matter what religion they were' and his mother was a good woman; 'we were brought up to love humankind.'[38]

I interject now a first sceptical question on behalf of anyone who is wary vis-a-vis my naive hypothesis. The question might go like this: as what is here documented so far are the explanations put forward by rescuers many years after the events to which their explanations relate, how good a guide can these be to their motives at the time? How indicative is what they say now of what they felt, what really moved them, then? There are a number of things one can offer in response to this question. First, since what I report these rescuers as saying is what rescuers seem to say, not just here or there, but quite generally and consistently, is it not likely to tell us something about what they actually felt at the time? Or must we rather suppose on the part of all these people a systematic – a common – misconstrual of their own reasons? Second, what they now say quite generally and consistently seems likely on the face of it to be as good a guide to their reasons as anything imputed to them on the basis merely of a current philosophical commitment. Third, one can try also to discover what was said by such people *then*. The evidence I have been able to gather about this suggests it might not have been all that different from what they say now.

A young French Catholic, Germaine Ribiere, in the period before anyone in the Church hierarchy in France had spoken out against the persecution of the Jews there, committed her feelings about this to the diary she kept. 'I ache for them in my whole being, I ache for my Jewish brothers and sisters,' she writes when seven thousand Polish Jews are rounded up in Paris; and then, after she has visited two internment camps, 'Total contempt for the human being.' She speaks to a rabbi, saying she will help in any way she can. Another entry by her reads, 'Humanity is the body of Christ. One part of that humanity is being tortured. . . . and we look on in silence as the crime is being perpetrated.' (Today, incidentally, Ribiere tells her interviewer also, 'My mother raised us to have respect for life.') When finally a small number of bishops do break their silence, what do they say? They speak the same sort of language as Germaine Ribière. The Archbishop of Toulouse, Jules Gérard Saliège, writes in a letter of August 1942, 'it has been destined for us to witness the dreadful spectacle of children, women and old men being treated like vile beasts. . . . The Jews are our brethren. They belong to mankind.' A few days later in a letter to be read within his diocese, the Bishop of Montauban, Pierre-Marie Théas, similarly proclaims, 'all men . . . are brothers, because they are created by the same God . . . all, whatever their race or religion, are entitled to respect. . . . The current anti-semitic measures are in contempt of human dignity.'[39]

That was then. When therefore, now, another woman, Marie-Rose Gineste, who spent four days on her bicycle delivering Monsignor Théas's letter and then took charge at his request of the hiding of the Jews of Montauban, says, 'It was all about human justice . . .', how plausible actually is it to suppose she would have expressed herself very differently at the time?[40] Or we may take the example of Pieter Miedema. He was a minister in the Dutch Reformed Church in Friesland; as he has been incapacitated by a stroke, his wife, Joyce, now speaks for him. The Miedemas hid Jews in their own home, and he, the minister, was also active in finding hiding places for them elsewhere in the area. He had to go on the run at one point in order to avoid arrest or worse. Pieter Miedema has declined to be honoured by Yad Vashem, having done only 'what everyone should have done'. Joyce Miedema now construes his thinking so: 'if you opt against opening your home and heart to an innocent fugitive, you have no place in the community of the just'; you choose 'the worst solitude a man can discover: his own exclusion from the family of man.' One might be tempted to take this for a merely second-hand sentiment – except that it was part of a sermon given by Miedema at the time, which his wife says will stay in her mind always, 'word for word'.[41]

Or, again, there is the example of Zofia Kossak-Szczucka. A Catholic author and right-wing nationalist, she wrote a leaflet protesting against the murder of the Jews of Poland and helped to found Zegota, the organization for aiding them. She was caught and sent to Auschwitz where she spent nearly a year. On her release, she became active in the rescue of Jewish children. Szczucka's writings of the period give expression both to some anti-semitic convictions and to an energetic appeal on behalf of the Polish Jews. In one piece, she writes that after the war they will be told, 'Go and settle somewhere else.' But now they 'are the victims of unjust murderous persecutions' and 'Christ stands behind every human being. . . . He stretches His hand to us through a runaway Jew from the ghetto the same way as He does through our brothers.' In the protest leaflet, Jews are described by her as the 'enemies of Poland'; but also as 'condemned people' and 'defenceless people', 'insane from grief and horror'. Their present plight Szczucka calls 'your fellow man's calamity'.[42]

That also was then. Today, another Polish Catholic writer and anti-semite, Marek Dunski, explains himself as follows. His motivation arose from his religious convictions. 'One could not simply allow a person to die.' In wartime, he says, evidently generalizing from his own case, people recur to more basic things: 'They tend to see a person as a human being. This is what happened with the Jews. They were not seen as Jews but as human beings.' Or the individual Jew was seen simply as 'a hurt, suffering being'. Dunski speaks as well, in connection with the aid he brought to a threatened Russian soldier, of not having 'any special fondness for Russians', yet of feeling 'that a human being ought to be saved at any price.' Marek Dunski had a part in the rescue of several hundred Jewish children. His reasons as given do not strike me as any less to be relied on for having been articulated later than Szczucka's similar ones.[43]

Some readers may be starting to wonder, secondly, why the material I have cited does not reflect (what we know to be the case from the review of literature in the previous section) that there were rescuers who helped their friends. It does not reflect it yet. Only because I have not got there yet. I was coming to them. Here is one category of such rescuers.

Bert Bochove and his first wife Annie (now deceased) hid a friend of Annie's when she came and asked for help. They then also hid thirty-six other people. Bochove says, 'it was easy to do because it was your duty', 'I got such satisfaction . . . from keeping people safe' and 'You help people because you are human and you see that there is a need.'[44] Tina Strobos's family, Social Democrats and atheists, hid Tina's best friend who was Jewish. The family had a tradition of helping others – refugees, miners' children. During the war they hid about a hundred people, though never more than five at a time: 'Some we knew, some we didn't.' Strobos says she believes in 'the sacredness of life'; today she gives talks to schoolchildren and tells them 'we have to be careful not to hurt others who don't belong to our little group.'[45]

Zofia Baniecka for her part would like children to know that there were people in Poland like Tina Strobos. Beniecka herself and her mother hid or found hiding places for Jews escaping from the Warsaw ghetto. One of these was a school friend – 'so of course I didn't turn her away.' But, as Baniecka also says, 'We hid at least fifty Jews during the war – friends, strangers, acquaintances, or someone who heard about me from someone else. Anyone was taken in.' Baniecka says she 'believe[s] in human beings'.[46] And then Jan Elewski. A Polish officer and leftist who protected his best friend from anti-semitic persecution before the war, he also saved seven strangers during the war by moving them to a more secure hiding place and supplying them with food there. He speaks of a 'feeling of duty' by contrast with the self-centredness of others who did not help; and of the thought that his family would have disowned him for 'not helping people who were being destroyed.' And Roman Sadowski also. He was a member of Zegota. He tried desperately to contact Jewish friends in the Warsaw ghetto when the deportations to the death camps began, but he failed and they perished. He then gave aid mostly to strangers: 'whoever turned to me, and whomever I could find.' Why? 'Their being Jewish did not play a part at all. Regardless of who they were, needing help was the criteria [sic] . . . Human life was at stake.'[47]

And Jean Kowalyk Berger. And Ada Celka. In the Ukrainian village in which the former lived, the Germans set up a labour camp and she saw there 'the cruelty . . . day after day.' She and her family agreed to hide a Jewish doctor who had earlier helped her. He arrived one night at their door, begging to be taken in. 'Then more people came during that night. . . . If you could have seen my house. . . . Everything was so difficult.' She describes how difficult. When she is asked why she helped, she says, 'When I saw people being molested, my religious heart whispered to me, "Don't kill. Love others as you love yourself."' Ada Celka, deeply religious as well, living in poverty in a one-room apartment with her sister and disabled father, took in the daughter of a Jewish friend. Herself a Pole, she also sheltered Russian partisans. 'What I did was everybody's duty. Saving the one whose life is in jeopardy is a simple human duty. One has to help another regardless of who this human being is as long as he is in need, that is all that counts.'[48]

It seems not uncommon amongst the Righteous: people who help friends or acquaintances and who help people other than friends or acquaintances, help people who are strangers to them; and who give universalizing reasons for doing what they do. About people like them it would seem safe to conclude that those reasons are not then merely rhetorical superstructures on or rationalizing derivations from friendship –

as the putative 'real' cause (or essence) of rescuer behaviour. What, however, of rescuers whose help was just for friends? Or just for friends and the relations of friends? Or whose help was primarily such? Here at least, it might seem clear, we would have come upon the Rorty sort of rescuer. I suggest, on the contrary, that that is not so clear. Let us consider first in this connection the story of Irene Opdyke.

Opdyke was a student nurse at the time of the invasion of Poland. She speaks of her mother as a strong influence – 'she never turned away anyone from her doorstep', 'always knew how to help' – and speaks of her own vocation to be a nurse likewise in terms of helping people. Opdyke was beaten and raped by Russian soldiers and later impressed into labour by the Nazis. Running an errand one day in the nearby ghetto she witnessed scenes of great brutality. 'Most of all, I remember the children', she says. Opdyke decided that 'if the opportunity arrived I would help these people.' She subsequently befriended twelve Jews employed in the laundry at her place of work. As she puts it, 'I didn't have a family. They were persecuted. It was a human bond.' When she then learned of a move impending to liquidate the ghetto, she managed to hide and finally save these friends, at a not insignificant personal cost to herself. She says 'that we belong all together. That no matter what a person's colour, race, religion, or language, we are created by one God'; and that 'all human beings belong to one . . . family.'[49]

Did Irene Opdyke save her friends only because they were her friends? Or did she save them because of the moral commitments she tried to live by, of the kind of person she was? Or: what was the balance between her feelings of friendship and her more general values or moral impulses, in moving her to act on behalf of people threatened? This question, actually, does not seem all that interesting in relation to Opdyke herself. She plainly had enough reasons, and good ones, to act as she did; and since she herself lays emphasis upon reasons of both kinds, who else could presume to say exactly what the balance was between them? But the question of the balance, of the interrelationship between different sorts of reason, does not closely depend, as it happens, on the chronology or details of Opdyke's particular story. It is of much broader applicability. For it would seem to be the case with those rescuers who came to the aid of friends, acquaintances and other such connected folk, that they also will generally explain themselves in the way we have begun to be familiar with, giving expression to universalist commitments. They – also – say the kind of thing that Rorty suggests rescuers would not usually have said.

Hela Horska, a doctor's wife, who hid the young son of one of her husband's patients and eventually thirteen other members of his family as well, says: 'All my life I worked for social causes. . . . It did not matter who it was if someone needed help I had to give it. . . . I helped because a human being ought to help another.' Albert and Wilma Dijkstra sheltered people Albert knew from his home town. The Dijkstras speak in terms of hiding 'Jewish friends . . . in danger' – and also of their belief 'that life is sacred', of their 'concern [having] always been with human life and not to whom it belongs', of not 'distinguishing [in this regard] between Christian and Jew, German and Dutch'. Gitta Bauer, who hid a family friend, says it was not a big decision: 'She was a friend and she needed help.' Bauer also says that her father had taught her, 'Jews are people like you and me only with a different religion. And that's it.' She has always been 'concerned about racism of any kind'. Libuse Fries brought aid to a workmate (her husband-to-be) in The Wresienstadt, and she helped his sister also and was imprisoned for doing so. Fries was brought up, she tells, 'to love nature and all human beings'; she 'thought it was inhuman to take young people from their families for no reason.' Germaine Belline and Liliane Gaffney, a mother and daughter, helped many Jewish friends: two brothers, their sister, her children, a niece, 'cousins of cousins'. They say: it felt 'natural' because these were friends; and '[t]he one thing I could never stand as a child is injustice'; and 'if you didn't live for others . . . it wasn't worth living. To be human we need each other.'[50]

And one 'Stanislaus' who had Jewish friends in the Warsaw ghetto nearby, and who together with his mother gave out much help, to friends and others – soup, shelter, finding hideouts. His reasons: 'Human compassion.' And Louise Steenstra who lost her husband, killed in their home by German soldiers for hiding a Jewish friend. She and her husband could not be 'insensitive', she remembers, to the fate looming over the various friends they helped: 'we felt so sorry for those Jewish people with their kids screaming when the Nazis came in the night to pick them up'; '[w]hen you are the mother of one child, you are mother to them all.'[51] And Gustav Mikulai who, 'see[ing] poverty and injustice all around [him]', became a Social Democrat in his youth, and who all his life has 'had three passions: music, women and Jews' – one of whom he married. He hid his wife and in-laws, and indeed together with a friend 'all the Jews we could'. He was 'sort of drunk with [his] rebellion against the horrible injustice' to them. 'It was a terrible time for humanity.' And Orest Zahajkewycz and Helena Melnyczuk, brother and sister, who hid friends in their home and whose father 'was always trying to help somebody', and who have tried to teach their own children 'to be human' and do the same. They also recall that period, by contrast, in terms of its 'horror – that one human being could do this to another.'[52]

And then, to finish with this grouping in my quasi-sample of rescuers, there is Stefania Podgorska Burzminski. She gave refuge in her apartment to the son of a Jewish woman she worked for, and later to his brother and his sister-in-law; in all, to thirteen people and 'for two winters'. Pivotal to her story as she tells it is this:

Before the war everyone shopped and talked together and everything was fine. But then there was the segregation and the mark of the Jewish star, and that was confusing for me. One day I saw a Jewish boy on the street, about nine years old, and another boy came up to him and said, 'You are a Jew!' and he hit him. A man, just an ordinary worker, saw it and said, 'Why would you do that? He's a boy just like you. Look at his hands, his face. There's no difference. We have enemies now from another country who say there's a difference, but there isn't.' So the boy who hit the Jewish boy looked sad and said, 'Oh, all right, I'm sorry.' I listened to him and I came home and I looked at my hands and I said, 'No, there is no difference.' So, you see, I listened and I learned.

Learned just about helping fellow denizens of Poland perhaps? Today, Podgorska voices a concern with the need to 'teach people humanity'.[53]

Now, it might be suggested that with rescuers whose aid was (or was primarily) to people more or less closely connected to them, the articulation of universalist motives and humanist principles *can* be discounted. They helped whom they knew, you see, and everything else would be at best well-meaning sentiment. But for my own part I do not see how this could possibly be asserted with any confidence, much less explanatory authority. That someone is a friend is in itself, of course, a perfectly good reason for helping them. On the other hand, the pertinent context here is one in which an inestimably large number of people precisely did not help friends, neighbours and other acquaintances. They stood by, looked on or turned away, whether in fear or shame or merely with indifference, as the Jews they knew were taken away or fled. In that sense, as a matter of ethico-sociological generalization, friendship or familiarity plainly is not a sufficient condition of one person's coming to the aid of another in serious jeopardy. If against this background so many of the rescuers who gave help to people close to them tell universalizing stories about what they did and who they are, as well as or sometimes rather than citing friendship and the like, on what basis can it be claimed that their universalizing stories vouchsafe us nothing of what 'really' impelled them?

It might now in turn be said, though, that this reasoning can be reversed against me. How many people also, it will be pointed out, professing similar moral viewpoints to all these rescuers, did not bring aid to Jews in danger. It is, again, an inestimably large number. The argument does not discomfit me, however, nor is the case so reversed genuinely symmetrical with the one it supposedly reverses. For I do not seek to belittle or minimize the part which might have been played by friendship and other particularist loyalties in contributing to individuals' motives for rescue. I simply meet here the effort to belittle or minimize the part played by universalist moral attachments, setting down what I have found. Nor does setting it down imply any claim that, as a matter of ethico-sociological generalization, universal moral attachments might on their part be a sufficient condition of rescue. The point is only that it is a complicated question just what combination of reasons, motives and other factors – temperamental, situational and so on – does, and just what combination does not, move people to act under risk for other people; a question to which no one, so far as I know, has the answer, if indeed there is *an* answer. All I do is report that a universalist moral outlook appears to have had a very significant part in motivating Jewish rescue. Many rescuers give voice to it and few do not. At the same time, no rescuer I have come across overtly repudiates it. To be sure, there were such people about also, at that time. They seem not to have been heavily involved in helping Jews is all. We know what some of them were doing.

A third and last query on behalf of the sceptical: Are there, then, no rescuers within my sample who are of that sort who say 'fellow Milanese . . . fellow Jutlander'? In fact, only one case I have been able to discover perhaps fits here. It is a Dane, unnamed in the source in which I find him, who says, 'The main reason I did it was because I didn't want anybody to hurt my friends, my neighbours, my fellow countrymen, without cause.' Even he makes some additional remarks as well, of seemingly broader scope, but ambiguously so. I mark him down as one for Richard Rorty anyway. This Dane is (if he is) a rare figure in the present company.[54]

It is another case, rather, that captures what seems to be the more general situation with rescuers who refer to their communities. Aart and Johtje Vos gave shelter in their home near Amsterdam to many who needed it, at one time hiding more than thirty Jews as well as a few other people. She, Johtje, says: 'We never talked about Jews [in Holland]. They were all just Dutch, that's all.' And he, Aart, says: 'Holland was like a family and part of that family was in danger. In this case, the Jewish part. The Germans were threatening our family.' This seems clear enough. But there is more. Aart Vos also recounts how one day after a bombing he found a wounded German soldier and helped him back to his camp. Asked by friends how he could bring himself to 'save a German', he replied, 'My wife and I were brought up to have respect for life.' Johtje Vos, relating the same incident elsewhere, puts it that their friends reproached Aart with helping the enemy and that his response to them was, 'No, the moment the man was badly wounded, he was not an enemy any more but simply a human being in need.'

And, this episode aside, Aart and Johtje Vos, looking beyond themselves and their children, that is, beyond their own family to a wider Dutch 'family', patently look further still. Johtje says that both she and Aart were brought up not to be prejudiced on grounds of 'race, colour, creed, nationality, or whatever . . . so it came very naturally to us to consider Jews just like us. We thought of them as human beings, just as we were.' Your response in that situation, she also says, depends on 'the results of your upbringing, your character, on your general love for people. . . .' Again: 'We helped people who were in need. Who they were was absolutely immaterial to us. It wasn't that we were especially fond of Jewish people. We felt we wanted to help everybody who was in trouble.' During the war, Aart says, he 'thought it wasn't possible that on this little planet people could do [the sort of things they did] to each other.'[55]

Just as friendship, as we have seen, need not be the only reason of someone who goes to the aid of a friend, so a commitment to compatriots, fellow citizens or other locally specific communities does not have to exclude more general humanitarian concern. With the rescuers the common pattern would seem to be that it did not. And is this so surprising? Mutual loyalty or solidarity within such communities can, it is true, be of an exclusionary sort; or it may sometimes simply relate to matters in which a more extensive identification would not be – for *those* matters – appropriate. It is also the case, however, that a person who says 'Dutch, just like us', 'fellow Dane' and so forth, may be appealing to a notion of civic equality and reciprocal obligation closely tied, as a matter of historical and cultural fact, to wider egalitarian, humanistic, universalist values. Especially when what is at stake is a matter of life, death or grave suffering, to think, 'Dutch like the rest of us', may only be to think, 'Another *person* in the Dutch community'. It need not be very different from thinking, 'Fellow human being.'

Such, at any rate, commonly was the case with the rescuers. Like Aart and Johtje Vos, those of them who allude to the specificities of community invariably point beyond these as well. Marion Pritchard who had a part in saving more than a hundred Jews says, 'In Holland, the Jews were considered Dutch like everyone else.' She learned tolerance from her father, 'more accepting of all people and their differences than my mother', and was imbued early on 'with a strong conviction that we are our brothers' keepers'. Decisive for Pritchard was the experience of happening to witness Nazis loading, throwing – 'by an arm, a leg, the hair' – young children, taken from a Jewish children's home, on to trucks. 'To watch grown men treat small children that way . . . I found myself literally crying with rage.' Pritchard's words do not, to me, encourage the inference that it was the 'Dutchness' of these victims that was for her the key thing.[56]

In turn, a certain 'Johan' explains himself so: 'The main reason was because I was a patriot. I was for my country.' He continues: 'The Germans robbed people of their freedom. And when they started taking the Jewish people, that really lit my fire. . . . I really became full of hate because they took innocent people – especially when they took little kids. That was the worst.' This same 'Johan' says he learned from his parents that 'Jews were just people'. His mother would never 'look down' on anyone. 'She would always appreciate what people were worth.' And then John and Bertha Datema recall some of their wartime reactions. John: that 'those people are Dutch, Jewish or not, they are Dutch'; and that 'I had witnessed more human suffering than I could cope with.' And Bertha: 'Every wasted life is another nail in Christ's body. When a child is destroyed, all of us become orphans.' And Helene Jacobs, a German rescuer for whom 'A community which destroys a part of itself on purpose, out of hatred, gives itself up. It degenerates. This happened in our country.' Jacobs explains her own rescue work like this: 'They were people who were in danger and I wanted to help them. It was as simple as that.' And like this: 'I always knew how dangerous it was, but I did it for humanity, and because I was a patriot.'[57]

Who here, once again, can claim to know the exact balance of these rescuers' reasons: between community, country or patriotism on the one hand; and humanity; children; people in danger or trouble or need, on the other?

I have now given, in any event, some account of rather more than half of the rescuers in my sample. Considerations both of space and for the patience of the reader deter me from relating, even in the truncated and reduced forms I have had to adopt for the stories I have told, the other stories remaining. But the stories left untold tell just the same story as the stories told. I let the subjects of them, of the ones I cannot tell, pass here finally in brief, anonymous parade.

There are the rescuers who speak of parents. 'My mother was always concerned about everyone else.' 'I remember my mother being a person who always wanted to give from her heart.' 'My mother always reached out to others and she taught all of us to do that, too. . . . I think it's in our blood.'[58] And there are the rescuers who helped save children: one who says, 'I believe in people', and who felt (at the age of forty-two), 'My life is past, but the children . . . have their life before them'; one who did what she did because 'All men are equal' and for 'no other' reason; one who 'cried when [he] went into the ghetto and . . . children clamoured after [him] . . . for help'; one who reflects that 'there are a lot of people who have no faith in human kind . . . they're only afraid for their own kin and not for yours or his or hers'; one who 'understood what it meant to be a Jew' when a six-year old fugitive girl said what her family name had been and what it was now; and one who remembers, similarly, the anguish of the child 'who does not know why she cannot use her real name' – and who speaks as well of the preoccupation with justice and injustice that has guided her, the rescuer, all her life.[59]

Then there are those who talk about persecution: like the woman who gives as the reason for her actions that 'they [the Jews] were persecuted not because of what they did but because of the way they were born'; and the woman who says, 'that he was a hunted man was all I needed to know'; and the man brought up in the belief 'that it was inadmissible to persecute people because of their race or religion'; and the man for whom the Holocaust started 'in the hearts' of people, for '[as] soon as you go and say "That Jew!" or whatever, that's where it starts. . . . As soon as you put one race higher than another one .. . .'[60] This last man says also, 'if the moment's there and there's somebody in need, you go help, that's all.' He touches a pervasive theme. The rescuers speak like this: 'to give help to those who are in need'; and 'one has to help all that need it'; and 'I just had to help people who needed help and that was that. I was always ready to help the needy, always'.[61] And the rescuers speak like this: 'the worst off were the Jews. So one had to give help where people were most help-less.. . .'; and 'I had to help. After all, the Jews were the most helpless people'; and 'anyone who needed help had to get it. Jews were in a specially dangerous situation . . . they had to be helped the most'; and 'My home is open to anyone in danger.'[62]

Such are the things rescuers say. They talk of their 'feeling of justice'; of learning early 'to fight for . . . justice' and early about 'helping others'; of growing up without anyone making 'a distinction between people of other religions'.[63] They say: 'There is no greater love than sacrificing your own soul for another's soul', and 'I was an old pacifist', and 'I would have helped anyone.'[64] One man says, 'I cannot stand violence.' He says, 'As a child I was taught an individual has human dignity. . . .' Another man says that what he did just had to be done – 'They suffered so much.' One woman says her mother was such an unjust person that she, the daughter, developed a strong sense of justice by reaction. She says, 'I didn't help only Jews. I helped everyone who was being oppressed because of their politics or ideas'. She says, 'all my life I've been for the peaceful coexistence of all people, of all colours and religions.'[65]

It could be that these rescuers are, all of them, mistaken; that they are really wrong about their reasons. Or it could be, on the other hand, that Richard Rorty is wrong about the Righteous.

IV

In setting out Rorty's view at the beginning of this essay, I reported the claim he makes that it is a 'weak' explanation of a generous action to say 'because she is a human being'. It turns out that this is itself only a weak version of his claim. For he goes on in the same place to suggest that, so far as identifying with humanity goes, in fact 'no one . . . *can* make *that* identification'; to him it seems an 'impossible' one.[66] Yet, the rescuers here, to say nothing of anyone else, appear to think they *can* make that identification – via notions of plain need and suffering; of human dignity and vulnerability; of equality, or justice, or a belief that we are all the children of one God. One man, indeed, finds it possible to explain himself in terms of a still wider sort of identification. This is Stefan Raczynski (the very last story to be told), whose 'father loved his fellow man' and who with the father sheltered on their farm some forty Jews, people escaping from a killing site in the nearby Polish forest. Raczynski says: 'It was a natural thing to do, like when you see a cat on the street, hungry, you give it food. When the Jews started coming from the forests and they were hungry, we gave them food. . . .'[67]

Now, there is a certain irony to be noted about all this. For not only is sympathy for the need or suffering of another being – human or sometimes 'even' animal – a perfectly well-known impulse after all, and also motive or reason for action. But Rorty himself, as anyone familiar with his work will be aware, rather makes something of the fact that human beings share a common capacity for suffering. Sharing this, they are able, evidently many of them, to reach beyond fellow townsfolk and fellow bocce players. So how does it happen, then, that Rorty should deliver himself of the speculation he does about the rescuers? Let it suffice to say here that two voices contend for the ear and soul of Richard Rorty. One of these is the voice of a good, old-fashioned liberalism, of which he is an impressive and eloquent spokesman. It enjoins us to be sensitive to the susceptibility of others to pain and humiliation. It tells us, following Judith Shklar, that cruelty is the worst thing we do. But these themes push Rorty, willy-nilly, towards a notion he would shun, the notion, namely, of a *common human nature*. The second voice that calls to him cannot stand for that. It is the voice, this one, of 'anti-essentialism'; and of 'anti-foundationalism'; and also, it would seem, of anti-universalism – from which, however, the first voice, speaking of plain, never-ending human suffering, continues to beckon him away. This is a pervasive tension in Rorty's thought. I take up *its* story elsewhere.

Referring, in another essay from *Contingency, Irony, and Solidarity*, to the work of Michael Oakeshott, Rorty commends to us the suggestion that morality be thought of 'as the voice of ourselves as members of a community, speakers of a common language.' If we see it so, he says, it will be impossible then to think 'that there is something which stands to my community as my community stands to me, some larger community called "humanity" which has an intrinsic nature.'[68] But I say: on the contrary. It is a triumph of our species, one of its most luminous achievements, to have found its way to this thought and the universalist moral principles which harmonize with it; and those like these Righteous among the Nations who managed to live by such principles under terrifying pressure are the glory of humankind. While one should not make too much perhaps of the influence of high philosophical discussion on the wider social and political culture, one can only wonder nevertheless whether what anyone really needs right now is the effort and the energy being poured out, by philosophers, theorists of language and culture, would-be radicals, feminists, breathless messengers of the end of nearly everything, to impugn such ways of thought – as weak; impossible; or sometimes even just malign, discourse of domination and what have you.

V

I cannot forbear to tell here, finally, of a curious coincidence; or so at any rate it was for me. At a late stage in the work for this foregoing essay I came upon a reference to an old article about Father Marie Benoit: yet one more

rescuer, of some renown, so-called Ambassador of the Jews. This reference
interested me not only because of the subject of the article but also because
of its author: one James Rorty. I just had to pursue it, didn't I? James
Rorty turns out to have been Richard Rorty's father.

This is what he wrote about the attitude of rescuers: 'Men and women of
every class and creed, in all the occupied countries, consciously risked
death and torture simply because they were revolted by the ugly cruelty of
the Nazis. . . . Instinctively they rejected what seemed and was a betrayal
of our common humanity. . . .' That seems to capture well the authentic
voice of the people now called Righteous.[69]

NOTES

1. The story is from Gordon J. Horwitz, *In the Shadow of Death: Living Outside the Gates of Mauthausen*, London 1991, pp. 124–43. Regarding conditions at Mauthausen, see also Robert H. Abzug, *Inside the Vicious Heart*, New York 1985, p. 106.
2. Richard Rorty, *Contingency, Irony, and Solidarity* [henceforth CIS], Cambridge 1989, pp. 189–91.
3. For another response to these passages in Rorty (and a good laugh), see Terry Eagleton, 'Defending the Free World', in *Socialist Register 1990*, pp. 85–6.
4. For a discussion of the issues, see Michael R. Marrus, *The Holocaust in History*, London 1989, pp. 55–107. Elsewhere Marrus and his co-author write: 'Generalizations break apart on the stubborn particularity of each of our countries.' See Michael R. Marrus and Robert O. Paxton, 'The Nazis and the Jews in Occupied Western Europe, 1940–1944', *Journal of Modern History* 54 (1982), p. 713. For comparative figures on Jewish losses, see Israel Gutman (ed.), *Encyclopaedia of the Holocaust* [henceforth *Encyclopaedia*], 4 vols, London 1990, volume 4, pp. 1797–1802.
5. Philip Friedman, *Roads to Extinction: Essays on the Holocaust*, New York 1980, pp. 411–14.
6. Rorty, CIS, p. 191.
7. Philip Friedman, *Their Brothers' Keepers*, New York 1978, pp. 30–32.
8. See, for example, Richard Rorty, *Essays on Heidegger and others*, Cambridge 1991, p. 1; 'Thugs and Theorists', *Political Theory* 15 (1987), pp. 564, 572, 578 n. 23; and 'Feminism and Pragmatism', *Radical Philosophy* 59 (Autumn 1991), pp. 5, 12 n. 18.
9. Andre Stein, *Quiet Heroes: True Stories of the Rescue of Jews by Christians in Nazi-occupied Holland* [henceforth Stein], Toronto 1988, p. 93.
10. Louis de Jong, 'Help to People in Hiding', in Michael R. Marrus, (ed.), *The Nazi Holocaust 5: Public Opinion and Relations to the Jews in Nazi Europe*, 2 vols, Westport (Connecticut) 1989, volume 2, p. 639. Regarding the burdens on women, see: Stein, pp. 7, 47, 188, 191–4; Samuel P. Oliner and Pearl M. Oliner, *The Altruistic Personality: Rescuers of Jews in Nazi Europe* [henceforth AP], New York 1992, pp. 83–4; and Gay Block and Malcka Drucker, *Rescuers. Portraits of Moral Courage in the Holocaust* [henceforth Block], New York 1992, pp. 63, 82.
11. For some accounts of such cases, see Nechama Tec, *When Light Pierced the Darkness* [henceforth Tec], Oxford 1986, pp. 63–8.
12. See Moshe Bejski, 'The "Righteous among the Nations" and Their Part in the Rescue of Jews' [henceforth Bejski], in Michael R. Marrus, *The Nazi Holocaust 5* . . . , volume 2, pp. 452–3; and *Encyclopaedia*, volume 3, pp. 1280–81.
13. Block, p. 252.
14. Yehuda Bauer, *The Holocaust in Historical Perspective*, Seattle 1978, p. 77; Bejski, p. 461.
15. Tec, pp. 115–9, 127–8; Oliners, AP, pp. 127–9. See also the results of a study by Manfred Wolfson reported in Lawrence Baron, 'The Holocaust and Human Decency: A Review of Research on the Rescue of Jews in Nazi Occupied Europe' [henceforth Baron], *Humboldt Journal of Social Relations* 13 (1985/86), pp. 239–40.

16. Friedman, *Roads to Extinction*, p. 414; Pierre Sauvage, in Carol Rittner and Sondra Myers (eds.), *The Courage to Care: Rescuers of Jews During the Holocaust* [henceforth Rittner], New York 1986, p. 137; Sarah Gordon, *Hitler, Germans, and the 'Jewish Question'*, Princeton 1984, pp. 218–21; and Baron, pp. 239–40.

17. Bauer, *The Holocaust in Historical Perspective*, p. 76; Tec, pp. 127–8; Oliners, AP, pp. 159–60; and Baron, pp. 239–40.

18. Tec, pp. 137–9, 145–9; Oliners, AP, pp. 155–7; Baron, pp. 239–40; P. M. Oliner and S. P. Oliner, 'Rescuers of Jews During the Holocaust' [henceforth RJ], in Yehuda Bauer and others (eds.), *Remembering for the Future* [henceforth RFTF], 3 vols, Oxford 1989, I, pp. 510–13; Mordecai Paldiel, 'The Altruism of the Righteous Gentiles' [henceforth Paldiel], RFTF, I, p. 520.

19. Cf. the remarks of Paldiel, pp. 520–1.

20. Perry London, 'The Rescuers: Motivational Hypotheses about Christians Who Saved Jews from the Nazis', in J. Macaulay and L. Berkowitz (eds.), *Altruism and Helping Behaviour*, New York 1970, pp. 241–50.

21. Douglas Huneke, 'Glimpses of Light in a Vast Darkness', RFTF, I, pp. 489–90, and 'A Study of Christians Who Rescued Jews During the Nazi Era', *Humboldt Journal of Social Relations* 9 (1981/82), p. 146 [henceforth, respectively, GL and SC]; Samuel P. Oliner, 'The Need to Recognize the Heroes of the Nazi Era', in Michael R. Marrus, *The Nazi Holocaust 5 . . .* , volume 2, p. 482, and 'The Unsung Heroes in Nazi Occupied Europe', *Nationalities Papers* 12 (1984), p. 135 [henceforth NR and UH]; and Tec, pp. 152, 154.

22. Huneke, GL, p. 489, and SC, p. 146; Oliner, UH, p. 135, and NR, p. 479. And cf. Oliners, AP, p. 142, and RJ, p. 509.

23. Baron, pp. 243–4; Oliners, AP, p. 176.

24. Tec, p. 181; Paldiel, p. 520.

25. Huneke, GL, p. 491, and SC, p. 146.

26. Oliner, NR, pp. 480, 482, and UH, pp. 134–5; Baron, pp. 245, 239–40.

27. Tec, pp. 129 (and 227), 178 (and 233); Oliners, AP, p. 81.

28. Oliners, AP, p. 115; Tec, p. 227.

29. Tec, p. 178.

30. Bejski, pp. 460–61; Stein, p. 310; Eva Fleischner, 'Can the Few Become the Many? Some Catholics in France Who Saved Jews During the Holocaust' [henceforth Fleischner], RFTF, I, pp. 241, 243; Kristen R. Monroe and others, 'Altruism and the Theory of Rational Action: Rescuers of Jews in Nazi Europe' [henceforth Monroe], *Ethics* 101 (1990), pp. 117–18, 122; Huneke, SC, pp. 146–7, and GL, p. 491.

31. Oliner, UH, pp. 134–5, and NR, p. 482; Oliners, RJ, pp. 507–9, and AP, pp. 163–70, 287; Tec, pp. 132, 145, 154; Paldiel, pp. 522–3.

32. Cf. Richard Rorty, *Consequences of Pragmatism*, Hemel Hempstead 1982, pp. xxix–xxx.

33. Though rescuers are mostly identified by their real names, in some of the sources I draw upon they are given fictitious ones to preserve confidentiality. As the sources themselves make it clear which practice is being followed, I simply use the names given, real or fictitious as the case may be.

34. Their story, like many here, is told in the wonderful book of Gay Block and Malcka Drucker, *Rescuers*, pp. 62–7. For Douwes, see also *Encyclopaedia*, volume 1, pp. 401–2.

35. Block, pp. 52, 57; Rittner, pp. 59, 65.

36. Tec, pp. 134–5, 139–40, 177–8; Rittner, p. 89; Bejski, pp. 468–70. For Duckwitz, see also *Encyclopaedia*, volume 1, p. 409.

37. Stein, pp. 18–20, 32; and pp. 183–5, 187, 191.

38. Rittner, p. 43; Block, pp. 232, 226. For Graebe, see also *Encyclopaedia*, volume 2, pp. 599–600, and Martin Gilbert, *The Holocaust: The Jewish Tragedy*, London 1987, pp. 476–8.

39. Fleischner, pp. 234–7; Friedman, *Their Brothers' Keepers*, pp. 49–50.

40. Block, pp. 128–31.

41. Block, pp. 68–71; Stein, pp. 58–9

42. Tec, pp. 107–8, 111–12.

43. Tec, pp. 101–6, 175.

44. Block, pp. 42–46; Monroe, pp. 107, 118

45. Block, pp. 84–9.
46. Block, pp. 163–5.
47. Tec, pp. 133–4, 160–1, 177.
48. Block, pp. 237–40; Tec, pp. 145, 165 (original punctuation).
49. Block, pp. 192–6; Rittner, pp. 44–51; Monroe, pp. 107, 119.
50. Tec, pp. 70–71, 165–6; Stein, pp. 222–4, 245; Block, pp. 136–41; 208–11; and 94–7.
51. Oliners, AP, pp. 193–9; Block, pp. 58–61, and Stein, pp. 102, 134. Steenstra's story is given under a fictitious name in Stein. I have felt free to use her real name here because it is given in Block, presumably with her agreement.
52. Block, pp. 220–3; pp. 241–5.
53. Block, pp. 180–5.
54. Oliners, AP, pp. 203–4.
55. Block, pp. 78–83; Rittner, pp. 24–7; Oliners, AP, pp. 215–20, 228. See my remarks at n. 51 above. They apply here too, to Johtje Vos.
56. Block, pp. 33–41; Rittner, pp. 28–33.
57. Oliners, AP, pp. 142–4; Stein, pp. 141, 144, 166; Block, pp. 149–52.
58. Block, pp. 166, 176, 215.
59. Block, pp. 204–7; Oliners, AP, p. 213; Block, pp. 188, 26, 48, 102–5.
60. Block, p. 77; Fleischner, p. 239; Block, pp. 114, 27.
61. Block, p. 32; Rittner, p. 107; Tec, pp. 170, 167.
62. Tec, pp. 176, 177, 177; Stein, p. 266.
63. Block, pp. 124, 118, 142.
64. Block, pp. 249, 146; Tec, p. 176.
65. Block, p. 172; Fleischner, p. 238; Block, pp. 153–7.
66. CIS p. 198; emphases in the original.
67. Block, pp. 197–201.
68. CIS p. 59. Compare the words of Maria Langthaler quoted at the beginning of this essay.
69. James Rorty, 'Father Benoit: "Ambassador of the Jews". An Untold Chapter of the Underground', *Commentary* 2 (December 1946), pp. 507–13, at p. 513. On James Rorty, see Alan M. Wald, *The New York Intellectuals*, Chapel Hill (N. Carolina) and London 1987, pp. 54–5 and passim.

GLOBALISATION AND THE STATE

Leo Panitch

> Alice never could quite make out, in thinking it over afterwards, how it was that they began: all she remembers is, that they were running hand in hand, and the Queen went so fast that it was all she could do to keep up with her: and still the Queen kept crying 'Faster! Faster!', though she had no breath left to say so.
>
> The most curious part of the thing was, that the trees and the other things round them never changed their places at all: however fast they went, they never seemed to pass anything . . .
>
> 'Well, in *our* country,', said Alice, still panting a little, 'you'd generally get to somewhere else – if you ran for a long time as we've been doing.'
>
> 'A slow sort of country!' said the Queen. 'Now, *here*, you see, it takes all the running *you* can do, to keep in the same place. If you want to get somewhere else, you must run at least twice as fast as that!'
>
> – Lewis Carroll, *Through the Looking Glass*

I. Introduction

Think of the Red Queen's Garden as capitalism. The relentless search for markets and profits brings about faster and faster changes in production and space, industry and commerce, occupation and locale, with profound effects on the organisation of classes and states. It is through this ferocious process of extension and change that capitalism preserves itself, remains capitalism, stays the same system. This paradox, or rather this dialectic, can only properly be grasped if we understand that the "bourgeoisie cannot exist without constantly revolutionising the instruments of production, and thereby relations of production, and with them the whole relations of society."[1] This was not an understanding merely appropriate to what happened to the world in the first half of the 19th century: it is no less appropriate to understanding what has happened over the second half of the 20th, and to what is taking place in the world today.

Now think of Alice, frantically running alongside the Red Queen, as the labour *movement*, or the social *movements*, or the broadly defined "Left".

For all the running they have made in this century, for all the mobilisation and reform, even the moments of revolution and national liberation, the world today is most certainly still very much capitalist, indeed it would seem ever more so. Of course, this does not mean that the world is unchanged from what it was, and this is partly due to the effect of those who have contested and thereby either insulated themselves against or modified the vast transformations wrought by the bourgeoisie. But the institutions of the Left, not least the once powerful Communist and Social Democratic parties, increasingly could not even keep pace and lost more and more initiative to the forces of capitalist change. Their original ambition *to get somewhere else*, to a social order beyond capitalism – that is, to socialism, however conceived – more or less gradually gave way to attempts at adaptation and accommodation to the dynamics of capitalist change. Yet the only result has been that they became more and more ineffective in their attempts to tame the market, and the social forces they had once mobilised and spoken for have become more than ever the victims of ruthless capitalist change.

It has become quite commonplace to recognise that some fundamental rethinking is required by the Left. But all too often such rethinking is still cast in terms of grabbing hold of the bourgeoisie's hand and trying to run faster and faster to match the pace of changes set by contemporary capitalism. This involves a fundamental strategic misconception. If effective forms of movement ever are to reemerge on the Left, they will have to be less about keeping up with or adapting to capitalist change, but rather more about developing the capacity to mobilise more broadly and effectively *against* the logic of competitiveness and profit in order eventually *to get somewhere else*, that is, to an egalitarian, cooperative and democratic social order beyond capitalism. To run, even twice as fast, on capitalism's terms will not in fact lead somewhere else at all.

These considerations are especially germane in light of the challenge posed by what has come to be known as 'globalisation'. The apparent subjection of even advanced capitalist social formations in recent decades to the competitive logics and exigencies of production, trade and finance undertaken on a world scale has entailed, as Robert Cox contends, "subordination of domestic economies to the perceived exigencies of a global economy. States willy nilly become more effectively accountable to a *nebuleuse* personified as the global economy; and they were constrained to mystify this external accountability in the eyes and ears of their own publics through the new vocabulary of globalisation, interdependence, and competitiveness".[2] Notably, for Cox, as for David Gordon, globalisation reflects less the establishment of a stable new international regime of capital accumulation than an aspect of the decay of the old 'social structure of accumulation';[3] as Cox puts it, the tendency to globalisation is "never complete", and there is "nothing inevitable" about its continuation. "Any attempt to depict it must not be taken teleologically, as an advanced stage towards the inevitable completion of a latent structure. Rather it should be taken dialectically, as the description of tendencies that, as they become revealed, may arouse oppositions that could strive to confound and reverse them."[4]

Most accounts of globalisation, however, see the process as irreversible, and in this perspective the predominant strategic response becomes one which invariably tends to see the strategies, practices and institutions of the Left as perhaps having been appropriate to an earlier 'national' stage of capitalism but as having now been rendered outmoded and outdated by globalisation. Just like Alice before she stepped through the looking glass, it is as though the Left used to be able to get somewhere else by running on the terrain of the nation state, but now that capital had escaped the nation state, the Left will have to learn to run with the bourgeoisie across the terrain of the globe. This approach has recently been well represented by David Held, for instance, for whom globalisation implies a distinctively new "international order involving the emergence of a global economic system which stretches beyond the control of a single state (even of dominant states); the expansion of networks of transnational linkages and communications over which particular states have little influence; the enormous growth in international organization which can limit the scope for action of the most powerful states; the development of a global military order . . . which can reduce the range of policies available to governments and their citizens." Since this new global order has apparently escaped the control of democratic institutions located at the national level, Held concludes that his means that "democracy has to become a transnational affair." Strategic priority must be given to "the key groups, agencies, associations and organizations of international civil society", extending their capacity as agencies for democratic control through an appropriate recasting of the territorial boundaries of systems of accountability, representation and regulation, fortified by entrenched transnational bills of social, economic and civil rights.[5]

While characterisations of globalisation as a qualitative new phase of capitalism such as these depart sharply from those who have understood capitalism as a "world system" from its inception, in terms of the implications of globalisation for the institutional capacity and strategic focus of the Left, the dilemma is precisely the same one as posed long ago by world system theorists. Thus Wallerstein:

"While the multiple political organizational expressions of the world bourgeoisie – controlling as they did *de facto* most state structures – could navigate with relative ease the waters of murky geographical identity, it was precisely the world's workers' movements that felt obliged to create national, that is, state-wide, structures, whose clear boundaries would define and limit organisational efforts. If one wants to conquer state power, one has to create organizations geared to this objective. Thus, while the world bourgeoisie has, when all is said and done always organised in relationship to the world economy . . . the proletarian forces – despite their internationalist rhetoric – have been far more nationalist than they claimed or their ideology permitted . . . these movements are caught in a dilemma. They can reinforce their state power, with the advantage of holding on to a foothold in the interstate system, but they face the risk of making the detour the journey, in Hobsbawm's phrase. Or they can move to organise transnationally, at the great risk of losing any firm base, and at the risk of internecine struggle, but it may be that power is only truly available at the world level.[6]

Even those less inclined to reduce the tradition of socialist internationalism to mere rhetoric, nevertheless still see the prime cause of the weakness of the Left today in terms of internationalism having "changed sides", as Perry Anderson recently put it: "The new reality is a massive asymmetry between the international mobility and organization of capital, and the dispersal and segmentation of labour that has no historical precedent. The globalisation of capitalism has not drawn the resistances to it together, but scattered and outflanked them. . . . The age continues to see nationalisms exploding like firecrackers across much of the world, not least where communism once stood. But the future belongs to the set of forces that are overtaking the nation-state. So far, they have been captured or driven by capital – as in the past fifty years, internationalism has changed sides. So long as the Left fails to win back the initiative here, the current system will be secure."[7]

There are a number of problems with this way of approaching the Left's strategic dilemmas in the face of globalisation. The premise that globalisation is a process whereby capital limits, escapes or overtakes the nation state may be misleading in two senses. First, there is often an overestimation of the extent to which nation states were capable of controlling capital in an earlier era; it is as if the Left's mode of practice was adequate in relation to the nation state and thus encourages a similar mode to be adopted at the global level: the problem is just one of running faster on the new terrain. But even for those not given to such illusions, there is a tendency to ignore the extent to which today's globalisation both is authored by states and is primarily about reorganising, rather than by-passing, states; it promotes, in this sense a false dichotomy between national and international struggles and diverts attention from the Left's need to develop its own strategies for transforming the state, even as a means of developing an appropriate international strategy.

II. The Internationalisation of the State

Any attempt to reassess Left strategies in the context of globalisation must begin with the understanding that although the nature of state intervention has changed considerably, the role of the state has not necessarily been diminished. Far from witnessing a by-passing of the state by a global capitalism, what we see are very active states and highly politicised sets of capitalist classes hard at work to secure what Stephen Gill in his essay in *The Socialist Register 1992* (primarily focusing on European Union but pointing to much broader tendencies of this kind) aptly termed a 'new constitutionalism for disciplinary neo-liberalism'.[8] In the past year alone, we have witnessed, not only with the GATT at the world level but also with the North American Free Trade Agreement (to be examined in some detail later in this essay) at the regional level, states as the authors of a regime which defines and guarantees, through international treaties with constitutional effect, the global and domestic rights of capital.

This process may be understood in a manner quite analogous to the emergence of the so-called laissez-faire state during the rise of industrial capitalism, which involved a very active state to see through the separation of polity from economy and guarantee legally and politically the rights of contract and property. We may recall, with Corrigan and Sayer, the long "revolution in government" in England that stretched from 1740 to 1850: "we should understand . . . what later became celebrated and dominant as 'political economy' to be simultaneously the discovery of economy (and 'the economy' argued for as a self-sufficient 'private' realm governed by the laws of the market) and a politicization of a moral code (entailing specific forms of 'policing') which makes that possible."[9] Similarly, as regards the emergence of the modern corporation in the United States through the 19th century, Alan Wolfe showed this could not properly be understood as "a triumph of laissez-faire. Laws could be changed only if the bodies that passed them were controlled; this meant that in order to take the corporation out of the public sphere and place it in the private one, the industrialists had to enter the public sphere themselves. Ironically, a political battle had to be fought in order to place an important – in the nineteenth century perhaps the most important – institution outside of politics, one had to have power in the state in order to make it impotent. Few clearer examples exist of how the struggle over legal parameters cannot be accepted as a given but becomes part of the activity of the state itself.. . ."[10] We are living through something like this in our own time: capitalist globalisation is a process which also takes place in, through, and under the aegis of states; it is encoded by them and in important respects even authored by them; and it involves a shift in power relations within states that often means the centralisation and concentration of state powers as the necessary condition of and accompaniment to global market discipline.

It must be said that most contributions to understanding the role of the state amidst the contemporary process of globalisation have lagged behind the process itself, and on the whole remained quite thin, at least in comparison with two key contributions which were made on the subject two decades ago. In 1971 Robin Murray offered a seminal contribution to what he termed "the territorial dialectics of capitalism" to the end of developing "a framework which would allow a more substantial approach to the problem of the effects of an internationalization of capital on existing political institutions."[11] The importance of his contribution was that, far from conceiving this as a process which could be understood in terms of capital "escaping" the state, Murray demonstrated to the contrary that as capital expanded territorially one of the key problems it had to confront was how to try to ensure that state economic functions might continue to be performed. At issue was the structural role of the capitalist state in relation to "what may most aptly be called economic *res publica*', those economic matters which are public, external to individual private capitals". This included guaranteeing property and contract; standardising currency, weights and measures; ensuring the availability of key inputs of labour, land, finance, technology and infrastructure; general macroeconomic orchestration; regulation of conditions of work, consumption and external diseconomies such as pollution; and provision of ideological, educational and communications conditions of production and trade. And alongside the performance of these *intranational* functions there stood the function of *international* management of external relations pertaining to any or all of these dimensions. Any capital which extended itself beyond the territorial boundaries of a state which had heretofore performed these functions had to either take these functions on themselves or have them performed by some other public authority. Historically this was often accomplished through colonialism and then neo-colonialism. In the contemporary era, and especially as regards the advanced capitalist states, it has primarily been a matter of "states already performing or being willing to perform the functions of their own accord", so that foreign capital came to be serviced on the same basis as domestic capital.

To speak in terms of functions is not necessarily improperly "functionalist" insofar as the range of structures that might undertake their performance, and the conditions which might mean their non-performance, are explicitly problematised. Murray explicitly did this, including by addressing the possibility that "the contradictions of the international system will be such as to prevent their fulfilment at all." Yet Murray saw no reason why, despite the major increase in the internationalisation of trade, investment and finance capital in the 1950s and 1960s, the performance of both intranational and international state functions could not continue to be contained within the system of nation states. Especially as regards "the *intranational* performance of public economic functions for extended capital", Murray stressed the positive advantages to capital in being able to play off one nation state against another: "Thus, even where there is extensive territorial non-coincidence between domestic states and their extended capitals, this does not imply that the system of atomistic nation states is outdated. The [notion] . . . that 'multinational corporations and nations are therefore fundamentally incompatible with each other' is not necessarily true."[12]

On the other hand, Murray discerned the contradictions entailed in a process which was exposing exchange rates and national monetary systems to an international money market, easing the process of international speculation and opening sources of credit outside the control of national authorities: "There is accordingly a tendency for the process of internationalization to increase the potential economic instability in the world at the same time as decreasing the power of national governments to control economic activity within their own borders." Attempts by states to correct balance of payments deficits in the context of this economic instability led to the adoption of policies which "further weaken the national capital and increase the domination of foreign capital within the national economy." Murray concluded from this that, precisely because capital was always a political opportunist which would take support from whatever public authority it could, ". . . existing states often suffered a decrease in their powers as a result of internationalization . . . [yet] weaker states in a period of internationalization come to suit neither the interests of their own besieged capital nor of the foreign investor."[13] As if recognising the unresolved ambiguities in his approach over whether the territorial dialectics of capital extended or diminished the role of the state, Murray ended his article by calling for an "elaboration of the connections between not only states, but the states and their capitals".

Three years later, in a brilliantly original analysis, Nicos Poulantzas took up exactly where Murray left off by explicitly problematising the notion of states and 'their' capitals, and insisting that "common formulations of the problem such as 'what can – or cannot – the state do in the face of the great multinational firms', 'how far has the state lost powers in the face of these international giants?' are fundamentally correct."[14]

Poulantzas's immediate concern was with understanding the dominant role that American capital had come to play in Europe, including the process whereby European states "take responsibility for the interests of the dominant capital." This not only involved granting concessions and subventions to American capital of the same type as it granted to indigenous capital, but also acting as a "staging post" by supporting American capital in its further extension outside Europe. This could "go so far as to help American capital circumvent the American state itself (the anti-trust legislation, for example). The international reproduction of capital under the domination of American capital is supported by various national states, each state attempting in its own way to latch onto one or other aspect of this process." This did not mean (in contrast to Murray) that the state policies weakened national capital, but rather that its industrial policies increasingly were concerned with promoting "the concentration and international expansion of their own indigenous capital" by linking it with the international reproduction of American capital.[15]

The concentration of power by transnational capital did not take power away from the state; rather, "the state intervenes precisely in this very concentration":

The current internationalization of capital neither suppresses or by-passes nation states, either in the direction of a peaceful integration of capitals 'above' the state level (since every process of internationalization is effected under the dominance of the capital of a given country), or in the direction of their extinction by an American super-state, as if American capital purely and simply directed the other imperialist bourgeoisies. This internationalisation, on the other hand, deeply affects the policies and institutional forms of those states by including them in a system of interconnections which is in no way confined to the play of external and mutual pressures between juxtaposed states and capitals. These states themselves take charge of the interest of the dominant imperialist capital in its development within the 'national' social formation, i.e. in its complex relation of internalization to the domestic bourgeoisie that it dominates. This system of interconnections does not encourage the constitution of effective supra-national or super-state institutional forms of agencies; this would be the case if what was involved was internationalization within a framework of externally juxtaposed states and capitals. These states themselves take charge of the interests of the dominant imperialist capital in its complex relation of internationalization to the domestic bourgeoisie."[16]

Transnational capital's interpenetration with domestic bourgeoisies may have rendered the notion of a national bourgeoisie increasingly arcane, but even an internal bourgeoisie "implicated by multiple ties of dependence in the international division of labour and in the international concentration of capital" still maintained its own economic foundation and base of capital accumulation at home and abroad, as well as exhibited specific political and ideological features with autonomous effects on the state. Nor was this struggle one in which only dominant classes and fractions were at play: ". . . while the struggles of the popular masses are more than ever developing in concrete conjunctures determined on a world basis . . . it is still the national form that prevails in these struggles, however international they are in their essence. This is due for one thing to uneven development and the concrete specificity of each social formation; these features are of the very essence of capitalism, contrary to the belief upheld by the various ideologies of 'globalisation'."[17]

Poulantzas's unsurpassed contribution was to remind us that the internationalization of the state was a development which could not "be reduced to a simple contradiction of a mechanistic kind between the base (internationalization of production) and a superstructural cover (national state) which no longer corresponds to it." Nor could the state be reduced to "a mere tool or instrument of the dominant classes to be manipulated at will, so that every step that capital took towards internationalization would automatically induce a parallel 'supernationalization' of states." If the focus of attention was put, rather, on relations and struggles among social forces, we would see that these did not shift to some hyperspace beyond the state. Rather, global class interpenetrations and contradictions needed to be understood in the context of specificities of the nation state's continuing central role in organising, sanctioning and legitimising class domination within capitalism.

III. The Antinomies of Robert Cox

It was only with Robert Cox's *Production, Power and World Order* in 1987 that a full-scale study of the internationalization of the state appeared which was founded on a historical materialist understanding of the role of "social forces in the making of history" (the book's sub-title) rather than a false counterposition between globalising capital and the power of states. The impact of Cox's book in challenging the dominant realist approach to the study of international relations has been comparable to the impact of Miliband's *The State in Capitalist Society* challenge to the pluralist approach to the study of comparative politics almost twenty years earlier. Writing over a decade later than Murray and Poulantzas, moreover, Cox was in a better position to analyse the changing modalities of the internationalisation of the state induced by the new era of economic instability and crisis since the mid-1970s.

Cox's approach, like Murray's, is grounded in his understanding of "indispensable functions" the state has to perform in a capitalist society, from guaranteeing property and contracts to dismantling obstructions to markets to ensuring the soundness of money. Thus, "the specializations of functions and centralization of state power" of the 19th century liberal state, which appeared "to contradict the principle of abstinence from intervention", actually involved "no contradiction, since to allow the market mechanism to function without disturbance required the sanction of coercive force, and to ensure this force was not to be used in particular interests but to defend the system as a whole required the creation of a specialized state apparatus."[18] A recent critique of the Coxian approach by Peter Burnham for allegedly failing to recognise that "the state meets the interests of capital-in-general by enforcing the discipline of the market through the rule of law and the rule of money", is in this sense entirely misplaced.[19] Cox is concerned, however, to go beyond this: ". . . in order to comprehend the real historical world it is necessary to consider distinctive *forms of state* . . . [and] the characteristics of their historic blocs, i.e., the configuration of social forces upon which state power ultimately rests. A particular configuration of social forces defines in practice the limits or parameters of state purposes, and the modus operandi of state action, defines, in other words, the *raison d'état* for a particular state." Within these parameters, the state exercised power and choice in the organisation and development of production and classes, although its actions "in these matters are, in turn, conditioned by the manner in which the world order impinges upon the state."[20]

It is in the specific context of the rise and fall of the hegemonic world order of *Pax Americana* that Cox situates the internationalisation of the state. Under the decisive shift in "relative economic-productive powers" in favour of the United States and its "unquestioned leadership" outside the Soviet sphere after 1945, the "putting into place of the new order involved the transformation of state structures" from those which had existed in the pre-war non-hegemonic system of nationalist/welfare states. That the new order entailed *a transformation, not a diminution, of the state* – a reorganisation of the state's structure and role in its external and internal aspects – is the decisive point. Within the framework of interstate agreements forged at Bretton Woods – and under the continued surveillance, incentives and sanctions of new international financial institutions (the IMF and World Bank) which "behaved as accessories to U.S. policy" – *Pax Americana* "was held in place by a configuration of different forms of state whose common feature was the role each played in adjusting national economic policies to the dynamics of the world economy." The process of establishing and internalising a "notion of international obligation" to the world economy constitutes, for Cox, "the meaning given to the term *internationalizing of the state*":

> *First*, there is a process of interstate consensus formation regarding the needs or requirements of the world economy that takes place within a common ideological framework (i.e., common criteria of interpretation of economic events and common goals anchored in the idea of an open world economy). *Second*, participation in this consensus formation is hierarchically structured. *Third*, the internal structures of states are adjusted so that each can best transform the global consensus into national policy and practice, taking account of the specific kinds of obstacles likely to arise in countries occupying the differently hierarchically arranged positions in the world economy.[21]

It will be noted that whereas Poulantzas proceeded from *within* ("states themselves take charge of the interests of the dominant imperialist capital in its development within the 'national' social formation"), Cox proceeds from the *outside-in*, beginning with international consensus formation and attendant agreements and obligations to which internal state structures are then adjusted. To be sure, Cox is careful to say that this "was not necessarily a power structure with lines of force running exclusively topdown, nor was it one in which the bargaining agents were whole nation states." Bureaucratic fragments of states engaged in a process of bargaining, with the hegemonic power structure "tacitly taken into account", and, "through ideological osmosis, internalized in the thinking of participants".[22] Whereas in the interwar era, the state's political accountability was solely turned inward so that the state acted as a *buffer* protecting the domestic economies from external forces, the internationalisation of the state after 1945 involves establishing a compromise between the international and domestic obligations of states. The state now takes the form of a *mediator* between the externally established policy priorities and the internal social forces to which it also still remains accountable. "The centre of gravity shifted from national economies to the world economy, but states were recognised as having a responsibility to both."[23]

The state was not less "powerful" in terms of controlling the national economy than before the war. State intervention, as Cox points out, had proved incapable of pulling the economy out of the 1930s Depression;

before the war no less than after the war, the state was primarily reactive, lacking "the ability to conceive and carry through an organization of production and distribution that would replace the market. It could tinker or 'fine tune'; it could not design."[24] Rather than a loss of power, the internationalisation of the state after 1945 reflected a shift in power inside the state, entailing "a restructuring of the hierarchy of state apparatuses." In appearance there was "virtually nothing" to signal this change in structure; rather the goals pursued and the uses to which the structures were put changed. Agencies with direct links to the "client groups of national economy", such as ministries of labour and industry and institutions of tripartite corporatism that had developed in the inter-war era, were not displaced. Indeed they, and the social forces attached to them, remained "relatively privileged" and even "preeminent". But they were subordinated to prime ministerial and presidential offices, foreign offices, treasuries and central banks in such a way that they became "instruments of policy transmitted through the world-economy linked central agencies."[25]

A new stage in the internationalisation of the state has arisen, however, in the wake of the crisis in the post-war order that emerged from 1968–75, a crisis which has led to the further expansion of "the breadth and depth of the global economy", even while undermining American hegemony. The internationalising of production and finance that grew through the 1950s and 1960s under the umbrella of *Pax Americana*, together with domestic inflationary pressures, industrial militancy and declining profits under conditions of full employment, engendered this crisis; the Bretton Woods exchange rates arrangement was abandoned, and the limits of the domestic fine-tuning capacity of tripartism were severely tested. Although Cox thus sees the crisis as having been generated as much by domestic contradictions as international ones, he nevertheless once again portrays the reconstruction of the state in the new era from the outside-in. A "new doctrine" redefining the role of states "was prepared by a collective effort of ideological revision undertaken through various unofficial agencies – the Trilateral Commission, the Bilderberg conferences, the Club of Rome, and other prestigious forums – and then endorsed through more official agencies like the OECD."[26] This doctrine, virtually identical as Cox portrays it to the governing philosophy of what he calls the Thatcher-Reagan hyperliberal state form ("the fullest, most uncompromising instance of a liberal state"[27]), attacked the post-war compromise in both senses of the term: the domestic compromise which tied in labour and welfare interests; and the international compromise of mediating between national interests and the global order. Inside the state, there is a further shift in power away from those agencies most closely tied to domestic social forces and towards those which are in closest touch with the transnational process of consensus formation. As summarised by Cox in his essay in *The Socialist Register 1992*:

LEO PANITCH 71

There is, in effect, no explicit political or authority structure for the global economy. There is, nevertheless, something that remains to be deciphered, something that could be described by the French word 'nebuleuse' or by the notion of 'governance without government'.

There is a transnational process of consensus formation among the official caretakers of the global economy. This process generates consensual guidelines, underpinned by the ideology of globalisation, that are transmitted into the policy-making channels of national governments and big corporations. . . . The structural impact on national governments of this centralisation of influence over policy can be called the internationalising of the state. Its common feature is to convert the state into an agency for adjusting national economic practices and policies to the perceived exigencies of the global economy. The state becomes a transmission belt from the global to the national economy, where heretofore it had acted as the bulwark defending domestic welfare from external disturbances. Power within the state becomes concentrated in those agencies in closest touch with the global economy – the offices of presidents and prime ministers, treasuries, central banks. The agencies that are more closely tied with domestic clients – ministries of industries, labour ministries, etc, – become subordinated. This phenomenon, which has become so salient since the crisis of the post-war order, needs much more study.[28]

It will be recalled that Cox had identified this same shift in power as the constitutive element in the reconstruction of the state in the Bretton Woods era. Although he does not make this explicit, it appears that now the corporatist and welfarist state apparatuses and the social forces allied with them lose the "preeminent" and "relatively privileged" position they had previously retained. But since they had already been substantively rendered "secondary" even in the post-1945 era,[29] the substantive change he has in mind in the post-1975 era appears to have to do with the role of the already dominant state apparatuses of treasuries, central banks, prime minister's offices, etc. They seem less and less to be in a *bargaining* relationship with the forces representing the global economy, and more and more their agents.

The limits of the "outside-in" orientation of Cox's approach to the internationalisation of the state become revealed here. The notion of the state becoming a "transmission belt from the global to the national economy" is not only too formal in its distinction between global and national economy, but also too "top-down" in its expression of power relations.[30] It would appear that in his 1992 essay Cox conflated some aspects of the internationalisation of the state going on since 1945 with developments that have taken place since the crisis of the mid-1970s. We seem to move directly from the state as a *buffer* (or now "a bulwark") to that of it being a *transmission belt*, skipping over the post-war stage of the state as a *mediator* between the global and the national, with accountability going both ways. But even if this was an understandable telescoping of his theorisation for the purposes of a brief essay, a framework that traces the internationalisation of the state as a process that takes us from *buffer* to *mediator* to *transmission belt* in relation to global capital is perhaps too brittle.

I would argue instead that the role of states remains one not only of internalising but also of mediating adherence to the untrammelled logic of international capitalist competition within its own domain, even if only to ensure that it can effectively meet its commitments to act globally by policing the new world order on the local terrain. It is in terms of the difficulty of such mediation that Cox's own insights on "the tendency toward limited democracy" as a means of limiting popular domestic pressures on the state can, in fact, best be appreciated. What needs to be investigated is whether the important shifts in the hierarchy of state apparatuses really are those which bring to the fore those most involved with the international "caretakers of the global economy", or whether a more general process is at work, determined more from within the state itself, whereby even those agencies without such direct international links, but which nevertheless directly facilitate capital accumulation and articulate a competitiveness ideology, are the ones that gain status, while those which fostered social welfare and articulated a class harmony orientation lose status. Whether that loss of status is considerable, or even permanent, however, partly depends on the transformations which these latter agencies are today going through in terms of being made, or making themselves, more attuned to the exigencies of global competitiveness and fiscal restraint. Ministries of labour, health and welfare are perhaps not so much being subordinated as themselves being restructured.

As for the structure of power at the international level, a "nebuleuse" or a "governance without government" is not well captured through the notion of a "global centralisation of influence over policy" and the "transmission belts" which emanate from them. Indeed, in an insightful passage in *Production, Power and World Order* Cox himself traced the "decline of centralized management characteristic of the world economy of Pax Americana" so that the world economy increasingly was better represented as "a system than as an institution." Whereas in the 1960s he identified a set of institutions with the U.S. Treasury at the apex and its policy criteria being internationalised through the IMF, World Bank and other such agencies, "during the 1970s, private transnational banks assumed such an important role that the top management structure could no longer be convincingly represented exclusively in terms of state and interstate institutions." The key development here was that "private international credit expanded for lack of any agreement on how the official intergovernmental structures in the system could be reformed. The impasse on reform was the consequence of stalemate between the United States and the European countries on the future role of the dollar. . . . In the absence of agreement on management by official institutions, dollar hegemony shifted to the financial market, that is to say, to the very largely unmanaged dollar itself. . . . Authority weakened at the apex of the international financial system. Crisis did not produce effective centralization. U.S. power was too great to be brought under any externally imposed discipline but was no longer great enough to shape the rules of a consensual order."[31] Cox does not see this problem has having been resolved by the early 1990s. Indeed, he stresses in his 1992 essay the "parlously fragile condition" of international finance in a context where not even the G-7 governments have been able to "devise any effectively secure scheme of regulation".

It becomes particularly clear here that there is an unresolved antinomy in Cox. On the one hand, there is one image of an increasingly centralised supranational management structure, founded on ideological consensus among the elites that populate transnational institutions and forums. He claims that the disintegration of the norms of post-war hegemonic order led to an intensification among the advanced capitalist countries of "the practice of policy harmonization [which] became correspondingly more important to the maintenance of consensus. The habit of policy harmoniz-ation had been institutionalized during the preceding two decades and was, if anything, reinforced in the absence of clear norms. Ideology had to substitute for legal obligation."[32] Is it this that transmits and links policy hyperliberal policy from country to country? On the other hand, there is another image of an unregulated system of international finance – which appears to be unregulated, moreover, in good part because of an inability to forge policy consensus at an interstate level.[33] Is it this system of international finance that internationalises the state, making accountable national policy makers of whatever ideological orientation?

The antinomies in the Coxian framework, as the emphasis shifts back and forth from social force to ideology to institution to system has led one recent critic, looking for a more orthodox and neater pattern of determina-tions, to throw up his hands in frustration at an approach which

> . . . in its frantic attempt to escape the twin evils of 'economism' and idealism offers little more than a version of Weberian pluralism oriented to the study of the international order. . . . Variables which comprise a social order – the economy, the polity, the civil society – are given no overall structure but rather each has a real autonomy which preclude overdetermination. . . . This factor approach is reflected in Cox's analysis to the effect that in the interaction between material capabilities, ideas and institutions no determinism exists, and relationships are reciprocal. The question of lines of force is an historical one to be answered by a study of the particular case. However laudable in theory, the true consequence of this position is to produce a pluralist empiricism which lacks the power to explain either the systemic connection between values, social relations and institutions or the extent to which the historical appearance of capital as a social relation transforms the social order in such a way that all relations are subsumed under the capital relation as the basis for valorisation.[34]

If the charge of a certain empiricism is perhaps not entirely off the mark, the general level at which Burnham demands primacy to be given to "the capital relation" is hardly any answer. Indeed, Cox would readily grant determination at this level but then ask: so what? We have already seen that Burnham's critique of the Coxian approach for allegedly failing to recognise that "the state meets the interests of capital-in-general by enforcing the discipline of the market through the rule of law and the rule of money", is entirely misplaced. Cox explicitly recognises this, as we have seen, as regards both the liberal state of the mid-19th century and the hyperliberal state of the late 20th century; but what he wants to know is *what disciplines the state to do this* – and what makes it do it again in another form in another historical conjuncture? The role of the state is not best conceived as something given by the capital relation once and for all; but neither it is best conceived in terms of a transmission belt from the global economy to the national economy.

The role of each state is still determined by struggles among social forces always located within each social formation. Even though these social forces are also, to recall Poulantzas, "implicated by multiple tiers of dependence in an international division of labour and in the international concentration of capital" and although the struggles may be seen as "more than ever developing in conjunctures determined on a world basis", the specific national form still prevails in these struggles due to uneven development and the specificity of each social formation. (Is it really to international finance that governments in London or Ottawa are accountable when they prepare their budgets? Or are they accountable to international finance because they are accountable to the City of London or to Bay Street?) Is it precisely in light of domestic as well as international concerns about the continuing salience of popular struggles at the level of the nation state that we need to locate current attempts at constitutionalising neo-liberalism. The internationalisation of the state in the 1990s appears to be taking the form, in the continuing absence of the ideological consensus or capacity to bring about a transnational regulation of capital markets, of formal interstate treaties designed to enforce legally upon future governments general adherence to the discipline of the capital market. This arises out of a growing fear on the part of both domestic and transnational capitalists, as the crisis continues, that *ideology cannot continue to substitute for legal obligation* in the internationalisation of the state.

IV. Forced to be Free: The State and North American Free Trade

The North American Free Trade Agreement which came into effect on January 1, 1994 most certainly fits the bill of constitutionalising neo-liberalism. Far more important than the reduction in tariffs, as President Clinton himself repeatedly intoned in the fevered run-up to the congressional vote on NAFTA in November, were the guarantees it provided for American investment in Mexico. As Ian Robinson has put it in one of the best analyses of the deal, international trade agreements like NAFTA not only "prohibit discrimination between national and foreign owned corporations [but also] create new corporate private property rights, possessed by both national and foreign investors. . . . It will function as an economic constitution, setting the basic rules governing the private property rights that all governments must respect and the types of economic policies that all governments must eschew."[35]

NAFTA's Investment chapter proscribes attempts by governments to establish performance requirements on foreign TNCs (excepting in the Auto sector) and defines investor rights which are protected under the agreement very broadly to include not only majority shareholders but minority interests, portfolio investment and real property held by any company incorporated in a NAFTA country regardless of the country of origin. The Monopolies and State Enterprises chapter requires public enterprises not only to operate "solely in accordance with commercial considerations" and to refrain from using "anticompetitive practices" such as "the discriminatory provision of a monopoly good or service, cross-subsidization or predatory conduct" (all of which is the bread and butter of TNCs themselves), but also requires public enterprises to minimize or eliminate any nullification or impairment of benefits" that investors, broadly defined as above, might reasonably expect to receive under NAFTA. The Intellectual Property Rights chapter, which grants up to 20 year copyright protection to a vast array of trademarks, patents, semiconductor and industrial designs, trade secrets, satellite signals, etc., goes furthest of all to "extend existing property rights by quasi-constitutionally protecting them against future democratic governments with the threat of trade sanctions . . . even though the effect of these rights is to restrict rather than enhance the free flow of ideas across national boundaries . . ."[36]

Taken together, these various provisions have the effect of redesigning the Mexican and Canadian states relation to capital to fit the mould made in the American metropole by establishing and guaranteeing state defence of "new private property rights that go well beyond those recognised in Canadian and Mexican law, if not that of the United States."[37] What is particularly important to stress, however, is that *this is not something imposed on the Canadian and Mexican states by American capital and state as external to the latter; rather it reflects the role adopted by the Mexican and Canadian states in representing the interests of their bourgeoisies and bureaucracies as these are already penetrated by American capital and administration.* As John H. Bryan, Jr., President of Sara Lee Corp. put it, the "most important reason to vote for NAFTA is to lock in [Mexico's] reforms".[38] This was all the more pressing insofar as there was a widespread awareness among North American elites (long before the Chiapas revolt on the day NAFTA came into effect) of popular discontent with the hyperliberal policies Mexico had adopted over the past decade, and a concern that any eventual opening up of Mexico's limited democracy might endanger the reelection of a PRI government. Shortly before the passage of the Agreement, an article in the Toronto *Globe and Mail's Report on Business* quoted Alvaro Cepeda Neri of Mexico City's *La*

Journada as saying: "The booty of privatisation has made multimillionaires of 13 families, while the rest of the population – about 80 million Mexicans – has been subjected to the same gradual impoverishment as though they had suffered through a war."[39]

But the Mexican state was not only acting in terms of the interests of its domestic bourgeoisie, nor even just concerned with providing further security guarantees to American capital in Mexico. It was also, in Poulantzas's terms, "taking responsibility for the interests of the dominant capital" by endorsing NAFTA as an exemplary "staging post" for a renewed American constitutionalising of neo-liberalism on a global scale. The Chairman of Saloman Inc. did not mince his words when he said that the defeat of NAFTA "would be a slap in the face to all leaders in the Western Hemisphere who have chosen the capitalist road over government-controlled economies."[40] Indeed, if, as the Foreign Affairs Committee Chairman in the House of Representatives, Lee Hamilton, put it, "the question is U.S. leadership in the world", it is notable that the greatest threat to NAFTA came from the opposition within the United States itself. The side deals on the environment and labour undertaken by Clinton were designed to allow for the necessary compromises within the American social formation: this succeeded to the extent that this divided the environmental movement; if the labour side deal failed to do the same, it was because, not surprisingly, it did not go as far as the environmental side deal and did not allow Canadian or American groups affected by NAFTA to challenge the non-enforcement of Mexican labour laws.

As regards the economic woes of the heartland of the empire, it is clear that the direct impact of NAFTA can only be minuscule. As Lester Thurow pointed out, a worst case scenario would entail the loss of 480,000 American jobs over the next five years; the best case would see the addition of 170,000 jobs:

> "The small stream of jobs produced or lost by NAFTA will not be noticed in a sea of 130 million American workers. . . . With a gross domestic product (GDP) only 4 to 5 percent of the United States, Mexico will not be an economic locomotive for America. . . . From 1973 to 1992 the per capita American GDP after correcting for inflation rose 27 percent. Yet over the same period average wages for the bottom 60 percent of male workers fell 20 percent in real terms. . . . Earnings prospects are collapsing for the bottom two-thirds of the work force. . . . After suffering two decades of falling real wages it is not surprising that Ross Perot can appeal to millions of Americans who lash out at the Mexicans in their frustration. . . . America is now a First World economy with a large, growing Third World economy in its midst."[41]

The Canadian experience under NAFTA's predecessor, the U.S.–Canada Free Trade Agreement (FTA), which served as the first staging-post for hemispheric free trade and even for the Tokyo round of GATT, certainly demonstrates that the constitutionalising of neo-liberalism exacerbates rather than contains the tendencies of the new global capitalism to generate successive social as well as economic crisis. The most recent study of Canadian employment trends since the inauguration of the FTA not surprisingly begins with a quotation from a currently popular Leonard Cohen song: "I have seen the future, brother; it is murder":

"Official unemployment rose from 7.5% to 11.3% from December 1988 to August 1993. The ranks of the jobless swelled by 576,000, bringing the total to 1.6 million. Adding those who dropped out of the work force, the unemployment level rose to 2 million, doubling from 7.5% to 14%. If we include involuntary part-time workers which amounts to hidden unemployment, the "real" unemployment rate is currently 20% of the work force. . . . Free trade supporters, though admitting that jobs have been lost in the low wage/low skill sectors of the economy, claim that the FTA is assisting the high-tech sectors, which comprise the emerging new economy of the 21st century, to grow and create high value added permanent jobs. The record of the first four years does not bear this out. . . . It is clear that despite positive signs in a few subsectors [only four – pharmaceuticals, computer services, accounting services and management consultant services – to a total of 28,000 new jobs], the job creation numbers are miniscule. There is no sign of an expanding knowledge economy (either in manufacturing or services) to absorb the 434,000 workers displaced from the old and new manufacturing/resource economy, the 111,000 construction workers and the 104,000 workers displaced from the private sector, old and new, service economy due to restructuring and recession. The public service sectors – education, health and social services, and government administration – absorbed 148,000 workers, but, given, the extreme financial stress that these sectors are currently experiencing and the disinclination to change policy direction, even partial absorption by public sectors is not likely to continue in the future. The future is indeed bleak."[42]

It was a mark of how deep the lines of American imperialism ran in Canada that every issue, from social policy to defence to Quebec's status in Canada, was interpreted during the course of the 1988 federal election through the prism of the pros and cons of the FTA. All sides of the debate took the position that the free trade agreement was a historic departure, an epochal turning point for Canada. Either it would finally free Canadian business from the fetters of tariffs and regulation, expose it fully to the rigour of competition, lay open a vast continental market for exports and investment; or it would mean the end of Canada as we have known it for 121 years, shifting our economic axis southward, imposing the rule of business, destroying the welfare state, undermining Canadian culture, subverting national sovereignty. Both views were misleading. The outcome of the free trade election marked not a new chapter, but rather the punctuation mark on a very long historical sentence of economic and cultural integration with American capitalism.

Canada's particular status as a rich dependency in the American Empire rested on the fact that like the United States, and partly due to its geographic and cultural proximity to the United States, the development of capitalism in Canada was predicated on a class structure which facilitated capitalist industrialisation.[43] A high wage proletariat and a prosperous class of small farmers drew American capital to Canada not only in search of resources, and not at all in search of cheap labour, but to sell to a market distinctly similar to the American. The national tariff designed to integrate an east-west economy and protect Canadian industry from competition from the south (and the flight of Canadian workers to the south) had the paradoxical effect of inducing the first American TNCs to jump the tariff barrier and sell to Canada's (and sometimes through Canada to the British Empire's) mass market. They were welcomed with open arms by the state as good corporate citizens, and funded by Canada's substantial and powerful financial capitalists. Through the course of the first half of the twentieth century, Canada moved from formal colonial status as a privileged white Dominion in the old British empire to a formally independent, but in reality quite a dependent status in a new kind of imperialism amidst a degree of direct foreign (American) ownership unparalleled anywhere on the globe.

Yet this status was still a privileged one, and Canadians shared in the spoils that went with American hegemony in the post-war order. Any dependent country has a degree of autonomy: this is especially true of a rich one with a substantial industrial proletariat not as easily subjected to the same pressures as American workers to accede to imperial demands of unswerving loyalty in a Cold War and therefore more open to socialist political ideas and mobilisation. Canada's welfare state, however poor a cousin to those in northern Europe, eventually came to surpass what the New Deal had inaugurated in the U.S. This gave Canada a badge of civility compared with American society. Some public corporations and regulatory bodies took on the additional role of protecting what residual autonomy Canadian economy and culture could retain. But in doing this, they did not so much challenge the fact of, as negotiate the scope of, Canada's dependency.

From this perspective, we can see that the free trade treaty of 1988 was designed not to inaugurate but rather to constitutionalise, formalise and extend Canada's dependence on the U.S. in a world now marked by economic instability amidst rampant financial speculation and strong trade rivalries. Far from wanting to prove their entrepreneurial virility by taking the risk of becoming globally competitive, Canadian domestic capital sought to minimise the risk that Americans, when in protectionist mood, might treat them, their exports and investments, as merely "foreign". In turn, the Canadian government promised to give up those weak devices it had hereforeto retained as a means of negotiating the scope of dependency. Margaret Atwood (like Cox, following Antonio Gramsci) used a very Canadian metaphor to describe what the Mulroney government had done in entering into the FTA: the beaver was noted in medieval bestiaries for biting off its own testicles when frightened and offering them to its pursuer.

Even so, the free trade agreement failed to remove all restraints on American protectionism. Many opponents of the FTA pointed this out, implying they might be content with the deal if it promised even fuller integration. But what most opponents were really objecting to was the whole dependent path of Canadian development: they wanted to avoid a punctuation mark being put at the end of Canada's long sentence of dependence. To defeat the deal would be to leave open the possibility of a "nevertheless" or a "however" – which might yet be written at some point in the future. They were encouraged by the emergence of a visible strain of anti-Americanism, even of anti-imperialism. An indigenous cultural community had long been straining to define Canadian identity in the face of dependence. The labour movement, once a strong if subordinate sponsor of continentalism, had also experienced a shift towards Canadianization as the American labour movement proved ever weaker and more abject in the face of economic instability. And considerable domestic ecology, peace, and feminist movements had emerged, often with socialists in leadership positions, and with greater salience in relation to Canadian governments than such movements had in the United States.

The anti-free trade forces were encouraged as well by the fact that the Canadian electorate showed no great enthusiasm for the Reagan-Thatcher hyperliberal state model. Just as the 1980s began, Canadians had opted for a Liberal platform which promised to install a "fair tax" system rather than supply-side economics, and to foster a Canadian capitalist class with distinctive national goals and ambitions through the National Energy Programme and a strengthened Foreign Investment Review Agency. It had indeed been in reaction to all this, as well as to cries for protectionism in the U.S. Congress, that the business community launched free trade and pursued it with such remarkable unanimity. When the NEP was established, Canadian capitalists, no less than American ones, were determined, not only to get rid of it at the first opportunity, but to disable permanently such interventions by the state. They feared that popular pressures were pushing the state to become, not the hand-maiden to business it had usually been, but a countervailing power to it. Not just fear was at play here, but also greed: some elements of Canadian business had become full players on a continental plane while others harboured ambitions that they too might reap substantial profits if Canada embraced its continental destiny. This demonstrated that the point had long passed when business in Canada was interested in 'reclaiming' the Canadian economy.

The continuing political predominance of business, despite the mood of the electorate and the volubility of progressive forces, was seen when opposition from a unified capitalist class destroyed the tax reforms advanced in the 1981 Budget, and when the Liberal government responded to the recession of 1981–2 by removing the right to strike from some one million of the three million organised workers in Canada. Yet the ideological impact of hyperliberalism still remained limited. In 1984 even the Conservatives sensed that they could not get elected on a Thatcher-Reagan platform. Mulroney ran a typically Canadian brokerage campaign promising everything to everybody, and declaring the welfare state a sacred trust. This did not make it a sacred trust, of course, given the powerful business pressures to which the government was beholden. But it emboldened people to defend the welfare state as soon as the Tories tried to undo it.

The decision to go for the free trade agreement, under considerable pressure from the Business Council on National Issues (a powerful lobby which grouped together the most powerful domestic and American corporations), thus took on a double purpose: to make permanent the dominance of business by formalising continental integration in the face of American protectionism and Canadian economic nationalism; and to introduce Reaganomics by the back door of the free market ethos and provisions of the free trade deal. A popular coalition, funded by the labour movement and led by the leadership of the above-mentioned 'new social movements', marshalled against the FTA with remarkable fervour and determination to force the free trade election of 1988. But it must be admitted that this coalition, and much less the opposition parties, never really made clear what their alternative really was. The experience with the 1980-84 Liberal Government showed that a policy for more economic independence and social justice could not rely on the cooperation of business. Yet the anti-free trade coalition were afraid to spell out the conclusion that the alternative had to involve fundamental challenges to capital's power and radically democratising the state. They were afraid to do so because the Canadian people had been so little prepared for such a departure, with the NDP's (Canada's social democratic party) failure in this respect particularly glaring.

Alongside a trenchant critique of the details and implications of the FTA, the anti-free trade coalition took a different tack. And it proved a shrewd one. They chose to mythologize the Canadian state as if it had always been a repository of Canadian independence and social justice. This was myth indeed. But nationalisms are built on myths, and this one became uncontested in the election with remarkable ideological consequences. The small badge of civility which a welfare state lends to Canadian social life in comparison with the American laid the basis for Canadian national identity to be defined in the 1988 election in almost Scandinavian terms, where pride in the welfare state was rather more justified. In this context, the outcome of the free trade election was, despite the narrow victory by the Tories, and the subsequent introduction of the FTA, rather ambiguous. Certainly, the victory of the business forces confirmed the historical trend toward continental integration. An exclamation mark had been added to Canada's historical sentence of dependence.

Paradoxically, the election also confirmed the absence of an ideological mandate to carry through Reaganomics in Canada. The Tories and the business community accepted the anti-free trade forces definition of patriotism as at least involving a defence of the welfare state. The freedom to trade and invest by business was bought at the ideological cost of pledging allegiance to medicare and other social programmes. In so far as the popular coalition forged during the campaign against free trade set the terms of the debate, and forced their opponents to adopt a defence of the welfare state as a central element in the definition of "Canadianism", they provided a strong ideological basis for defensive struggles. The seeds of the destruction of the Conservative Party, reduced in the subsequent 1993 election to only two seats in the House of Commons, were sown amidst the ambiguity of their 1988 victory on free trade. The challenge for the Left remained to enlarge the framework of struggle. A defence of the welfare state promises only stalemate so long as the power and mobility of capital remains untouched. In the context of Canada's reinforced dependency amidst global economic instability and financial speculation, a clear alternative to free trade and unbridled capitalist competition still remains to be articulated.

V. A Progressive Competitive Alternative?

There are those who . . . believe that we can take on the challenge of competitiveness *and* retain our socialist values; indeed they believe that competitiveness will create the very economic success essential to sustaining social programs. They are mistaken. In the first place they are wrong because, in the particular case of Canada, there is no capitalist class with the interest or capacity to develop a strong industrial base. . . . But they are more than just mistaken. The framework for competitiveness they invite us to accept is ultimately dangerous. . . . Once it is accepted, its hidden aspects . . . such as attacks on social programs – quickly reassert themselves. Once we decide to play on the terrain of competitiveness, we cannot then step back without paying a serious price. Having legitimated the importance of being competitive (when we should have been mobilising to defend our social values), we would be extremely vulnerable to the determined attacks that will inevitably come in the name of "global realities". . . . The competitive model ultimately asks how the *corporate sector* can be strengthened. Our perspective asserts that it is the very strength of that sector that limits our freedom and belittles the meaning of "community".
Gindin and Robertson, Canadian Auto Workers (CAW)[44]

The global recession of the 1990s is testimony to the economic failure of global hyperliberalism. Far from state policies having no effect, global trade competition among states has ushered in "an unstable vicious circle of 'competitive austerity'" whereby the cumulative effect of each state's policies is immense in the misery it causes. As Greg Albo summarises this: "each country reduces domestic demand and adopts an export-oriented strategy of dumping its surplus production, for which there are fewer customers in its national economy given the decrease in workers' living standards and productivity gains all going to the capitalists, in the world market. This has created a global demand crisis and the growth of surplus capacity across the business cycle."[45] Unfortunately, however, the programme for a more progressive form of competitiveness which has been advanced by most mainstream parties of the centre-left does not constitute much of an alternative. For a considerable period through the 1970s and well into the mid-1980s, a large portion of the Left refused to acknowledge that the crisis of the Keynesian/welfare state was a structural one, pertaining to the very nature of capitalism and the contradictions it generates in our time. Their response to the crisis, clearly visible in the Canadian free trade debate, was to point to the relatively low unemployment levels in Sweden as evidence of the continuing viability of tripartite corporatism in sustaining the Keynesian/welfare state.[46] This involved, however, ignoring or downplaying the very contradictions and conflicts that were undermining even the Swedish model, and eventually this naive stance was displaced by an attempt to emulate those countries which were most successful in the export-led competitive race. But rather than allow bourgeois economists calling the tune with their neo-liberal logic of deregulation, free markets, privatisation and austerity to dictate the terms of the race, a 'progressive competitiveness' strategy is advanced by intellectuals on the Left (from social democratic to left-liberal to a good many erstwhile marxists) whereby labour and the state are urged to take the initiative and seize the hand of business in making the running towards competitive success.

At the core of the strategy, still largely inspired by a different facet of Swedish corporatism, is to support and guide both workers and capitalists towards high-tech/high-value-added/high wage production. The key to this is public policy promoting the widespread training of a highly skilled, highly flexible and highly motivated labour force, and encouraging enterprises to take full advantage of recent technological developments in microelectronics, to the end of producing high quality commodities at high productivity levels through flexible production methods. Equally founded on an acceptance of the irreversibility of globalisation, but convinced that its connection with hyperliberalism is only a matter of the ideological colouration of politicians too closely attached to bourgeois economists, this approach still wants to give strategic priority to the state. Once shorn of an ideology of free markets as the premise of state policy in the process of globalisation, the 'progressive competitiveness' strategy expects the state to be able to sustain a substantial social wage if it explicitly connects welfare and education to the public promotion of flexible production and technological innovation in those particular sectors which can "win" in a global export-led competitive race. Relative prosperity (clearly based on an extension of the advantages of relative over absolute surplus-value extraction) would fall to those states which can guide capital and labour to adopt this 'smart' competitiveness strategy. With all its emphasis on training, this is indeed a strategy which is precisely about *learning* how to run twice as fast amidst globalisation.

That such a strategy is both chimerical and dangerous is, in fact, already demonstrated by the experience in North America both by the Clinton Democratic administration and the Ontario NDP government elected in 1990. It presents a programme of vast economic readjustment for both labour and capital, with blithe regard for how, in the interim, the logic of competitive austerity could be avoided; it presumes that mass unemployment is primarily a problem of skills adjustment to technological change rather than one aspect of a crisis of overproduction; it fosters an illusion of a rate of employment growth in high tech sectors sufficient to offset the rate of unemployment growth in other sectors; it either even more unrealistically assumes a rate of growth of world markets massive enough to accommodate all those adopting this strategy, or it blithely ignores the issues associated with exporting unemployment to those who don't succeed at this strategy under conditions of limited demand (and with the attendant consequence this would have for sustaining demand); it ignores the reality that capital can also adapt leading technologies in low wage economies, and the competitive pressures on capital in this context to push down wages even in high tech sectors and limit the costs to it of the social wage and adjustment policies so central to the whole strategy's progressive logic in the first place. It is hardly surprising that Albo in this context comes to the conclusion that even "the progressive competitiveness strategy will be forced to accept, as most social democratic parties have been willing to do, the same 'competitive austerity' as neo-liberalism . . . as a cold necessity of present economic conditions."[47]

Robert Cox, who terms this strategy "state capitalist", and sees it as the only possible medium-term alternative to the hyperliberal form of state, makes it quite clear that it "is, in effect, grounded in an acceptance of the world market as the ultimate determinant of development":

> The state capitalist form involves a dualism between, on the one hand, a competitively efficient world-market oriented sector and, on the other, a protected welfare sector. The success of the former must provide resources for the latter; the sense of solidarity implicit in the latter would provide the drive and legitimacy for the former. . . . In its most radical form, state capitalism beckons towards an internal socialism sustained by capitalist success in world-market competition. This would be a socialism dependent on capitalist development, i.e. on success in the production of exchange values. But, so its proponents argue, it would be less vulnerable to external destabilization than attempts at socialist self-reliance were in weak countries . . ."[48]

Cox sees this option ("with or without its socialist colouration") as largely limited to late industrialising countries (such as France, Japan, Germany, Brazil, South Korea) with strong institutional and ideological traditions of "close coordination between the state and private capital in the pursuit of common goals." He is well aware that this type of state capitalism, while incorporating that portion of the working class attached to the world-market-oriented sector or employed in the welfare services sector, would nevertheless exclude many people ("disproportionately the young, women, immigrant or minority groups, and the unemployed") who would remain in a passive relationship to the welfare services and without influence in policy making. Amidst anomic explosions of violence from these groups, Cox expects that the state capitalist alternative's "historic bloc would be thin" and that this might entail the kind of repression and insulation from democratic pressures which would particularly make illusory the prospects the state capitalist strategy holds out for an "internal socialism". Still, as of 1992, Cox took the position that state capitalist strategies in Japan and Europe constituted "the only possible counter-weights to total globalization at the level of states". He held out particular hope that the European Community, where the "unresolved issue over the social charter indicates a stalemate in the conflict over the future nature of the nation state and of the regional authority" might yet bring to the fore "a capitalism more rooted in social policy and more balanced development", one reflecting the continuing influence of social democratic and older conservative traditions. Given the limited medium-term options of those on the Left who are looking for an alternative that would go beyond choosing between rival forms of capitalism, Cox urges them to look positively upon "the ideological space that is opened by this confrontation of hyper-liberalism and state capitalist or corporatist forms of development".[48]

Yet what is the evidence of such a confrontation? Cox exhibits here an unfortunate tendency to turn juxtaposed ideal-types, constructed for the purposes of analytic clarity, into real-world confrontations for which there is all too little evidence. The institutional and ideological structures that Cox points to as the basis for a state capitalist 'progressive competitiveness' alternative to hyperliberal globalisation are in fact being subsumed as subsidiary sponsors of globalisation in a manner quite analogous to the way Cox saw tripartite institutions of national economic planning as having become subsidiary elements in adjusting domestic economies to the world economy in the post-war order.

Both in Europe and in North America, ministries of labour (and the tripartite forums and agencies they sponsor) as well as ministries of welfare and education, are being restructured to conform with the principles of global competitiveness, but their capacity to retain their links to the social forces they represent in the state rests on their ability to tailor this reconstruction along the lines of 'progressive competitiveness' principles. In this way, key social groups that would otherwise become dangerously marginalised as a result of the state's sponsorship of global competitiveness may become attached to it by the appeal a progressive competitiveness strategy makes, especially through the ideology and practice of training, to incorporating working people who are unemployed and on welfare (or who soon might be) as well as the leaders of the unions, social agencies and other organisations who speak for them. Insofar as they are successful in this, moreover, ministries of welfare, education, labour, regional development, etc., may prevent their further loss of status in the hierarchy of state apparatuses and even recapture some of their previously foregone status. Insofar as it undertakes no greater challenge to the structure of the state or to the logic of global competitiveness than that of insisting that more, rather than less, state economic orchestration can be a more effective, and at the same time a more humane, handmaiden to competition, the 'progressive competitiveness' strategy ends up being not an alternative to, but a subsidiary element in, the process of neo-liberal capitalist restructuring and globalisation.

The 'stalemate' over the European Social Charter sustains this interpretation. In North America, the most-oft cited guarantee that the progressive competitiveness strategy will not coalesce with the logic of competitive austerity is the European Community's Social Charter. It is pointed to as a model for other international agreements which would constitutionalise a high level of labour rights, social standards and corporate codes of conduct. On this basis, Robinson argues: "If globalization can mean more than one thing . . . then the irreversibility of globalization no longer necessarily leads to neo-conservative economic and social policy prescriptions. In this light, national competitiveness, too, can mean more than one thing, depending upon whether it is achieved by cutting labour and environmental costs to TNCs, or promoting technological innovation and reducing the social, political, and environmental externalities associated with largely unregulated global market competition."[50] This approach almost always involves vastly inflating the salience and significance of the European Social Charter, or, where its weakness is acknowledged (as Robinson does), fails to inquire whether the reason "the most powerful labour movements in the world have made only very limited progress towards an adequate EC social dimension" is because of its incompatibility with even the 'progressive competitiveness' strategy of global competitiveness. The trenchant critique made by Robinson of NAFTA's side deals as a cosmetic means of buying off domestic opposition is not apparently seen by him, and so many others, as entailing a deeper lesson regarding such incompatibility.

Alain Lipietz has recently provided a chilling account of how moderate EEC social democrats "set up a Europe of traders and capital", hoping that a social dimension would follow, but failing to understand that they had already "thrown away their trump cards by signing the Single Act of 1985":

A single market for capital and goods without common fiscal, social and ecological policies could not fail to set off a downward competition between member states, each needing to bring its trade into balance. To deal with the threat of 'social dumping', Jacques Delors counted on a push *after the event* by unions in peripheral and social democratic countries to impose common statutory or contractual bases throughout the community. This has not happened, despite the (half-hearted) protestations of the European parliament . . . attempts to harmonise VAT failed . . . [and] lack of harmonization on capital taxation is much more serious. . . . Even more serious was the surrender over social Europe. In September 1989, The European Commission proposed an insipid Social Charter. . . . In December 1991, at Maastricht . . . legislative power in Europe was handed over to coordination by national governments; a state apparatus on auto-pilot. Social Europe was once more sacrificed, and reduced to a 'zero-Charter', with Britain opting out. . . . In essence, as it is presently emerging, Europe will be unified only for the sake of capital, to allow it to escape from state control; that is, from the tax authorities and from social legislation."[51]

It is, of course, not really an escape from state control. Lipietz's account would make no sense if it were. The governments of Europe are not trying to assert a control over capital at the nation state level while at the same time trying to foreswear control at the regional level. The states, including the social democratic-led ones, as Lipietz avers, are the political authors of the Europe of traders and capitalists. Of course, they reflect capital's domination in each social formation in doing so, but it must also be said that the notion that this capital is ready to sustain, as the basis of regional trade rivalries, a rival state capitalist form "rooted in social policy and territorially balanced development" is belied by all the facts before us. Indeed, Cox may have been closer to the mark when he suggested in 1987 that the decline of American hegemony and the competitive pressures in the world system were acting on all states in such a way as to encourage an "emulative uniformity".[52] But his expectation at that time that this might involve common "adoption of similar forms of state-capitalist development geared to an offensive strategy in world markets and sustained by corporatist organization of society and economy" only rings true if we see state capitalism, as we have suggested, not as an alternative to hyper-liberalism but rather a subsidiary element sustaining competitive austerity, even in Europe. As Albo notes: "it is not the Anglo-American countries who are converting to the Swedish or German models but Germany and Sweden who are integrating the 'Anglo-American model'. . ."[53]

Even if American hegemony in international institutions has declined somewhat the continued direct imbrication of American capital in Europe as a powerful social force with which the European bourgeoisies remain interpenetrated still induces an "emulative uniformity". Poulantzas may have been wrong in his estimation in 1974 that each of the European bourgeoisies were too enmeshed in a structure of dependence on American capitalists to allow for a major extension of intra-regional cooperation in Europe. But he was not wrong in insisting that American capital must not be seen as standing outside Europe rather than a strong presence within it. Indeed, part of the reason for the failure of a 'Social Europe' has also to do with the mobilisation of American firms in Europe against it from the early 1980s on.[54] The multidimensional spread of direct foreign investment, with mutual interpenetration among European, Japanese and American capitals reinforces this tendency for emulative uniformity.[55]

VI. Conclusions: 'It ain't over 'til its over'[56]

It would indeed appear that there is no way of honestly posing an alternative to neo-liberal globalisation that avoids the central issue of the political source of capitalist power, globally and locally: the state's guarantee of control of the major means of production, distribution, communication and exchange by private, inherently undemocratic banks and corporations. It is inconceivable that there can be any exit from today's crisis without a planned reorientation and redistribution of resources and production on a massive scale. Yet how can this even be conceived as feasible, let alone made a basis for political mobilization?

This essay has suggested that those who want to install a "transnational democracy" in the wake of the nation state allegedly having been bypassed by globalisation simply misunderstand what the internationalisation of the state really is all about. Not only is the world still very much composed of states, but insofar as there is any effective democracy at all in relation to the power of capitalists and bureaucrats, it is still embedded in political structures which are national or subnational in scope. Those who advance the nebulous case for an "international civil society" to match the 'nebuleuse' that is global capitalist governance usually fail to appreciate that capitalism has not escaped the state but rather that the state has, as always, been a fundamental constitutive element in the very process of extension of capitalism in our time.

Sol Picciotto, who himself wants to give strategic priority to 'international popular organisation' as the best way forward, is nevertheless careful to warn against "naive illusions that social power exists quite independently of the state", and calls for "more sophisticated analyses of the contradictions of the state and the ways they can be exploited to build the strength of popular movements, while remaining aware that the national state is only a part of the overall structure of power in a global capitalist society."[57] The international constitutionalisation of neo-liberalism has taken place through the agency of states, and there is no prospect whatsoever of getting to a *somewhere else*, inspired by a vision of an egalitarian, democratic and cooperative world order beyond global competitiveness, that does not entail a fundamental struggle with domestic as well as global capitalists over the transformation of the state. Indeed, the contemporary era of the globalisation of capital may have finally rendered the distinction between national and foreign capital more or less irrelevant as a strategic marker for the Left. The two centuries-old search for a cross-class "producer" alliance between labour and national capital as an alternative to class struggle has taken shape in recent years in the form of the progressive competitiveness strategy, but its weaknesses have been very quickly revealed in the context of the globalisation of capital.

It is necessary to try to reorient strategic discussions on the Left towards the transformation of the state rather than towards transcending the state or trying to fashion a progressive competitive state. At the most general level this means envisaging a state whose functions are not tied to guaranteeing the economic *res publica* for capitalism. We have seen how the internationalisation of the state entails a turning of the material and ideological capacities of states to more immediate and direct use, in terms of both intranational and international dimensions, to global capital. The first requirement of strategic clarification on the Left must be the recognition that it must seek the transformation of the material and ideological capacities of states so that they can serve to realize popular, egalitarian and democratic goals and purposes. This does *not* mean attempting to take the state as it is presently organised and structured and trying to impose controls over capital with these inappropriate instruments. Nor does it mean trying to coordinate such controls internationally while resting on the same state structures. The point must be to restructure the hierarchy of state apparatuses and reorganise their *modus operandi* so as to develop radically different material and ideological capacities.

"One of the principal tasks of the capitalist state", David Harvey notes, "is to locate power in the spaces which the bourgeoisie controls, and disempower those spaces which the oppositional movements have the greatest potential to command."[58] The Left must take this lesson out of the book of capital to the end of relocating power to the benefit of progressive social forces. The same might be said about the important role the state can play in the distribution of time as an aspect of power. Radical proposals coming forward on the Left today for a statutory reduction in the working day to as little as four hours are not only directed at coping with the appalling maldistribution of employment in contemporary capitalism, but as Mandel and Gorz both stress, are designed to establish the conditions for the extension and deepening of democracy by providing the time for extensive involvement in community and workplace decision making.[59]

To emphasise the continuing importance of struggles to transform the state does not mean that territorial boundaries within which claims to state sovereignty are embedded ought to be seen as immutable. One of the important insights of Poulantzas was to point to the regional disarticulations that resulted from the extended reproduction of international capital within the framework of existing nation states. The integration of national with international capital upsets the old bases for national capital's unity; and at the same time regional discontents with state policies which are increasingly articulated with the needs of the global economy have provided fertile ground for a resurgence of old nationalisms with a separatist purpose. Right-wing nationalisms, and the parochialisms and intolerances they both reflect and engender, must be combatted on every front. But it is not always necessary for the Left to oppose the break-up of an existing state, just as it is not wise to dismiss out of hand attempts at international rearticulation of sovereignties through the creation of regional federations. The question is only whether the locus of power is thereby shifted to those spaces wherein democratic and inclusive movements which are oppositional to capital can expand their spaces and powers through a reorganisation of sovereignties.

For instance, while left-internationalists usually shake their heads in dismay at the apparent stupidity of Quebec leaving the Canadian federation at the very moment when France should be joining a federal Europe, it is by no means necessarily the case the existing Canadian federal state lays a firmer foundation for democratic challenges to capital than would close and amicable cooperation between an independent Quebec and a restructured Canadian state. Indeed more might be expected from two nation states each of whose *raison d'etat* was expressly more egalitarian and democratic in purpose rather than binational and territorial (*Ad Mare Usque Ad Mare*, it has often been pointed out on the Canadian Left, does not quite match *Liberty, Equality and Fraternity* as an expression of *raison d'état*). Nor should it be necessarily thought that a federal Europe must be one that necessarily extends democratic powers rather than disperses them more thinly in relation to a greater centralisation of state powers oriented to fulfilling capital's *res publica* on a continental terrain. Moreover, a federal state composed of the *existing* states of Europe is one that continues to rest on the *modus operandi* of these states. As every Canadian knows, capitalist forces are as capable of playing off the units of a federation against one another and against the centre, as they are of doing so with sovereign nation states; indeed the process may be more easily obscured behind an interminable debate over the division of constitutional powers.

Alain Lipietz, while taking as "a starting point that the struggles and social compromises are still settled at the level of the old-established nations of Europe", would like to see social and political unification as quickly as possible insofar as this would be democratically structured so as to overcome the terrible condition of competitive austerity. But he admits that while it "is better to have a Europe which is progressive (in the alternative sense of the word) than a France, a Sweden, etc, which are progressive in isolation . . . the present dilemma does not lie here. We are asked to choose between a Europe of *possibly* alternative states, and a united Europe which is liberal-productivist. My response is that if this is the choice, the first solution is better. . . ." He admits that in the short term it is unrealistic to expect a united Europe to be based on anything other than 'liberal-productivism'. But it is no less unrealistic to expect that this will change in the future without a prior change in the configuration of social forces and restructuring of state apparatuses in the member countries.[60]

A 'possibly alternative state' to those sponsoring globalisation amidst competitive austerity today would have to be based on a shift towards a more inwardly oriented economy rather than one driven by external trade considerations. This in turn would have to mean greater emphasis being placed on a radical redistribution of productive resources, income and working time than on conventional economic growth. This could only be democratically grounded, as Albo puts it, insofar as "production and services [were] more *centred* on local and national needs where the most legitimate democratic collectivities reside." Democratically elected economic planning bodies at the 'micro-regional' level, invested with the statutory responsibility for engineering a return to full employment in their communities and funded through direct access to a portion of the surplus that presently is the prerogative of the private financial system to allocate, should be the first priority in a programme for an alternative state.

This alternative could not be realised without at least some trade controls and certainly not without quite extensive controls over the flow of capital. (Indeed, it is improbable that such capital control can be realised without bringing the financial system within the public domain and radically reorganising it in terms of both its structure and function. This used to be known, when the Left was still innocent about its terminology, as the 'nationalization' of the banks). Of course, this would necessarily require interstate cooperation to install managed trade (rather than autarky) and to make capital controls effective. Have we then gone through this exercise only to come full circle – right back to the internationalisation of the state? Certainly not. International agreements and treaties between states will most certainly be required, but they will have the opposite purpose to the constitutionalising of neo-liberalism: they will be explicitly designed to permit states to effect democratic control over capital within their domain and to facilitate the realization of alternative economic strategies.

The feasibility of this alternative scenario rests entirely on conditions that still remain to be established. It is all too easy to predict the immense pressure and exertion of naked power that would emanate from international capital and dominant states to a country that was even near the point of embarking on such a strategic alternative; all to easy (and, of course, intentionally or unintentionally demobilising) because what it ignores are the prior material and political conditions that would bring the possibility of change onto the historical agenda. Some of these are material in the economic-technical sense of the term. Thus, even the technical feasibility of short-term capital controls is an open question today. Yet the instability of the world financial system is such that we are likely to see the 'discovery' of means of control and regulation, whether before or after an international financial collapse. But it is, above all, the political conditions that need to be created. The impact of domestic and external resistance is unpredictable in abstraction from the character, strength and effectiveness of the social forces that will mobilise within states and put the alternative on the agenda. Cox is extremely insightful on this when he insists at the end of *Production, Power and World Order* that once "a historical movement gets underway, it is shaped by the material possibilities of the society in which it arises and by resistance to its course as much as by the . . . goals of its supporters". Yet this is why, he insists, that "critical awareness of the potentiality for change . . . concentrates on the possibilities of launching a

social movement rather than on what that movement might achieve. . . .
In the minds of those who opt for change, the solution will most likely be
seen as lying not in the enactment of a specific policy program as in the
building of new means of collective action informed by a new understanding of society and polity."[61]

This will happen within states or it will not happen at all, but it will not
happen in one state alone while the rest of the world goes on running with
the bourgeoisie around the globe. Alternatives arise within international
political time: the movement-building struggles arise in conjunctures
which are, as Poulantzas understood, more than ever determined on a
world basis. Movements in one country have always been informed and
inspired by movements abroad; all the more so will this prove to be the case
as opposition builds to the evils globalisation is visiting on peoples rights
around the globe, increasingly also including the developed capitalist
countries. There is no need to conjure up out of this an 'international civil
society' to install a 'transnational democracy'. Rather we are likely to
witness a series of movements arising that will be exemplary for one
another, even though national specificities will continue to prevail. It is to
be hoped, of course, that these movements will as far as possible be
solidaristic with one another, even though international solidarity movements cannot be taken for alternatives, rather than as critical supplements,
to the struggles that must take place on the terrain of each state.

There is a stifling tendency on the Left today to draw facile lessons from
previous failures of attempts to escape from the logic of globalisation. The
limits faced by the Alternative Economic Strategy in Britain in the
mid-1970s and the French Socialist programme at the beginning of the
1980s are particular favourites employed to 'prove' that capital has the
unchallengeable power to escape the state. But was there even the political
will in these cases, let alone the movement or the material conditions, to
try to escape the control of capital? Franqis Mitterand had learned to
"speak socialist", in the immortally cynical words of Gaston Defferre, but
what failed in 1981–82 was primarily an attempt at a Keynesian reflation at
a very inopportune moment rather than the far more radical assault on
capitalism that had been envisaged in the 'Programme Commune'. And
while U.S. Secretary of State William Rodgers harboured "cosmic" fears
in 1976 that Tony Benn might precipitate a policy decision by Britain to
turn its back on the IMF which might in turn lead to the whole liberal
financial system falling apart, Rodgers quickly found he could count on the
support of the rest of the Labour Cabinet let alone the Treasury and the
Bank of England and the MI5.[62]

It is time the Left stopped reading its own faulty memory of such past
moments into all potential futures. It would seem that the last word, like
the first, belongs to Lewis Carrol's *Through the Looking Glass*:

'That's the effect of living backwards', the Queen said kindly; 'it always
makes one a little giddy at first ---'
'Living backwards!' Alice repeated in great astonishment. 'I never heard
of such a thing!'
'--- but there's one great advantage in it, that one's memory works both
ways."
'I'm sure *mine* only works one way,' Alice remarked. 'I can't remember
things before they happen.'
'It's a poor sort of memory that only works backwards,' the Queen
remarked.

NOTES

1. *Manifesto of the Communist Party*, Karl Marx, *The Revolutions of 1848: Political Writings, Volume I*, D. Fernbach, ed., London 1974, p. 70.
2. Robert Cox, "Global Perestroika", in R. Miliband and L. Panitch, eds., *New World Order? The Socialist Register 1992* p. 27.
3. David Gordon, "The Global Economy: New Edifice or Crumbling Foundations?", *New Left Review* 168, March/April, 1988.
4. Robert Cox, *Production, Power and World Order*, New York, 1987, pp. 253, 258.
5. David Held, "Democracy: From City-states to a Cosmopolitan Order?", *Political Studies*, XL, Special Issue, 1992, pp. 32–4.
6. Immanuel Wallerstein, *The politics of the world-economy*, Cambridge, 1984, pp. 10–11.
7. Perry Anderson, *Zones of Engagement*, London 1992, pp. 366–7.
8. Stephen Gill, "The Emerging World Order and European Change", in Miliband and Panitch, eds., *New World Order?* London 1992, pp. 157–96.
9. Philip Corrigan and Derek Sayer, *The Great Arch: English State Formation as Cultural Revolution*, Oxford 1985, p. 105.
10. Alan Wolfe, *The Limits of Legitimacy*, New York 1977, p. 22.
11. Robin Murray, "The Internationalization of Capital and the Nation State", *New Left Review* 67, May-June 1971, pp. 84–108.
12. Ibid., p. 102, citing *Monthly Review* of November 1969, p. 12.
13. Ibid., p. 109.
14. Nicos Poulantzas, *Classes in Contemporary Capitalism*, London 1974, pp. 70–88.
15. Ibid., p. 73.
16. Ibid.
17. Ibid., p. 78.
18. Cox, *Production, Power and World Order*, op. cit., (henceforth *PPWO*), pp. 132–3.
19. Peter Burnham, "Neo-Gramscian hegemony and the international order", *Capital and Class*, 45, Autumn, 1991, p. 90.
20. *PPWO*, pp. 105–6.
21. *PPWO*, p. 254.
22. *PPWO*, pp. 256–9.
23. *PPWO*, pp. 254–5.
24. *PPWO*, pp. 189.
25. *PPWO*, pp. 214, 220–1, 228, 266, 281.
26. *PPWO*, pp. 259, 282–3.
27. *PPWO*, p. 289.
28. Cox, "Global Perestroika", *op. cit.*, pp. 30–1.
29. See *PPWO*, p. 266 and p. 283.
30. See *PPWO*, p. 259, for an earlier use of this term.
31. *PPWO*, pp. 300–3.
32. *PPWO*, p. 259.

33. To be sure, Cox sees even this system to some extent in ideological and institutional terms: "The capital markets in question cannot realistically be thought of as nonpolitical. They are not cast in the classical model of an infinity of buyers and sellers of money; rather they are composed of a limited number of oligopolists whose consensus can be ascertained by a few telephone calls and whose individual judgements are based on a balancing of financial risk-taking and prudence, of political pressures and personal prejudices." *PPWO*, p. 301.

34. Peter Burnham, "Neo-Gramscian hegemony and the international order" *Op. cit.*, pp. 77–8.

35. Ian Robinson, *North American Free Trade As If Democracy Mattered*, Canadian Centre for Policy Alternatives, Ottawa, 1993. Two other excellent analyses are: Christian Deblock and Michele Rioux, "NAFTA: The Dangers of Regionalism", *Studies in Political Economy* 41, Summer 1993, pp. 7–44; and Ricardo Grinspun and Robert Kreklewich, "Consolidating Neoliberal Reforms: Free Trade as a consolidating framework" forthcoming in *Studies in Political Economy* 43, Spring 1994.

36. Ibid., p. 2.

37. Ibid., p. 20.

38. *Business Week*, November 22, 1993, p. 34.

39. *The Globe and Mail Report on Business*, Toronto, November 1, 1993.

40. *Business Week*, November 22, 1993, p. 35.

41. Lester Thurow, "An American Common Market", *The Guardian Weekly/The Washington Post*, November 21, 1993.

42. Bruce Campbell (with Andrew Jackson), *"Free Trade": Destroyer of Jobs. An Examination of Canadian Job Loss under the FTA and NAFTA*, Canadian Centre for Policy Alternatives, Ottawa, 1993, pp. 1–6.

43. See my "Dependency and Class in Canadian Political Economy", *Studies in Political Economy* 6, Autumn, 1981, pp. 6–33.

44. Sam Gindin and David Robertson, "Alternatives to Competitiveness" in D. Drache, ed., *Getting on Track: Social Democratic Strategies for Ontario*, Montreal, 1992, pp. 32–3, 39.

45. Greg Albo, "'Competitive Austerity' and the Impasse of Capitalist Employment Policy" in this volume.

46. See the critique of this position in my *Working Class Politics in Crisis*, London 1986, esp. chs. 4–6; and in my "The Tripartite Experience" in K. Banting, ed., *The State and Economic Interests*, Toronto 1986.

47. Albo, *op. cit.*

48. Cox, *PPWO*, pp. 292–4.

49. See "Global Perestroika", *op. cit.*, esp. pp. 31 and 41; and *PPWO*, esp. pp. 292 and 297–8.

50. Robinson, *op. cit.*, p. 44.

51. Alain Lipietz, *Towards a New Economic Order*, Oxford 1992, pp. 156–9.

52. *PPWO*, pp. 298–9.

53. Albo, *op. cit.*

54. See John Lambert, "Europe: The Nation-State Dies Hard", *Capital and Class*, 43, Spring 1991, esp. p. 16. For a somewhat different appreciation of Poulantzas's contribution to that offered here, see Sam Pooley, "The State Rules, O.K.? The Continuing Political Economy of Nation States" in the same volume, pp. 65–79.

55. See *PPWO*, p. 360; and Harry Magdoff, "Globalization – To What End?", *The Socialist Register 1992*, pp. 44–75.

56. With apologies to Yogi Berra.

57. Sol Picciotto, "The Internationalisation of the State", *Capital and Class* 43, Spring 1991, p. 60.

58. David Harvey, *The Condition of Postmodernity*, Oxford 1989, p. 237.

59. Ernest Mandel, *Power and Money*, London 1992, esp. pp. 202; and André Gorz, *Critique of Economic Reason*, London 1989, p. 159.

60. Lipietz, *op. cit.*, p. 135.

61. *PPWO*, pp. 394–5.

62. See Daniel Singer, *Is Socialism Doomed?*, Oxford 1988; and Leo Panitch, "Socialist Renewal and the Problem of the Labour Party" *The Socialist Register 1988*; and Panitch and Miliband, "The New World Order and the Socialist Agenda", *The Socialist Register 1992* (esp. fn. 24).

CAPITALISM AND THE NATION STATE IN THE DOG DAYS OF THE TWENTIETH CENTURY

Manfred Bienefeld

Introduction

With global capitalism triumphant, the idea that humanity must ultimately choose between socialism or barbarism would seem preposterous if working people's historic gains were not being reversed, if political extremism was not flourishing, if economic and social polarisation were not growing, if nations and societies were not disintegrating, if ethnic, religious and imperialist wars were not proliferating and if lean and mean ideologies were not diluting compassion and destroying the meaning of responsible citizenship. As it is, it is not so surprising that some people claim to be able to hear the faint hoofbeats of barbarism in the stillness of the early dawn.

The hegemonic ideology counters such hysteria by endlessly repeating its dog-eared promises of progress and efficiency, but careful observers note that, as they lose credibility, these promises are being steadily diluted. Gone is the dream of the leisure society, along with that of full employment, that of a regular, secure job and that of a compassionate society. Is there an end to this? And where does barbarism begin?

A new realism is changing the terms of our debates. The ghost of Malthus stalks the land declaring human progress a delusion, asserting the iron law of poverty, defining the crisis of the developing world as a problem of 'surplus population'. The ghost of Hitler beckons with dreams of pure ethnic or religious states, promising desperate people some ground on which to make a stand against the faceless forces destroying their lives. And in the belly of the beast, the ghost of Reagan poisons the political process with its insidious appeals to a crass individualism that teaches people to hate taxes and politics and to put their trust in personal wealth, however obtained.

And now some influential mainstream voices claim to have heard the hoofbeats at close range and have declared barbarism imminent and inevitable, allegedly driven by 'exogenous' factors, like population growth, resource scarcity (sic) and 'differences among civilizations'.[1] Taking the social and political disintegration that attends globalisation as a

94

given, they announce barbarism's arrival and tell people they must accept it. Once again, it seems that 'there is no alternative'! And if globalisation continues, unchecked, they may be right.

Samuel P. Huntington forecasts a future full of bloody 'culture wars' spawned by 'differences among civilizations' which he claims to be 'not only real' but 'basic'.[2] This crude and ultimately racist assertion obviously need not be true since history is full of examples of cultural assimilation and coexistence. But it is actually coming true as globalisation forces weak, indebted and disempowered nations to accept policies that radically expose them to fierce competitive pressures from an unstable and volatile global economy. Under these conditions they are often unable to maintain the delicate political balances on which social cohesion, political stability and cultural coexistence so often depend.

More recently Robert Kaplan has delivered a similar message, inviting us to think about the 'extremely unpleasant' possibility that the world faces 'an epoch of themeless juxtapositions, in which the classificatory grid of nation-states is going to be replaced by a jagged-glass pattern of city-states, shanty-states, nebulous and anarchic regionalisms'. Today's West Africa is said to be the picture of this future, showing

> what war, borders, and ethnic policies will be like a few decades hence . . . West Africa is becoming *the* symbol of worldwide demographic, environmental and societal stress, in which criminal anarchy emerges as the real "strategic" danger. Disease, overpopulation, unprovoked crime, scarcity of resources, refugee migrations, the increasing erosion of nation-states and international borders, and the empowerment of private armies, security firms, and international drug cartels are now most tellingly documented through a West African prism. . . . (It) provides an appropriate introduction to the issues . . . that will soon confront our civilization . . . it is a microcosm of what is occurring, albeit in a more tempered and gradual manner, throughout . . . much of the developing world; the withering away of central governments, the rise of tribal and regional domains, the unchecked spread of disease, and the growing pervasiveness of war.[3]

But Africa was not always like this, nor was its present plight inevitable. The comprehensive disaster that has befallen it was ushered in when its intransigent creditors imposed radical neoliberal policies on weak, indebted and distressed economies. It was their claim that these policies would lead to accelerated development,[4] but they actually led to a predictable disaster. Thus, in 1983, a reviewer of the World Bank's 'Berg Report' wrote that he regarded

> the document as a whole fundamentally wrong in its analysis; self-serving in its implicit allocation of responsibility for current problems; misleading in its broad policy prescriptions, and totally unrealistic both with respect to the social and political implications of its 'solutions' and with respect to its assumptions about real aid flows, price and market prospects for African exports and the robustness of Africa's struggling institutional structure.
>
> It is both arrogant and meaningless for the Bank to assert in that context that . . . the way forward lies through a greater concern with technical expertise and a greater reliance on the market. Such advice cannot be followed for any length of time under current circumstances because the social and political consequences . . . would be so dramatic that the policies would be devastated by the political whirlwinds which would be unleashed. As in the past

these domestic political responses could then be blamed for the disasters which follow, rather than being seen as more or less direct consequences of the acceptance of the(se) externally designed policy prescriptions.[5]

By 1985, the World Bank complained that 'borrowers and lenders often fail to take account of the institutional, social, and political rigidities that restrict a country's capacity to adjust';[6] and by 1988, its Chief Economist for Africa lamented that 'we did not think that the human cost of these programs could be so great, and economic gains so slow in coming'.[7]

Neoliberalism was not the only cause of Africa's problems but its crude ideological prescriptions made many bad situations worse. Certainly the current turmoil was not the inevitable result either of government intervention in the economy, or of the tribal or ethnic heterogeneity of most African states. The latter claim is especially pernicious in its implicit suggestion that only ethnically homogeneous states can be viable, a misconception based on the tautology that successful states eventually appear homogeneous. Moreover, it ignores the fact that ethnic homogeneity is an illusion, as illustrated by the fact that many Ethiopians used to think the Somalians lucky because they all came from the same tribe; until that country exploded into clan warfare.

This does not mean that culture or history do not matter; only that the trajectory of history is not genetically defined; and that material circumstances have a powerful bearing on the scope fur cultural coexistence or merger. That scope is reduced when nations lose their sovereign power to mediate potential internal conflicts and to manage the competitive process in ways that are sensitive to domestic social and political circumstances. The resulting risks are even higher in the case of technologically and administratively weak, or politically and culturally divided, societies like those of Africa. Which is why the imposition of these policies was especially indefensible there, and why it is now so distressing to see the perpetrators blame the victims.

Lest anyone doubt the ability of neoliberal policies to produce disastrous results when applied radically and insensitively to inappropriate situations, they need only look to Eastern Europe. Here these policies have decimated living standards and undermined institutions, social cohesion and political stability. As a result, the growth rates of secessionist movements, civil wars, ethnic conflicts, racism and fascism have been rivalled only by those of crime, poverty, prostitution and the Warsaw stock market index.[8] And amidst this carnage the IMF and the US government insist that these policies must be sustained or intensified, even as they profess their deep commitment to democracy. But,

by demanding draconian economic changes, by giving full unconditional support to the Yeltsin team and by ostracizing the previous Parliament – thereby contributing to the collapse of the political centre – the Clinton Administration (along with the international financial institutions) has contributed to the Zhirinovsky phenomenon . . . Ironically, what the West predicted would happen without Yeltsin – that is, the rise of a nationalist-

Communist movement – has happened because of him . . . The boosters of shock therapy should be chastened by what they have wrought. In the future they must pay more attention to the virtues of stability and consensus.[9]

Of course, the market extremists will deny responsibility and blame some allegedly exogenous factors (like corruption or the lack of entrepreneurship) for these failures, apparently unaware that policies must be designed for the real world, not for the text book models.[10]

It should be a sobering thought that the same institutions that are 'managing' these developments in Africa and Eastern Europe are using the same logic and the same policy prescriptions to push globalisation in the rest of the world. Their performance in these regions can leave no doubt in anyone's mind as to their commitment to these policies and their determination not to be deflected from them by mere political opposition or by some 'transitional' costs, no matter how high, how general or how permanent.

That is why the prophets of barbarism must be taken seriously, but it is also why we must reject their phoney fatalism. So long as globalisation continues to undermine the capacity of national governments to manage the competitive process in accordance with socially and politically derived limits and priorities, West Africa and Eastern Europe do afford us a glimpse of our future. But it will be so only if we allow it to be so; if we remain deaf to the cries of help from the societies presently being destroyed; or to the voices of those who still believe in the possibility of building stable, prosperous societies in which people can live in harmony with nature and with each other, while spending less time in less stressful, more interesting jobs and devoting an increasing part of their lives to social and cultural pursuits. Technology has made this dream a possibility; politics must realise it.

This dream is all but universal, and it contains the essence of the socialist dream. Its realisation must be the central focus of our political efforts to develop a plausible politics for the twenty first century. And our struggle must begin by rescuing the secular, territorial nation state from those who would abandon it, and from those who would replace it with the disastrous notion of ethnic or religious states. We must do so not because, once rescued, the nations state would necessarily allow us to achieve our goal, but because its loss would leave us in a barbaric global wilderness for a hundred years.

To those arguing that we must accept a barbaric future because there is no alternative, we reply that the prospect of barbarism will provide the stimulus needed to renew the struggle for democratic socialism, now as in the past.

Positive Promises and Hegemonic Ideologies

Meanwhile the mainstream continues to promise prosperity and welfare gains through globalisation, while downsizing its promises in accordance with the harsh facts of economic life. But it is gradually losing its capacity to persuade a sceptical population that globalisation serves their long term interests and this threat to its status as a hegemonic ideology has led to two responses: more rhetoric about measures to ameliorate the transitional welfare losses responsible for this erosion of support; and a much heavier emphasis on the alleged irreversibility of globalisation. The message is now subtly altered to read: the process serves your interests, as well as possible, under difficult circumstances; transitional costs can, and will, be substantially ameliorated; and, in any event, 'there is no alternative'.

Given that what appears to be possible under these conditions does not include full employment, or protection of incomes, of the social wage or of working conditions, it is not surprising that this message is difficult to sell to a generation that has just lived through twenty-five years of that which is now said to be impossible, namely stable and dynamic growth, with full employment, increasing income equality, increasing leisure, improved working conditions and social and political stability. To such people these promises look more like threats.

But then, these promises were even further diluted in an even tougher and more realistic restatement of the positive promise of globalisation in Robert Reich in *The Work of Nations*.[12] Since Reich's previous work had emphasised the important positive contributions historically made by national industrial policies, and since he writes as a political liberal, explicitly concerned with the welfare of America's working people, it comes as a surprise that he now accepts globalisation as the only option, even though he acknowledges that it threatens to undermine the living conditions of the majority of those people. So what is the promise held out by this vision of globalisation? And how plausible are the arguments that lead to these conclusions?

Reich believes that globalisation implies a peaceful, prosperous and dynamic future for the world economy as a whole, but that only a minority of America's working people are in a position to share in the resulting benefits. Meanwhile, the majority face a long term decline in their standards of living, unless their skills can be substantially enhanced. The central challenge is, therefore, 'whether there is still enough concern about American society to elicit sacrifices' to finance the training that would 'help the majority regain the ground it has lost and fully participate in the new global economy'. Unfortunately, in the absence of any external threat to the US, after the collapse of the Soviet Union, 'it is far from clear . . . whether it is possible to rediscover our identity, and our natural responsibility' to the degree necessary.

Despite his explicit concern for the welfare of America's working people, and his appeals to the charitable instincts of America's skilled (comprador?) elite, Reich's argument provides that elite with the perfect rationale for a unilateral declaration of independence. By accepting that in a global world the legal, moral and material foundations of citizenship have become all but meaningless, he legitimises and encourages the view that individuals have no self interested reasons to be concerned about the welfare of their fellow citizens; that a failure to fund the training on which the future welfare of the majority depends, would have no significant impact on that elite's quality of life. No wonder that Reich ultimately has so little faith in his own appeals to that rich minority's charitable instincts. One can but agree that, in a world as Reich presents it, the minority would be most unlikely to rise to the challenge that he poses.

Reich's analysis is based on four indefensible premises. Globalisation is inevitable and irreversible; a globalised world would provide the rich minority with a steadily improving quality of life; a world of five billion individuals would be dynamic and efficient; and America's (and the world's) working majorities could be rescued from impoverishment by increased training. These premises engender complacency among an elite that actually has a lot to lose from unchecked globalisation, and false hopes among a working majority whose economic decline is not going to be arrested by training funded through the charitable (or waning patriotic) instincts of the fortunate few. Let us examine these premises more closely.

Irreversibility, Inevitability and the Real World

Reich's conclusion that globalisation must be accepted as a *fait accompli* must be, and is, primarily based on its assumed irreversibility. It cannot be based on any positive benefits, since these accrue only to a minority, while the majority is threatened with an open ended, permanent decline in its standard of living. Moreover, this decline could only be averted if the skilled minority were prepared to finance the upgrading of their skills out of compassion, or a vestigial sense of social responsibility which Reich considers no more than a remote possibility, since that minority is rapidly divesting itself of the responsibilities of citizenship. On these terms, no responsible union leader, or citizen, could consider accepting globalisation on its merits, which is why Reich has to base his case for its acceptance on the claim that there is no choice, that globalisation is inevitable and irreversible.

To emphasise this fact he begins with a graphic description of a world in which alternative 'national' policies have become more or less inconceivable. In this world, a nation's citizens are no longer 'bound together . . . by a common economic fate' and

As almost every factor of production – money, technology, factories, and equipment – moves effortlessly across borders, the very idea of an American economy is becoming meaningless, as are the notions of an American corporation, American capital, American products, and American technology.

In response, America can only try 'to increase the potential value of what its citizens can add to the global economy, by enhancing their skills and capacities and by improving their means of linking those skills and capacities to the world market'. Only then could it alter the fact that, at present, only 'a small portion of America's workers' are able to seize the opportunities presented by globalisation, while 'the majority of Americans (are) losing out in global competition'. Unfortunately, such an initiative is not very likely 'when the very idea of an American economy is becoming meaningless', and since things may get a lot worse yet. Indeed, with the collapse of its traditional 'enemy' in Eastern Europe, America may face an even more dramatic political disintegration.

America may simply explode into a microcosm of the entire world. It will contain some of the world's richest people and some of the world's poorest, speaking innumerable languages, owning many allegiances, celebrating many different ideals. These individuals will be efficiently connected to the rest of the globe – both economically and culturally – but not necessarily to one another. Our collective identity will fade. There will be no national purpose, and no pretence of one.

Reich can only accept this disastrous vision of the future because his belief in the irreversibility of globalisation appears to be absolutely unconditional, and because he appears to believe that such an America could remain dynamic, efficient and stable enough to provide the skilled elite (his 'symbolic analysts') with a steadily improving quality of life. The former assumption is illogical and untenable, as argued below, the latter is unlikely to prove justified, as the following two sections will show.

The irreversibility of globalisation cannot be treated as unconditional since both the erosion, and the restoration, of national sovereignty is necessarily a matter of degree. Hence, when extreme consequences threaten, the demand for policy reversals at the margin can and will become overwhelming. The limits of the politically possible will alter. People will demand consideration even of policies that may initially be difficult to implement, remembering that short term pain can be justified by long term gain. In this process, things deemed impossible yesterday, will emerge as feasible options today. Who could have imagined the New Deal in 1929. And who would have thought that in 1992 *The Economist* would call for a restoration of international capital controls, or that, in the same year, a regular correspondent of the *Financial Times* would argue that the 'nationalisation of the banks' was now the only way to deal with Britain's financial woes?[12] Unfortunately Reich quite inexplicably chooses not to explore or discuss such possibilities, but to declare the 'old nationalist policies' unconditionally off limits and irrelevant. This is a shame, and a worry.

The worry turns to confusion, or consternation, when Reich reveals, much later in the book, that he also believes that any attempt to reverse globalisation would be necessarily bad. Thus, whatever the circumstances, he warns that nations must,

> eschew trade barriers . . . as well as obstacles to the movement of money and ideas across borders . . . (because these) . . . would only serve to reduce the capacity of each nation's work force to enjoy the fruits of investments made in them.[13]

But if this is true, then why is America's majority now threatened with a pervasive decline in a standard of living that was sustained over many years and that was achieved at a time when profits were higher, labour less well trained, the economy more protected and productivity lower? And how does he reconcile this claim with his earlier work showing that many of the nationalist policies he now decries were not detrimental to welfare or efficiency? And why the earlier emphasis on irreversibility? Ultimately one suspects that it is Reich's commitment to globalisation itself that has become unconditional, though for reasons that remain unclear.

The irreversibility of globalisation becomes important for its proponents only when its inherent desirability is in doubt. At that point the argument for globalisation must come to depend on the stick, rather than the carrot. It must now be accepted, however reluctantly, because there is no alternative. But this demobilising conclusion follows only if the process is truly irreversible, because it is driven by some exogenous factor, like technical change. The implication would be quite different if the driving force turned out to be primarily political, namely the rules and regulations of institutions designed to produce and protect the globalisation process because it serves certain specific interests at the majority's expense. In this case the claim that these policies were irreversible would cease to be demobilising and would turn into a rallying cry for those who recognise that the interests of the majority require a reversal of those political choices.

So is globalisation technologically driven? The claim is most common and most plausible in the case of financial deregulation where the proliferation of electronic media has, indeed, created formidable problems for national regulators. However, even here, the evidence shows the claim to be clearly indefensible. In fact, financial deregulation was, and is, primarily politically driven.

The claim that financial regulation has become impossible for technical reasons is obviously untenable. First because many of the world's most successful economies were slow to liberalise their financial markets and still regulate them extensively today.[14] Second, because, where there is the political will, as with the laundering of drug money, regulation is generally agreed to be feasible, even though it may be difficult. Third, when the World Bank advises countries to liberalise financial markets slowly, in order to minimise the risk of speculative destabilisation, it implicitly confirms both that such regulation is currently occurring and that it is feasible in future.[15] And, finally, the fact that almost everyone accepts global financial regulation as both necessary and feasible, implies the feasibility of national regulation, both because global regulation is far more difficult, and because it would, in any case, require regulators to monitor transactions at some sub-global (or national?) level.

The inescapable conclusion is that financial liberalisation is politically driven, and that technology has been both a means and an excuse. The incentive was the opportunity to make enormous fortunes by creating mountains of credit – and debt – 'in a wonderful country called Offshore . . . where there were no rules at all, because there was no country'.[16] And those fortunes continue to grow, despite the global economy's sluggish performance. In fact, 1993 was a bumper year for the folks in finance, as

> Goldman, Sachs offered bonuses of at least $5 million each to its 160 partners . . . the top hedge funds reaped profits of hundreds of millions of dollars, and a fund's manager gets the lion's share of that . . . even the not so top dogs made out like bandits (so that) hundreds of investment bankers who aren't partners will clear the million dollar bonus hurdle . . . and even junior investment bankers, five years out of business school will take home bonuses of $250,000'.[17]

And all this in a country where 'real average wages have declined by 18% between 1972 and 1990',[18] where unemployment remains persistently high, where poverty is on the rise, where urban decay has reached unimaginable levels and where the casualisation of labour is rampant. The real question is not whether this pattern of development is reversible, but how long it can last?

To be sure, for the moment these 'deregulated financial markets' have given those who control the flows of international finance a 'stranglehold . . . on government monetary policy',[19] and a veto power over attempts to reregulate finance. But before those same people start talking about irreversibility and 'the end of history', they might reflect on the fact that it is the real economy that ultimately gives money its value. With electronic money, you can't even light a fire to keep warm.

In the final analysis, financial regulation depends on the political will to enforce adequate sanctions, so that, given the risk of discovery, the majority of people will observe the law. The fact that such laws can always be technically evaded (by some, for a time) is not an argument against them or their enforcement, any more than the existence of unsolved murders constitutes an argument against the homicide laws. In fact, the biggest obstacle to the enforcement of financial regulations today, is not the computer or the fax machine, but the poisonous individualism of the eighties which has undermined people's willingness to observe the law by corroding the ethical and ideological foundations on which law enforce-ment, taxation and the ability to justify social investment ultimately rest. But such fashions change. People are not born with such venal views, and throughout history, popular uprisings have persuaded many a surprised ruling class suddenly to rediscover its sense of social responsibility when it thought it no longer needed one.

The alleged irreversibility of globalisation will be increasingly challenged as more people experience its costs and recognise that these are not due to minor or temporary disturbances afflicting a small minority, but are part of an open ended and long term challenge to the majority's quality of life. Once that majority also understands that the obstacles standing in the way of a reversal of these trends are not immutable historical laws or technological inevitabilities, but political choices imposed on them by a venal and short sighted minority, the time will be ripe for change.

In the meantime, it is worth nothing that the global elite itself clearly does not believe in irreversibility. Otherwise it would not be so actively creating new international institutions and agreements to threaten any country contemplating such a reversal with collective retaliation. And the range of policy instruments being made subject to retaliation in this way is constantly being extended by agreements like the Canada-US Free Trade Agreement (CUFTA), the North American Free Trade Agreement (NAFTA) and the Uruguay Round of the GATT, which are all much more than trade agreements. They are explicit attempts to roll back national sovereignty.

Thus, the new GATT agreement has so narrowed the range of policy options available to governments in the developing world that a critic, writing before the final agreement was signed, described its potential impact as follows:

> The powers and position of TNCs would be enhanced, the sovereign space of countries would be reduced and the process of transnationalisation of the world economy (and of the Third World) would be carried forward to an extent where it would not be easily reversible. It will divide the world between the "knowledge-rich" and "knowledge-poor", with the latter permanently blocked from acquiring the knowledge and capacity to be rich. . . . In economic and social terms, Third World countries and their people could be said to be on the point of being rolled back to the colonial era.[20]

Some take comfort in the thought that countries generally only enter such agreements voluntarily, but this is to ignore the fact that what appears to be voluntary, is often tinged with more than a hint of blackmail and coercion.[21] Moreover, these governments in question frequently do not represent the national interest in any real sense. In fact, governments dominated by small global elites or by international capital, often seek to enter such agreements to protect their interests from domestic political challenges.

Canada's experience provides a particularly explicit example. Thus, when its Mulroney government broke an explicit promise by announcing its intention to seek a Free Trade Agreement with the United States, the Minister for International Trade, told a reporter that 'the main reason' why Canada needed such an agreement was 'to ensure that no future Canadian government could ever return to those bad old nationalist policies of the past'![22] It is a sad comment on Canada's democracy that this treasonable and utterly undemocratic statement did not lead to the Minister's, let alone the Government's resignation.

In such a world, collective security takes on a whole new meaning, as the national fractions of a global elite seek multilateral protection from domestic political forces, be they Chiapas Indians, Moscow conservatives or persistent social democrats. But, as these elites sit ensconced in their rich ghettoes, behind their electric fences and their security guards, declaring this new world inevitable and irreversible, their actions speak louder than their words. And these show clearly that they know it is not so.

Globalisation is not inevitable and certainly not irreversible. Moreover, the main obstacles to its reversal are the institutional and legal barriers erected by international capital to extend its power and to protect its interests. This means that something can be done. And, eventually, something will be done. We can only hope that when countries finally begin to push for policy reversals at the margin, those who are now holding the world to ransom do not make good on their threats to respond with massive retaliation. And if they do, we must hope that the world's intellectuals have not been so mystified and suborned that they blame the ensuing disaster on those who dared to begin the reversal of a process that was always bound to lead to disaster.

What future awaits the 'fortunate few'?

The second promise of Reich's argument is that globalisation promises the skilled minority a wonderful future of health, wealth and happiness in a stable, dynamic and efficient world. Even though Reich points out that 'the peace of mind potentially offered by platoons of security guards, state-of-the-art alarm systems, and a multitude of prisons is limited',[23] there is no doubt that he presents their future as a beguiling and seductive one. Globalisation will serve their long term interests and they are quite rational, from a self interested point of view, to be preparing to 'complete their secession from the union'. Moreover, by doing so, they will not significantly impair their quality of life.

But this vision is based on a narrow, materialistic definition of the quality of life, an extremely individualistic view of the world and a naive view of the political process. In fact, the mismatch between this vision and the actual future is likely to be even greater than that between today's Los Angeles, and the 1994 Los Angeles people would have imagined in the fifties.

The truth is that in an ever more fragmented, volatile and competitive world this minority's gains will be shallow and precarious. Material gains will be offset by other losses, like increased personal and economic insecurity, more fragmented and transitory family and community relationships and an increasing incapacity to protect spiritual, ethical or environmental standards from erosion by the forces of competition. In fact, it is doubtful whether such a society could prevent competitive pressures from pushing people systematically beyond the limits of the law in the desperate struggle for economic survival. Corporate competition would come to resemble the world of organised crime, where people have to take responsibility for their own security and for the enforcement of contracts and the law, as each actor defines them.

Life will become extremely uncertain, even for the fortunate few. Their skills will be constantly threatened by technical change, by competition and by changing patterns of corporate control over assets (physical and financial), the knowledge and the media outlets, needed for the minority to exercise its skills. In short, the markets for those skills will become ever more unstable and oligopolistic. The Russia of the nineties will be the model of this future; a future that will be truly barbaric, as law enforcement is 'privatised', economic security is abolished and trust is all but eliminated. In such a world, even the elite's quality of life would be desperately low by any reasonable definition.

The 'Malibu forever' future that Reich promises the global elite is thus a delusion. In the fiercely individualistic and competitive world that he envisages, society will lose its capacity to manage the resulting centrifugal forces. Efficiency will eventually take a back seat to survival, and technology will lose its lustre and even its value. In a chaotic and barbaric world a computer cannot do much to raise efficiency. Indeed, for most of the people trapped in such a nightmare, it will be just another useless thing you cannot eat.

These issues are politically important because it is not unreasonable to think that, given a clearer appreciation of the future that actually awaits them, many members of the global elite would be willing to sacrifice some personal income in return for the chance to live in diverse, peaceful communities able to satisfy the basic human need for 'both affection, generated in small groups, and respect, gained by activities that are consonant with community values and that respond to shared concerns'.[24] Unfortunately, such choices are now being unwittingly foreclosed in the insane scramble for a socially destructive form of efficiency that is being enforced by today's unregulated competitive markets. People must be freed from the misapprehension that increased wealth necessarily means increased choice and, hence, increased happiness. We need to give more thought to the choices foreclosed in the process of attaining that wealth. Too often our political choices are pre-empted by hostages that have been given to fortune in the process of creating undesirable and irrational economic obligations.

As Stephen Marglin has reminded us,

We torture language when we say our young people "choose" to join one or another of the authoritarian or destructive cults that abound. Many of them seem to be searching, however desperately, for the community and family that our single-minded attention to GNP has helped to destroy. In short, rather than expanding the domain of choice uniformly, growth expands choice in some dimensions but restricts it in others.[25]

And globalisation is foreclosing many choices as it shapes the choices of the future. Even if the global elite could continue to enjoy an ever rising aggregate income, it would have to endure its good fortune in a grim world ravaged by crime, social polarisation, political instability, the intensification of work, personal isolation and pervasive economic insecurity. No doubt people would adjust to such a life and they might even come to love it, given the alternative of life among the dispossessed. But that does not mean they would have chosen it had they been given a genuine choice. At the end of the day, what they get will not be what they would have wanted, had they made their choices before the options were decimated. That is why time is of the essence.

Instability and Inefficiency in a Globalised World

But the news for the global elite and others is even worse than this, since an unregulated global economy is unlikely to remain dynamic and efficient, so that not even the promise of higher aggregate material incomes is likely to be fulfilled. Although most mainstream economists insist on claiming that further economic liberalisation will always tend to increase both efficiency and total output, those claims are based more on ideology and (bad) theory, than on history or science.

Most neoliberals do not appear to realise just how much is implied by their injunction that even a minimalist state must be responsible for contract enforcement. This is not simply a matter of drafting some laws, paying a police force and hiring some prosecutors. It requires the creation of a society in which the vast majority of people are prepared to obey the law voluntarily, settle most of their differences without recourse to the law, or to violence; pay their taxes because they are 'the price of civilisation';[26] restrain their search for immediate personal advantage in line with ethical standards; and ultimately define their self interest as members of society, not as pure individuals.

Reich clearly values people's sense of social responsibility but fails to realise that, in its absence, contract enforcement at reasonable cost becomes impossible. And with it goes the promise of efficiency, prosperity and stable growth, on which the prosperity of the skilled minority also depends.

Nor can the contract enforcement function be delegated upwards to the global level as is suggested when people propose global regulation, say, of something like finance. This is to confuse a political task with a technical one. Such regulation has to be embedded in a political process capable of writing rules with enough legitimacy to allow them to be enforced at reasonable cost and with a minimum of coercion. It is because globalisation is not creating such a framework, that the word does not describe a positive process of global construction, but a negative process of national disintegration. Moreover, effective international regulation will only become possible when stable and cohesive nation states, broadly representative of their people, cooperate to establish and enforce mutually agreeable rules at an international level. In the same way as those nation states should be based on smaller, viable communities through which people could exercise their responsibilities as citizens and define themselves a social beings.

The issue of contract enforcement is but one of the many ways in which the social and political context has to be a critically important determinant of economic efficiency. Competition cannot lead to true and sustained efficiency unless it is embedded in a social and political matrix capable of restraining the struggle for economic efficiency sufficiently, to allow society to make genuine choices trading efficiency off against other objectives like environmental protection, social cohesion, political stability or the ability to maintain full employment. But such choices can only be made within political entities that have sufficient sovereignty to enforce them, and that are sufficiently open and democratic to legitimise them. Such entities are termed 'generic nation states' for the purposes of this discussion and they are an essential prerequisite for the efficient functioning of markets.

More broadly, economic theory itself understands quite clearly that the consequences of the deregulation of markets can range from increased efficiency and growth to chronic instability and even crisis, depending on the place, the extent and the context of that deregulation. And the process of globalisation has tended to push deregulation too far, too fast almost everywhere, partly because the debt crises have increased the leverage of those who benefit from globalisation, and partly because the destruction of the sovereign powers of nation states makes it more difficult to manage the resulting pressures in accordance with local circumstances. As a result, it becomes more and more difficult to make good economic or social policy as globalisation increases the distance between the policy makers and the real world. The result is a reminder that 'the quality of information on which all investment decisions must rely tends to deteriorate with distance'.[27]

Globalisation has made national economic management far more difficult, but it has not created a global economy. Indeed, even in finance, where this process has probably gone furthest, it remains true that 'there are only limited examples of truly global financial services, markets or products'. Moreover, even the trend has not been uniformly in the direction of more globalisation, as indicated in a February 1993 issue of the

AMEX Bank Review, which reported 'an observed retreat of financial firms away from global expansion, returning to national/local bases' and then explained this 'observed withdrawal of financial firms from their global ambitions (as) more a reflection of the over capacities in certain markets'.[28]Those global markets that do exist are largely unregulated and this has tended to make them relatively volatile, unpredictable and irrational. They have performed poorly by almost any standard; they are partly responsible for the global economy's present inability to return to steady growth; and they are substantially responsible for the disaster that befell so many developing economies in the eighties; and there is every reason to think that they will generate similar, or larger, problems in the future. Certainly the record of the recent past lends little support to the claim that globalisation will foster dynamic economic growth. In fact, fifteen years of aggressive neoliberal deregulation have produced the most disappointing economic performance since the war.

That unregulated markets should have performed so badly should not have come as a surprise. Frank Hahn, writing from a neoclassical perspective, warned in 1982 that the neoliberal 'advocates say much more than even pure theory allows them to say, and infinitely more than the applicability of that theory permits'.[29] In particular, they fail to take adequate account of the dangers posed by the inherent instability of the investment function, whose dependence on highly subjective expectations can potentially lead it to generate large and extremely wasteful deviations from an economically efficient growth path. That is why so many successful countries used various non economic mechanisms to manage their economies at the national level. His argument is worth citing at some length.

> If the invisible hand is to operate there must be sufficient opportunities for intertemporal and contingent intertemporal trade. In fact that there are not enough of these opportunities. The lack of contingent markets means that the market economy is associated with more uncertainty than pure theory allows. The lack of intertemporal markets means that great weight must rest on market expectations. The Rational Expectations hypothesis substitutes an internal and psychic hand for the market. Each individual somehow has learned how the invisible (hand) would have performed if it had been given markets within which to perform. If it is agreed that this is not of high descriptive merit, there is, in fact, no obvious mechanism by which intertemporal decisions can be co-ordinated. This was Keynes's view. I have yet to see it refuted. The French drew the conclusion that they at least required indicative planning. The Japanese have for a long time employed non-market institutions to supplement private investment decisions. In Germany, the banks seem to act as market substitute. In Britain, where politicians now follow gurus rather than arguments we are all set to rely on the invisible hand doing a job which, in practice, it will not and cannot do.[30]

Five years later, a paper by Professors Dornbusch and Frankel showed that exchange rates had become far more volatile since their deregulation in the seventies, and that the proportion of those fluctuations that could be explained by changes in the underlying economic fundamentals – ie relative inflation rates, productivity growth, costs of production – was 'close to zero'![31] The fluctuations were therefore irrational, costly and distorting.

Another study, assessing the performance of deregulated international exchange rate markets led Paul Krugman to a forthright and blunt conclusion that stands in sharp contrast to the repeated claims that the deregulation of these markets must yield substantial benefits and poses no speculative risks.

> At this point, belief in the efficiency of the foreign exchange market is a matter of pure faith; there is not a shred of positive evidence that the market is efficient, and . . . similar results obtain for other asset markets . . . that is, both the bond and the stock market. . . . The bottom line is that there is no positive evidence in favour of efficient markets, and if anything a presumption from the data that (these) markets are not efficient. . . . The important conclusion . . . is that we are freed from Friedman's . . . argument . . . that an efficient market could not exhibit destabilizing speculation. . . . Now we know that in fact no evidence supports this hypothesis – that is one maintained purely on faith.[32]

This is a devastating conclusion for those, including Reich, who confidently assert that globalisation will yield efficiency gains, and that its reversal must yield commensurate losses. In their more candid moments, the World Bank and the IMF also acknowledge the ambiguity of the impact of deregulation. The Bank has even described the seventies lending spree, that created the devastating debt crisis of the eighties, as evidence 'that competitive financial markets . . . can still make mistakes', having already pointed out that deregulated financial markets frequently 'tend towards instability and fraud'.[33]

The IMF, too, has discovered a downside to its financial policy prescriptions. It has warned that financial liberalization 'may . . . result in destabilizing and inefficient capital market speculation';[34] and that the economic recovery of the early nineties has been so slow and hesitant because the collapse of earlier speculative booms has led to 'the wealth losses and financial sector repercussions associated with asset price declines (that) have restrained consumption and investment'.[35] The same point was made rather more forthrightly in 1991 by a senior US banking official who declared that 'the borrowing binge of the past decade is the key reason why lending is tight'.[36]

The problems to which these statements refer are not minor ones. The human, social and economic losses imposed on much of the developing world by the debt crisis of the eighties were enormous, as are the costs of the delayed recovery of the early nineties. Moreover, the mechanisms that produced these problems, as well as the $5 million annual bonuses for the partners at Goldman, Sachs, remain in place and are presently stimulating new speculative asset inflations whose costs will come due in a few years time. Undoubtedly they will again be paid for by the poor and the middle classes of the world through wage reductions, cuts in social services and taxes to fund public bailouts of the same speculators who caused the problem in the first place, whose losses are, in fact, merely paper losses reflecting the reversal of irrational and unwarranted speculative gains.

Only a Gilbert and Sullivan opera could do justice to this global shell game. Until it is written, some passages from a recent IMF report on *International Financial Markets* will serve. Referring to recent difficulties encountered by banks in various industrial countries, the report says,

> A crucial question to ask . . . is why after a long postwar period of stability have banking problems become so widespread and occurred with such frequency? What is it that induces banks in different countries to abandon – seemingly periodically – the principles of sound banking. Although no single answer can do full justice . . . at least one common thread running through many recent banking crises merits attention. That thread is the recognition that the competitive pressures unleashed by financial liberalization do not merely increase efficiency; they also carry risks, as banks and other institutions alter their behaviour to ward off institutional downsizing.
>
> Faced with a potential downsizing of their operations, many banks responded to this new, less hospitable environment by increasing the riskiness of their portfolios.
>
> In the end, the increased risks taken by banks were often exposed and turned into losses by a significant shift in economic conditions. . . . Where these risks were not adequately protected . . . the losses subsequently spilled over into the public domain.[37]

A rough translation of this tortured language would begin by recalling the warning delivered to the Canadian government by the Chairman of Sun Life Assurance, to the effect that 'a very liberal regulatory regime is an invitation to get yourself into trouble'.[38] The 'trouble' in question results from the speculative bubbles often created by the credit expansion made possible by deregulation. Participation in these binges is all but obligatory since fund managers who fail to participate will generally be unemployed long before their caution is vindicated. After all, to most people, $5 million in the hand makes the number of birds in the bush academic.

Ironically, the cautious fund managers who did not participate in such booms would not even turn out to be right from his institution's, or profit maximising client's point of view, though he would be right from the economy's point of view. Such boom/bust cycles are, indeed, highly undesirable and wasteful; distort prices and misallocate capital; re-distribute income in a highly regressive manner; and bankrupt many otherwise viable and desirable businesses. But from a narrow institutional perspective he would have missed out on a 'glorious' opportunity to cash in on the run up of the boom and, if he'd been clever enough to bet on the subsequent fall in the futures market, he could have made big money in both directions. George Soros, now famous for making one billion dollars in ten days speculating against the British pound, explained it all in his book *The Alchemy of Money*.

> Commercial banks . . . seek to maximize their profits within the framework of existing regulations and they cannot afford to pay too much attention to the systemic effects of their activities. A commercial banker who refuses to go after what seems like a profitable business is liable to be pushed aside, and even if a bank decided to abstain there are many others anxious to take its place. Thus, even those who realized that the international lending boom was unsound found themselves obliged to participate or lose their places.

There is an important lesson here: participants are not in a position to prevent a boom from developing even if they recognize that it is bound to lead to a bust. That is true of all boom/bust sequences. Abstaining altogether is neither possible nor advisable. For instance, in my analysis of mortgage trusts I clearly predicted a bad end, yet my advice was to buy now because the shares would have to rise substantially before they crashed.[39]

To be fair to Soros, he wrote all this as a warning, making it clear that he considered these events to be wasteful, destructive and inherently undesirable. Indeed, he even identified and advocated the only solution that is available to deal with such problems when he said:

The lesson to be learned is that financial markets need to be supervised. Only some kind of intervention, be it legislative, regulatory, or a gentle hint from a central bank, can prevent boom/bust sequences from getting out of hand.[40]

Unfortunately, globalisation makes this more difficult by undermining the national capacity to regulate these processes. As a result, boom/bust cycles proliferate and expand, leaving Mr. Soros to make more billions in 1993 as one of the most successful hedge fund managers on Wall Street. It was not as if he hadn't warned us.

And the gyrations continue. Asian property and stock market shares are the current favourites. The results will be the same, only more so. And their costs will come on top of those still being borne from the previous cycles. These things don't come cheap, as the IMF reminds us.

When such banking and financial crises occur, their resolution can be costly. For example it has been estimated that the saving and loan crisis on the United States carried a $180 billion price tag for the tax payer (equivalent to over 3 percent of GDP).[41]

No wonder governments everywhere have to cut social services and curb their profligate spending on education and unemployment insurance. No wonder social democracy is on the run. Somebody has to pay for those $5 million dollar bonuses!

Eventually these bills will become unpayable. Once wages have been slashed to the bone, unemployment insurance abolished and everything from policing to education privatised, the bailouts will have to stop, since, by then, public sector revenues will have collapsed as the real economy falters under the weight of accumulated debt, the burden of unemployment and weak consumer spending. Then there will be a financial crash, maybe a depression and if we are unlucky, a war. And soon economists will start preaching the benefits of deregulation again. Or maybe not?

The possibility of another depression has even been raised in the pages of *The Economist* which published a special section on international finance that began by noting that, in the eighties, the world economy had undergone a 'decisive change' in which 'many of the boundaries between national financial markets (had been) dissolved'. The results were said to be disturbing, since 'the trend towards financial integration . . . makes exchange rates ever more volatile, harder to control, more disruptive of economic policy-making and ever more of a nuisance to companies that trade and invest across borders'. In fact, 'financial dread' was said to be 'the mood of the moment', including dread of another depression.

> The changes in international finance of recent years have not made . . . a crisis any less likely. In some ways, quite the reverse. . . . Just as the new international dimension of finance has added to some risks that may help to start a crisis – greater instability in currencies, faster transmission of economic disturbances across borders, new opportunities for leverage, increased susceptibility to the illusion of liquidity and so on – so it has also weakened (or anyway complicated) the traditional remedies of economic policy. In the new world of finance, the seas are rougher and the life-rafts flimsier.[42]

The bottom line is that unregulated markets are dangerously unstable and ultimately economically inefficient. At the same time, their social and political consequences are both deeply undesirable and ultimately unsustainable. In Karl Polanyi's words 'such an institution could not exist for any length of time without annihilating the human and natural substance of society'.[43] And globalisation is nothing but a renewed attempt to create such an impossibility. There can be no such thing as one single global economy, since there is – and there could be – no meaningful global political process to manage that market. And without such management, a global market could not function either efficiently or effectively. That is why

> it was not simply 'capitalist production' which historically demonstrated its relative superiority in the competitive struggle. It was 'capitalism, as organised in an effective, modern nation state', which must claim this distinction. The qualification is most important.[44]

For all these reasons, Reich's naively optimistic prognosis for America's (and the globe's) fortunate minorities misses the mark. Even this group has many reasons to be concerned about the future if globalisation continues on its present course. It must be persuaded by argument and by the threat of political opposition to accept a political compromise through which it can regain its social and political legitimacy, in return for agreeing to recreate sovereign political spaces within which capital, labour, and other constituencies can bargain and in which the resulting agreements can be enforced, in which the political process can establish social, political, ethical and environmental priorities and trade them off against efficiency; and in which full employment can be pursued as an overriding priority. In the early post war era, capital was persuaded to accept such an agenda due to the realism inspired by the disaster of the twenties, the depression, the war and the communist threat. We can only hope, this time, a similar result can be achieved with less costly and terrible inducements. The first step is to disabuse the fortunate few of the notion that all is well for them. It is not.

Why is the training solution so popular when it can't work?

This brings us to the fourth and last pillar of Reich's liberal version of the neoconservative defence of globalisation, namely the claim that the majority of America's working people, who are threatened by globalisation, can be 'saved' by training schemes financed by the fortunate few. This claim is crucial, since no ideology could hope to remain hegemonic by promising the majority of the population steady immiserisation, on top of the chronic economic insecurity and the social disintegration people are already being asked to accept as an inevitable part of this lean and mean world. Unfortunately the promise that training will – or even could – protect the threatened majorities of the world from a pervasive decline in their standards of living is totally implausible.

The training gospel has three features that explain its enormous popularity in circles otherwise adamantly opposed to government intervention in the economy. It is vague enough that it can be supported by almost everyone; it implicitly places the blame for their plight on the victims; and, if successful in increasing their supply, it will actually reduce the 'privileges' enjoyed by the few workers still able to command a high wage. Let us explore each of these features in turn.

Why the broad appeal? Training is a motherhood issue because it sounds positive but has so little content that it is compatible with any political position. A commitment to training need not lead to any action, partly because it is so difficult to tell whether it has done so. This is because every country is already training people on a large scale; no one knows what sort of training is actually needed in a globalising world; any training initiatives will remain subject to the existing fiscal constraints; and the success or failure of training schemes is very difficult to establish since no one can be expected to forecast the detailed skills required. The market establishes success or failure *ex post*. Hence this commitment need not and often does not lead to significant action or expenditure. At the same time, the training issue can be used to undermine some remaining bastions of opposition to the rollback of the welfare state. As a result, adoption of the training myth can actually lead to 'less than nothing' as far as working people are concerned.

For example, the issue can be, and is being, used to undermine the principle of unemployment insurance. If skills are the central problem, then the state can limit its responsibility to the provision of some training, however flimsy or irrelevant, and then wash its hands of the unemployed. This represents an abdication of a fundamental social and moral responsibility, in a world in which access to productive assets and opportunities is increasingly restricted by highly concentrated and oligopolistic property rights. And the training myth makes it easier for the state to slide out from under this obligation by diverting unemployment insurance funds to training schemes that would have been created in any case. In addition, the focus on training can also provide a good platform from which to intensify the attack on working conditions more generally. Slogans like the need for 'permanent retraining' or for 'lifetime learning' are widely used to describe and justify the casualisation of labour which is creating a world in which workers are paid what it takes to get them to the factory gate each day, hoping the straw boss will give them the nod. This is the ultimate logic of the fully deregulated labour market now being touted as the next big policy issue by the international financial institutions.[45] And finally, the training issue provides a good basis from which to push education, even further into a purely instrumentalist path, leaving ideas like education for its own sake, for socialisation or for citizenship, to fall by the wayside. More choices foreclosed!

The second feature that makes the emphasis on training so attractive to many is that it makes the individual responsible for his or her plight. To reject this argument is not to reject the ideal of personal responsibility, or to deny the value of training. It is to question the implicit removal of responsibility from an economic system in which unregulated markets are undermining the social fabric, misallocating resources, reducing efficiency on any reasonable definition and destroying people's access to work under conditions compatible with broader social and ethical objectives.

The idea that it is the deficient skills of the unemployed that are the cause of their problem also implies that training could restore full employment – in good jobs! But, this claim really cannot be taken seriously. Since millions of highly trained people are unemployed today, the argument must assume that someone, somewhere knows a different kind of training that would alter this outcome, at an acceptable cost and within an acceptable time frame. But this is simply foolishness, even though there is no shortage of snake oil peddlers claiming to have solutions among the ranks of the management gurus and the 'Training for Success' entrepreneurs.

The third reason for the popularity of the training panacea in right wing circles is the fact that the good jobs now held by Reich's skilled minority, command high wages because of their relative scarcity. If training initiatives had a significant impact on the supply of those skills, this would tend to reduce those wages – or 'privileges'. Although it would also raise the standard of living of some of the marginalised majority, the ultimate result would be to increase the proportion of working people in the marginalised group, at least so long as labour remained in surplus at the global level. This is because in a competitive economy with surplus labour, the wage is determined by labour's supply price, irrespective of its average productivity.

Ultimately, the threat to the majority of the world's working people will only be lifted with the arrival, or the achievement, of global full employment and that is not imminent or likely in the absence of a global political mechanism to make it happen. Until then, globalisation will continue to depress the direct wage, the social wage and the living conditions of most working people and this will intensify if access to productive assets, including information and knowledge, is placed even more firmly in the hands of large corporate entities that have no explicit social responsibilities and that cannot be directly influenced through democratic political processes.[46] In such a world, the main impact of training will be to reduce the size of the 'fortunate minority' and increase the size of the 'declining majority'.

To solve the unemployment problem, capital and capitalists, must once again be embedded in a system in which the pursuit of profit is undertaken within clearly defined social and political constraints, including the need to construct jobs and careers in ways that accommodate the needs of individuals as people, and the needs of communities as social and cultural entities. In the absence of such conditions, full employment will either remain an unattainable mirage, or be achieved at such a desperately low level of wages and under such deplorable social and working conditions that it will be self-defeating and ultimately even inefficient.

Of course, training could improve the position of specific groups, like Reich's American majority, or maybe Canada's workers, since it is possible for a society to capture a larger share of the good jobs that remain in a slowly growing, 'downsizing' world. However, such success will be largely (even if not entirely) at someone else's expense, and can therefore be expected to lead to increasing conflict. Moreover, success in that struggle is most likely to be achieved by countries able to maintain a high degree of social cohesion and political stability, precisely because efficiency is increasingly a social phenomenon, depending on reliable human relations, social stability, good communications and low costs of law enforcement or essential environmental clean ups. Ironically, countries that have achieved success on such a basis, are currently being pressed to alter their policies by countries that have been far less successful, but that have more power. In this way, inferior policies (both economically and socially) are displacing superior ones. In fact a Toronto based consultant recently reported a conversation in which a former US trade negotiator is said to have acknowledged that, in his opinion, Japan's industrial policies have been very successful but, since the US could not reproduce them, the Japanese would have to be persuaded, or forced, to abandon them. Whether true or not, the report illustrates some of the dangers, and the potential irrationality, one should expect when intense economic rivalry occurs in an unregulated world.

Finally, training must not be treated as a 'cargo cult'.[47] To be effective, it must always be accompanied by other initiatives and by investment in infrastructure, industry and technology. In fact, a recent comprehensive study of this issue concluded that success is likely only when 'investment in vocational education (occurs) . . . in those skills relevant to rapidly growing industries, and, more generally, in industrially dynamic economies'.[48] The same was true if education was to have an impact on poverty:

to reduce poverty, the public sector has to invest in education, to plan balanced growth, and to manage an incomes policy that "lifts all boats".[49]

Of course, the training mystique, like the promise of prosperity, is rapidly losing credibility as growing armies of retrained people wait for the illusory good jobs. Thus Canada, which has strongly encouraged students to study science and engineering for many years, has just been told that

> because of the slow economy, cost reductions and corporate efforts to improve productivity, there will be little or no growth in R&D employment (in Canada) over the next five years. . . . (since) the current aim of the corporation is to achieve higher productivity with the same or already diminished number of employees.[50]

To assess the training argument in the face of such evidence, one cannot just 'take everything as given' and tell the frustrated graduates they must make the best of an uncertain world. One needs to acknowledge that the training argument was used to sell a very risky policy to people who feared just such an outcome. Those who claimed that other good jobs would come along, now have a responsibility to justify those claims, not so that we can gloat at their discomfort, but so that people will be a little less gullible next time around.

Ultimately the claim that training would protect the majority never had a chance because it was both politically and analytically wrong. It was politically wrong, because the promised training effort never had a chance of materialising, since financial constraints were bound to get in the way of good intentions;[51] since the fortunate few were never likely to fund those activities on a charitable basis, (as Reich anticipated); and since many politicians never had any intention of keeping those promises.[52] It was analytically wrong because even if a big training effort had been funded, it would not have solved the problem. In fact, even of the relatively few people that were trained for high skill jobs in Canada, only a few got even close to a well paying, secure job. In the world as presently constructed, training would not have solved the problem even had there been much more of it.

Protectionism: The Great Taboo of the Postmodern Age

For all these reasons, even Reich's sober reassessment of globalisation's promise is far too sanguine. Irreversibility is a threat, not a promise; the global elite's future is not assured; and the majority's immiserisation will not soon be arrested. Barbarism beckons unless the mindless destruction of the social fabric and of existing political identities is arrested, but this cannot begin until the discussion of protectionism can be rescued from the realm of religious fanaticism and returned to that of rational discourse. It has become the great taboo of the age. Economists regularly frighten the children, and each other, with gruesome tales of the ravages inflicted by this unspeakable evil: in the thirties, in the developing world and, especially, in their economic models. As with all irrational taboos, the foundation of this repressed hysteria is pure ideology. The true believers espouse it as a matter of faith, while those whose interests it serves, worship it as the basis of their power.

The endlessly repeated claim is that protectionism, in all its various forms, would reduce welfare, destroy efficiency and increase conflict. That is the message that reaches the people after the complex underlying debates have been simplified for public consumption by the media, the respectable experts and the great institutions, established to pronounce on such matters – and to promote globalisation. To hear them say it, one would think the truth about these matters had been unambiguously established. Thus, the Managing Director of the IMF told the world at the end of the disastrous eighties that:

> There is at the present time a kind of silent revolution in the world. More and more countries recognize that there are good policies and there are bad policies . . . that removing all structural impediments to growth is the only way to progress.[53]

Such blanket assertions cannot begin to be supported by the empirical evidence, by history or even by neoclassical theory. What support they do have stems almost entirely from models constructed on the assumption that economic liberalisation increases efficiency, growth and welfare; models based on a theory that defines optimal outcomes as, 'outcomes produced by perfectly competitive markets'. When economists abandon this tautology and address the real world, blanket condemnations of protection, or of national intervention, turn out to be utterly untenable.

In fact, the case for positive industrial strategies, using a variety of protective devices to build a strong national industrial and technological base, is both historically and theoretically strong. At a minimum, this is because many economies do not possess the internal conditions needed to respond positively and constructively to an intensification of international competition, and 'when the first-best policies are either unavailable or damaging on other dimensions, a proindustry trade regime has a second-best role to play'.[54]

The theoretical case for a proactive industrial policy has a long history,[55] and was confirmed once again by the experience of the East Asian NICs,[56] leading one authority to remark that

> the typically applied rule of thumb in evaluating infant industry protection – learning periods of about five years and a maximum effective production of 10-20 per cent optimally administered through subsidies rather than tariff or import controls – would seem to be much too conservative, judging at least from the historical experience of South Korea and Taiwan.[57]

These insights were reflected in the so-called 'new trade theory', which showed that, even within a neoclassical framework, a number of interventionist policies in trade and industry can be shown to enhance efficiency and strengthen the relative competitive position of the instigating economy, once oligopoly, imperfect information flows, externalities and learning effects are taken into account.[58] However, by undermining the general case for economic liberalisation, this argument opened a Pandora's Box of possibilities and reminded everyone how little economists had to contribute to policy discussions in an imperfect, disequilibrium world.

Many economists must therefore have been relieved when these open ended policy conclusions were generally reversed, once the threat of trade (or other?) retaliation was taken into account. Retaliation could be shown to negate both the advantages to the instigating country and the potential efficiency gains. On this basis, the consensus in favour of market deregulation and non-intervention was restored, though with some notable exceptions.[59] Indeed, the case now appeared even stronger because it could claim to have taken full account of real world imperfections.

But there is all the difference in the world between a defence that rests on the intrinsic merits of non-intervention, and one based on the threat of retaliation. The latter is essentially a coercive argument and, moreover, applies only to individual economies making policy choices within a particular international trade regime, that defines the likelihood and the extent of retaliation. In such a case, the threat of retaliation has to be factored into any decision, but even then, it does not have to be accepted as immutable. Trade regimes are subject to change in time.

For a discussion of the merits of particular international trade regimes, the fact that a wide range of interventionist, national policies can be dynamically efficient has far reaching implications, however. If global efficiency and welfare are to be maximised, such trade regimes should give member states enough sovereign power to make use of such dynamically efficient interventionist policies, and protect them against unwarranted retaliation for doing so. That is what the early Bretton Woods agreement attempted to do, with its explicit provision for capital controls and for temporary trade restrictions (when 'material damage' was inflicted on an economy). And it was this feature of the agreement that allowed member states to sustain full employment, and to implement national political compromises on issues like income distribution, working conditions and social conditions. This in turn contributed to the fact that the period during which these rules prevailed was the most stable, egalitarian and successful period of economic growth in history. There is no reason why the world could not do as well in future, if it restored the necessary conditions of national sovereignty. Unfortunately, the international trade regime is currently being pushed in exactly the opposite direction from that required.

As for the historical evidence regarding protection, the two most common generalisations are that the depression of the thirties conclusively demonstrated the evils of nationalism and protection, and that the great success of the early post war period illustrates the desirability of trade liberalisation. Neither claim is persuasive.

Polanyi's interpretation of the depression is very different and far more persuasive. It argues that the terrible events of the thirties were the painful and ultimately inevitable result of the excessive economic liberalisation of the twenties, which had produced ever greater economic, social and political turmoil. The resulting contradictions eventually triggered political upheavals in which societies reasserted control over their economies in ways ranging from those of the Fascists, to the New Deal and to Sweden's social democracy.[60]

This argument is far more plausible than that which claims that, after decades of success and prosperity, governments suddenly abandoned free trade in favour of protectionism for no material reason, and then added insult to injury by massively deflating their economies in the midst of a recession.[61] In fact, Polanyi's account brilliantly documents the world's long desperate struggle, under the leadership of the League of Nations, to use neoliberal policies to resolve the persistent contradictions then afflicting the world economy; and as, despite the intensity and the persistence of these efforts, the debts, the economic imbalances and the social dislocation continued to grow, eventually producing painful and, in some cases, barbaric policy reversals.

Polanyi's account of the twenties ought to sound eerily familiar to students of today's crisis. The problems that had accumulated and that eventually had to be resolved, included: an explosion of unserviceable debt that eventually induced economic stagnation, low investment and rising unemployment; extreme economic instability, leading to speculative boom/bust cycles that misallocated resources; fuelled economic insecurity and destroyed otherwise viable assets and skills; and a dramatic increase in income inequality, which undermined the moral and political legitimacy of political and economic systems.

The converse claim that the extended economic boom of the post-war period can be ascribed to economic liberalisation was always less well founded and has been further discredited by the deplorable economic, social and political results associated with accelerated economic deregulation over the past two decades. Indeed, these have recently persuaded even *The Economist* to call for the restoration of some national controls over capital,[62] recalling an earlier assessment that had appeared in *The Financial Times* in the wake of the 1987 stock market crash, which had echoed Polanyi's assessment of the depression, by suggesting that there might now be an urgent need to reassess the merits of deregulation and globalisation.

> The post-war economic system was designed by people who had endured the chaos of the 1930s. They may have erred too far on the side of controls and constraints on markets – *although it is at least arguable that the "golden era" of trade expansion was possible only because the regime governing capital flows was so illiberal* (emphasis added).

It now seems increasingly clear, however, that the reaction against government intervention and managed markets in the 1970s and early 1980s went too far. There was a pervasive
retreat from responsibility.[63]

By now that retreat from responsibility has gone very much further and
the difficulties standing in the way of its restoration have grown; but so has
the recognition that there is a problem and that it requires a solution. This
will eventually provide the basis for the political response that is needed.
And that political response can only occur within sovereign political
spaces, within which a democratic process can define and implement the
kind of framework that is required if markets are to serve societies, rather
than destroying them.

Towards a Positive Nationalism

So far this paper has argued that globalisation is essentially a destructive
process, creating a world that will not be stable, efficient or socially
desirable. As it gradually destroys the capacity of nation states to manage
economic processes to some broad social purpose, it does not, and cannot,
replace these capacities at a global level. As a result the competitive
process will become increasingly unstable and destructive, threatening
social cohesion, political stability and human welfare. Even economic
efficiency, the one thing the process was supposed to deliver with certainty,
is increasingly undermined by instability, uncertainty, speculation, the
persistent creation of excess capacity and the stifling presence of unserviceable mountains of debt. And there is no reason to believe that this process
is about to stabilise. In fact, the opposite is more likely, as contradictions
grow more severe and as governments further lose their ability to deal with
domestic fiscal problems and external obligations in ways that can be
reconciled either with their social responsibilities or with the need for
internal political stability.

The current situation is made more dangerous because the international
financial institutions have clearly decided that the way out of this impasse is
to accelerate further the deregulation of markets, focusing especially on
the deregulation of labour markets which is likely to have particularly
explosive social and political consequences. It is nothing short of incred-
ible, that these institutions are advocating the US labour market model for
Europe, thereby revealing the full extent of their inability to distinguish
between socially destructive and socially desirable sources of efficiency.
Together with their demonstrated willingness to accept unlimited social,
human and economic costs as the price of transition in Eastern Europe, no
one can doubt their open ended commitment to the ideology of the
market. Although, within that paradigm they would prefer to see welfare
conditions improve, this is a secondary concern which must be addressed
within the framework of 'sound economic policies'. They do not entertain
the thought that, in an unregulated world, it is those 'sound policies' that

create the 'facts of economic life' within which welfare services, labour laws, social services and progressive income taxes have to be progressively dismantled, because 'efficiency' demands it.

The solution to this crisis will not, therefore, come from those international institutions, as some optimists believe. And this is not only because of their blinkered ideological approach, but also because they are not embedded in a political process that could make their policies truly sensitive to local circumstances, or that could lend those policies the legitimacy they need to be effectively implementable. 'Generic nation states' have been defined as the political entities that must fulfill those tasks. But what are their prospects? Is their resurgence a real possibility, or is it a functionalist dream? And if their revival is possible, is it likely to take a positive or desirable form? The answers to these questions are far from clear.

The need for such states arises from the fact that unregulated markets are not viable, not efficient and not socially desirable. That is why the link between nation state and market has been so very close from the outset; why both emerged more or less simultaneously in history. Mercantilism was the economic ideology of the monarchical state, but its limitations were exposed with the accelerated growth of rationalism and commerce in the eighteenth century. This new world demanded a new way of defining the link between the individual and society, as the divine right of hereditary status and the absolute teaching of the church lost their power to induce people to internalise the rules and values of the social order. A new basis had to be found for providing people with the possibility of defining themselves as members of 'a society', as social beings. And this vacuum was filled intellectually by theories ranging from Rousseau's social contract, in which the object was achieved almost entirely through positive inducement (the carrot), to the Hobbesian state, reluctantly accepted as a necessary evil (the stick). In practice, the void was filled by nationalism, a term that first came into use in the middle of the eighteenth century and that dominated the landscape by its end. As compared to the monarchical state, the nation was an egalitarian, populist concept, and those who brought it into use tended to equate 'nation' with 'people'.

> It was the 1750s . . . that saw new intellectual distinctions being made between the monarchical state (the government) and the nation. In 1755 an obscure (French) cleric named G. F. Coyer, condemning his more sophisticated contemporaries, began to preach that no love was so pure as that felt for the nation, and that this embraced both the state and all orders of society. Amidst the growth of French cultural nationalism . . . a new political attitude, a "new patriotism", . . . was coming into existence, pairing together king and the whole French people as the proper objects of patriotic feeling'. These inchoate beginnings appear to have culminated in the concept of 'nationalism' only after the French Revolution had brought these beliefs to power – and to grief – in a major nation.[64]

Ever since, the nation state has been an essential mechanism for the management of increasingly complex societies and economies. Some regard it as the root of all evil; others as a means through which humanity can aspire to the highest ideals of selfless devotion to society. And both may be right, since nationalism has probably approximated both judgments at some time or other. The truth is that the political content of this political entity is undefined, and must remain so. It is, after all, one of the purposes and attractions of national sovereignty to enable societies to make choices that allow them to be different; to live by different cultural or social norms; to set different priorities between efficiency and other social objectives.

But why, at the dawn of the twenty-first century, should we pin our hopes of rescuing the social vision with which we began, on the nation state? Has this particular political and ideological solution to the problem of reconciling our individuality with our essence as social beings, not been overtaken by history? And do we not know that the nation state has historically been merely a vehicle for capital to enforce the logic of the market, while covering its tracks with fine sounding phrases about social responsibility and patriotism?

These fundamental questions have to be incorporated into the discussion of the 'generic nation state'. The question that is posed by history, is: In what form can we realistically hope, at the end of the twentieth century, to redefine and reconstruct political entities that would allow us to manage the increasingly destructive and irrational forces of global competition, while providing individuals with the capacity to define themselves as social beings and while containing the risk of conflict between such political entities? The 'generic nation state' is defined as any political entity that performs the first two of these functions. The answer to the third has to be defined in terms of some positive model of international cooperation, that will protect the sovereignty of those generic states and discourage predatory behaviour through collective security provisions.

This paper cannot hope to deal adequately with these enormous issues. It will merely reflect on some of the difficulties that will be encountered as we prepare to meet this challenge. Three questions will be addressed: Why nation states? What are the prospects for a restoration of national sovereignty? And, what are the prospects for a restoration of a positive, humane nationalism?

The focus on nation states derives primarily from a pragmatism born of a total inability to conceive, let alone construct, a meaningful political process at the global level. The truth is that Trotsky and the international socialists were always right, analytically, but their message was always politically useless. In fact, it tended to lead either to paralysis or to a Warrenite[65] acceptance of globalisation as a positive process, left to develop the forces of production and the conditions for socialism. Well, we are there now. The forces of production have been developed to a level that unquestionably makes it possible to provide all people with a comfortable material existence with only a moderate expenditure of effort by each person. But where are the conditions for socialism? As we address the question of how to bring those forces of production under social control, we must begin somewhere, and it cannot be the world. Not only would this be utterly impractical, it would imply and require a degree of centralisation in a political discussion and organisation that would be extremely dangerous, and very difficult to reconcile with the diversity that is surely one of our objectives. In short, just as global financial regulation can only be built on effective national regulatory systems, so the global management of the competitive process, or of a socialist economy, must be built on sub global units, namely our 'generic nation states'.

The emphasis on 'generic' nation states makes the point that these need not be the existing nations, as bequeathed by history; that it is possible for these to be either larger, supranational entities (like Europe), or smaller, sub-national ones (like Croatia). However, this does not mean that such changes should, or could, be achieved or undertaken lightly. They are always fraught with enormous dangers and will almost always be positively retrograde when they lead to a demand for ethnically defined states, on the spurious grounds that only such states are legitimate or viable. The current proliferation of such demands reflects the growing instability and economic insecurity spawned by globalisation and the growing inability of existing, territorial states to manage the regional or ethnic issues within their borders. But the creation of ethnic splinter states will not solve these problems and will generally create new and even bigger ones. After all these little states will still have the global market to contend with. In short, the resurgence of the ethnic state must be regarded as a major step in the direction of barbarism. Once the rights of citizenship depend on our ethnic genealogy, we will all end up living in apartheid South Africa.

The future must lie in restoring the sovereignty of existing territorial states, within which such ideals as equality, non racism and an unqualified acceptance of a sense of social responsibility are, at least, conceivable and realistic objectives. That sovereignty must then be used to create the political space that is needed to restore the gentler, more humane societies that people clearly want, and that they know to be possible. On such secure foundations, such nations could then possibly seek to unite with others in larger regional political entities (such as Europe), once a sufficiently coherent political process has allowed the conditions for democratic legitimacy to be established at that higher level. The power to manage the centrifugal forces of competition should then reside at these higher levels, embedded in regional political process. And the space thereby created for social and cultural diversity should be used to give more power to lower levels of government and administration, and to the organs of civil society. The principle of subsidiarity is a useful way of thinking about this devolution of power, although its real impact will naturally depend on the way it is actually defined in practice.[66]

But even if a focus on the nation state could be defended, is it a feasible or realistic objective today? No doubt much conspires against it. Indeed, most of this paper has shown that globalisation has substantially under-mined the material base of the nation state and has erected serious institutional obstacles to block attempts to reverse this process. However, it has also shown that those developments are not inherently irreversible, and that the growing conflict between the demands of an increasingly unstable and illegitimate economic system and gradually disintegrating social systems, are presently transforming the political landscape and shifting the limits of the politically possible. It is in this context that it is vitally important to channel people's rising anger in a positive and con-structive direction, rather than allowing it to sweep them away on the rising tide of fascism, monarchism, religious fundamentalism or ethnic nationalism.

Of course, the fate of recent social democratic governments shows clearly just how difficult it is to realise any alternative vision, no matter how moderate, in the world as presently constructed. But these failures must merely lead to a redoubling of our efforts, secure in the knowledge that the consequences of the present policies will continue to swell the ranks of the politically disaffected and will continue to intensify and legitimate the search for an alternative. After all, who would have thought that, in 1992, one would find a long time correspondent of the *Financial Times* of London considering the nationalisation of the banks as a serious policy option for Britain?

> The latest analysis from the invaluable Professor Tim Congdon . . . which examines the current state of British banks, savings institutions and insurance companies . . . describes a catastrophe waiting to happen. . . . This crisis of the financial intermediaries rules out any domestic recovery for years, even assuming that it can be contained. Congdon puts the earliest date at the late 1990s. That could be optimistic. The private sector's boot-straps are broken. . . . There is one tried and proved remedy: bank nationalisation.[67]

In short, people are seriously discussing policy choices that would have been deemed unthinkable only a few years ago. This does not mean that they are now on the side of the people. They may want to nationalise the banks in order to bail out the speculators with public money. But the change is significant because it means that new political coalitions are possible, new possibilities are arising. Moreover, through links between similar coalitions in many nations, one can begin to discuss the shape of a new set of international institutions, that must one day be constructed to secure and protect national sovereignty in a context where member states are encouraged and advised to use their sovereign powers to pursue domestic full employment growth, as an overriding priority, and to reconcile their other objectives and their trading relationships with that commitment.

Such initiatives may not succeed immediately, since the obstacles now standing in their way are formidable. But the struggle must continue, because the current process is not viable and, unless the explosive political forces now being generated, can be channelled in a positive direction, barbarism may become the only option. Let us remember that it is not the option people would choose. And that if they appear to choose it at some stage, it will be because they were given the choice only when it was no longer a choice, but a *fait accompli*.

And so we come to the final question: What chance of a positive, constructive nationalism? Again, there can be no doubt that the odds are long. The post war world demonstrated that it is possible for nations to provide a context within which working people can strike bargains with capital that can transform their lives, allowing them to live a better, more secure life, working in more pleasant working conditions for higher wages and in relatively stable communities. Historically these gains were enormous, though enormous problems also remained. But it represented a historic achievement, and there was no reason, in principle, why that process could not have continued, if those political entities had retained sufficient control of their economies to allow those national bargaining processes to continue. But once capital slipped out from under these arrangements, it soon undermined them through the forces of unregulated international competition. The rest, as they say, is history.

Now some would argue, with some reason, that it is not possible to manage capital. That the dissolution of that post war phase of stable, widespread prosperity was inevitable and that social democrats never seem to learn. They make a very important point that needs to be addressed when we discuss the kinds of controls that should and could be exercised over the competitive process in order to ensure that it can serve our social objectives. Here, another version of the principle of subsidiarity might again be helpful: allow as much freedom for decentralised decision making in the market, as is compatible with the objective of a dynamic, stable economy capable of functioning within socially and politically defined constraints reflecting social, political, cultural, ethical and environmental objectives. No doubt that question will never be answered definitively, but then, only a fool would expect it to be. Bertrand Russell once said: 'Education is a process of becoming confused at a higher level'. To which we need only add that: 'History is the ultimate process of education'.

NOTES

1. S. P. Huntingdon (1993) 'The Clash of Civilizations' *Foreign Affairs*, Summer.
2. S. P. Huntington (1993) 'The Clash of Civilizations' *Foreign Affairs*, Summer. It is surely appropriate that this prediction of inevitable culture wars should emanate from the same

mind that coined the phrase 'forced draft urbanisation' to describe the flood of refugees created by U.S. bombing and defoliation campaigns at the height of the Vietnam war. Since urbanisation was universally associated with 'development', he described this displacement of rural people as an unexpected benefit of those campaigns.

3. R. D. Kaplan, 'The Coming Anarchy' *Atlantic Monthly*, February 1994, pp. 46 and 48. All of the following quotations are from this article.

4. World Bank (1981) *Accelerated Development in Sub-Saharan Africa: an Agenda for Action*, World Bank: Washington D.C.; also known as 'The Berg Report', after its chief author Elliot Berg.

5. M. A. Bienefeld (1983) 'Efficiency, Expertise, the NICs and the Accelerated Development Report', *IDS Bulletin*, 14:1, Institute of Development Studies: Sussex UK, pp. 18 and 22.

6. World Bank (1985) *World Development Report 1985*, World Bank: Washington D.C., p. 2.

7. Cited in *The Toronto Globe and Mail*, 22nd June 1988.

8. This rose by over 700 percent in 1993 and was, therefore, termed the most successful stock market in some of the financial press. No doubt this was meant to be whimsical. The 'market' trades in the shares of seven firms, and is a particularly crass example of a speculatively driven, destabilising and irrational phenomenon.

9. Editorial *The Nation*, 3/10 January, 1994, p. 3/4.

10. The World Bank has actually described the policy prescriptions which it imposed on its clients during the first decade of its policy lending, as 'text book' policies which took inadequate account of local social and economic realities. World Bank, *Adjustment Lending: An Evaluation of Ten Years of Experience*, Washington, D.C.: World Bank, 1988, p. 66.

11. The arguments presented in Reich's book attracted special attention because the author was a leading liberal democrat, who has since become Secretary of Labour in an administration that garnered much electoral support by voicing 'grave, but unspecified' reservations about NAFTA, and then proceeded to make its passage an overriding policy priority, achieving its Congressional victory on the basis of a Republican majority voting with Democratic minority. R. B. Reich, *The Work of Nations*, New York: Vintage Books, 1992. The quotations which follow all come from pages 3 to 8, or 321 to 323.

12. Laurence Harris *The (London) Financial Times*, October, 1992.

13. Reich, op. cit., p. 312.

14. This has been especially true of Japan and South Korea. Thus a special report on 'offshore banking in Asia', in the *Far Eastern Economic Review*, described the rapid expansion of this phenomenon in each of seven Asian countries and then concluded with a report on Japan which declared that in Japan such flows were still almost completely under the control of the government authorities. Typically, the Review then proceeded to denounce the 'anachronistic bureaucratic culture' that was clearly impeding progress in Japan. This despite the fact that the section had begun by announcing that the entire offshore phenomenon was primarily driven by the desire to avoid taxation! *Far Eastern Economic Review*.

15. Obviously if one can deregulate slowly, then the degree of regulation is matter of policy choice, not a technological given. These issues are more extensively discussed in M. A Bienefeld 'Financial Deregulation: Disarming the Nation State', *Studies in Political Economy*, No. 37, Spring 1992.

16. A. Smith, *The Roaring Eighties*, Toronto: Summit Books, 1988, p. 19.

17. Amey Stone, 'Sorry, This Year your bonus is only . . . \$5 million', *Business Week*, 17 January 1994, p. 27.

18. A. Donner, 'Canada's Economic and Industrial Outlook', Speaking Notes (mimeo), January 1994.

19. J. Toporowski, 'Why the World needs a Financial Crash' *The (London) Financial Times*, February 1986, p. 21.

20. C. Raghavan, *Recolonization: GATT, the Uruguay Round and the Third World*, London: Zed Books, 1990, p. 45.

21. CUFTA, NAFTA and the Uruguay Round were all negotiated against the background of the implicit or explicit threat of trade sanctions. The fact that these threats were usually not 'official' threats made by the negotiating parties does not preclude their effectiveness.
22. Pat Carney as cited in *The Toronto Globe and Mail*.
23. Reich, op. cit., p. 302.
24. A. Etzioni, *An Immodest Agenda: Rebuilding America Before the 21st Century*, Toronto: McGraw-Hill, 1983, p. 33.
25. S. Marglin, The Wealth of Nations' in *The New York Review*, XXXI:12, July 19, 1994, pp. 41–44. (A review of I. M. D. Little *Economic Development: Theory, Policy,* and *International Relations*, New York: Basic Books, 1984)
26. This felicitous phrase was coined by one of FDR's advisors and is a useful antidote to the fecklessly selfish messages emanating from the tax revolts of the neoliberal age.
27. Economic Council of Canada, *A New Frontier: Globalization and Canada's Financial Markets*, Ottawa, 1989, p. 25.
28. AMEX Bank Review, *Globalisation, Regional Blocks and Local Finance*, 20:2, 22 February 1993.
29. F. Hahn 'Reflections on the Invisible Hand', *Lloyd's Bank Review*, No. 142, April 1982, p. 20.
30. Ibid., p. 12.
31. R. Dornbusch and J. Frankel 'The Flexible Exchange Rate System: Experience and Alternatives', Paper presented to the International Economic Association Basle Round Table conference on *Survival and Growth in a Polycentric Economy*, October 1987.
32. P. Krugman 'The Case for Stabilizing Exchange Rates', *The Oxford Review of Economic Policy*, 15:3, Autumn 1989, pp. 65–66.
33. World Bank, *World Development Report 1989*, World Bank: Washington D.C., p. 4.
34. IMF, *Staff Studies for the World Economic Outlook*, Washington D.C.: IMF, August 1989, pp. 8–9.
35. IMF, *World Economic Outlook*, IMF: Washington D.C., October 1993, p. 10.
36. *The Toronto Globe and Mail*, 8 October 1991, p. B6.
37. IMF, *International Financial Markets: Part II. Systemic Issues in International Finance*, IMF: Washington D.C., pp. 2/3.
38. John McNeil, Chairman of Sun Life Assurance Co. of Canada as cited in K. Dougherty, 'Open war feared in finance reform', *The (Toronto) Financial Post*, 13 November 1990.
39. G. Soros, *The Alchemy of Finance*, Toronto: Simon and Shuster, 1987, p. 100.
40. Ibid., p. 101.
41. IMF, *International Financial Markets: Part II. Systemic Issues in International Finance*, IMF: Washington D.C., p. 2.
42. 'Peaceful Co-existence' in 'World Economy: Survey' section, *The Economist*, 19th September 1992, p. 46.
43. K. Polanyi, *The Great Transformation*, p. 3.
44. M. A. Bienefeld 'The International Context for National Development Strategies: Constraints and Opportunities in a Changing World' in M. A. Bienefeld and M. Godfrey (eds) *The Struggle for Development*, Toronto: Wiley, 1982, p. 31.
45. IMF World Economic Outlook, IMF: Washington D.C., October 1993, Chapter IV.
46. For a fuller discussion of this issue see: M. A. Bienefeld 'Basic Needs in the Competitive Economy' *IDS Bulletin*, Sussex (England): Institute of Development Studies (University of Sussex), 9:4, June 1978; and M. A. Bienefeld 'The International Context for National Development Strategies: Constraints and Opportunities in a Changing World' in M. A. Bienefeld and M. Godfrey (eds) *The Struggle for Development*, Toronto: Wiley, 1982.
47. The term stems from several documented instances in which residents of some remote Pacific islands, responded to the cessation of air traffic at the end of WWII by clearing 'runways' in the bush, hoping that this would bring back the planes on which they had come to depend for many things.
48. W. H. Haddad, M. Carnoy et al 'Education and Development: Evidence for New Priorities', *World Bank Discussion Paper No. 95*, Washington D.C.: World Bank, 1990, p. 49.
49. Ibid., p. 15.

50. P. Hadekel 'Future bleak for R&D students' *The Ottawa Citizen*, 24 December 1993, p. F1. The article summarises the findings of a survey of the research and development spending plans of 160 companies, undertaken by the Conference Board of Canada.

51. The mainstream would argue that these financial constraints would have been worse without their liberalisation policies. However, this claim is generally no more than a pure tautology, reflecting their unshakeable, but indefensible, faith in the idea that freely functioning markets yield optimal results. The neoclassical theory of the second best shows that this faith is utterly misplaced when applied to the real world. It shows that even if one accepts all of the restrictive and unreal assumptions of that theory, it is impossible to say anything about how the removal of some market imperfections will affect a world with many such imperfections. The result may be an increase or a decrease in both welfare and efficiency. In the real world, on the other hand, we have seen that leading neoclassical theorists, the World Bank, the IMF and The Economist all accept that it is likely that the liberalisation of the global economy – and especially that of global financial markets – has led to unnecessary instability, excessively high risk taking, inordinately high interest rates, an extensive misallocation of resources reflected in a stifling burden of uncollectible debt and unwarranted and unethical shifts in income distribution.

52. Maybe the most crass example of this process was the promise of 'special compensation' for Canadians who stood to lose their jobs as a result of the CUFTA. This was much advertised and promised and played a significant role in calming people's fears. Then, immediately after the agreement was signed, the government announced that it could not keep this promise because it was impossible to tell which people lost their jobs as result of the agreement, and which lost their jobs for other reasons. The case is noteworthy because it is so obvious that the government was fully aware of this difficulty from the outset, and because it did not feel the need to mince words or to allow a decent interval to elapse before telling people they had been had.

53. IMF, *IMF Survey*, 18 October 1989, p. 290.

54. D. Rodrik, 'Conceptual Issues in the Design of Trade Policy for Industrialization', *World Development*, 20:3, 1992, p. 312.

55. F. List, R. G. Harris, *Trade, Industrial Policy and International Competition*, Toronto: UofT Press, 1985.

56. R. Wade *Governing the Market*, Stanford University Press, 1992.

57. H. D. Evans *Comparative Advantage and Growth: Trade and Development in Theory and Practice*, London: Harvester Wheatsheaf, 1989, p. 309.

58. P. Krugman, 'Scale Economies, Product Differentiation, and the Pattern of Trade', *American Economic Review*, Vol. 70, 1980, pp. 950–59.

59. Some neoclassical economists did not share this view and concluded that, even after accepting the risks of retaliation, there was still a case to be made for 'targeted, firm specific intervention' designed to strengthen specific, high value added parts of the manufacturing sector. In Canada this view eloquently and forcefully presented by Professor Richard Harris in a study written for the *Royal Commission on the Economic Union and Development Prospects* ('the McDonald Commission'). However, the Commissioners, in their wisdom, summarily dismissed this argument without refuting any of its central propositions. See R. G. Harris, *Trade, Industrial Policy and International Competition*, Toronto: UofT Press, 1985.

60. For a fuller discussion of this argument and of its relevance to the current crisis, see M. A. Bienefeld, 'The Lessons of History and the Developing World', *Monthly Review*, 41:3, July–August 1989.

61. Kindleberger. Galbraith.

62. 'Peaceful Co-existence' in 'World Economy: Survey' section, *The Economist*, 19th September 1992, p. 46.

63. M. Prowse, 'The message of the markets', *The (British) Financial Times*, 24th October 1987, p Weekend FT 1.

64. G. Newman, *The Rise of English Nationalism*, London: St Martin's Press, 1987, pp. 162–163.

65. Bill Warren *Imperialism: Pioneer of Capitalism*.

66. Subsidiarity is defined as a principle which states that, given certain defined objectives, power should remain at the most decentralised level that is compatible with their successful achievement.

67. L. Harris, 'Time to nationalise private sector debt', *The (London) Financial Times*, 19th October 1992, p. 23.

GLOBALISATION AND STAGNATION*

Arthur MacEwan

It is relatively clear that globalisation, the international spread of capitalist exchange and production relationships, is a very destructive and painful process. The implementation of the North American Free Trade Agreement (NAFTA) will provide some very stark examples over the next several years. In Mexico, peasants are likely to suffer final extinction as a class, as they are driven off the land by competition from large scale U.S. grain producers. In the United States, many workers with relatively low levels of skills and task-specific skills – such as broom makers in Alabama, glass makers in West Virginia, and workers connected to auto production throughout the country – will lose their jobs or see their wages dramatically reduced.

Moreover, there is good reason to believe that NAFTA, like other steps in globalisation, will generate greater income inequality both between and within countries. During the last few decades, as we have witnessed a surge in the spread of capitalism, we have also seen a widening of the income gap between the underdeveloped and developed economies. Within the United States, as the country's economic integration with the rest of the world accelerated after 1970, so too was there a marked rise in income inequality that became particularly evident in the 1980s. One widely quoted figure captures the sad spirit of the era: between 1977 and 1989, the richest 1% of families in the United States obtained 60% of the after-tax income gain. Within Mexico, recent years have also seen rising inequality, especially since the middle of the 1980s when the government began to move strongly with its programme of neo-liberal 'reforms'. Indeed, a worsening distribution of income was the general rule in Latin American countries during the 1980s, a decade in which the debt crisis brought the full burden of globalisation to bear upon the region.[1]

Greater income inequality is not the only social failure generated by the success of globalisation generally and by NAFTA particularly. Environ-

---

*An earlier version of this paper was presented at a Seminar on 'The Worlds Today: Circumstances and Alternatives,' Centro de Investigaciones Interdisciplinaria en Humanidades, Universidad Nacional Autonoma de Mexico, Mexico City, December 7, 1993.

mental destruction is surely exacerbated with the success of globalisation. The greater mobility of capital makes it more and more difficult for citizens of any one political unit to organise and use their government to impose regulations on polluting firms.

Perhaps the most damaging social contradiction of globalisation is its impact on democracy. NAFTA provides the illustration of the general process because this agreement enshrines 'the market' as the principle by which economic activity shall be organised in North America. It does so by direct statement of principles; it does so by prohibiting governments from developing new public sector productive activities; and it does so by effectively limiting the power of governments to regulate private business (directly excluding some forms of regulation and restricting others by giving business greater mobility to escape onerous rules). NAFTA, then, is quite explicitly an agreement that pushes out the boundaries of unfettered capitalist production, and in so doing it limits democracy by limiting people's power to exercise political control over their economic lives.

These social contradictions of globalisation – these social failures associated with the successful spread of capitalism – should come as no surprise. Even at its best, capitalist development is a process of 'creative destruction', to use Joseph Schumpeter's famous phrase. As accumulation takes place, competition forces firms to be creative in order to survive, and those firms that are not creative are destroyed. In a world of markets and competition, winners are matched by losers, and creation and destruction become one and the same. Losers, however, are not simply impersonal firms or abstract inefficient technologies. In the real world, losers are people, sometimes capitalists, but always workers, individually and as communities. 'Creative destruction' means the unemployment of real workers, the destitution of real communities, devastation of the environment, and disempowerment of the populace.[2]

Of course people do not sit idly by while all this takes place, and globalisation's social contradictions continually give rise to popular protest movements. Those of us who have opposed NAFTA can take some satisfaction from the fact that, as the historian and activist Jeremy Brecher pointed out in *The Nation* (December 6, 1993), '. . . elements of the struggle against NAFTA prefigure a movement that could radically re-shape the New World Economy. . . . For the first time in many years [in the United States], substantial numbers of people mobilised to act on broad class interests.' Such movements are always desirable. Even if all they do is effect marginal improvements of the current order, marginal improvements are better than no improvements.

Growth or Stagnation?

However, there is the more substantial question of whether or not these popular movements are likely to bring about larger changes, structural alternatives, something really different. The likelihood of larger changes depends to a great extent on whether or not globalisation will generate a renewal of economic growth. Globalisation has always produced social contradictions and protest movements, but economic growth has generally contained these movements and limited the emergence of alternatives. As we approach the end of the century, however, the world economy is mired in stagnation – relatively slow economic growth – and any appraisal of alternatives must involve a prognosis of that stagnation and of its relation to globalisation.

At first blush, it would seem folly to argue that globalisation is likely to be associated with continuing stagnation. After all, in the history of capitalism, globalisation and growth appear to have been tightly connected, mutually reinforcing processes at the foundation of the system. Observing this apparent historical relationship, proponents of a more open international economy have promised great gains – all the benefits of more economic growth – as we accept the neo-liberal order of globalisation embodied in NAFTA and other agreements. But there are problems. Let me cite four:

First: The current neo-liberal globalisation is not the same as the general historical spread of capitalism. It is one thing to say that globalisation and growth have gone hand-in-hand in the history of capitalism, but quite another to claim that neo-liberal policies of unregulated international commerce and reduction of state services have been a foundation of capitalist expansion. Virtually every country that has achieved some successful economic development – from the United States and Great Britain in an earlier era, to Japan and South Korea in more recent decades – has done so with active state intervention in economic affairs, particularly with extensive state regulation of foreign commerce. (As is hardly necessary to point out, the converse is not true. There are many cases where state intervention in foreign commerce has not led to any growth success. The historical record seems to indicate that such state intervention is a necessary but certainly not sufficient element in achieving economic growth.)

One of the ways that state intervention has played a major role is through the promotion of industries with substantial technological externalities (positive impacts on technological development elsewhere in the economy). During the industrial revolution of the late 18th century, British industry flourished behind tariff barriers averaging 50% in manufacturing sectors. After World War II, while Japanese tariffs were not high, the government maintained tight direct controls over both imports and direct foreign investment, encouraging the development of Japanese-owned firms in such key industries as automobiles and computers. In addition, developmental states have used a variety of fiscal and monetary mechanisms, specific subsidies, and at times state-sponsored firms to pursue national development. In some cases, states have pushed their country's firms toward an external orientation and achieved success through export led growth; South Korea provides the most important recent example. In no case, however, has successful export-led growth been directed through the sort of deregulation that might be called 'free trade', the sort of deregulation that is called for in the neo-liberal project.[3]

Of course the United States today has passed through its period of initial development, and, however large a role state control of external commerce played in that initial development, a regime of 'free trade' might yield substantial growth gains in the current era. There is no doubt that many large U.S. firms will garner major benefits from the imposition of NAFTA and other parallel agreements. They will gain access to markets and resources, and they will be less constrained by local regulation.

Yet gain for large U.S. corporations is not the same thing as growth of the U.S. economy. Over recent decades the foreign operations of U.S.-based firms have maintained their share of world exports while their U.S. operations have dwindled in relative importance. For example, between 1966 and 1984, the U.S. share of world manufactured exports declined from 17.5% to 14.0%. Yet U.S.-based multinationals' share in world exports actually rose slightly in the period, from 17.7% to 18.1%; the 'parent' firms' declining share was more than balanced by a rising share of their foreign affiliates.[4] Certainly, British experience at the end of the last century indicates that there is no necessary equation between the international success of national capital and the growth success of the national economy. On the contrary, that historical example suggests that, as important segments of capital become more international in their orientation, they are less willing to support the types of state policies that would yield national growth. Industrial policies and programmes to develop the national labour force, for example, are of little interest to firms committed to and dependent on overseas operations; indeed, in so far as those policies and programmes carry a cost – as they always do – such firms are likely to oppose them.[5]

Second: When globalisation has been associated with rapid growth, that growth has had historically specific causes and cannot be attributed to globalisation per se. This argument has been most fully developed by Harry Magdoff and Paul Sweezy, and it rests on a distinction between the current era (really the last century) of monopoly capitalism and an earlier era of smaller scale, more competitive capitalism.[6] The very large firms that emerged at the end of the 19th century in the United States and other advanced capitalist countries have a tremendous capacity to expand production. Moreover, as they have centralised wealth to a very great degree, they have greatly increased their capacity for savings. Growth will then take place if this massive capacity to save can find sufficient outlets through equally massive investment opportunities. The problem is that there is nothing within the system – within the normal spread of capitalism and the everyday technological innovation, opening of new markets and exploitation of new resources – that assures sufficient investment opportunities will in fact be available. When rapid growth does come, it is the result of particular causes – epoch making innovations such as steam power and the railways or a set of events that provides an extremely favourable business environment.

The quarter century following World War II was one of these 'extremely favourable' periods. Following the war, rapid economic growth in the U.S. and elsewhere was generated by: postwar reconstruction; technological spin-offs from war production; pent-up demand for consumer durables; the stability within international capitalism provided by the relatively great power (hegemony) of the United States; and the large demand provided by a growing economic role of the government, most notably in its military spending. These particular factors – and one might name others – were by their nature either ephemeral (postwar reconstruction) or self-limiting (the growing economic role of the government). They could generate a period of rapid growth, but they could not provide a foundation for indefinite rapid growth. By the 1970s, these factors had run their course, and we entered the current era of stagnation. (The mid-1980s saw a limited renewal of growth in the United States, based largely on a new military build-up and massive government fiscal deficits, but it did not, and could not, last.)

The question then arises whether or not further globalisation – NAFTA, extension of GATT, greater access for U.S. firms to Asian markets – could again provide the circumstances necessary for a new round of rapid growth. The answer seems clearly negative, unless it can be shown how this new globalisation creates conditions of the sort that have led to rapid growth in the past. There is no reason to think that the expansion of the system's realm of operation in and of itself will do the trick.

Third: When globalisation generates inequality, it tends to undermine growth. The problem of secular stagnation due to limited investment opportunities might be reduced were globalisation to yield a sufficient expansion of consumption demand or to provide the foundation for a renewal of government spending. Yet the growing inequality that is likely to be associated with the sort of neo-liberal globalisation embodied in NAFTA will tend to move things in the opposite direction. By providing U.S. firms with access to production sites in Mexico and through direct provisions in the agreement, NAFTA is part of a broad strategy by U.S. firms that gives emphasis to deregulation and cost cutting. This strategy, however, also tends to force down wages and curtail social spending, so any gains from lower costs tend to be off-set by losses from weakened demand. Moreover, the neo-liberal ideology that helps drive NAFTA also tends to limit the extent to which governments can stimulate demand by classical Keynesian policy. (Supporters of NAFTA in the United States argue that, by opening Mexican markets, the agreement will strengthen demand for U.S. goods. While there will likely be some short run gains, as a longer run prognosis, this analysis repeats the classic error of mercantilist ideology – that exports can grow without a counterbalancing growth of imports or foreign investment.)

Furthermore, both within the realm of government demand and in the private sector, there is a sense in which stagnation and inequality are circularly reinforcing processes. Slow growth and inequality have contributed to the huge build up of debt, in the United States and in the Third World.[7] The debt burden then becomes a restraint on private and public spending, and slow growth and inequality are thus perpetuated.

The restraints which inequality places on growth are not only on the demand side. Low wages may reduce the rate of technological progress as well. It is widely recognised that during the 19th century, technological advances in the United States were especially rapid due, at least in part, to the shortage of labour and relatively high wages (as compared to Europe). High wages led U.S. firms to innovate more rapidly. Today, as U.S. firms gain greater access to low wage labour in Mexico and elsewhere, the pressures tend to run in the opposite direction. Moreover, low wage levels tend to contribute directly to slower rates of labour productivity growth. The globalisation strategy of U.S. business appears to be based on the perception of wages only as a cost of production. But, quite clearly, in production wages are an incentive as well. Strategies which suppress wage costs also suppress that incentive.[8]

In the context of NAFTA, it is worth noting that greater inequality in the United States is not likely to be balanced by rising wages and greater equality in Mexico. Wages in the United States will be suppressed not so much by the actual movement of production to Mexico (from which Mexican workers might gain) but by the threat of such movement. Furthermore, while the Mexican government continues its inegalitarian policies – suppressing and controlling unions, tax policies that favour the wealthy, programmes supporting a reconcentration of land holding – any movement toward equality will be greatly hampered. Finally, NAFTA will lead to the inundation of Mexico by imports of goods which are produced more cheaply in the United States. Grains are the most dramatic example. Also, U.S. service industries are likely to force many small scale Mexican operations out of business. The result will be a huge displacement of Mexican peasants and workers, swelling the ranks of the Mexican reserve army of labour and keeping wages at a minimum. In the real world of unemployment, less regulation of trade is more likely to lead to a waste of resources than to a more efficient allocation of resources.

Fourth: When globalisation has been most effective as a foundation for economic growth, a firm institutional basis for international stability has existed. As I have pointed out already, successful globalisation has not meant a simple expansion of the realm of unregulated markets. When it has been most effective in generating rapid growth, globalisation has taken place under the aegis of a powerful state – a super imperial power – that has been able to regulate international affairs and provide a stability that encouraged business expansion. This argument has been usefully articulated in the context of the social structure of accumulation theory, which asserts that, in any epoch of successful capitalist development, expansion has been based on and organised by a set of social institutions. This set of institutions, which regulates the otherwise self-destructive operations of markets, includes at least institutions of labour relations, state operations, and international affairs. Here it is only necessary to point out that the regulating institutions of international affairs are absent in the current surge of globalisation.[9]

The problem is apparent when this era is compared with earlier eras when globalisation has been relatively successful (in terms of growth) – for example, the middle of the 19th century when British hegemony provided stability and the post-World War II quarter century when U.S. hegemony played a similar role. In each of these eras there existed an industrial leader, a relatively unchallenged political-military authority, and a set of financial relations that established a matrix for the operation of markets. Globalisation could proceed apace, enhance the imperial power's realm, and strengthen the entire system (though, in the contradictory nature of things, overextension ultimately contributed to the end of hegemony).

In the current era, in spite of the fact that the U.S. stands alone as a super power, it is not able to provide imperial stability. It is no longer a clear industrial leader. International financial arrangements are in flux and unstable. The great military power of the U.S. seems ineffective – at best – in maintaining the sort of stability that would be needed for a new era of expansion. In this context, the implications of globalisation are very different. Neo-liberal globalisation – the spread of a system without sufficient means of regulation – contributes to the instability of the system and therefore undermines, rather than enhances, growth.

Alternatives to Globalisation

I think that these various points at least give us some reason to anticipate that the era of slow economic growth is not likely to be brought to a quick termination by the current surge of globalisation. In the 'creative destruction' of capitalist development, we appear to be at a point where the 'destructive' aspects are relatively large compared to the 'creative'. This means that in North America – and elsewhere as well – the popular movements that are energised by the social contradictions of globalisation are likely to have some impact, and it becomes especially meaningful to speak of alternatives.

But what kind of alternatives? Is there any reason to believe that the current forces being generated by globalisation and stagnation might connect to the widely shared goal of establishing a more egalitarian and democratic society? What is different about the current situation that might provide a basis for optimism? What lessons might we draw from the analysis of globalisation and stagnation that could help move things along?

While answers to these sorts of questions require a certain amount of speculation, there are certain observations that seem reasonable. To begin with, it seems useful to recognise that globalisation has made some dramatic changes in the economic relationships among working people in different parts of the world, particularly in the relationship between workers in the United States and workers in Mexico and other relatively poor countries. With the reduction in barriers to trade and with the spread of capitalist production relationships, workers in the different parts of the world economy are producing the same things in the same ways for the same markets. Ironically, by thus being in competition with one another, they have a common interest which creates a material basis for solidarity.

This material basis for solidarity becomes clear if we compare the currently emerging situation with the stereotypical situation of an earlier era in which Third World workers were producing raw materials for export to the advanced countries, and workers in the advanced countries were transforming these raw materials into manufactured goods. In those circumstances, lower wages in the Third World could directly benefit workers in the advanced countries. Lower wages for copper miners, sugar cane cutters, or banana plantation workers in the Third World could mean lower prices in the United States. Workers in the advanced countries would then tend to lose as wages rose in the Third World.

Now consider the implications of lower wages at the Ford plant in Hermosillo. One implication may be cheaper cars in the United States, but the much more profound, immediate and obvious impact is lower wages for auto workers in the United States. As globalisation has succeeded in making different economies more and more alike, in transferring technology across national boundaries, and in placing workers in competition with one another, it has succeeded in creating a basis for international labour solidarity. Workers in Michigan and Morelos now have a relation like workers in Illinois and Indiana.

Of course a common material relationship does not translate directly into concerted political action. Competition among workers in different nations can contribute to reactionary nationalism, xenophobia and conflict. Also, along with globalisation, there appear to be greater divisions among different strata of workers within nations, and major cities have a striking duality – as New York and Los Angeles, for example, bridge the entire gap from the pinnacles of wealth and power to the depths of Third World poverty all within a few city blocks. Yet a common material interest across international boundaries does create a strong potential, perhaps even a necessary condition, for common action. By creating this common material interest, globalisation offers some hope for overcoming national divisions and increases the likelihood of effective international working class politics.

Globalisation, furthermore, is changing the structure of the work force – in the United States, in Mexico, and everywhere else – in ways that create new possibilities for political action, both locally and across international boundaries. One of the most profound changes is the feminisation of the paid labour force. The spread of capitalist production relations has meant the elimination of home production, the traditional realm of women. As women have entered the paid labour force, they have often been the ones most subjected to international competition. The high rate of employment of women in the maquiladoras and in assembly production in the United States illustrates the special position of women in the emerging globalised economy.

The special position of women has some significance in any discussion of alternatives because, certainly in the United States and it seems in many other countries as well, political struggles associated with women are among the most dynamic parts of popular protest movements. Moreover, struggles in which women play a major role have a good chance of being more broadly oriented struggles. Because of their experiences as women, women workers are particularly likely to build connections between workplace and community.

The issue of 'community' has an important role in the development of alternatives to the current dynamic of globalisation. One of the reasons for the widespread, negative visceral opposition to globalisation – whether in the form of opposition to NAFTA or as opposition to corporate takeovers in the United States by foreign-based multinationals – is that people see this phenomenon as undermining whatever control they retain over their own economic lives and, along with this, threatening the security of their communities. Sometimes this opposition appears as irrational and, as such, is derided by the proponents of globalisation. Why oppose NAFTA when U.S. firms have been investing in low wage countries for years? Why oppose the corporate takeover by a multinational based in London or Frankfurt of a multinational base in Manhattan when all make decisions on the same basis? Popular protest movements, however, are quite rational in directing their actions at these highly visible symbols of the marketisation of our lives.

Struggles for the maintenance of community against marketisation – against the subjugation of other social values to consideration of private profit – provide clues on how to shape alternatives in the current period. People's desire to maintain community is closely connected to their desire for meaningful democracy, real control over the affairs that affect their everyday lives. It is impossible to destroy local and national communities, the realms in which people most strongly identify with one another, and at the same time build a democratic society.[10]

In addition, the value that people place on community – tangible, intelligible relations to other people with whom they feel a historical bond – tells us something about the way to shape economic programmes. For example, it suggests that economic programmes based on export expansion cannot meet people's needs. Export-led growth can be a basis for rapidly rising national income – though where it has been most successful, we should note, it has not been associated with the neo-liberal 'free trade' dogma. But if we define economic programmes in terms of our ability to penetrate foreign markets, then at every step of the way we will be confronted by conflicts between the maintenance of community and economic success.

In the same way that export-led growth comes into recurring conflict with the maintenance of community, it is always a threat to establishing a more equal distribution of income. If we say that the primary criterion on which to base an economic programme is our success in international markets, then we must take the steps that are necessary to succeed in international markets. Often, those steps will mean limits on wage increases or movement of firms to lower wage regions, restrictions on social programmes, tax incentives for corporations, and other policies which favour the wealthy over the poor.[11]

Most important, perhaps, an economic programme that is defined by an external orientation rules out the kinds of controls that are necessary if any nation is going to pursue policies of full employment. Full employment is important because it is probably the single most powerful programme leading to a more equitable distribution of income. Also, people cannot live fulfilling lives without meaningful work, and full employment improves the likelihood that meaningful work will be available. Yet full employment fiscal and monetary policies, in the United States or in any other country, cannot be implemented without constraints on external commercial relations, including controls on trade and capital movements. Foreign commerce of all sorts has a role in any reasonable economic programme, but the problem is to subordinate economic exigencies to social goals and social values; that cannot be done in an export-led programme.

Alternative economic programmes that call for greater income equality, full employment, and an inward economic orientation have a connection to our current condition of stagnation. Equality, full employment and the strengthening of community are not simply nice things to wish for, but they are also policies that address the conundrum of stagnation. As I have suggested above, one of the roots of stagnation is the great inequality that exists – in the world and within many countries, including the United States and Mexico. Demands for equality are therefore demands for a reform that is consistent with both the needs of those at the bottom of the economic hierarchy and the system's needs for stability and survival. Full employment and greater income equality would do far more to extend the market than would any programme of opening new markets for exports. (I should point out that it is quite possible that such a connection would not exist, that doing what is socially desirable would not be consistent with overcoming stagnation. If stagnation resulted from an excessive wage squeeze on profits, then greater income equality would hardly be an economic solution, however socially desirable.)

Similarly, if stagnation is perpetuated by the instability of international affairs, then less not more reliance on international economic connections seems appropriate. Without a strong imperial power to enforce stability, placing greater and greater emphasis on international economic ties would exacerbate a downward spiral of stagnation and instability. In some quarters, a similar definition of the problem leads to policies for recreating a strong imperial power, but I doubt that it is possible to do so and it is certainly not desirable. The proper responses to stagnation, then, are reforms that lead in the direction of strengthening community and building an inward oriented economic alternative.

Strategic Difficulties

As I have indicated, these statements about alternatives are necessarily in the realm of speculation. As such, they are not only vague but also potentially self-contradictory. On the one hand, for example, I have given emphasis to the possibility of international solidarity among workers as a basis for building stronger social movements toward alternatives. On the other hand, I have said that one response to globalisation should be a focus on community as the basis for our economic alternatives. It is not clear how these two arguments fit together.

Perhaps, however, the apparent contradiction between a movement based on international working class solidarity and a focus on community can be transformed into a positive element in the construction of an alternative to the present course of globalisation. After all, progressive social movements are frequently confronted with the task of building broad solidarity while at the same time recognising the differences and divisions among the various constituencies of that movement. More and more, the Left has moved toward the position that greater strength for the broad movement depends upon a positive acceptance of the differences. For example, no effective working class struggle can fail to give prominent positions to the particular interests of peoples of colour or of women. Certainly, insofar as the Left has explicitly recognised and embraced these 'particular interests', the progressive movement as a whole has been stronger. Similarly, in recognising the particular interests of communities, it is likely that an international working class movement would be strengthened. At the same time, local community struggles would be more powerful tied to a larger movement. None of this eliminates the potential contradiction between the international and community components of progressive opposition to globalisation. Yet it is useful to see this problem as one form of a recurring difficulty in which building a powerful oppositional movement means continually dealing with tensions among its particular components; and it will never do to ignore or suppress those tensions.

Similarly, other problems in the alternative agenda I have suggested can be successfully dealt with only after they are explicitly recognised. One especially important example is also connected to the focus on community, for a focus on community can be an apologia for reaction, xenophobia, and the imposition of traditional forms of exploitation and oppression. Control of foreign commerce easily becomes a rationalisation for a conservative nationalism, and in the United States this means racism as well. The way in which a progressive position and a reactionary position have this sort of relation and potentially dangerous connection is suggested by the rather unusual left-right coalition in the United States that emerged in opposition to NAFTA.

The dangers evident in such a coalition should lead the Left to rethink some of its traditional responses to globalisation. In particular, traditional forms of protectionism and the arguments in support of protectionism can quickly become the basis for a reactionary politics. The protectionist position singles out and gives special emphasis to one type of threat to workers, the threat from foreign competition. In the rhetoric of protectionism, 'our' jobs are being moved abroad where foreigners – 'they' not 'us' – will reap the benefits. In fact, workers' jobs are continually threatened in many ways: by the vicissitudes of the business cycle, technological change, intra-national movement of capital, and just plain poor management, as well as by foreign competition. Most broadly, workers' jobs are continually threatened by the efforts of employers to raise profits. A progressive response to the job loss of globalisation would place it in this larger context and demand a general protection for jobs, not simply a protection from foreign imports. As a practical matter, workers need to be protected from job loss associated with globalisation, but a struggle for particular practical policies needs to be connected to a broader ideological struggle. Otherwise, focusing singularly on job loss to foreign competition, the Left will simply become the tail on the dog of nationalist – which is to say reactionary – rhetoric.

One more problem faced by the forces opposed to the current course of globalisation lies in the fact that programmes to overcome stagnation and restore growth to the world economy only exacerbate environmental destruction. Economic growth has long been a pillar of Left programmes, and our critique of capitalism has given a central position to the system's failure to expand sufficiently rapidly to provide jobs in the wealthy countries and to overcome poverty in the Third World. The environmental crisis forces a re-examination of this analysis, but, in fact, the analysis has always been a weak one.

It is one thing to say that capitalism is in crisis because of stagnation and that within capitalism more rapid growth is the only means to stem the emergence of opposition. These are points I have stressed in the preceding pages. It is quite another thing to say either that more rapid economic growth would solve the fundamental social problems of capitalism or that beyond capitalism growth would be a key to social progress. Capitalism needs growth because it cannot tolerate any far reaching redistribution of income. Yet it is the great maldistribution of income that gives rise to our most severe social problems – everything from street crime and homeless-ness to racial conflict and meaningless work. A Left agenda that gives prominence to the redistribution of income would make far more sense than an emphasis on economic growth.

Redistribution of income in itself does not eliminate environmental problems, but it makes an important positive contribution to the solution of these problems. Greater equality reduces both the necessity of and the pressures for economic growth, and thus gives greater leeway for the economic organisation that avoids destruction of the environment. Within the current social framework, economic well-being almost necessitates environmental destruction; and, ironically, environmental destruction may be greater during an era of stagnation than during more rapid expansion as private individuals and firms become more and more desper-ate for economic survival. (Consider for example, the environmental destruction of tropical rain forests in the Third World under the pressure of the debt crisis or the destruction of temperate rain forests in the U.S. Pacific Northwest under the pressure of high unemployment rates.) By giving prominence to equality over economic growth, anti-globalisation forces might find one of their strongest arguments.

I cannot pretend that these brief comments do away with the ambiguities in my agenda for alternatives to globalisation. And the list of problems in my agenda could surely be extended. All I can say in defence of my ambiguities is that the current course of affairs has many more problems. At least the alternatives I have discussed have the merit of being grounded in the economic realities of globalisation and stagnation as they confront us today. These realities are wreaking havoc on the peoples of North

America, and on the peoples of the rest of the world as well. We had better find some alternatives.

Nobody said it would be easy!

NOTES

1. On the income gap between rich and poor countries see Harry Magdoff's 'Globalization: To What End?' in Ralph Miliband and Leo Panitch, editors, *The Socialist Register, 1992: New World Order?* Monthly Review Press, New York, 1992. The figures on U.S. income distribution changes in the 1980s come from the Congressional Budget Office as reported in the New York *Times* of March 5, 1992. Data for Mexico are available from the Instituto Nacional de Estadistica, Geografia e Informatica: Encuesta Nacional de Ingresos y Gastos de los Hogares. Also, see George Psacharopoulos et al, *Poverty and Income Distribution in Latin America: The Story of the 1980s*, The World Bank, Human Resource Division, Latin America and the Caribbean Technical Department, Regional Studies Program, Report No. 27, revised April, 1993. For a useful analysis of the connection between globalisation and inequality in the U.S., see Edward E. Leamer, 'Wage Effects of a U.S.-Mexican Free Trade Agreement', Working Paper No. 3991, National Bureau of Economic Research, Cambridge, February, 1992.
2. Schumpeter develops the concept in Chapter VII of *Capitalism, Socialism and Democracy*, Harper & Row, New York, 1950. While using Schumpeter's phrase, I should note that not much of the rest of the argument here is consistent with the ideas that Schumpeter develops in that chapter. He uses the concept of creative destruction largely in explaining the success of capitalist development, whereas I am trying to use it in explaining the contradictions (potential failure) of capitalist development.
3. This line of argument is developed in Arthur MacEwan, 'Technological Options and Free Trade Agreements', Working Paper 93–05, Department of Economics, University of Massachusetts – Boston, October, 1993, where more complete references are provided.
4. See R.E. Lipsey and I.B. Kravis, 'The Competitiveness and Comparative Advantage of U.S. Multinationals, 1957–1984', *Banca Nazionale del Lavoro Quarterly Review*, No. 161, 1987, p. 151.
5. See E.J. Hobsbawm, *Industry and Empire*, Penguin Books, London, 1969.
6. The argument, which is also associated with Paul Baran, is developed in various places; see, for example, Harry Magdoff and Paul Sweezy, *Stagnation and the Financial Explosion*, Monthly Review Press, New York, 1987.
7. See Arthur MacEwan, *Debt and Disorder: International Economic Instability and U.S. Imperial Decline*, Monthly Review Press, New York, 1990. Also, see Robert Pollin, *Deeper in Debt: Changing Financial Conditions of U.S. Households*, Economic Policy Institute, Washington, D.C., 1990.
8. Empirical evidence on the correlation between inequality and slow national growth is not well developed. Yet the evidence that does exist does not give much support to the idea that a low wage, inequality strategy is likely to yield rapid economic expansion. Some limited empirical evidence and the technology and incentive arguments are discussed in MacEwan, 'Technological Options and Free Trade Agreements', as cited above.
9. The social structure of accumulation argument is developed in David M. Gordon, Richard Edwards, and Michael Reich, *Segmented Work, Divided Workers: The Historical Transformation of Labor in the United States*, Cambridge University Press, New York, 1982.
10. The connection of community to the controversies over international commerce is usefully developed by Herman E. Daly and John B. Cobb, Jr., *For the Common Good: Redirecting the Economy Toward Community, the Environment, and a Sustainable Future*, Beacon Press, Boston, 1989.
11. At least some on the Left, however, ignore these sorts of arguments and assert that a progressive economic programme – at least in Mexico and elsewhere in Latin America – should be built on the basis of export-led growth. See, in particular, Jorge Casteneda, *Utopia Unarmed: The Latin American left After the Cold War*, Alfred Knopf, New York, 1993.

'COMPETITIVE AUSTERITY' AND THE IMPASSE OF CAPITALIST EMPLOYMENT POLICY

Gregory Albo

1. The Impasse of Capitalist Employment Policy

Keynes closed his *General Theory* with the warning that 'it is certain that the world will not much longer tolerate the unemployment which, apart from brief intervals of excitement, is associated – and, in my opinion, inevitably associated – with present-day capitalistic individualism'. Despite Keynes's conviction that 'a right analysis of the problem [would] cure the disease', present-day capitalism is again associated with mass unemployment.[1] This represents a remarkable reversal of the postwar 'golden age' of high growth and low unemployment. In the period from 1966–73 a state of virtual full employment was reached, with unemployment falling below 3 per cent in many states, with Germany and Japan even suffering serious labour shortages. From the oil shock of 1973 to the 1981–82 Volcker recession, mass unemployment spread across the OECD area, accompanied by accelerating inflation, giving rise to the awkward, if descriptive, term stagflation. Despite the recovery of the mid-80s and the squashing of inflation, the majority of the advanced capitalist bloc continues to be characterized by low-productivity increases, 'jobless growth' and steadily mounting unemployment. Even in the case of what often has been misleadingly referred to as the 'great North American jobs machine' unemployment has failed to drop back to pre-crisis levels.

The stagnation of industrial production since the recession of 1991–92 has added further to employment problems. The subsequent 'sick recovery' has shown scarce job prospects (with rates of new job creation in North America running at about one quarter of previous recoveries). Stagflation has fallen into 'disinflation' but still without growth. Across the OECD zone unemployment rates are now typically double, and often three and four times, what they were during the 'golden age of capitalism'. The proportion of the population actually engaging in paid work contributing to the total social product has, for the most part, been declining.[2] Fewer people are working at full-time jobs – and often at longer hours – while more people are not getting enough – or any – hours of work. The

144

proportion of the population dependent on income transfers has, consequently, been secularly increasing.

The shift in the principal doctrines of employment policy since the onset of the crisis has been, perhaps, even more remarkable than the rise in unemployment. The postwar period was dominated by a form of keynesianism commonly referred to as the neoclassical synthesis, or, less favourably by Joan Robinson, as bastard keynesianism.[3] This keynesian view held that the unemployed were involuntarily out of work and represented unutilized resources that could be mobilized to increase output. Capitalist economies, keynesians argued, can get stuck at high levels of unemployment: nominal wages tend to be 'sticky' downwards so that real wages might not fall to clear the market; similarly, declines in interest rates might not cause capitalists to invest and thereby to take up more workers. In either case, there is a lack of *effective demand* due to the collapse of the marginal efficiency of capital (expected profits). Full employment can be restored only by raising effective demand by increasing private or public consumption, bolstering investment levels or by finding new foreign markets. The point was well summed by Keynes in *The General Theory*:

> The celebrated optimism of traditional economic theory, which has led to economists being looked upon as Candides, who, having left this world for the cultivation of their gardens, teach that all is for the best in the best of all possible worlds provided we will let well alone, is also to be traced, I think, to their having neglected to take account of the drag on prosperity which can be exercised by an insufficiency of effective demand. For there would obviously be a natural tendency towards the optimum employment of resources in a society which was functioning after the manner of the classical postulates. It may well be that the classical theory represents the way in which we should like our economy to behave. But to assume that it actually does so is to assume our difficulties away.[4]

Following the stagflation experience, there are few adherents to the keynesian view today that increasing aggregate demand, in either the form of consumption or public investment, will have much effect in stimulating economic growth or lowering unemployment. Even when there exists real effective demand shortfalls at the national level, due to slower investment or to the pursuit of restrictive budgetary policies to control domestic costs for international competitiveness, particularly by the G7 group at the core of the world economy, it is doubtful that a stimulative package would call forth private sector investment at levels high and enduring enough to recreate an economic boom. It is even more unlikely that demand stimulation at the national level – or even the supra-national level such as Europe – can solve the long-period unemployment problem which now exists. (Nor can the international mechanisms and institutions that might supply stable, long-term, balanced aggregate world demand be identified or foreseen.)

The general crisis of unemployment since 1974 has shattered postwar capitalist employment policy centred on keynesianism. All sides of the political spectrum have seemed to come to agreement on two fundamental points as necessary to soak up the massive global labour surpluses: the need to provide a supply-side stimulative package to spur renewed accumulation, and maintenance, if not strengthening, of a liberal regional and global trading regime, through the economic integration proposed by the European Economic Community and the North American Free Trade Agreement, or via the multilateral General Agreement on Trade and Tariffs.

The right's supply-side strategy has focused on breaking the institutional rigidities built into the Fordist postwar system that limited market discipline, protected workers' bargaining power and, through productivity sharing, maintained aggregate demand. Improved market flexibility would, it is contended, increase the returns to capital and, in turn, the rate of capital accumulation. The social democratic left's supply-side strategy has also attempted to increase flexibility and competitiveness, but in this case by stimulating the introduction of flexible automation through the systematic introduction of new technologies by industrial policies and tax incentives and by developing highly-skilled workers through modernised training regimes. In either the neo-liberal or 'progressive competitiveness' strategies, the employment policy conclusions run parallel: rapid economic growth, export-oriented industrial policies and freer trade are the only hope to bring unemployment back down to the 'full employment' levels of the postwar 'golden age of capitalism'. There is no alternative to supply-side strategies of 'liberal-productivism' for each firm, region or country to win a place in the competitive battle for world market shares and to solve the unemployment crisis.

The neo-liberal view, in its original monetarist or more recent variants, contends that unemployment is a *specific, individual, voluntary* problem of the labour market.[5] Individual firms and workers voluntarily make, accept or refuse wage offers. Unemployment is essentially a result of real wages asked being too high and profits too low, consequently leading to fewer job offers, a lower rate of investment and the use of labour-saving techniques. Attempting to lower real wages through inflation, as keynesian stimulus does, soon leads to workers' wage expectations adapting, leaving the aggregate labour supply unchanged. Unemployment remains at its natural, or voluntary, rate of unemployment (which is re-defined more precisely as the non-accelerating inflation rate of unemployment). Demand stimulus, therefore, does not affect real output and thus levels of employment in the long-term.

In this view, lowering the natural rate of unemployment depends upon lowering inflation, so that capitalists can have more certainty about their investments, and de-regulating non-market barriers which prevent real wages from falling in the labour market and thus preventing new hires and higher levels of productivity and investment. The measures to improve labour market flexibility are primarily 'defensive' in nature, that is, they involve rolling back institutional securities for workers built into the postwar labour market and welfare state. This defensive flexibility includes: reducing trade union power; minimizing the welfare disincentives to work; improving information flows and labour mobility; leaving investment in training to individual decisions on their 'human capital' needs; and eliminating market restraints, such as minimum wages and unemployment insurance, which limit downward wage flexibility. By moving to an unregulated free market, economic adjustment would instantaneously produce market-clearing wage levels (with the principle of substitutability of labour and capital making any bias to capital-using technological change unimportant except for determining the rate of growth). In effect, Say's Law is restored, and all unemployment is a voluntary, individual choice given existing competitive conditions in the market.

In one form or another, the neo-liberal approach has dominated the agenda of employment policy since the late 1970s. It has not stood up very well against actual economic experience. At the most basic level, the neo-liberal position has never provided a satisfactory explanation as to why the natural rate of unemployment should vary so much over time, between countries, or for any number of institutional reasons. Rather than exhibiting any tendency 'toward an optimum employment of resources', more than anything else, as Keynes warned, the natural rate seems to track the historical rate of unemployment. Bringing down the rate of inflation and increasing wage flexibility through the 1980s has not meant a reduction in unemployment. On the contrary, fiscal and monetary restraint have contributed to the deflationary tendency of the crisis by squeezing down social and wage costs thereby taking demand out of the system (in the process seriously damaging the neo-classical notion of a vertical Phillips curve at a natural rate of unemployment).

Indeed, the spread across the capitalist bloc of neo-liberal policies of keeping wage increases below productivity growth and pushing down domestic costs has led to an unstable vicious circle of 'competitive austerity': each country reduces domestic demand and adopts an export-oriented strategy of dumping its surplus production, for which there are fewer consumers in its national economy given the decrease in workers' living standards and productivity gains all going to the capitalists, in the world market. This has created a global demand crisis and the growth of surplus capacity across the business cycle. The structural asymmetries in the payments position of the major countries, notably the deficit of the U.S. which has played the role of absorbing other countries' export surpluses since the postwar period, have thus proven intractable. As a result, unemployment is spiralling upward even in the centre economies of Japan and Germany which are running payments surpluses. So long as all countries continue to pursue export-led strategies, which is the conventional wisdom demanded by IMF, OECD and G7 policies and the logic of neo-liberal trade policies, there seems little reason not to conclude that 'competitive austerity' will continue to ratchet down the living standards of workers in *both* the North and the South. Only the most dogmatic of market economists, of which there are all too many today, can still hold that neo-liberal policies offer a route out of the jobs crisis. (Or they must at least concede that these policies can only be sustained by further 'Brazilianization' of having the working classes of the North and the South bear the burden of adjustment imposed by the contradiction between the international payments constraint and export-oriented policies.)

2. Competitiveness and the Production of Skills

The social democratic supply-side perspective also stresses the need for labour market flexibility 'to compete in the new global economy' to maintain domestic employment. In this case the focus is less on increasing wage and market flexibility which, it is argued, has caused the income and work polarisation of the 1980s. Rather, the notion is of an offensive flexibility whereby the training of highly-skilled workers contributes, or indeed causes, the successful integration of new technologies and flexible workplace adaptation to shifting market demand for products. The lack of an appropriate skill profile of the labour force and a dynamic training regime, this view contends, causes a mismatch between workers' skills and the demand for labour as a result of technological change. The mismatch is registered in slow industrial adjustment to market changes and thus higher rates of unemployment. By re-training and adjusting workers' skills, the dislocations from technological change will eventually work themselves out as firms adapt to the new competitive conditions at higher levels of output. In its essence, this position was elaborated best by Joseph Schumpeter:

> Economists have a habit of distinguishing between, and contrasting, cyclical and technological unemployment. But it follows from our model that, basically, cyclical unemployment is technological unemployment. . . . We have seen, in fact, in our historical survey, that periods of prolonged supernormal unemployment, coincide with the periods in which the results of inventions are spreading over the system.[6]

The high unemployment levels confronting the advanced capitalist countries today, then, are caused by a shift to a new technological paradigm: the end of the mass production processes of Fordism and the transition to the new flexible work processes and automated factories brought about by the microelectronics revolution. The period of economic transition across this 'industrial divide' can be shortened, however, by re-tooling of factories and rapid adjustment of work skills to meet the new competitive conditions. This position suggests that supply, in this case the supply of skilled labour, will create its own demand, and that the processes of national adjustment, and existing demand conditions, provide no significant long-term barrier to lowering unemployment. Successful microeconomic adjustments on the supply-side will lead to desired macroeconomic results on the employment side. This view can be termed the *'progressive competitiveness'* model – adapted by social democratic parties across the OECD and by the Democratic Clinton regime in the U.S. – of creating globally competitive, high value-added firms using highly skilled workers. Training policy is, in this model, the cornerstone to job creation and an alternate response to the 'competitive austerity' resulting from neo-liberal labour market strategies.

But how should we think of training policy within capitalist societies and can we infer the employment conclusions drawn by the 'progressive competitiveness' strategy? Since the publication of Harry Braverman's remarkable book, *Labor and Monopoly Capital*,[7] there has been a verita-ble explosion of studies of the capitalist labour process. Braverman's own view that the structural tendency of modern capitalism is to uniformly extend Taylorism, and thus de-skill workers, is limited. Not only does he fail to fully account for a differentiation of skills across occupations, his thesis also appears historically bound to the deep separation of conception from execution characteristic of Fordism. Yet, even more insensitive to skill differentiation has been the view, associated with Michael Piore and Charles Sabel's *The Second Industrial Divide*,[8] that microelectronics leads to a uniform process of skill enrichment. This latter sentiment has charac-terized most recent writings on the skills impact of the new production concepts and is central to the progressive competitiveness model.

The real lesson of the many studies of the labour process, however, is that a *social choice* is involved in the organization of the workplace, albeit a choice severely constrained by the relations of production particular to capitalism.[9] This dynamic relationship between technological changes, work organization and skills has been neglected until recently.[10] Depend-ing on whether one was reading the economics or sociology literature, technology or organizations caused a certain type of labour process and hence a specific national growth model. But as Michael Storper notes:

> In reality, both 'firms' and 'industries' are being redefined, such that the notion of returns as strictly internal loses its meaning in any dynamic, historical sense. In sum, in functioning industrial systems, both the division of labour and technological innovations tend to be endogenously and dynamically reproduced and are, in turn, mutually reinforcing.[11]

An important factor affecting this social choice – little considered because of the assumption of either progressive or regressive advance of worker skills through the growth of the market – is the 'technical capa-cities' of the national labour force and the role of the training process in determining what goes into the labour process. With the old technological paradigm of Fordism in decline, the development of 'technical capacities' also raises fundamental political questions. If the labour movement should support the end of Taylorism – one of its historical demands for the re-uniting of head and hand – on what basis should it commit itself to upgrading the skills of workers so as to expand the capacities for self-management? How should the productivity gains from more flexible work processes be shared-out so as to increase employment and equalize income?

The failure to take up these questions, at least within North America, is witnessed most clearly in the 'human capital school', the position which has dominated the analysis and policies of training since the 1960s, and is most associated with neo-liberal employment policies.[12] The conceptual core of human capital theory is the view that individuals invest in themselves (in job search, information sources, qualifications, migration) for the sake of future monetary returns – a return on investment in skills (non-pecuniary returns from education being ignored or reduced to a monetary value). As one of the founders of the school, T.W. Schultz, put it:

> Labourers have become capitalists not from a diffusion of the ownership of corporation stocks, as folklore would have it, but from the acquisition of knowledge and skill that have economic value. This knowledge and skill are in great part the product of investment and, combined with other human investment, predominantly account for the productive superiority of the technically advanced countries.[13]

At the level of the firm, individual enterprises respond to relative costs of factor inputs, including varied types of skilled labour, and then set the demand for labour. Even with non-homogeneous units of labour, production functions substitute units of labour and capital at the margin with no substantive, or at least dynamic, variation in technique. At the level of the individual, price signals are sufficient to yield the required investment in skills and thus supply of skilled workers. For firms or individuals training occurs by comparing the cost of investing in skills with the additional revenues earned. In short, human capital theory suggests that the labour market yields *private* market signals to individuals which are not at variance with the *social* signals for the economy and society as a whole.

But the treatment of skills as acquired individual attributes tradeable in the market, and thus a claim for a high wage based on a high marginal productivity, is seriously flawed. One of the tenets of dual labour market theory which still merits attention is that the labour market is something less than homogeneous in its treatment of individual workers and in its structure. The earnings of workers are significantly influenced by factors such as gender, age, race, and social origin, so they cannot be reduced simply to a return on investment in human capital. As well, systematic barriers to occupational mobility and employment instability for one group of workers can be contrasted with the stable employment advance through internal labour markets of firms for other workers.[14] Regardless of whether such a strong dualism should be attributed to technology and market structures, specific skills learned through on-the-job training tends to be limited to core workers in technically advanced firms. The market alone does not provide either adequate skills or stable employment. Thus, the dualists pointed out, if investment in skills is important, it is unlikely to be adequately provided in terms of volume or of equal access for all workers by the market. Public programmes for training and employment are essential.[15]

Apart from the lack of training due to differences of industry structure, there are additional reasons to suggest that the problems of market failure extend to individual firms and eventually across the economy.[16] Firm investment in training resides with the individual worker and not in physical assets; the 'human capital' attached to the trainee is thereby mobile. This is especially the case for what Gary Becker calls 'transferable skills and competencies'.[17] These general skills will increase individual productivity equivalently for any enterprise, and contrast to the specific training that increases individual productivity primarily in the firm providing the training (although little training is completely specific to a single firm). Skills provided by general training are, consequently, in danger of being 'poached': individual firms may forego the costs of training, finding it instead to their advantage to bid trained workers away from the training firm by providing a higher wage. If this occurs on a wide enough scale, training firms would cease to train for they would lose their investments. In other words, markets with 'poachers' and 'trainers' are unstable; market failures in this type of 'employer-centred' system will lead to skill shortages. So governments, again, have a role to play in the provision of training either by a grant-levy scheme to equalize private training or through institutional public training programmes providing a collective good.

The expansion of state training programmes in the 1960s and 1970s to cope with the problem of poaching sparked a further response, particularly in Britain, Canada and the U.S., from human capital theorists to re-establish the primacy of a private market in training – a response now embedded in the neo-liberal labour market policies of the Anglo-American countries.[18] The human capital theorists contended that, at least theoretically, the market would provide specific skills. Yet they also agreed that firms would be unwilling to finance *general* training that involved costs that could not be recouped because of poaching. The problem, however, was not market-based training, but trainee wages that were too high relative to their marginal product. If these wages were brought in line, either by wage subsidies or lowering trainee allowances and minimum wages, poaching would be pointless as all firms would undertake training. The market would again supply price signals appropriate to socially efficient training levels.

This neo-liberal strategy of privatizing training had disastrous consequences for workers and skills training throughout the 1980s as firms failed to provide adequate levels of trained workers, and workers dropped out of training programmes because of a lack of decent living allowances. Unskilled workers on training programmes, moreover, often became little more than subsidized waged labour, especially in the British and Canadian training programmes, on the basis that any paid work provided basic training for further employment. The return to market-driven training, therefore, represented the market failures of insufficient volumes of training and a social polarisation amongst the recipients of training.

The 'progressive competitiveness' advocates of training policies for more flexible workplaces, moreover, began to point to more fundamental limits of market-driven training which were blocking skills adjustment (and thus allowing unemployment unnecessarily to climb). The problem of training market failure, for example, meant that a labour market intelligence network was still required, but the rush to privatization had seriously compromised the capacities of the labour exchanges (a key project of social democratic reformers since the turn of the century). For instance, formal training for higher education or technical training tends to leave the costs (foregone income and direct outlays) with the individuals. As predicted by human capital theory, 'workers pay for their own schooling'. But imperfections in the capital market, especially equal access to loans for trainees of different social origins, will remain. Substantial financial programmes and trainee allowances – which also involve occupational selection decisions by the state on what to provide funding for – will be required. There is, furthermore, unlikely to be perfect information about occupational choices, for youth and older workers in particular, so skill 'investments' will not necessarily be efficient. The typical activities of labour-market boards – counselling, job banks, placement, mobility – remain imperative if the market is not to undersupply skills. Limiting skilling to calculations of returns on investment will, in fact, yield fewer returns in terms of skilled workers than if training and education are viewed as social rights to be guaranteed by the state.

A period of transition between techno-social paradigms will compound all these problems into serious obstacles to adjustment and high unemployment. The problem of poaching, for example, will tend to intensify in market-driven training systems in a transitional period. Few skills are exclusively firm-specific and bidding wars will ensue for workers with the new skills in demand. So unless rigid internal labour markets are in place, or the firm is in a monopsony position, capitalists will, in general, underinvest in training. Firms in a competitive cost crunch, moreover, are likely to cut training costs as a first step to cutting labour costs (as has happened as a result of more open economies and import pressures during the 1980s). As a result of these two pressures, skill shortages will appear in recoveries from recessions which, in turn, will spur poaching from weaker firms (many of which will be start-up new technology companies). In a period of a technological paradigm shift, training failures will inevitably lengthen the period of adjustment and provide the basis for wrenching levels of unemployment for countries pushed down the neo-liberal path as weak firms lose their skilled workers and competitive edge.

Finally, the neo-liberal defence of market-based training, critics pointed out, depends upon static parameters in the demand and supply of labour in the short period (and pure flexibility of skills and wages in the long period). This assumes that individual capitalists know *ex ante* the appropriate skills to even new techniques and that *ex post* these skills will be supplied to meet the aggregate needs of all capitalists. But this is not likely, given the fallacy of composition problems underpinning the logic, to be the case. An *oversupply* of high-level general skills in the labour market will in fact make for an easier transition to more advanced production techniques and a more flexible workforce to meet changing market demands. This is the foremost principle drawn by the 'progressive competitiveness' strategy from the training policy debate: product strategies are linked to available skills and technological advance places a premium on highly-skilled workers.

The systemic failure of the market to provide comprehensive training suggests that skills may be seen best as a 'public or collective good'. In a powerful series of essays, Wolfgang Streeck has argued precisely this point:

> . . . the fundamental uncertainty for employers recovering their training expenses in an open labour market . . . turns skills, from the viewpoint of the individual employer, into a collective good. If an employer provides training, he is no more than adding to a common pool of skilled labour which is in principle accessible to all other employers in the industry or locally, many of which are his competitors. . . . As a result, there will be a chronic undersupply of skilled labour. . . . In this sense, I regard skills as an example of what I described as collective, social production factors which capitalist firms, acting according to the rational utilitarian model, cannot adequately generate or preserve.[19]

This is an important conclusion, and one that can be widely endorsed: if left to the market, training will occur, and powerful corporations like IBM may even provide high quality training and develop strong internal labour markets, but these will be isolated 'islands of excellence'. Non-market training institutions are essential to the adequate provision of skills (particularly to the access to skills by individual workers in marginalized social groups). A neo-corporatist training regime, as argued by Streeck and endorsed by the 'progressive competitiveness' strategy, would be a preferred option to the market.[20] In this view, firms, regulated by corporatist structures like the German Works Councils, are the ideal places for training. State training programmes, like markets, may equally fail to provide the needed 'collective skills good'. Schools are not the ideal places to create work skills even if the skills needed are general and polyvalent. This does not mean that formal classroom training is absent – even the famous German apprenticeship system includes this component; but it does mean that on-the-job training is suited best for producing the dynamic training regime and skills attributes, including the 'socialization in work-related values', demanded by 'the new competitive conditions in world markets'.[21]

The obstacles to a successful corporatist strategy along German lines are enormous in the Anglo-American countries where the experience of on-the-job training is mixed and the political conditions to produce works councils are decidedly remote. Even when the state has extensively regulated on-the-job training, it often has meant little more than firms providing brief, firm-specific training for semi-skilled workers. In introducing the Japanese flexible work processes, firms have used training as much for the inculcation of 'corporate culture' as for actual skills training. On-the-job training for peripheral workers, moreover, has often simply meant brief periods of employment without the skills upgrading necessary to improve labour market chances in the long-term (and certainly not the development of the skills requisite for more active citizenship in the broader community). Publicly provided programmes, and institutional training centres supplying formal qualifications, have been essential to providing skills and broadening access to training. A strong public core to training is often seen, therefore, as necessary in North America to facilitate adjustment to the new work processes and to have productivity gains spread across the national economy.

These three principal means of regulating the training of workers – the market, corporatist institutions, or the state – are rooted in different societies in quite distinct ways. In Japan, a highly segmented, formal schooling is followed by extensive training at the firm level, with the firm's investment maintained by extremely rigid internal labour markets. Germany appears as the example par excellence of corporatist regulation of training. An extensive adult and secondary vocational education structure is added to a highly developed apprenticeship system, jointly regulated by unions and management through works councils. Sweden, in contrast, has a strong public component to training, particularly for the unemployed and to encourage worker mobility, supervised by the National Labour Market Board. The North American 'market model' of training has been more varied and institutionally unstable: Canada and the U.S. have alternatively relied upon 'poaching' skilled workers from other nations through immigration, public training programmes targeted at the disadvantaged or the highly qualified, and firm-specific market supplied skills.

These different national forms of producing skills have become important, according to the progressive competitiveness model, to current industrial restructuring. The production of skills and the type of national training regime are important not just for flexibility in general but the *kind* of flexibility firms will adopt. The old mass production processes of Fordism tended to rely on a sharp separation of conception and execution. The rigid differentiation of tasks produced a skill polarisation: conception concentrated in specialist technical skills in design offices; skilled manufacturing and trades jobs filled by apprenticeship or specialist training; and a mass of unskilled assembly jobs with limited specific training tied to a minute division of labour. In contrast, flexible automation tends to use reprogrammable technologies to re-integrate production and design.

Work organisation can consequently be more flexible, in responding to differentiated product demand. Flexible automation, moreover, requires workers that are more flexible, emphasizing multi-tasking and multi-skilling, general skills rather than specific ones, and analytic and problem-solving abilities rather than mere procedural capacities. Thus skills are likely to be decisive to a re-organized labour process – both to exploit the potential productivity of new technologies and to involve workers directly in improving productivity – for firms attempting to export high value-added products.[22]

Yet just as Fordism differed between nations, the 'progressive competitiveness' strategy contends there is unlikely to be a uniform adaptation of a new form of work organization under a regime of flexible automation. As Arndt Sorge and Malcolm Warner have emphasized, training and qualification structures appear linked to technological adaptation but are embedded in national traditions.[23] The availability of highly skilled workers in countries with strong training institutions permits quick re-deployment of labour to new technologies and products which, in turn, helps preserve the skills base and competitiveness. In contrast, in countries with weak skilling structures and old products, a low skills equilibrium seems to develop which forces downward economic adjustments to compete on the basis of costs. In other words, there appear to be national forms of flexibility, dependent upon the training regime, in responding to market uncertainty and new product demands. The task of employment policy is, then, to upgrade the national training regime. Within social democratic thinking, this conclusion has been most forcefully stated by the Canadian Steelworkers:

> What has become known as the high-skill business strategy refers to a cluster of business strategies that are compatible with secure jobs providing fair wages. . . . The high-skill option requires businesses to pursue strategies of increasing value-added rather than strategies to reduce labour's share in existing value-added. . . . We need enlightened management who recognize the importance of competing in higher value-added markets on a high-skill basis. . . . Once there is a commitment to truly developing worker skills and their roles in a workplace, workers will be partners in building toward sustainable prosperity in their workplaces and communities.[24]

If a country, or region for that matter, is to keep its export share, or increase it to boost employment levels, employment policy must have as its central concern the production of skills. Training leads to jobs, and highly-skilled training is the basis for the good jobs in high-value added, globally-competitive firms that will put an end to 'competitive austerity'.

The training policy regime advocated by the progressive competitiveness strategy is superior to the neo-liberal model in terms of both the analysis of market failure in the provision of skills and the positive role that training can play in adjustment. The insight that training structures can act as a leverage to improve firm level adjustment to the demand and quality of products, for instance, is important. Similarly, the conclusion that highly-skilled, involved workers can begin to reverse the deskilling of work under Taylorism, and add to labour productivity, is a result with important implications for the labour movement as a whole. To the extent that worker involvement and training policy are collectively negotiated with organized workers at the plant level, and through elected works councils at the sectoral level, there is the *potential* capacity to make material advances to worker self-management that has been limited by the management rights clauses that were part of the Fordist productivity-sharing bargain.

But it is not possible to generalize, as is done by the progressive competitiveness strategy, that upgrading skills in line with the new technologies will resolve the problem of unemployment. This position must assume that levels of unemployment have not been secularly increasing for some time (a questionable proposition for the OECD zone). It must further assume that the volume and distribution of hours of work is, more or less, already adequate. Present unemployment can then be posed as essentially an adjustment problem caused by lags in skill development in response to new technologies and competitive conditions. These assumptions are problematic: numerous studies have shown that the level of unemployment has been increasing for some time for any degree of capital utilization suggesting a growing surplus labour force; as well, the level of unused capacity has been increasing indicating growing demand problems. In these conditions, training will raise the average level of skills, but it will not mean more jobs will be available.

The progressive competitiveness strategy hinges, then, on sustained high rates of growth in world (not necessarily national) markets to lower unemployment. This depends upon a number of equally strong and dubious assumptions. It depends, for example, on higher value-added production spreading across the national economy so as to replace lower value-added standardized production being lost to low wage producers and regions. This entails the very large risk that the de-industrializing sectors will decline at a faster rate, and with greater employment losses, than the rate of expansion of sectors of high technology. The high technology sectors being boosted must also see no cost advantage to moving to low wage production sites (although there is ample evidence that they do and that developing countries are able to supply skilled workers). Export growth in high technology sectors, moreover, must be more rapid than previous levels of export growth if unemployment is not to grow because of higher capital-labour ratios in these sectors relative to the declining low-wage sectors.

It is an extremely suspect proposition that rapid enough accumulation can be achieved in world markets to accommodate all the countries and regions engaged in this high-growth, high-productivity, high-tech export-oriented strategy. That would take a near-miracle in itself. Yet more basically the extension of the export-oriented strategy beyond a single country ignores the simple problem of who is going to bear the payments deficits as all companies and countries squeeze costs to pursue the high value-added, export-oriented industrialization strategies that is to solve the national umemployment crisis. Will it be the deficit-plagued U.S. and Canada? Will it be the export-oriented Japanese and German economies engaged in their own fiscal crises and trying to maintain payments surpluses to expand their spheres of influence? Can the Asian 'miracle economies' suddenly reverse their industrial structures and become launched on an import binge? Or, perhaps, the devastated economies and workers of Africa and South America could do the world economy a good turn?

The asymmetry of all countries pursuing export markets can only add to the competitive pressures to bargain down national wage and social standards. As low-wage zones increasingly adopt leading edge technologies – as mobile productive capital from the North establishes new plants in these zones because of their own high technology strategies – the downward wage pressure will accelerate (as it must with global labour surpluses). But, as has become all too evident, the bargaining down process takes demand out of the system, with no clear compensating source, precisely when more output is being put on the world market. The cumulative effect is to add to the realisation problems of growing surplus capacity and a further spiral of unemployment. The distribution of hours of work also polarizes to meet the new competition: multi-skilled core workers are pushed to work longer hours to recoup training investments, while peripheral workers and the unemployed scramble to get enough hours of paid work. The progressive competitiveness strategy is forced to accept, as social democratic parties have been willing to do, the same 'competitive austerity' as neo-liberalism, and further 'Brazilianization of the West', as a cold necessity of present economic conditions.

3. Beyond 'Competitive Austerity'?

The relationship of training regimes to overall employment policy retains a central importance. New qualifications and skills may affect the speed of adjustment for individual firms, or even countries if a strong training regime has been institutionalized. But there is no reason that this should increase the general volume of employment particularly as other firms and regions adopt (as they appear to be doing) the same progressive competitiveness strategy. Under these conditions national (or regional) employment is increased only to the extent somebody else (or some other region) is bested and put out of work. The distribution of work, but not its aggregate volume, is altered: the result is better-skilled workers but unemployed in the same number (or higher if all countries pursue cost-cutting to improve export competitiveness and take demand out of the system). Indeed, the rationalisation of production from the new work processes has not meant higher world growth rates so that productivity gains have largely been at the expense of employment causing the 'jobless growth' phenomenon. The productivity growth from new technologies has consequently been profoundly inegalitarian: the permanently displaced workers and unemployed suffer declining living standards; the re-trained multi-skilled worker often gains in greater job security and lower consumer costs; and the owners of capital, and their managers, take all the increases in productivity and output.

The danger in the present situation – and it is already a feature of current international conditions – is to push every country, and even the most dynamic firms embracing the new work processes, toward competitive austerity. Robert Boyer has captured well this dilemma:

> On the one hand, there is the opportunity to mitigate some of the worst features of fordism: less need for a hierarchy exercising authoritarian control, the possibility of doing away with tedious, dangerous, or purely repetitive jobs, opportunities of raising qualifications through general and adequate technical training. . . . But on the other hand not all companies or sectors are in a position to adopt this strategy: falling back on cheap, unskilled labour is a great temptation – and a very real danger, particularly as minimum wage levels are lowered. . . . Equally, it is not certain that computerization will undermine the historical division between manual labour and intellectual work. If some repetitive tasks can be abolished and others made potentially more varied and interesting, the rationalization and taylorization of intellectual work itself may occur.[25]

If the 'worst features of fordism' are to be avoided, then the question of unemployment must be directly confronted.

There have been few credible explanations of the post-crisis divergence in unemployment rates to be found in any of the explanations from either the demand or supply side. Numerous crossnational correlational studies seem to have conclusively demonstrated that there is no simple, uniform relationship between economic variables and the level of unemployment.[26] In general these studies have found various political variables, such as the extent of coporatism, the composition of the governing block, to be more telling. The conclusion drawn from the 'politics matter' studies is bold, and strikingly at odds with mainstream economic thinking: 'mass unemployment is unnecessary; full employment is a matter of (social democratic) political will.' This conclusion can be sustained, however, only at the most general level, in that some states have done better in *containing* the growth of mass unemployment, even while all states have been doing worse in employing their labour forces. It does point, however, in the direction of studying the particular history and economic institutions of national employment policies.

As Goran Therborn's book, *Why Some Peoples Are More Unemployed than Others*,[27] argues, the postwar national routes to employment success and unemployment disaster have been diverse. Some states, such as Sweden and Japan, have managed to perform relatively better in terms of unemployment, while other states, such as Britain, Canada, and the

Netherlands, have become high unemployment disasters. The allocation of unemployment within national labour forces, moreover, is distributed in strikingly different ways. Unemployment in Italy, for example, has tended to fall disproportionately on the young and women, whereas in Britain it has fallen more on males. Germans have withdrawn from the labour market with sharp declines in labour force participation (especially for older workers). The Swedes, in contrast, have expanded public employment and massively increased part-time work. North Americans have allowed the part-time, peripheral workforce to grow; at the same time average hours of work among core workers has increased. Although labour reserves appear as a fundamental feature of capitalist production within all these countries, and have grown in importance since the crisis, capitalist societies exhibit an extraordinary range of possibilities for the distribution of and paid work and social arrangements for containing unemployment.

Even in the narrow keynesianism of the neoclassical synthesis, there was an important rejection of some of the defences of pure market economies. Keynesian reasoning laid to rest the doctrine of Say's Law – a mainstay of neoclassical economics since the 19th century – that supply creates its own demand by generating the income to purchase the output produced making slumps, and labour surpluses, impossible. The keynesian revolution suggested that capitalist economies, and especially labour markets, are not self-adjusting to fluctuations in supply and demand: as a result of expectations about the future, market adjustments can move as easily away from 'full employment equilibrium' as toward it. This conclusion contained a broader implication, one little noted except within the marxian tradition: economic adjustment takes place in real *historical time* and under the constraint of existing *economic institutions*.

Michael Kalecki pointed out that there are essentially three ways to bolster effective demand for employment: deficit spending through higher public investment or subsidies to private consumption; stimulating private investment by lowering interest rates or tax concessions; and, finally, redistribution of income (and work) from higher to lower income classes. The policy path pursued over the postwar period has had important implications for the post-crisis capacity of national states to contain unemployment.

Keynesian policies relied extensively on fiscal policy (and partly monetary policy) attempting to stimulate private investment and much less on deficit spending, increasing consumptions or redistribution. This budgetary approach entailed keeping private sector growth rates as high as possible through ever greater cuts in corporate taxes, subsidies and tax incentives to keep investment levels increasing, and to offset the capital-using bias of technological change (given relatively constant hours of work and distributional shares). The economies of North America were the examples, par excellence, of this method of keeping employment high. As traded goods began to occupy an increased share of domestic production, the national economies which had adopted this strategy have had to engage in ever-increasing levels of competitive bargaining to attract or keep capital. The weak labour market and training structures developed over the postwar period added to the North American employment problem: skilled workers had either been 'poached' from Europe or left to the random individual decisions of the private sector; the rapid labour supply growth which had fed postwar 'extensive accumulation' now translated into the massive growth of low-waged job sectors; and workers with 'good jobs' in unionized firms were forced into concessions bargaining to keep capitalists in their communities and to hold off the swelling rolls of unemployed and low paid workers queuing up for the good jobs promised by the 'American way of life.'

Although deficit spending was never extensively engaged in for macroeconomic stabilisation, European states, more than North American ones, stimulated public investment, and expanded the size of their public sectors, using the investment as a platform for continual modernization of infrastructure and industry. But the end of the 'golden age' and the competitive pressures of more open economies also showed the limits of this strategy. To the extent the European statist strategy disengaged a larger proportion of annual output from the market economy, and to the extent it contributed to the maintenance of a labour process model using the most advanced techniques and work processes effectively involving workers, this method helped to stabilize employment fluctuations and to keep employment high.

But the 'eurosclerosis' disease of institutional rigidities in the labour market that served as the basis for containing unemployment became an obstacle with increased capital mobility: European capitalists took their investments to where wages and work standards were lower or where the rate of return was higher (as in the U.S.), effectively shutting down domestic accumulation. To try to keep investment at home and to hold market shares, European states also have been forced to hold back the public sector, to allow increased industrial rationalization and shedding of workers, and to raise interest rates. France's socialist reflation of the early 1980s, for example, had more successes than often given credit for in terms of avoiding the extensive downturn of the rest of the OECD area, and in rationalizing industry from nationalizations. But the keynesian reflation could not be sustained on its own against a world economy marching to the tune of restraint and capital mobility. The jobless rates in France, therefore, did not stay down once the reflation ended. The French socialists subsequently moved toward the neo-liberal approach of stimulating private investment, following the route adopted elsewhere, but had even less success in containing the drift toward persistent double-digit unemployment. As a result of these forces, mass unemployment has spread across the European states as well, notably in Germany, France, and Italy, which had adopted the public sector route to maintaining high employment. Along with North America, they too have pursued neo-liberal adjustment policies and export-oriented development at the end of the 1980s, allowing unemployment to rise (although still distributing it differently).

Kalecki's first two ways to full employment, deficit spending and stimulating private investment, appear to have reached their limits as a means to avoid competitive austerity. This leaves the third option to full employment of redistributing income, and, more particularly today, of redistributing work. Kalecki's third option of redistributing income was barely evident at all (and of work even less so) over the postwar period. The maintenance of private ownership of the means of production limited the possibilities for redistribution of income for it also would have sacrificed Keynes's famous 'animal spirits' inducement to invest. This was, as Leo Panitch has argued, one of the main failures of the income policies to constrain wage pressures that were a part of full employment economies: they attempted to freeze the distributional shares of income between the social classes and fell apart on the basis of that contradiction.[28]

Redistribution of income, was limited therefore, to countries that could build up solidaristic institutions within the labour market to redistribute wages to the lower paid, and that had the political capacity to drive up tax rates to provide a pool of funds to be redistributed through the welfare state. This situation was limited, for the most part, to Sweden. But even in this case, with the foremost political conditions for maintaining employment, the economic strategy still entailed the postwar fordist fixation of keeping growth rates as high as possible, to avoid disturbing the unequal class structure by promising workers a share of growing output, and rationalizing the industrial structure to maintain export markets. As the golden age growth slowed, the Swedish model, too, confronted difficulties in containing unemployment: the solidarity wages policy and tax loads both reached an impasse vis-a-vis workers initially and subsequently capitalists. Sweden, therefore, had to engage in a continual series of competitive devaluations to export its unemployment elsewhere, and to maintain the competitiveness of its export-driven economy. Sweden's active labour market policies also had to change emphasis by the end of the boom in the 1970s from aiding adjustment to directly supporting employment.

As the 'golden age' was ending, therefore, the Swedish model was under strain. The Meidner Plan to socialize capital in the late 1970s attempted to confront these difficulties directly by radically extending social ownership. But the labour movement was only able to advance the Plan in a most limited, and essentially irrelevant, way. The defeat of the Meidner effort to bring capital more firmly under democratic control prepared the basis for the reversals of the 1980s. Swedish capital began to break openly with the postwar compromise, attacking the welfare state, opposing further tax burdens (despite the enormous concentration of wealth), and actively internationalizing financial and productive capital. The increased capital mobility, at the same time the social democratic government sought to improve profits to maintain its export-oriented strategy, eventually raised a new limit on Swedish employment policy: it blocked Sweden's ability to use competitive devaluations to export its unemployment.

The maintenance of low unemployment through the 1980s consequently depended less on Sweden's progressive competitiveness strategy, as social democrats continue to try to argue, and more on *'shared austerity'* amongst the Swedish working class through the 'spreading of employment.' These policies have included the holding back on the rationalisation of plants, the extension of public sector employment, and reductions in the average hours worked per worker. Yet even *'shared austerity'* had reached its limits in the early 1990s. It could only be sustained as long as the labour market institutions built up over the postwar period had the ideological support for solidaristic wage and work policies amongst workers *and* Swedish capital was willing to allow a *national* bargain to share productivity gains. With the fall 1991 election of a bourgeois government neither condition still held. As a result, Swedish unemployment has rapidly shot up, more than doubling in a year, in the process destroying the illusions which have captivated social democrats around the world of an export-led progressive strategy for competitiveness.

The Swedish experience of 'shared austerity' contains two important lessons for socialist economic strategies. The first is that the employment impact of slower economic growth can be distributed in different ways, although they largely entail spreading employment across the working class. With limited or declining employment growth in the manufacturing sector, the spread of well-paid work depends upon workers as a whole paying more taxes, taking home less pay and working less. This has the positive benefits of increased leisure and better public services and environment, but less private consumption.

The second lesson is that it is difficult politically to sustain employment-spreading as long as it is limited to 'socialism in one class' or if capital is freed from having to make a national bargain. The social democratic left's response to the economic crisis throughout the 1980s has been that capital could not be attacked. Above all else, profits had to be improved for international competitiveness and thus to sustain employment and the welfare state. With the end of the Swedish experiment in 'shared austerity', this is no longer a plausible line of argument. This strategy has allowed capital to free itself from national controls and the traded sector to dominate domestic production needs. Not even Swedish social democracy has been able to withstand the vicious circle of competitive austerity. The global keynesianism or supranational regulation that might manage the world market has proven a deceptive political project and an elusive means of economic management. There is no intellectually honest response from the left to the economic crisis, particularly with respect to unemployment, that does not involve political restraint on the power of capital and a substantial redistribution of work and resources.

The impasse of capitalist employment policy is linked, based on the preceding analysis, to two broad factors: the crisis of Fordism and the end of keynesian employment policies on a national basis; and the growing contradiction between the openness of national economies in terms of trade and capital mobility and the lack of regulation, and the seeming impossibility of doing so under the present international regime, of the world market. The left's economic alternative must address both sides of the crisis. Two general principles seem central. First, the view now accepted amongst social democrats that the growth of unemployment is inevitable must be rejected: unemployment is the basis for the splitting of society into those who have paid work in core jobs and those excluded from either work or stable employment. The left's economic alternative must advance the principle that democratic citizenship proceeds from the right to work and the right to a decent income. Second, the political compromises at the international level necessary for long-term stability must be built around the principle of maximizing the capacity of different 'national collectivities' democratically to choose alternate development paths (socialist or capitalist), that do not impose externalities (such as environmental damage) on other countries, without suffering isolation and coercive sanction from the world economy.[29]

The implications of these principles is consistent with the analysis of employment policy that redistribution is central to addressing unemployment. An alternative model will have to entail a radical redistributional shift in terms of resources and new institutional structures: from the traded goods sector to the local and national economies; from the highest paid to the lowest paid; from those with too many hours of work to those with too few; from management dominated labour processes to worker controlled; and from private consumption-led production to ecologically-sustainable economies. A redistributional employment policy would contain some of the following components.

Inward Industrialization

It is difficult to envision either stable macroeconomic conditions or alternate development paths with continued internationalisation of production. The export-oriented strategies which have spurred competitive austerity will have to be replaced, therefore, by a process of inward industrialization. The inward-oriented strategy does not imply closing the economy from trade, but rather a planned expansion of domestic services and production to expand employment and increased control over the international economy to reinforce stable and divergent national macroeconomic conditions.

International trade will obviously remain important to reach certain economies of scale and to transfer new products and processes. But international trade and financial rules need to be restructured so as to allow for diversity of economic models rather than the homogeneity of 'competitive austerity' now demanded by IMF adjustment procedures. Inevitably this points to managed trade between national economies and reforming international institutions to impose symmetrical adjustment on deficit and surplus countries. Confronting present imbalances, for example, will require debt relief for the countries of the South and Eastern Europe so they can shift to meeting domestic consumption needs and expand trade within their zones.

Protectionism will also have to be allowed. It has proven impossible for surplus countries to inflate enough, or deficit countries to deflate enough, to restore balance (without further devastating job losses). Social tariffs are important to allow countries to adopt advanced environmental and work standards without loss of jobs and international sanction from 'worst-practice' production methods.

The corollary to diversity of development paths is the re-integration of national economies. The expansion of employment will depend, most notably, upon the redevelopment of urban economies and the fostering of a self-managed sector for community welfare and collective leisure.[30] Similarly, the limitations of market instability on employment will require the extension of national and sectoral planning structures to encourage future core industries, control the open sector and establish sustainable production. Inward industrialization will mean, therefore, production and services more *centred* on local and national needs where the most legitimate democratic collectivities reside.

Democratic Workplaces

A part of the economic crisis lies on the supply-side in the impasse of the Fordist labour process and the transition to flexible automation. Under the pressures of competitive austerity it is the 'worst features of Fordism' – speed-up, continued fragmentation of work, increased supervision of workers – which is going ahead. Even if there are productivity gains to be had by increased worker input into production, the political risk this entails for capital in terms of worker self-management has meant opposition. Capital will prefer to continue with Taylorism or negotiate involvement with the fewest workers possible. As the basis for the wage bargain, such a labour process will contribute to the polarisation of the labour market. An alternative model will, therefore, have to transform work relations. The left's project here has been longstanding: the collective negotiation over the terms of involvement in the labour process and an end of taylorism. This will, of course, imply negotiation over training and skills, but also move to incorporate product design and quality and even sectoral planning over what to produce.

Redistribution of Work

The crisis of Fordism has not only lowered the rate of productivity increases, it has also concentrated these gains in the hands of capital. It is fundamental to an alternative economic model to redistribute existing output more justly and to share-out further productivity gains equally. There are two important parameters to this principle to be accounted for. A just distribution of output requires that the unemployed be incorporated into the waged economy. As well, if sustainable production is a constraint, then increased production through working just as many hours is not a priority. Instead, existing work and future productivity gains would have to be shared so as to employ the jobless at decent incomes and increase free time as a central social objective. The employment crisis can only be resolved by directly confronting the redistribution of work-hours and income.[31] The social democratic embrace of keynesianism, and now progressive competitiveness, always sought solutions to unemployment and class divisions through faster growth and more output. This must now be firmly rejected as both unviable and undesirable.

As an economic system, capitalism rationalises social life for economic ends. This includes, as a fundamental element, the extension of worktime to lower costs. But the drive to continual technological change from competition also reduces the number of hours of work required to produce a given level of output. Thus, as an economic system, capitalism tends to produce long hours of work for some and a lack of hours, or unemployment, for others. The labour movement has consistently had to apply its alternate logic on this system to free time for leisure and ensure that work is solidaristically shared. Some of the dimensions of redistributing work are, although politically difficult, straightforward: overtime limits, restrictions on 'double-dipping' by professionals, extension of vacations, flexible work-scheduling, increased possibilities for unpaid leave, yearly education and training days, and collective negotiation by worksite of jobsharing to spread existing work. The major dimension for dealing with unemployment is, however, a reduction of standard worktime that is sharp and general. To be at all effective in dealing with current unemployment levels, it must be faced that the hours reduction will have to be accompanied by a decline in real wages (partially offset by productivity gains and a decline in unemployment claims) so as to redistribute both work and income. It is precisely because wages will have to shift in the short-run that worktime reduction must be solidaristic: apply equally to the public and private sectors and squeeze wage differentials so as to preserve the purchasing power of the lowest paid. As unemployment declines, productivity gains can then be shared-out in both increased purchasing power and declines in worktime. The struggle over the redistribution of work and income must become central to employment policy if the unemployment crisis is to be addressed.

Employment Planning

The components of an alternate employment policy have in common the need for economic planning to constrain the market. Capitalist employment policies have typically left employment planning to the aggregate assessment of labour market trends and the targeting of training. The local component of employment planning has been labour exchanges which served as labour market intelligence networks and a location for job listings and counselling. Even the Swedish labour market boards never developed a local planning capacity or direct democratic accountability to the communities they served. Indeed, they have never been able to fully move beyond their adjustment role for competitiveness allocated to them under the Swedish model. An alternative employment policy will have to develop local democratic administrative capacities for both the technical and political basis to address the redistribution of work.

Democratic employment planning has a number of dimensions. The 'golden age' simply ignored environmental issues, but it seems clear that an alternate model must have this as a binding constraint on production. This will have to be encompassed within employment planning for sustainable production will entail 'dirty' industries of declining jobs, the distributional consequences of slower growth, and the planning for new employment in non-resource intensive services. With the dramatic lowering of the amount of labour employed in the manufacturing sector, employment planning will have a large component directed at the service sector. This should radically centre our attention on the type of service sector that should be supported in terms of jobs and organizational structure. In particular, employment should be developed in the so-called 'third sector', that is, the self-managed community services (either newly formed or partly devolved from traditional state administration) such as cultural production, environmental clean-up, education and leisure. In order to absorb the unemployed, these activities will have to be planned. Locally elected labour market boards – which would govern over all work-related issues – should have as part of their mandate the determination of socially-useful activities and the planning for local employment.

The present political situation of competitive austerity does not lend itself to an alternate economic policy. It cannot proceed simply on the basis of economic necessity. The basis for an alternate social project must be found on the political grounds of social justice and the extension of democracy as a substantial redistribution of resources and power lies at the heart of any real solution to the contemporary unemployment crisis.

4. Mass Unemployment and National Economic Policy

It would be rash to be optimistic on the future of the labour market and unemployment in the advanced capitalist zone. The constraints of the international order on national employment policy are severe. The pressures produced by open economies, with extensive capital mobility and global labour surpluses, have gutted the capacity of national governments to regulate employment levels through the type of aggregate measures which were part of postwar keynesianism.

Many keynesians concede that the increased openness of economies and the internationalization of production has shifted the economic terrain. 'Keynesianism in one country' is no longer seen as viable as demand stimulation on a national basis is simply dissipated through either imports or capital outflows. Reflation will, therefore, have to take place on a supranational basis. This view has been argued by many advocates of economic integration associated with international economic institutes and a significant section of the social democratic movement. They seek to either co-ordinate a worldwide reflation or to recreate a viable economic space so that stimulation is not lost through leakages.[32] Yet even if the two premises of this view are granted – the combination of unused capacity and economic openness – its viability is deeply suspect. There are no substantive mechanisms for co-ordination or instruments for reflation at the international level; nor is the political means by which they could be implemented apparent, given the competition which still exists between capitalist nations and the spatial specificity of production structures. It is quite unclear, therefore, what it means to reduce unused capacity (and unemployment) at the international level, as this includes the vastly different national production structures and unemployment experiences of, for examples, Japan, Canada and Britain. Does global stimulation increase the exports of – and consequently reduce their unemployment – the industrial belts of Japan or the Atlantic provinces of Canada? In any respect, this solution returns to the myopic social democracy of the postwar period of attempting to resolve the capitalist unemployment problem through higher growth, with the distribution and production questions being ignored and the environmental one ultimately being damned.

Much of the social democratic movement has consequently drifted to sub-national levels of government, or specific industrial sectors, where some level of industrial capacity exists, and developed the 'progressive competitiveness model' as an alternative to neo-liberalism and keynesian reflation. Training policy has become the centrepiece of this strategy:

employment will result from highly skilled workers improving the competitiveness of high value-added firms selling on the world market. But this export-oriented strategy, too, has become incorporated in the pressures producing competitive austerity throughout the world economy and converged with neo-liberalism. Its advocates must confront the harsh fact that it is not the Anglo-American countries who are converting to the Swedish or German models, but Germany and Sweden who are integrating the 'Anglo-American model' of income and work polarisation. Toyota is laying-off and breaking life-time employment guarantees, the Volvo plant in Kalmar is closing and the postfordist future of full employment in high value-added export-oriented firms now looks like one of the most pot-holed detours taken by the left in the 1980s.

As the golden age of capitalism was at its end in the 1970s, Joan Robinson, the foremost analyst of postwar employment policy, made the following bitter observation on the keynesian experience: 'Growth of wealth has not after all removed poverty at home, and 'aid' has not reduced it abroad. Now unemployment exacerbates social problems and embitters politics. In this situation, the cry is to get growth started again.'[33] Two decades later, with a persistent lengthening of the unemployment queues, the supply-side 'cry to get growth started again' is even more pitched. But now there is clearly even less reason to believe, and ecological and redistributive reasons actively to oppose, the supply-sider's proposition that better microeconomic performance leading to faster economic growth is capable of resolving the capitalist unemployment problem. Upon surveying the wreckage produced by these views there is, indeed, good reason to adopt Robinson's dismay.

Yet there is as well, on this point, a lesson still to be absorbed from Keynes on national economic policy:

> . . . if nations can learn to provide themselves with full employment by their domestic policy (and, we must add, if they can also attain equilibrium in the trend of their population), there need be no important economic forces calculated to set the interest of one country against that of its neighbours. There would still be room for the international division of labour and for international lending in appropriate conditions. But there would no longer be a pressing motive why one country need force its wares on another or repulse the offerings of its neighbours, not because this was necessary to enable it to pay for what it wished to purchase, but with the express object of upsetting the equilibrium of payments so as to develop a balance of trade in its own favour. International trade would cease to be what it is, namely, a desperate expedient to maintain employment at home by forcing sales on foreign markets and restricting purchases, which, if successful, will merely shift the problem of unemployment to the neighbour which is worsted in the struggle, but a willing and unimpeded exchange of goods and services in conditions of mutual advantage.[34]

Keynes's position still seems to be essentially correct. It strikes at the core of the present impasse of capitalist employment policy, where the demands for rationalization of all aspects of economic and social life for international competitiveness, so as to dump unemployment on other regions and countries, have become incessant. But for an employment

GREGORY ALBO   169

policy to move beyond competitive austerity today, however, will require a much bolder political, economic and ecological project than Keynes himself was ever capable of envisioning.

NOTES

1. J.M. Keynes, *The General Theory of Employment, Interest and Money* (London: Macmillan 1936), 381.
2. See: B. Rowthorn and A. Glyn, 'The Diversity of Unemployment Experience since 1973', in S. Marglin and J.Schor, eds., *The Golden Age of Capitalism* (Oxford: Clarendon 1990).
3. See: F. Burchardt, et al., *The Economics of Full Employment* (Oxford: Basil Blackwell 1944); D. Worswick, 'Jobs for All?' *The Economic Journal*, 95 (March 1985); and R. Solow, 'Unemployment: Getting the Questions Right', *Economica*, 53: supp. (1986).
4. Keynes, *General Theory* 33–4.
5. See: M. Friedman, 'The Role of Monetary Policy', *American Economic Review*, 58 (March 1968); and M. Bruno and J. Sachs, *The Economics of Worldwide Stagnation* (Oxford: Oxford University Press 1985).
6. J. Schumpeter, *Business Cycles, Vol. 2* (New York: McGraw-Hill 1939), 515. Also see: OECD, *Employment Growth and Structural Change* (Paris: OECD 1985).
7. (New York: Monthly Review Press 1974.)
8. (New York: Basic Books 1984.)
9. On the different factors shaping the skilling process see: S. Wood, ed. *The Degradation of Work* (London: Hutchinson 1982); E. Batstone, et al., *New Technology and the Process of Labour Regulation* (Oxford: Clarendon 1987), Ch. 1; and R. Allen, 'The Impact of Technical Change on Employment, Wages and the Distribution of Skills: A Historical Perspective', in C. Riddell, ed., *Adjusting to Change: Labour Market Adjustment in Canada* (Toronto: University of Toronto Press 1986). Especially fascinating on this issue, in relation to economic performance, is: T. Nichols, *The British Worker Question* (London: Routledge 1986).
10. R. Hyman and W. Streeck, eds., *New Technology and Industrial Relations* (Oxford: Basil Blackwell 1988); A. Sorge and M. Warner, *Comparative Factory Organization* (London: Gower 1986); and M. Maurice, F. Sellier and J. Silvestre, *The Social Foundations of Industrial Power* (Cambridge: MIT Press 1986).
11. 'The Transition to Flexible Specialization in the U.S. Film Industry', *Cambridge Journal of Economics*, 13:2 (1989), 197.
12. RI1For surveys see: A. Ziderman, *Manpower Training: Theory and Policy* (London: Macmillan 1978); M. Blaug, 'The Empirical Status of Human Capital Theory: A Slightly Jaundiced Survey', *Journal of Economic Literature*, 14 (1976); and D. Gordon, *Theories of Poverty and Underemployment* (Lexington: D.C. Heath 1972). It should be noted that human capital theory, in its early or more recent variations, is more concerned with market-based financing of training than with the dynamic relationship between skills and production. Entrepreneurs are responsible for innovations. But new developments in neoclassical economics are beginning to raise some similar concerns. See: F. Green, 'Neoclassical and Marxian Conceptions of Production', *Cambridge Journal of Economics*, 12:3 (1988).
13. 'Investment in Human Capital', *American Economic Review*, 51 (1961), 3.
14. See: A. Lindbeck and D. Snower, *The Insider-Outsider Theory of Employment and Unemployment* (Cambridge: MIT Press 1988).
15. See: *Theories of Poverty*, 92–4 and 122–4; and G. Cain, 'The Challenge of Dual and Radical Labour Market Theories to Orthodox Theory', *Journal of Economic Literature* 14 (1976).
16. Ziderman, *Manpower Training*, 34–9; and J. Davies, 'Training and Skill Development', in Riddell, ed., *Adapting to Change*. The problem may also be stated as follows: the contradiction between the generality of a particular skill in terms of its training content (potential transferability) and the generality of the investment (potential mobility of the trainee).

17. *Human Capital* (New York: National Bureau of Economic Research 1964).
18. The theoretical points in contention can be seen in: Ziderman, *Manpower Training*, 48–54; Davies, 'Training', 182–4; and W. Streeck, 'Skills and the Limits of Neo-Liberalism: The Enterprise of the Future as a Place of Learning', *Work, Employment and Society*, 3:1 (1989), 92–7.
19. Streeck, 'Skills and the Limits of Neo-Liberalism', 94.
20. Streeck's case is most directly presented in his 'Neo-Liberalism and Skills'. Also see: P. Senker, 'Technical Change, Work Organization and Training', *New Technology, Work and Employment*, 4:1 (1989).
21. *Ibid.*, 96–9.
22. Although differing in their assessment of flexible automation, several authors note the new skills profiles: R. Kaplinsky, 'Industrial Restructuring: Some Questions for Education and Training', *IDS Bulletin*, 20:1 (1989); A. Phillimore, 'Flexible Specialisation, Work Organization and Skills', *New Technology, Work and Employment*, 4:2 (1989); and P. Mehaut, 'New Firms' Training Policies and Changes in the Wage-Earning Relationship', *Labour and Society*, 13:4 (1988).
23. Sorge and Warner, *Comparative Factory*, 173–80; and C. Lane, 'Industrial Change in Europe: The Pursuit of Flexible Specialization in Britain and West Germany', *Employment, Work and Society*, 2:2 (1988).
24. *Empowering Workers in the Global Economy: A Labour Agenda for the 1990s* (Toronto: United Steelworkers of America 1991), 16–7 and 26.
25. R. Boyer, *The Search for Labour Market Flexibility* (Oxford: Clarendon Press 1988), 260. This choice has been discussed with respect to Canadian trade unions in: G. Albo, 'The "New Realism" and Canadian Workers', in A. Gagnon and J. Bickerton, eds., *Canadian Politics* (Peterborough: Broadview Press 1990).
26. See especially: M. Schmidt, 'The Politics of Unemployment', *West European Politics*, 7:3 (1984); G. Therborn, *Why Some Peoples Are More Unemployed Than Others* (London: Verso 1986); and F. Scharpf, *Crisis and Choice in European Social Democracy* (Ithaca: Cornell University 1991).
27. (London: Verso 1986.)
28. See Panitch's *Working Class Politics in Crisis* (London: Verso 1986).
29. This view has been developed in: M. Bienefeld, 'The International Context for National Development Strategies: Constraints and Opportunities in a Changing World Economy', in M. Bienefeld and M. Godfrey, eds., *The Struggle for Development: National Strategies in an International Context* (London: John Wiley & Sons 1982); and A. Lipietz, *Towards a New Economic Order* (New York: Oxford University Press 1992).
30. The problem of planning employment is linked to the reformation of the left's position on state administration. For a recent effort to do so see: G. Albo, D. Langille and L. Panitch, eds., *A Different Kind of State? Popular Power and Democratic Administration* (Toronto: Oxford University Press 1993).
31. The diversity of employment experiences through the 1980s has also amply illustrated that the labour supply must be considered as at least a medium term policy target. That is, countries have handled quite differently the size and composition of the labour supply in terms of access to paid, full-time work. As we confront the crisis of work, this needs to be brought more clearly into democratic deliberation, in terms of paid work as a right of citizenship for all ages, and the extent to which the national market should be open to labour flows, before the worst aspects of sexism, ageism, and xenophobia develop.
32. See: K. Coates and M. Barratt-Brown, eds., *A European Recovery Programme* (Nottingham: Spokesman 1993); M. Webb, 'International Economic Structures, Government Interests, and International Coordination of Macroeconomic Adjustment Policies', *International Organization*, 45 (1991); S. Holland, *Out of Crisis: A Project for European Recovery* (London: Spokesman 1983); J. Williamson, 'Global Macroeconomic Strategy', in Institute for International Economics, *Promoting World Recovery* (Washington: Institute for International Economics 1982); and F. Scharpf, *Crisis and Choice in European Social Democracy* (Ithaca: Cornell University Press 1991), 259–69.
33. *What are the Questions? And Other Essays* (Armonk: M.E. Sharpe 1980), 30.
34. *The General Theory*, 382–3.

GLOBALISM, SOCIALISM AND DEMOCRACY IN THE SOUTH AFRICAN TRANSITION

John S. Saul

"Democracy and the market": the ideology of the new globalism. Now, for better or worse, this phrase also epitomises a great deal of the currently dominant political discourse in South Africa as that country prepares for its first non-racial election on April 27th–29th 1994. For better? Obviously, we must celebrate the resonance of a moment that will mark – if all goes well – the removal of the last vestiges of the most resolutely institutionalised racist system in the world and the entry into office of Nelson Mandela and the African National Congress (ANC). But – for worse? – there does seem to be something all too anti-climatic about what is now likely to emerge from the current "transition to democracy" in South Africa, even assuming a reasonably clear passage to consolidation of a majority-elected government. Certainly, on the left (both inside that country and abroad), rather more was expected from the dramatic mobilisation of popular energies that, during the 1970s and 80s, came to stalemate the activities of the apartheid state and to pave the way for "negotiations". Recall Magdoff and Sweezy's confident assertion, less than a decade ago, that South Africa's

> system of racial segregation and repression is a veritable paradigm of capitalist superexploitation. It has a white monopoly capitalist ruling class and an advanced black proletariat. It is so far the only country with a well developed, modern capitalist structure which is not only objectively ripe for revolution but has actually entered a stage of overt and seemingly irreversible struggle.[1]

Or the formulation, of somewhat earlier vintage, of so astute an observer as Michael Burowoy who wrote that "by virtue of its history of struggles, its powerful state, its developed forces of production, the immiseration of its proletariat, the increasing insecurity of its white intermediate classes, and the merging of race and class, South Africa has become the arena of the prototypical Marxist revolution".[2] How romantic such expectations now sound.

There are, of course, those who will be quick to say "I told you so", leftists of various persuasion who have been, all along, suspicious of the ANC's own particular brew of petty-bourgeois African nationalism and quasi-Stalinist leftism. But more often than not such critics' points have been scored from abstract and rhetorical positions so far removed from the likelihood of being exposed to any "reality check" of their own as to be almost entirely unenlightening. Not that criticisms of the ANC are necessarily out of order. But if the real lessons of the current transition in South Africa are to be learned, any such criticisms cannot merely be extrapolated, with doubtful relevance, from some pristine set of revolutionary first principles. They must, instead, be grounded with reference to the real complexities of the situation – complexities dictated by the apparent imperatives of both global capitalism and the country's internal structure of power[3] – that have challenged the popular movement there. More generally, the difficulties of the ANC in sustaining an on-going transformation of South Africa actually evoke dangers and dilemmas that confront the left the world over. What alone distinguishes South Africa, perhaps, is that certain of these "dangers and dilemmas" are etched there all the more vividly against the backdrop of the high hopes that until so recently prevailed.

The present essay can say, concretely, only a limited amount about the details of the current election-centred transition itself, a transition which is still very much in train as this is being written (in February, 1994) and whose immediate implications will, in any case, be that much clearer to the reader by the time (after April) that this essay is finally published. Nor will it attempt a blow-by-blow account of the process of negotiations which, since Nelson Mandela's release from prison in February 1990, has prepared the ground for the forthcoming elections and set the stage for their immediate political aftermath. What it can seek to do, however, is to situate both these negotiations and the electoral process itself more firmly with reference to broader issues, in particular those embedded in the couplet "democracy and the market", invoked above. What, we should ask, is "democracy" actually likely to mean in the present South African context? Will the current situation draw to the fore the more empowering connotations of democratic practice, or its less empowering ones? What is both possible and "realistic" in this respect? And what of "market forces", world-wide and local, the centrality of which is now so crucial a premise in the ANC's thinking about the economy? How much space can be granted the free play of such market forces before the new government (or, more broadly, the popular movement itself) forfeits any real prospect of dealing with South Africa's vast social inequalities and pervasive discrepancies of economic power in a productive and "progressive" manner? And – a closely related query – what meaning, if any, can one hope to see attached to the notion of "socialism" in an emergent, post-apartheid South Africa?

To attempt to ground these difficult questions entirely adequately in South African realities would also stretch the limits of the present essay, of course. Perhaps it will be enough to demonstrate that such questions are those that many South Africans continue to ask themselves as they reflect on the profoundly contradictory nature of the transition that is unfolding in their country. There is, in any case, a second dimension to our discussion that is of even more general relevance. It concerns the notion with which we began this essay: "the ideology of the new globalism". In keeping alive a debate about transformation in their country, those South Africans who are now doing so also find themselves forced to face down a particular "tyranny of concepts" – regarding "democracy", regarding "socialism" – quite specific to the current global conjuncture. In accompanying their efforts, therefore, we can also learn something about the challenges – conceptual, practical – that confront us all.

I. To Craft Democracy: Delimiting the Transition Agenda

We will return to the question of "socialism". Can we not at least hail, quite unequivocally, the coming of democracy to South Africa? It would be difficult not to answer in the affirmative – but there are issues to be dealt with nonetheless. Certainly the process that is drawing South Africa towards elections remains a fragile one. Moreover, there is some question as to what meaning can be attached to this process even if it should prove to be successful in its own terms. Here much will depend on what, more generally, we take "democracy" to mean. This is not an innocent undertaking: the fact is that no word in the political lexicon is so ideologically charged as "democracy" has become. To understand fully the import of the South African case we must unpack this concept, and also take note of the considerable struggle that now, in the post-Cold War world, centres on attempts to assert ownership of it. At the same time, the very complexities of what is happening in South Africa provide a privileged opportunity for exploring issues – about "democracy", about "socialism" – that are of crucial importance to the redefinition of the left's project more globally defined.

Of course "democracy" has been placed on the agenda not by theorists, but by peoples: in Eastern Europe, in Latin America, in the Far East, in Africa. What is only slightly less remarkable, however, is the speed with which liberal and right-of-centre intellectuals (especially in the United States) have seized upon this world-wide popular initiative, seeking not only to turn "democratization" into an academic growth industry (the new *Journal of Democracy* is an important site for this activity) but also to direct, even domesticate, the process – precisely by taming and tailoring the concept itself. What we are witnessing, in essence, is a recycling of "modernization theory", that earlier attempt to make the American political system – or, rather, an heroic abstraction of it – a model for the world. "In fact", it is stated, "liberal democracies today are widely regarded as 'the only truly and fully modern societies'".[4] Startling, too, in this respect is the fact that many once familiar figures from the nether-world of American political science have resurfaced astride the current "global resurgence of democracy" – Samuel Huntington for example, and, *mirabile dictu*, the likes of Almond and Verba. Take, for example, the deployment of the hoary old ideas of the latter by Larry Diamond, a more youthful but already quite ubiquitous theorist of "democracy's third wave":

> Perhaps the basic tension in democracy is between conflict and consensus. Democracy implies dissent and division, but on the basis of consent and cohesion. It requires that the citizens assert themselves, but also that they accept the government's authority. *It demands that citizens care about politics, but not too much.* This is why Gabriel Almond and Sidney Verba, in their classic book *The Civic Culture*, call the democratic political culture "mixed". It balances the citizen's role as participant (as agent of political competition and conflict) with his or her role as subject (obeyer of state authority) and as "parochial" member of family, social and community networks outside politics. *The subject role serves governability while the parochial role tempers political conflict by limiting the politicization of social life.* (emphasis added)[5]

Much of the flavour of the current democratisation industry is captured in this passage. Central to the exercise is a reining in of the claims of democracy. But note that this self-conscious narrowing of the definition of global democratic possibility is consistent with emphases long current within mainstream (especially American) democratic theory. As Philip Green has argued extensively, such theorising has come to collapse the notion of democracy into that of "liberal democracy", the specific type of "democracy" familiar in the West. This system, defined by its theorists variously as "pluralism" and "polyarchy" and "democratic elitism" but labelled "pseudodemocracy" by Green, he describes as "representative government, ultimately accountable to 'the people' but not really under their control, combined with a fundamentally capitalist economy."[6] As he adds, this kind of democracy is "preferable to most of the immediately available alternative ways of life of the contemporary nation-state. But it is not democracy; not really."

To this limited version of democracy Green does juxtapose another "hidden" or "popular" face of democracy. For it is "the popular masses, not elites, who set the democratic agenda":

> We would do better, at least initially, to understand this hidden face of democracy as a series of moments: moments of popular insurgency and direct action, of unmediated politics. . . . We would do better to conceive of the real history of democracy as the history of popular struggle, in which the people learn, as Rosa Luxemburg put it, how to govern themselves. . . . To argue that only formal elections eventuate in representation is simply to argue by definition or to assume what has to be painstakingly proved. In this way the "democratic elitist" tends to make elections into virtually absolute trumps – the only legitimate method for ascertaining the will of the only definable cast of characters known as "the people". But then the "necessary condition" becomes the enemy of all attempts to eliminate injustices that are intrinsic to it; the good becomes the enemy of the better.[7]

"The great moments of the creative process", Green concludes, "are not parliamentary sittings or elections but strikes, demonstrations, marches, occupations, even funerals" and he proceeds to specify some of the ways in which the "direct expression" of "demands for equal rights" might possibly burst through the constraints of polyarchy. Moreover, it is in just this spirit that the noted Tanzanian writer and activist Issa Shivji has himself distinguished "liberal democracy" (as "part of the ideology of domination") from "popular democracy" – seen to be "an ideology of resistance and struggle".[8]

What these writers are grasping for is a definition of democracy geared to facilitating and/or expressing a wide-spread mobilisation of the hitherto powerless against the structures of their socio-economic subordination. Of course, identifying the programmatic substance of such a project (socialism?) in the face of the kind of difficult-to-discipline global capitalism that is presently so dominant is no easy task; we will have to discuss this issue more directly below (section III). It is also the case that the practical, day-to-day modalities of such a politics are much easier to conceptualise in an insurrectionary phase (South Africa, 1984–6, for example[9]) than in a situation of more "normalized" politics – when finding ways of consolidating the practice of "popular democracy" against the pull of routinisation dictates a search for entry points for struggle within relatively stable institutions. Still, the fact that the dominant voices seeking to frame the discourse about democracy in the current global conjuncture are not those of the Greens and the Shivjis does help render such a search that much more difficult to imagine. As a result, "what is missing" (in Anderson's pungent epitomisation of contemporary democratic thought) "is any conception of the state as a structure of collective self-expression deeper than the electoral systems of today. Democracy is indeed now more widespread than ever before. But it is also thinner – as if the more universally available it becomes, the less active meaning it retains."[10]

It will come as no surprise then that the bulk of the current literature on "the transition to democracy" is very far from allowing any notion of "popular democracy" to cast the claims for democracy in the Third World expansively. In fact this literature seeks, by and large, to define the terms of any such transition ever more narrowly. A classic instance is the much cited work of Giuseppe Di Palma in which he emphasises the importance to the "crafting" of democracies – defined as the "setting up [of] government in diversity as a way of defusing conflict" – of accepting certain stern limitations upon such efforts. As he argues, "one factor that reconciles to democracy reluctant political actors tied to the previous regime is that in the inaugural phase coexistence usually takes precedence over any radical social and economic programs".

Such precedence [Di Palma continues] stems from understanding the limits of democratic (and other politics) as natural harbingers of material progress. It stems as well from a fuller appreciation that wilfully using democracy as a Jacobin tool of progress not only is ingenuous but may also raise intolerable political risks; namely, authoritarian backlashes and, in anticipation, escalation into a virtuous "guided" democracy. Past democracies – the most instructive example from the 1930s being the second Spanish republic – have foundered on such Jacobin instincts. By giving reform precedence over coexistence and making support for reform the test of legitimacy, they have unintentionally fulfilled a prophecy: the losers would be unwilling to reconcile themselves to a nascent democracy. The example looms large among political practitioners in Europe and Latin America. Indeed, the importance of coexistence has not gone unnoticed, despite its significant policy sacrifices, by those who still sympathise ideally with a more Jacobin democracy.

There is some bluff "good sense" in this, of course. A preoccupation with the way in which a would-be democratic society develops norms of tolerance and due process is not an irrelevant one. Yet how easy it is for such an approach to emphasise this issue at the expense of any real concern about socio-economic outcomes, how easy for it to underwrite, conservatively, a tendency to "blame the (wilfully unrealistic) victims" rather than their oppressors for any transitions that fail. Di Palma, for example, is quick to identify "mobilisational models for the Third World" based on *dependencia* paradigms and undue popular suspicion regarding the role played by the "advanced industrial democracies" in the "global economic order" as representing a particularly clear danger to "democratic crafting". Not surprising, then, his comfortable conclusion that, currently, "democracy's *disengagement from the idea of social progress* [is] a silver lining because it has actually given democracy more realistic, more sturdily conscious grounds for claiming superiority in the eyes of public opinion and political practitioners" (emphasis added).[11]

To be sure, there is amongst such theorists some concern about the fact that, in Larry Diamond's words, "democracy cannot endure if massive inequality and exclusion go unchallenged". Moreover, "getting reform on the agenda requires that the disadvantaged and excluded economic groups organize and mobilize politically." Nonetheless, Diamond warns,

. . . if reform is to be adopted without provoking a crisis that might destroy democracy, the costs to privileged economic interests of overturning democracy must be kept greater than the costs of the reforms themselves. This requires realism and incrementalism on the part of those groups pressing for reform. It also requires sufficient overall effectiveness, stability and guarantees for capital on the part of the democratic regime so that privileged economic actors will have a lot to lose.[12]

Moreover, this concern for the sensibilities of capital, phrased here, commonsensically enough, in tactical terms, is merely one dimension of a much more fundamental conceptual slide – expressed in its most unabashed form in Diamond's influential work, but present in the bulk of this transition literature – from "democracy" *through* "liberal democracy" to (Diamond's own phrase) "liberal capitalist democracy". Fortunately, he writes, "the past four decades of Third World economic development have furnished invaluable lessons for distinguishing the policies that work from those that do not. Broadly speaking, market-oriented economies develop while state-socialist economies fall behind. Internationally open and competitive economies work; closed (or at least rigidly and persistently closed) economies do not. Economies grow when they foster savings, investment and innovation and when they reward individual effort and initiative. Economies stagnate and regress when bloated, mercantilist, hyperinterventionist states build a structure of inflexible favouritisms for different groups, curtailing change, experimentation, competition, innovation and social mobility."[13] This, then, is the loaded way in which Diamond and his colleagues lay the foundations of the case for their brand of "democracy".

Small wonder, then, that for Diamond the effort to create "a balanced [democratic] political culture – in which people care about politics but not too much" requires, "in Eastern Europe and much of the developing world, restraining the partisan battle [by] deflating the state and invigorating the private economy"! And beyond that – once again, at the conclusion of his text, we have the invocation of polyarchy and of "democratic elitism" – there lies the crucial role of "political elites" and of the pacts they create amongst themselves: "[E]lite actions, choices and postures can have a formative impact in shaping the way their followers approach political discourse and conflict. Opposing party leaders must take a lead in crafting understandings and working relationships that bridge historic differences, restrain expectations and establish longer, more realistic time horizons for their agendas. . . . [C]ompeting party elites must set an accommodating and civil tone for political life."[14]

We do well to be on our intellectual guard, then, as regards the "global resurgence" of democratic theory. Much of it carries a very conservative political charge. But it is not just conservatives who introduce narrowing perspectives into their vision of what a transition to democracy must imply in most contemporary settings. Take the analysis by Adam Przeworski of those transitions that involve the "extrication" (his term) of democracy from authoritarian regimes in which "political forces that control the apparatus of repression, most often the armed forces" remain strongly positioned. Under such circumstances, he argues, protagonists will agree (if it proves possible for them to agree at all) "to terminate conflicts over institutions because they fear that a continuation of conflict may lead to a civil war that will be both collectively and individually threatening. The pressure to stabilize the situation is tremendous, since governance must somehow continue. *Chaos is the worst alternative for all*" (emphasis added).[15]

This does suggest a limiting condition certainly and, since it is one that will prove most germane to the discussion of the current transition in South Africa, we will have to return to it. But there is more to Przeworski's argument. He seeks to remind his readers of other limitations on the transition by taking note, in terms that the Di Palmas and the Diamonds would be less inclined to use, of "the traditional dilemma of the Left": "that even a procedurally perfect democracy may remain an oligarchy: the rule of the rich over the poor. As historical experience demonstrates, democracy is compatible with misery and inequality in the social realm and with oppression in factories, schools, prisons, and families."[16] As for the Right its "traditional dilemma" has been "that democracy may turn out to be the rule of the many who are poor over the few rich"! Small wonder, he continues, that, in seeking to reconcile such polar opposites, "democracy has been historically a fragile form of organizing political conflicts".

The implication? "[A] stable democracy requires that governments be strong enough to govern effectively but weak enough not to be able to govern against important interests. . . . [D]emocratic institutions must remain within narrow limits to be successful."[17] Under such circumstances, Przeworski concludes, the best case scenario for the transition is one in which "Reformers" within the erstwhile power structure distance themselves from their own "Hardliners" and agree to negotiate a form of democratic outcome with "Moderates" within the democratic camp – those who, in turn, are prepared to distance themselves from the "Radicals" who occupy a position further over on the ideological spectrum. A Left bending over backwards to avoid chaos; a Left propitiating the powers-that-be; a Left that is nothing if not "prudent": such, then, is the shrunken vision of the transition to democracy that the realism of the epoch, advanced by both Right and Left, would seek to fashion for us.

II. Negotiations, "Elite-Pacting", Democracy: The South African Case

In many respects the current transition to democracy in South Africa would seem to fit, quite neatly, Przeworski's model. As Joe Slovo – senior ANC and South African Communist Party leader and an active player, both as participant and theorist, in the negotiations process that has unfolded in South Africa since Mandela's release – put the point in a celebrated 1992 intervention:

> The *starting point* for developing a framework within which to approach some larger questions in the negotiating process is to answer the question: *why are we negotiating?* We are negotiating because towards the end of the 80s we concluded that, as a result of its escalating crisis, the apartheid power bloc was no longer able to continue ruling in the old way and was genuinely seeking some break with the past. At the same time, we were clearly *not dealing with a defeated enemy* and an early revolutionary seizure of power by the liberation movement could not be realistically posed. This conjuncture of the balance of forces (*which continues to reflect current reality*) provided a classic scenario which placed the possibility of negotiations on the agenda. And we correctly initiated the whole process in which the ANC was accepted as the major negotiating adversary.[18]

"But what," Slovo then asks, "could we expect to achieve in the light of the balance of forces and the historical truism that no ruling class ever gives up all its power voluntarily? There was certainly never any prospect of forcing the regime's unconditional surrender across the table." Stating a similar point more prosaically, Steven Friedman summarises the negotiations moment as one in which "the balance of power and the potentially catastrophic effects of a descent into civil war dictate that negotiated transition rather than revolutionary transformation is the order of the day

– and that a settlement . . . requires significant compromises to allay the concerns of the white elite".[19]

Has the very process of negotiations witnessed a taming of the impulse towards genuine democratic empowerment in South Africa, as "Moderates" within the popular movement have had to rein in the "Radicals" in the name of realism? Clearly, if this were to prove to be the case it would be a particularly sorry outcome – especially so in light of the process that actually brought South Africa to the brink of its present "transition to democracy" in the first place. For that process has been defined, over the past two decades, by a remarkable series of those "great moments of the creative democratic process" identified earlier by Green as being so important: "strikes, demonstrations, marches, occupations, even funerals." Without doubt, mass action – first stirring in Durban and Soweto in the 1970s, then peaking in the near insurrection of 1984–6, and, ultimately, reviving in the late 1980s in the very teeth of the government's imposition of draconian emergency regulations – has been the key factor forcing the apartheid government onto the path of "Reform". And it has continued to be an important ingredient of the negotiations round as well, massive popular demonstrations demanding more rapid advance towards a democratic outcome having punctuated the negotiations at various key points during the past four years.

This political process has also meant the creation in South Africa of an infrastructure of popularly-rooted groups and organisations quite beyond anything seen elsewhere in Africa. Perhaps the trade unions have been closest to centre-stage in this, but civic associations, youth groups, education-focussed bodies (the NECC, principally), women's organisations and the like have all been a part of it. It is true that, especially beyond the union sphere, one could easily overstate the actual efficacy in organisational terms of many of these initiatives as well as the degree of internal democracy that, in practice, they manifested. Nonetheless, the mounting of such initiatives – which came to interface actively with the ANC and also to take its leadership when appropriate – did represent a major political accomplishment. Moreover, the whole process has seemed to promise the possibility that a populace so organised would to be able to continue to advance its claims in the post-apartheid period – even, if necessary, *against* the claims of its own ostensible political vanguard. There also developed, alongside this kind of practical politics, an important *theoretical practice*, a mode of discourse that served, simultaneously, both to encapsulate and to reinforce the most positive attributes of South Africa's emergent "Mass Democratic Movement". Created as much by those directly engaged in the political process as by professional intellectuals, this discourse highlighted a quite radical notion of the importance of "civil society" to the on-going struggle in South Africa, both before and after any elections that might occur.

At the same time, to return to the formulations of Slovo with which we began this section, there has been a strong counterweight within the negotiations process to any such positive pressures as are coming from below. This counterweight lies in the threat posed by both the potential for "chaos" and the exercise of countervailing power by "important interests", and it has come to loom large in the eyes of ANC negotiators. Thus the hard Right, both white and black, undoubtedly has demanded attention, as it has threatened, by word and by increasingly evil deed, to undermine the viability of any possible transition to democracy. This continues to be true to the present moment, of course. As I write, today's newspaper finds Mandela accusing Gasha Buthelezi and his Inkatha movement – quite plausibly in light of all that has happened in recent years – of a massacre of 15 young ANC election workers in a Natal village.[20] And, on my desk, a recent issue of *Southscan* highlights a "warning from the general staff of the SA Defence Force to President FW de Klerk about an extremely dangerous security situation in which the loyalty of a large number of officers could not be guaranteed"![21]

Nor has De Klerk, the ANC's main interlocutor during the negotiations, been an innocent bystander to all of this. Opinions differ as to how to interpret the role he has played. Still, it seems safe to say that, throughout the negotiations' process, he has proven himself to be a "Reformer" of a very particular type. Moved by circumstances quite literally beyond his control to a level of concession – the release of Mandela, the unbanning of the ANC, the entry into negotiations – towards the democratic forces far beyond anything deemed acceptable by his predecessor P. W. Botha, he has nonetheless continued, deep into the negotiations' process, to try to have it both ways: appearing to offer a measure of reform sufficiently expansive to possibly coopt ANC "Moderates" into settling for a "liberal capitalist democracy", while also attempting, rather incompatibly, to safeguard certain essential features of white minority rule. No mere prisoner of his police and military (although these have proven to be potentially crucial wild-cards in the situation), De Klerk seemed himself to have sanctioned wide-ranging efforts seriously to weaken the ANC.[22]

How are we to evaluate the compromises embraced by the ANC that such varied emanations of Right-wing intransigence have produced?[23] It is too early to say definitively, of course, since many important constitutional details remain to be ironed out by the newly elected parliament – sitting, as it also will, as constitutional assembly. But should one have misgivings about the acceptance of a "Government of National Unity" principle that will lock the ANC – for five years (should it win the election) – into working through a cabinet compulsorily inclusive of its chief rivals? And have too many concessions already been made in the direction of regional de-centralisation?[24] Or in the direction of ensuring the continuity of the present civil service? Certainly the ANC is a very long way from "smashing the state". But Joe Slovo, in his recent overview of this process, has insisted that such concessions be measured against how very much more both "Reform" and "Hardline" forces were actually demanding from the ANC going into the process.[25] And on this score he may well be right: perhaps historians will come to grant the ANC considerable credit for having managed to produce, out of such unforgiving conditions, even the relatively favourable constitutional results that they have.

But the main costs of negotiations may lie elsewhere, in any case – in the price exacted politically from the popular movement by the very nature of the process that has produced the new constitution. True, in Joe Slovo's opinion, this price need not prove to have been very high: he presents negotiations as offering "the possibility of bringing about a radically transformed political framework . . . which will result in the liberation movement occupying significantly more favourable heights from which to advance" towards "real people's power".[26] But has the politics of negotiations really provided so promising a stepping stone for the further mobilisation of continuing popular-democratic struggle? The fact is that there are already many within the ANC leadership who find themselves rather more comfortable with the kind of elite-pacting politics (polyarchy-in-the-making!) negotiations have encouraged than with any conception of "real people's power" and deep-cutting socio-economic transformation. And the kind of horse-trading politics that the GNU and other new structures will invite may merely reinforce such tendencies. Moreover, there is available within the ANC a discursive practice that could lend itself quite easily to a narrowing of the political agenda, a practice that, historically, has juxtaposed a "national-democratic" phase of struggle to any transformative/socialist one.[27]

The pressures upon the ANC to identify "upwards" within the worldwide and local class systems are strong, in any case. That there should be those within the movement who will be inclined to so identify need not surprise us. After all, it is well known that some within the ANC-in-exile had all along harboured aspirations that were quite petty-bourgeois nationalist in character, and they have been joined by others of similar stripe upon return. Indeed, as the elections approach an accelerating bandwagon effect is drawing even more such elements to the ANC's colours. These are not actors who, if "democracy" is to be the name of the game, will be terribly sorry to see a liberal democracy substituted for a popular one.[28] (And, of course, the same is true of the various international forces – the IMF and World Bank, the corporate sector and international aid community – that now crowd in upon the movement from all sides.)

Note, too, the irony that even some of the more progressive cadres within the leadership ranks of the ANC may find themselves lending support to such tendencies. After all, like all southern African liberation movements, the ANC had its own internal political practices moulded, at least in part, by the hierarchical imperative of organising for military purposes and protecting security in quite a hostile environment – and this within an exile milieu that surrounded the movement on all sides with few models besides the authoritarian practices of both conventional nationalist regimes in the host African countries on the hand and the Stalinist regimes of their Eastern European backers on the other. Many cadres formed by this experience are, on their return, at least as likely to be drawn – even if "for the very best of reasons" – towards top-down, hierarchical models of change management in which the populace is directed, disciplined, "mobilized", as they are to the rather messier business of helping facilitate more direct and unmediated expressions of popular energies and class demands. There are, in short, lessons in democracy for the ANC to learn as well as for its opponents.

It is worth reminding ourselves, therefore, that some critical discussion has continued, alongside the negotiations, as to whether the ANC might not in fact have pushed harder – perhaps realising thereby a less compromised constitutional outcome while also consolidating a rather more militantly democratic politics. Indeed, such discussion has occurred even within the ANC itself, some expressing the fear that concessions made by the ANC do indeed threaten to gut the capacity of a post-apartheid government to sustain any serious attack upon the severe socio-economic inequalities that characterise South African society. Near the mid-way point of the negotiations, for example, senior ANC cadre Pallo Jordan responded to the movement's own "Strategic Perspective" document by suggesting that the ANC might have lost track of its broader goals of democratic transformation and begun to make the lowest common denominator of constitutional agreement an end in itself.[29] Of course, there was a plausible, if predictable, response to this, the claim that Jordan ran the risk of substituting mere rhetoric for political realism – with Jeremy Cronin, SACP activist and one of the clearer thinkers in the camp of the democratic movement, writing in criticism of Jordan that, "to be sure, there are sometimes epic, all-or-nothing moments in politics. But when one is simply not in such a moment, then all-or-nothing tactics are liable to yield . . . nothing."[30]

And yet things were not quite so straightforward as this suggests, either. After all, it was Cronin himself who raised, at about this same time, closely related questions regarding the dangers of a negotiations process in which "mass action" came to be viewed merely as a "tap" to be turned on and off at the ANC leadership's whim as short-term calculation of advantage at the bargaining table might dictate:[31]

> It is critical that in the present we coordinate our principal weapon – mass support – so that we bring it to bear effectively upon the constitutional negotiations process. But we must not confine or inhibit mass struggle to this purpose. Instead we need to encourage, facilitate and indeed build the kind of fighting grassroots organizations that can lead and sustain a thousand and one local struggles against the numerous injustices our people

suffer. . . . Democracy is self-empowerment of the people. Unless the broad masses are actively and continually engaged in struggle, we will achieve only the empty shell of a limited democracy.[32]

For Cronin, as for others, it is the fact that such powerful popular energies continue to bubble up from the base in South Africa that gives politics there its peculiarly vibrant potential. Yet the question remains: will the emerging "democratic practice" of the ANC actually permit these energies to become focussed in such a way as to drive forward a process of genuine social transformation? Time alone will tell, although it is sobering to note, in this respect, a comment made by another prominent SACP/ANC militant, Raymond Suttner, in reflecting on Joe Slovo's recent celebration of the outcome of the negotiations process:

JS [Joe Slovo] is absolutely right to underline the massive victory we have scored at the negotiations. He fails, however, to mention that the past three years have also seen the transformation of our organisations, particularly the ANC. This transformation could have a serious, long-term impact. In particular, the negotiations have had a dissolving effect on mass organisation, a tendency for our constituency to become spectators. If we conduct the coming election campaign in a narrow electoralist manner, the dissolution could be deepened. Whatever the victory, we should not underrate the strong sense of demoralisation in our organisations.[33]

Need the drive for genuine democratic empowerment in South Africa find itself to be quite so compromised by the logic of negotiations and electoralism as this? And what, in any case, might such a drive actually mean in practice beyond these still relatively abstract invocations by Cronin and Suttner? It will be important, in this regard, to keep an eye on various concrete policy spheres in order to monitor whether assertions by the popular classes that promise both to redress their grievances and advance their long-term interests in structural change are to be facilitated by the ANC. A recent analysis by Henry Bernstein of developments linked to the agrarian question serves to give some sense of what a substantive politics of empowerment might actually begin to look like in that sector. Unfortunately, Bernstein's findings might also be considered to represent a particularly unsettling straw in the wind.[34]

Thus Bernstein, after a careful analysis of the need for dramatic changes in the allocation of land and rural opportunity, suggests the need for grass-roots mobilisation to make this possible. As he argues,

It is the political dynamic itself that provides a radical and potentially transformational content to any process of land and agrarian reform, rather than the scale of the immediate gains. The latter – how much land is redistributed in the foreseeable future, the conditions of redistribution and of the development of black farming – will be constrained by both the general balance of forces, and the time it will take for the rural masses to develop their political capacities and cohesiveness. However, the limits imposed by the balance of forces in any conjuncture of struggle are only known by pushing against those limits, and the developing capacity of popular social forces itself shifts the balance and extends the terrain of political possibility.

The perspective outlined here is not a fantasy of immediate and total ("revolutionary") transformation: it envisages individual (if not absolute) title to land and individual or household farming, not socialist property or production. It is rather an assessment of the politics of potential "structural reform" . . . as opposed to what is otherwise on offer: a limited "deracialization" of land and farming designed by experts, delivered by the state, and driven by the logic of the market. This path excludes the agency of those whose daily struggles for existence bear the deepest imprint of apartheid.

As Bernstein concludes his article (its themes dovetailing in many ways with those of the present paper), the "energies, hopes and ideas" of this latter group are "the most important political resource for 'structural reform' in the countryside". "It is not too late", he says, "for the ANC to start to connect with them". Unfortunately the overall thrust of his analysis does not find him overly confident that such a prospect will be realised.

And yet we must be careful not to overstate the case. It will not be entirely easy for any who have come of political age within an ANC culture to ignore the fact that there is a massive population of genuinely deprived people in South Africa. There is also the fact, emphasised earlier, that this population itself has certain organisational and ideological resources for pressing its own claims. Note, for example, the moment late in the negotiations process when COSATU demonstrated to ensure provisions favourable to labour (regarding lock-out clauses and other issues) in the draft constitution: in Slovo's words, "there cannot be the slightest doubt that the COSATU intervention, and the massive COSATU led demonstration outside the World Trade Centre, at the beginning of November[1993], had a positive outcome on the negotiating process." Moreover, as Slovo continues, "the capacity for this kind of pressure will remain critical in the coming weeks, months and years".[35]

Some would see another promising sign that the popular classes may indeed be empowering themselves in South Africa to lie in the burgeoning, as part of the on-going emancipation process, of forums for sectoral struggles – for, in effect, *sectoral democratization* – that have grown up alongside the more high profile negotiations' forum where national demo-cratisation has been on the agenda. Particularly important in this regard is the role played by the trade union movement. The alliance between the ANC and the country's largest trade union, COSATU, has been crucial to underwriting the politics of transition in South Africa. And recent efforts to consolidate a "Reconstruction Accord" between unions and the ANC represents a front where COSATU is seeking to extend that alliance in order to consolidate a workers' agenda for a post-election government.[36] But a second front upon which the unions are attempting to flex their class muscle more independently has been, precisely, the tripartite (unions-business-government) venue of the National Economic Forum.

Although some critics have seen participation in any such forum as representing a slide by the unions in the direction of cooptation and corporatism, the unions themselves have felt this to be an important context within which they can assert themselves. True, there is evidence that some ANC leaders are uneasy about this kind of autonomous realm of economic decision-making, however important it may have been in the past as one front of the popular challenge to the old system. Would they prefer, eventually, to draw national level decision-making back more firmly into the hands of the ministries they are about to inherit? Certainly activists in the education sector express parallel concerns. ANC cadres returning from exile are seen to have turned more easily to educational technicians (from SACHED, for example) than to the National Education Conference (born in the fires of mass struggle in the early to mid-1980s), for example. Here there is some suspicion that the nascent Education Forum – designed to facilitate, precisely, a sectoral democratisation of the education sphere – may already be losing pride of place amongst the ANC leadership to a more technocratic, government-centric definition of future education decision-making.

We will return to related themes in the next section of this paper, when we assess the possible programmatic content, in socio-economic terms, of policy-making by a future ANC government. Can we at least suggest here that the fate of the forums will be one significant index of the strength of impulses towards "popular democratization" in the new South Africa? In fact, unease regarding the ANC's possible long-term transformative intentions can run deep – the floating, at the National Union of Metalworkers' 1993 Congress, of the idea of launching a worker's party in order to keep progressive positions more firmly on South Africa's agenda offering a suggestive case in point in this respect. Nonetheless, most trade union efforts are still very much directed towards struggles within the ANC-led alliance itself in order to safeguard progressive policy initiatives at government level; COSATU's decision to place a number of its most prominent leaders on the ANC's electoral list offering a clear case in point of this.[37]

Not that the unions are the only actors in this process. Indeed, there are even those on the Left who fear that the better organised workers could take on some of the trappings of a "labour aristocracy" in the next round in South Africa: unless, that is, they become ever more integrally linked to other South Africans – in the rural areas, in the townships, in the shanty-towns – as part of a much broader alliance of social forces.[38] Hence the importance of Bernstein's preoccupations regarding the politics of the agrarian question. Hence the concern as to what kind of mobilisation for progressive, transformative purposes will prove possible in the townships (whether through the civic associations or their successors, whether within the fold of the ANC or outside it). And what of other assertions – on the gender front for example[39] – that also bear democratic promise: the promise of helping to confirm the continued existence of a popular, potentially hegemonic, political project and of contributing to the further deepening of it?

There remains, in short, a strong popular pull – from the streets, the country-side, the shop-floor – on the ANC and this must still be considered a real term in the South African political equation. Will the ANC come to embrace warmly such pressures from below, even further shape them towards progressive ends, as a way of beating off demands from the Right? Perhaps some promise in this respect can be found in a recent statement by Mandela when he warned workers gathered at the COSATU annual congress to be "vigilant": "How many times", he asked, "has a labour movement supported a liberation movement, only to find itself betrayed on the day of liberation? There are many examples of this in Africa. If the ANC does not deliver the goods you must do to it what you did to the apartheid regime."[40] True, this might merely be an invitation to trade unions to act as one more pressure group within a pluralistic model of democracy – even if the language used might seem to promise something more. But does it at least suggest that it is too early to despair of the possibility of a genuine struggle within the ANC over what form democratisation will take in the new South Africa?

Perhaps, with any luck, such a struggle could then produce a more promising outcome than Steven Friedman – one writer who has actually sought to view South Africa through the optic of the orthodox transition literature cited above – can readily envisage. In his article "South Africa's Reluctant Transition" – published in the *Journal of Democracy*, no less – Friedman has drawn centrally on a distinction of Benjamin Neuberger's: one that juxtaposes "two strains within African nationalism – the 'liberal democratic approach' which seeks pluralist democracy, and the 'national approach', which seeks 'national self-determination', defined as a state in which 'the citizens of the nation are ruled by kith and kin'".[41] For Friedman the latter pole, pulling towards authoritarianism, is very much a part of the ANC's political baggage. Nor is he entirely wrong; for this (and other) reasons there are, as noted above, lessons in democracy for many in the ANC to learn.

But what follows from this for Friedman? The very best that can possibly happen is that "leaders . . . strike a compromise that is finely balanced and sturdy enough to prevent destabilisation *from both left and right* and then to maintain support for it through a series of severe trials". Friedman is too well informed about the complexities of the South African case not also to emphasise that "the solutions required may not lie within the realm of possibility if divisions are as truly intractable as they seemed for much of 1992".[42] (And continue to be, in some ways, in 1994!) But he does ignore something else: not merely the difficulties but also the *probable costs* to vast numbers of South Africans of only going so far as to establish a conventional liberal democracy. Liberal democracy vs. authoritarianism, full stop: these are, in effect, the only resting places on his spectrum. And what of the inequalities that persist; must they merely be endured in the name of prudence and realism? Friedman, like many other contemporary students of the transition, does give us some plausible reasons to think that this might be so. Nonetheless, the fact – canvassed in this essay – that there is another form of democratic empowerment that must be considered is something he merely defines out of the analysis.

III. Stigmatizing Socialism: The Market as "Common Sense"

Why is this foreshortening of democratic expectation happening, even in places like South Africa where something more liberating might have been expected? Self-evidently, it has something important to do with the renewed strength of the Right in the post-Cold War epoch. But it also has something to do with the state of the Left. Consider the question: towards what end would any alternative, more "popular", form of democracy actually need to be mobilized? The conventional answer would once have been unequivocal: towards "socialism". Now few people seem quite so sure.

True, it is difficult to avoid the power of Marx's argument about democracy in *On the Jewish Question*, one that underscores the possible discrepancy between the appearance of formal political equality on the one hand and the reality of class inequality on the other. Recall Marx's argument. For him, "political emancipation certainly represents a great progress. . . . It is not, indeed, the final form of human emancipation, but it is the final form of human emancipation *within* the framework of the prevailing social order." Still, the freedom political emancipation embodies serves to reduce "man" (sic) to "abstract citizen", "infused with an unreal universality". In contrast, "human emancipation will only be complete when the real, individual man has absorbed himself into the abstract citizen; when as an individual man, in his everyday life, in his work, and in his relationships, he has become a *species-being*; and when he has recognized and organized his own powers as social powers so that he no longer separates this social power from himself as *political* power." The main effect of political revolution in the modern (capitalist) world is therefore quite paradoxical, in Marx's view: it has merely helped to "abolish" (or, perhaps better put, to obscure) "the political character of civil society", "emancipating [that] civil society from politics and from even a semblance of a general content" while "dissolving" the social relations that characterize it (notably class relationships) into an apparent congeries of (abstract) "individuals". Marx came to see the overthrow of the particular system of class power that so deeply shaped civil society under capitalism as necessary to giving real, human substance to any more narrowly-defined political emancipation.[43]

Of course, some on the Left have come to resist forging the link between democracy and socialism that would seem to follow from this analysis. Take, for example, the recent polemics of John Keane who actually sees the aspiration towards socialism as an *impediment* to realising progressive outcomes. Thus, the demand for socialism, in its desire to "destroy the division between civil society and the state"(!), is "undemocratic", while "the demand for democracy is much more subversive because it calls into question all heteronomous forms of power".[44] In this way Keane also seeks to remind us – as do Laclau and Mouffe in making related claims for the centrality of a non-foundationalist "radical democracy" – of the danger of allowing any excessive emphasis on class struggle to silent consideration on the Left of other liberatory assertions (premissed on gender and racial grounds, for example).

Over-stated? Perhaps most readers of the *Socialist Register* will find the terms of Andrew Gamble's riposte to these remarks by Keane (as well as to Laclau and Mouffe) more congenial. Gamble associates himself with critics of these theorists who are "disturbed [at] how sweeping is their condemnation of classical Marxism, and how flimsy and rudderless is the radical democratic politics they are proposing". "In order to give it some coherence", Gamble asserts, "they still have to draw on the concept of socialism and the socialist tradition". And "a socialism . . . without a workers' movement, without class analysis and class politics would hardly be socialism at all . . . [and] would become just another variant of liberalism."[45] To think otherwise, he implies, would cede far too much ground to those practitioners of capitalism who do *know* just how much their own class interests drive their undertakings and would like nothing better than to see the class struggle downgraded in importance.

There is also the simple fact that Marx's analysis of the logic of capitalism seems more relevant than ever in explaining the dynamics and depredations of capital's current global reach. As Perry Anderson argues, "intellectually, the culture of the Left is far from being demobilized by the collapse of Soviet communism, or the impasse of Western social democracy". After all, "the central case against capitalism today is the combination of ecological crisis and social polarization it is breeding", especially on the global plane, and "market forces", Anderson affirms, "contain no solution to these".[46] And yet: things are not really quite that simple either. After all, the real drag on the Left's self-confidence regarding the claims of "socialism" is not primarily to be found in the kinds of considerations raised by Keane, Mouffe or Laclau. Doesn't it lie, much more fundamentally, in the fact that we are much less confident than in the past about the possibility of actually realizing, in practice, a socialist alternative to globally ascendant capitalism? Thus Anderson qualifies the remarks just cited with the sobering reflection that "the case against capitalism is strongest on the very plane where the reach of socialism is weakest – at the level of the world system as a whole. . . . [T]he future belongs to a set of forces that are overtaking the nation-state. So far they have been captured or driven by capital – as, in the past fifty years, internationalism has changed sides. So long as the Left fails to win back the initiative here, the current system will be secure."[47]

Even more pertinently for present purposes, we can simply return to Przeworski's grimly "realistic" analysis regarding the necessary pull towards the Centre/Right in most, if not all, democratic transitions. For the fact is that this conclusion is framed for him by the simultaneous belief that there exists only very limited room for socio-economic manoeuvre in "Southern" settings: as he memorably states his point, "capitalism is irrational; socialism is unfeasible; in the real world people starve – the conclusions we have reached are not encouraging."[48] If socialism has long been the dream of those on the Left, many will see in Przeworski's stark formulation the very essence of their present-day nightmares. What, indeed, can the democracy of "popular struggle" possibly mean within the constricting circumstances dictated by an all too arbitrary but enormously powerful global capitalist system?

It is cold comfort to realise that liberal democratic thinkers have themselves virtually no resources within their own chosen framework with which to theorise the implications for them of the power relations of the new global economy; their response is, by and large, simply to ignore the issue[49] and get on with the further thinning out of their definition of democracy. The Left, of necessity, has had to take the question of global socio-economic structure more seriously as a constraint on their own hopes for meaningful democratisation – not least in the context of the South African transition. Must we lapse into Pzreworskian pessimism in this regard? Certainly, in the first instance, it must be acknowledged that there is absolutely nothing straightforward about developing a progressive economic policy, in South Africa or anywhere else for that matter, under current global circumstances. No-one but perhaps the more obtuse of "ultra-leftists" can any longer expect a revolutionary alternative to emerge full-blown or very quickly anywhere on the globe – even if South Africa, with its running start of mass mobilisation and popular contestation, did seem momentarily to be better positioned than most to keep the revolutionary flame alive. But has the momentum that might at least have sustained there a more subtle and apposite struggle for transformation also been lost?

It is perhaps too early to say so definitively, although there is good reason for concern. What, for example, are the implications of remarks like those of senior ANC negotiator Thabo Mbeki when he stated that, on economic matters, the National Party's positions "are not very different really from the position the movement has been advancing"?[50] Or the resonance of the following kind of smug report to be found in a 1993 issue of South Africa's *Business Day*:

> We can look with some hope to the evolution in economic thinking in the ANC since the occasion nearly three years ago when Nelson Mandela stepped out of prison and promptly reaffirmed his belief in the nationalization of the heights of the economy. By contrast, after delivering his organization's anniversary message last week, Mandela – supported by SACP chairman Joe Slovo – went out of his way to assure a large group of foreign (and

local) journalists that the ANC was now as business-friendly as any potential foreign investor could reasonably ask. He indicated further that ANC economic thinking was now being influenced as much by Finance Minister Derek Kays and by organized business as anyone else.[51]

And a plethora of recent statements by ANC leaders have rubber-stamped this apparent acceptance of the centrality of capitalist impulses to ANC economic plans – from the almost slavish solicitation of foreign and domestic investment and the easy acknowledgement of a key role for the IMF and the World Bank to the sometime temptation to reduce the concept of black empowerment to the question of creating a black business class![52]

Make no mistake: this is what one brand of "realism" has come to mean in South Africa. However, there are counter-tendencies – and they do have some real social weight behind them, notably within the circles of organised labour. While recognising as naive the notion of some immediate seizure of economic power and subsequent dictating of an entirely new logic to the South African economy, the bearers of such counter-tendencies do manifest a conviction that class struggle over social-economic outcomes can and must continue in South Africa. They seek to blend "realism" and militancy in such a way as, cumulatively, to hedge in the writ of capital and eventually, they hope, to tilt the balance of power away from it in some recognisably socialist manner. At its best, as I have argued, such activity begins to exemplify a project of what (drawing on the writings of the early Gorz and Kagarlitsky) I have characterised as "structural reform",[53] and what others in South Africa (albeit with somewhat different emphases) have labelled "radical reform" or "revolutionary reform".[54] This defines a project that promises to sustain the momentum of revolutionary change because it insists both that forces engaged in day-to-day contestation develop an increasingly clear and self-conscious sense of the long term goal of structural transformation that frames their immediate undertakings and that every such undertaking also contributes to the building of a stronger organisational base for other struggles that will be necessary in the future.

A statement by Enoch Godongwana, prominent trade unionist and presently Acting General Secretary of the National Union of Metal-workers (NUMSA), in a recent debate captures the tenor of this approach quite neatly. Acknowledging that, "if we want a socialist alternative in the absence of an insurrection, that poses a challenge for us", he proceeds:

> So we argue a socialist alternative, but within the constraints of saying we cannot simply storm and seize power tomorrow. Therefore we should be creative – how do we make sure that, in the process of struggling for socialism, we assert ourselves as a class with the objective of having a class rule . . . We must begin, while we assert a leading role in various areas of society, *to build certain alternatives within the capitalist framework that will tend to undermine the capitalist logic*. (emphasis added)[55]

Moreover, in the same debate, we find a senior ANC leader, Pallo Jordan, also expressing interest in this kind of strategy "which doesn't necessarily imply grabbing hold of the state or nationalisation of the commanding heights of the economy, but in a sense establishing a number of strategic bridgeheads which enable you to empower the working class and the oppressed, and from these bridgeheads you begin then to subordinate the capitalist classes to the interests of society in general."[56] And there is even a recent statement by Mandela himself in which he states that he does "not believe South African businessmen could be trusted to develop a post-apartheid economy without state intervention":

> We are convinced that left to their own devices, the South African business community will not rise to the challenges facing us. . . . While the democratic state will maintain and develop the market, we envisage occasions when it will be necessary for it to intervene where growth and development require such intervention.[57]

Of course, just what meaning contending class forces can be expected to breathe into such formulations in the post-election round in South Africa is an open question. This is already a controversial matter on the Left in South Africa, with a number of economic planning exercises already underway within the democratic movement being particularly worthy of attention in this regard. One of the most controversial of these is the work of the Industrial Strategy Project (ISP), an off-shoot of the COSATU-linked Economic Trends Group. The ISP has developed the model of an industrial strategy motored by a preoccupation with export markets, high tech production and the need to be competitive in international terms – with significant income and wealth redistribution seen as then flowing from the success of this newly burgeoning manufacturing sector (and from, in addition, a relatively unspecified programme of "urban reconstruction and rural reconstruction"). Class struggle? The problem, as ISP co-ordinator Dave Lewis sees it, is that "key fractions of capital do not necessarily have an interest in successful industrialisation or in high rates of economic growth". Just as the authoritarian military state disciplined capitalists in Korea, so workers in South Africa – acting through their unions and through worker participation in boards of directors – must now act "to subordinate the narrow interests of capitalists to the logic of capital"![58]

This model is certainly subject to criticism, Cronin, for example, balking at the image of workers mobilising to submit the capitalist class to the logic of capital and looking instead to the possibility of their submitting "the capitalist class to the logic of social need, of social demand, to the logic of a working class political economy". In addition, the ISP's powerful emphasis on "competitiveness" and an outward-looking growth strategy has been queried – not least by Canadian trade unionist Sam Gindin in a suggestive series of interventions.[59] It is also the case that a second model – one proposed, more recently, by the ANC's Macro-Economic Research Group (MERG) – has an economic agenda that seems more tilted towards creating an internal dynamic for the economy around the servicing of "basic needs"; this model foresees a beefing up of the state's role for this purpose, although it remains less clear on the question of just how directive an ANC state may have to be in pressing capital to play a more effective developmental role.[60] But such an approach can at least begin to touch base with other writings on the South African economy that have emphasised the possibilities of inward industrialisation, of "growth *through* redistribution" and of much more active kinds of direction of investment.[61]

Do such projections at least represent a thin edge of the wedge for eventual realisation of the kind of on-going and intensifying struggle on the socio-economic terrain envisaged by Godongwana and Jordan, as quoted above. Perhaps an even greater effort to close in on the prerogatives of capital along these lines could be expected to bear significant fruit – helping frame the choices of capitalists more firmly within a progressive, increasingly expansive definition of South Africa's possible socio-economic direction. A more transformative vision could also help tip the balance of current projections towards additional kinds of economic activities – less state-centred perhaps, but popularly and cooperatively driven. Might these not find South Africans being empowered to act to service their own immediate and pressing needs (housing is a good example) in creative, productive ways, ways that would help, precisely, to give socio-economic substance to the kind of broad-gauged, hegemonic political project hypothesised in the previous section?

To left and right, there are activists and analysts of the South African economy who think such "possibilities" are fanciful, of course. For some, the terms in which options are thus being cast are far too narrow, and they suggest, instead, the need for a shift "from basic needs to uncompromising class struggle" in which working-class leadership now positions itself to "give leadership to the spontaneous uprisings" that are sure to spring up in response to the anti-climatic nature of the post-apartheid dispensation for most South Africans.[62] Consider, as well, the arguments of Lawrence Harris, the well-known Marxist economist who, though British, has been close to ANC decision-making circles off and on over the years.

Not so long ago papers by Harris were instrumental in forging for the ANC a definition of a "mixed economy" that he presented, precisely, as able to keep alive the struggle for the long-term transformation of the South Africa economy.[63] A more recent article finds him now dismissing any possibility that the ANC can hope to lay the ground-work for socialist transition.[64] His present position rests on a critique of the claims of a revolutionary-cum-structural reform strategy (which he insists on caricaturing in presenting as a singularly unpromising corporatist tailing of capital).[65] And he concludes with an extended attack on Joe Slovo for the latter's apostasy in moving away from his far more straightforwardly militant positions of the 1970s. Harris is too good an economist not to offer some very compelling arguments in support of a pessimistic outlook on South Africa's future. We know what he is talking about when he quotes Slovo, against himself (circa 1976), as prophetic regarding the present moment in South Africa: "The national struggle is stopped in its tracks and is satisfied with the co-option of a small black elite into the presently forbidden areas of economic and political power"! Yet what is so depressing about Harris' approach is that – except for an all too abstract invocation of the good old days of the "Leninist tradition" (once also embraced but now abandoned by Slovo) – he spares himself, in his dismissal of current positions, the task of discussing what an effective revolutionary strategy for the present, actually existing, South Africa could possibly look like. This brand of intervention is probably as stultifying for development of the radical imagination in South Africa as any more self-consciously right-wing approach could possibly be.

Not that models that try to keep alive some sense of struggle vis-à-vis capital have been spared the scorn of more orthodox economists in South Africa. Harris may now think those in play to be far too meek, but Nicoli Nattrass, in a recent (and quite symptomatic) paper, attacks even the relatively mild proposals of the ISP and MERG as being notably adventurist.[66] While raising a range of more detailed questions regarding the specific modalities of intervening to shape capital's choices, her chief preoccupation remains, therefore, "the limits to pushing capital around". These limits, she suggests, are very strict . . . and, in her formulation, quite familiar: "Capital simply leaves (or does not enter) if the policy environment is unfriendly. Given the weakening of labour world-wide (as a result of prolonged recession), the increase in capital mobility and the expansion in overseas investment opportunities . . . the bargaining power of labour, like that of state planners, has been significantly eroded". Her conclusion: "It simply suggests that capital has to be courted rather than coerced."

Unfortunately – she represents a kind of mirror image of Harris in this respect – Nattrass excuses herself from the necessity to consider seriously the probable upshot of her own narrowing of alternatives. Is there any reason for us to think that capital – left free, in effect, to determine the terms of its own seduction – will actually produce any real economic transformation in South Africa? And if not, does she think the political situation is then likely to produce a viable equilibrium? In truth, for Nattrass politics is most likely to be defined as a vector for irrational intrusions into the technocratic world of rational economic decision-making.[67] However, back in the real world of class struggle – where capitalism can still be deemed to be "irrational" – we find ourselves drawn back to a more positive vision of politics, and to the link, apparently necessary, between real democracy and economic transformation 'socialism'.

For the model of revolutionary-cum-structural reform that might keep such transformation on the agenda premises a politics of popular empowerment in order to drive the process from below. As we have seen, there are tendencies at work within the ANC that might be narrowing its definition of democracy and the possible scope of popular assertions that might otherwise press against the apparent limits of the status quo. Moreover, the ANC's reluctance to present itself as an organisation that focuses, essentially, a class project (in however nuanced a form) can prove highly demobilising in its own right. Certainly left/social-democratic parties elsewhere that, once in power (as, now, "the government of all the people"), retreat from presenting themselves in these terms have usually wound up acting – in the name of "realism" and "pragmatism" – as spokespersons for the very worst kinds of market-liberal/monetarist policy packages. Could an intensification of differences over such issues ever find an ANC government turning repressively on the Left – "the Moderates" against "the Radicals", in effect – in the post-election world?[68]

Or will class struggle within and around the ANC draw from that organisation a level of creativity and leadership appropriate to the challenge that faces the popular movement in South Africa? Self-evidently, the realisation of an alternative vision of societal transformation, one premissed on the goal of socialism and the practice of structural reform, will not be an easy task. It is even possible that, between them, Harris and Nattrass are correct and that there is no "middle road" between an all too vague and nostalgic "revolutionism" and mere subservience to global capital's dictate. Small wonder if, under such circumstances, there are those now comfortably situated in the upper echelons of the ANC who can come to think socialism an irrelevance. As Colin Bundy has put the point: "There will be many who remain unconvinced. They believe that would-be socialists in South Africa are doomed to defeat; epochally quixotic, tilting forlornly at windmills driven for the rest of history by capitalist energies. To speak of 'prospects' for socialism, they say, requires a leap of faith." And "perhaps it does," Bundy concedes; at the very least it "requires stamina, creativity and collective resourcefulness."

But there is also something more that drives the search for such an alternative, an understanding (succinctly epitomised by Bundy) of the negative implications of not making it real:

> On the other hand: to imagine that a milder manner capitalist order can secure a decent future for the majority of South Africans – or that deracializing bourgeois rule will meet the aspirations of exploited and oppressed people – or that South Africa can somehow be absolved of its economic history and enter a future like that of Sweden or Taiwan: now that really requires a leap of faith.[69]

Does it also bear noting that, just as some within the ANC seem inclined to make just such a "leap of faith" to the right, it is possible to perceive the first indications of a waning self-confidence amongst the very western intelligentsia who so recently brought us the notion of a post-Cold War "end of history"? Take, for example, Robert Kaplan's recent, widely-read article on "The Coming Anarchy" (in *The Atlantic Monthly*[70]), an article which seeks to demonstrate "how scarcity, crime, overpopulation, tribalism, and disease are rapidly destroying the social fabric of our planet". It is true that, as Kaplan slouches from one catastrophic Third World setting to another, the general tone of his article remains far more sensationalist than analytical. And certainly he traces none of his litany of desperate conditions and escalating barbarism back to any possible contradictions in the global production system. Nonetheless, there are signs of an interesting failure of nerve to be found in this and various other current writings. After all, we might ask, how many basket-case economies can capital afford to walk away from before the shrinking horizons for expanded reproduction offered by such a world become a problem for it? Are these the circumstances under which the pendulum of power might begin to swing back in the direction of the popular classes, including within national boundaries? Might the space for imposing hegemonic, left-leaning projects on capital – in South Africa, more globally – and releasing socio-economic energies, creative and collective, from the base open up sooner than we think?

IV. Beggaring the Imagination: The High Costs of Global Ideology

Unfortunately, for the moment (as Bundy himself acknowledges), "leaps of faith" to the left are much less the norm than mere "commonsensical" acceptance, for better or worse, of the "inevitability" of a pretty unalloyed capitalism. In his response to John Keane, cited earlier, André Gamble wondered aloud as to "socialism's fate" in the contemporary world. At best, might this not amount to socialism's merely "lingering on as a critique of the shortcomings of liberalism, and as an analysis of the destructive effects of capitalist economics on individuals and communities"?[71]

For Gamble "there is another possibility": "The waning of belief in the methods and politics of state socialism makes possible the intellectual and political rebirth of the socialist project by setting free once more hopes of emancipation." But what if the "waning of belief" is in the very feasibility and efficacy of "the socialist project" itself – and of the practice of a genuinely "popular democracy" that might accompany it? For in South Africa, as elsewhere, it is not merely the strength of structural determinations that encourage people to reach this conclusion. There is also an autonomous cultural charge to what is happening. As we have seen, the threatened foreclosure of any sense of socio-economic possibility beyond "liberal capitalist democracy" involves both a hollowing out of language and a beggaring of the historical imagination. In part, this culture of ascendant global capitalism crystallises spontaneously, but it is also driven by active efforts at ideology-creation on the part of liberal and right-of-centre intellectuals. And the costs of the grim fecundity of such an ideology are likely to be very high indeed – not least in South Africa.

This is not the case simply because the operations of capitalism, un-alloyed and "irrational", will, in all probability, have little if any positive impact on the material lot of the vast majority of South Africans ("in the real world people starve"). It is also true because, at the cultural level, imaginations do not stand still. Thus, as argued above, the sidelining of socialist democracy may prove, in a world of continuing scarcity and inequality, to be a pyrrhic one for global capitalism in many settings. Frustrated, balked of a sense of alternative purpose at the level of socio-economic vision, feeling merely disempowered as potential class actors and therefore cast into a political vacuum, people begin to look elsewhere for presumptive routes to their salvation.

Sometimes this frustration may still be framed in broadly "Leftist" terms, the kind of populist-cum-racist rhetoric that has become the stock-in-trade of Winnie Mandela and others like her in their appeals to potentially disaffected youth.[72] In such a politics, South Africa's demo-cratic imperative can be seen merely to curdle and fester dangerously. But even more often, perhaps, popular frustrations will find voice through the politicised expressions of competing fundamentalisms: various extremes of religious, of racial, of national, of regional and ethnic mobilisation. "Chaos" can spring at least as much from such sources as from the threatened backlash of the powerful classes highlighted by Przeworski, and the unravelling of the social fabric that is currently occurring in various countries around the world offers grim testimony to that fact. How ironic if "barbarism" should break out not in spite of, but precisely because of, the limited nature of the transition to democracy that is currently being granted – in both theory and practice – global sanction.

South Africa does run great risk of unravelling along such lines: as is well known, virtually all of the divisions mentioned above are present and available for potential politicisation. True, there are many activists in South Africa, within and without the ANC, who are striving to avoid such a tragic denouement to their liberation struggle and wishing to attach a more expansive meaning to the transition currently afoot. Perhaps it is here that progressive theory also has a role to play: as guardian – against the pull of "the ideology of the new globalism" – of the political imagination. More than twenty-five years ago, Roger Murray asked pointedly of the future of socialism in Africa whether the "historically necessary" was really likely to prove the "historically possible".[73] We now have a much clearer sense of the costs to Africa of its not, as yet, having done so. All the more reason for us to ensure that, as a pendant to on-going struggle in South Africa and elsewhere, the historically necessary at least remain *the historically thinkable*.

NOTES

A preliminary version of this essay was first presented to the annual meeting of the (American) African Studies Association, Boston, December, 1993. I am grateful to Marlea Clarke, Dan O'Meara, Leo Panitch, David Pottie, Mike Zmolek and, especially, Stephen Gelb and Colin Leys for helpful comments on a subsequent draft.

 1. Harry Magdoff and Paul Sweezy, "The Stakes in South Africa", *Monthly Review* 37, 11 (April, 1986); they went on to state that "a victory for counter-revolution – the stabilization of capitalist relations in South Africa even if in somewhat altered form – would be stunning defeat for the world revolution."

 2. Michael Burowoy, "The Capitalist State in South Africa: Marxist and Sociological Perspectives on Race and Class", in *Political Power and Social Theory*, volume 2 (1981), p. 326.

 3. I have discussed some of these complexities in my "South Africa: Between 'Barbarism' and 'Structural Reform'", *New Left Review*, #188 (July–August, 1991) and, in an exchange with Alex Callinicos, in *New Left Review*, #195 (September/October, 1992).

 4. Larry Diamond and Mark Plattner, "Introduction" to their jointly edited volume, *The Global Resurgence of Democracy* (Baltimore: John Hopkins, 1993), p. ix.

 5. Larry Diamond, "Three Paradoxes of Democracy" in Diamond and Plattner, *op. cit.*, p. 103. See also Huntington's essay, "Democracy's Third Wave" in the same volume.

 6. Philip Green, *Retrieving Democracy: In Search of Civil Equality* (London: Methuen, 1989), p. 3. On the "pluralist" analysis (and endorsement) of liberal democracy see also David Held, *Political Theory and the Modern State* (Cambridge: Polity Press, 1989), chapter 2. As Colin Leys and I have summarized the relevant point elsewhere (in chapter 10, "The Legacy: An Afterword" of our *Namibia's Liberation Struggle: The Two-Edged Sword* [London: James Currey, 1994]), "In reality, . . . liberal democracy does not imply that citizens rule themselves, but that rule by elites is made legitimate by periodic elections, and – very importantly – by various ancillary mechanisms, above all the mediation of political parties." In that chapter – with reference to this definition and in ways suggestive for an understanding of the South African case – we also discuss the limitations of the "transition to democracy" in Namibia in the wake of that country's recent liberation from South African colonialism.

 7. Philip Green, "Introduction: Democracy as a Contested Idea", to his edited volume *Democracy* (Atlantic Highlands, N.J.: Humanities Press, 1993), pp. 14–15. See also Rick Salutin, *Waiting for Democracy: A Citizen's Journal* (Markham: Viking/Penguin, 1989).

 8. Issa Shivji, "The Democracy Debate in Africa: Tanzania" in *Review of African Political Economy*, #50 (March, 1991); as he further notes, "democracy, for most of us [African intellectuals], whether we like it or not, is associated with the organization of the state and government structures (Parliament, courts, parties, accountability, elections) rather than a summation of the experience of struggles of the majority. Of course, these are not mutually exclusive: indeed we will all swear by our political science text-books that they are not. And yet in practice, and in our theoretical and political practice, we rarely let loose of the apron strings that bind us to imperialism or the African state or both, we rarely deviate from liberalism; and in our case therefore compradorialism". What this demonstrates to Shivji is, among other things, "a total lack of faith in the masses of the African people".

 9. Perhaps too easy: it could be argued that, in the South African insurrection, the favoured rallying-cry of "ungovernability" (as in: "making the townships ungovernable") substituted all too easily for the more firmly grounded and organizationally developed politics that might have borne even greater long-term promise.

10. Perry Anderson, *A Zone of Engagement* (London: Verso, 1992), pp. 355–6.

11. Giuseppe Di Palma, *To Craft Democracies: An Essay on Democratic Transitions* (Berkeley and Los Angeles: University of California Press, 1990), pp. 22–4.

12. Diamond, "Three Paradoxes of Democracy", *op. cit.*, pp. 104–5. See also footnote 49, below.

13. Larry Diamond, "The Globalization of Democracy" in Robert O. Slater, Barry M. Schutz and Steven R. Dorr [eds.], *Global Transformation and the Third World* [Boulder: Lynne

Reiner, 1993]. For evidence that this is an extremely one-sided way in which to present the development record in Africa – to go no further afield – see the more balanced approach in Richard Sandbrook, *The Politics of Africa's Economic Recovery* (Cambridge: Cambridge University Press, 1993), and also Colin Leys, "Confronting the African Tragedy" in *New Left Review* (forthcoming [1994]). Diamond's formulations ignore, for Africa (to go no further afield), the catastrophic outcomes of most capitalist development strategies on the continent, as well as the crucial role the state (authoritarian, interventionist) has played in settings (the Asian NICs, for example) where capitalism has been more successful. Here, as so often in their "scientific" writings, Diamond and his colleagues in the democracy business are marketing almost pure ideology.

14. Diamond, "Three Paradoxes of Democracy", *op. cit.*, p. 106.

15. Adam Przeworski, *Democracy and the market: Political and economic reforms in Eastern Europe and Latin America* (Cambridge: Cambridge University Press, 1991), p. 85.

16. Przeworski, *ibid.*, p. 34. Bracket for the moment the fact that Przeworski seems here to be working with a concept of democracy that Green would probably label mere "pseudodemocracy".

17. Przeworski, *ibid.*, p. 37.

18. Joe Slovo, "Negotiations: What room for compromise?" in *The African Communist* #130 (3rd Quarter, 1992), pp. 36–7. This particular paper also found Slovo proposing – as a way of breaking the negotiations log-jam and hedging against right-wing backlash – "sweeping concessions to the government in the form of 'sunset clauses' in a new constitution", including a period of compulsory power-sharing and a significant guaranteeing of existing civil service and security force contracts, (as summarized by Paul Stober, "Slovo's 'sunset' debate is red-hot", *The Weekly Mail*, October 30–November 5, 1992, p. 16). Quite similar ideas were embraced, almost immediately, by the ANC leadership itself in its own important "Strategic Perspective" document.

19. Steven Friedman, "South Africa's Reluctant Transition", in *Journal of Democracy*, 4, #2 (April, 1993), p. 57.

20. "ANC blames Buthelezi for massacre", *The Toronto Star*, February 21, 1994, p. 14; Mandela cites Buthelezi – accurately enough, apparently – as having "gone so far as to say, he does not want to lie and to promise the people of Natal that there will be no bloodshed in the course of their campaign to disrupt the election".

21. "Top generals' warning to De Klerk may hide double agenda", *Southscan*, 9, #5 (4 February 1994), p. 33.

22. Future assessments of this period may actually find the extent of De Klerk's intransigence to have been, in some ways, "imprudent" from a "Reform" point of view. Permitting the ANC to advance more readily as a legitimately hegemonic force might have helped preempt some of the unravelling of South African society – evidenced in the rising tide of criminality, for example, and the increasingly fissiparous political tendencies – that has occurred since 1990. Perhaps some in the business community had reached this conclusion rather earlier, increasingly confident that the future policies of an ANC could be hedged in, in any case, by economic pressures. This will be a complex process for future historians to untangle; it is, for example, equally possible that at the outset of negotiations important elements in the business community were less confident than they were to become of their ability to control the socio-economic fall-out from political democratization. If so, they may have felt that De Klerk's delaying tactics bought them time to further soften up the ANC for their own purposes. Still, the fact remains that for such members of the corporate class nostalgia for racial domination in and of itself is likely to have been less of a complicating factor than for De Klerk and his fellow "Reformers" within the National Party. On this subject, see the section "Explaining De Klerk" (pp. 7–19) in my earlier essay "South Africa: Between 'Barbarism' and 'Structural Reform'", *op. cit.*

23. Note, too, that it is the very depth of such intransigence that, after a successful South African election, may force an ANC government into a (necessarily?) heavy-handed crack-down against various of the "Hardliners". If this should happen, it can be expected significantly to compromise the prospects of consolidating any kind of democratic culture in the new South Africa.

24. Especially if more such concessions were to come to this front: the recent offering by Mandela of even "greater regional powers and a constitutional principle that could be the

first step to an Afrikaaner *volkstaat*" – designed further to mollify the right-wing whites – is a particularly unsettling development in this regard. See Phillip Van Niekirk, "ANC, de Klerk reach out to right wing: Mandela, Pretoria offer concessions to lure black-white alliance back into election", *The Globe and Mail*, February 17, 1994.

25. Joe Slovo, "The Negotiations Victory: A political overview", *The African Communist*, #135 (Fourth Quarter, 1993).
26. Slovo, "Negotiations: What room for compromise?", *op. cit.*, p. 36. Moreover, he continues, "the negotiating table is neither the sole terrain of the struggle for power nor the place where it will reach its culminating point. In other words, negotiations is only a part, and not the whole, of the struggle for real people's power."
27. Perhaps this is why one will look in vain in the pages of the recent book which draws together Nelson Mandela's various public pronouncements since his release from prison in 1990 (*Nelson Mandela Speaks: Forging a Democratic, Nonracial South Africa* [New York: Pathfinder, 1993]) for the making of any real connection between the current process of ensuring democratization (much discussed) and the prospect, near or afar, of socialism (virtually unmentioned).
28. It is such actors who will be most ready to avail themselves of the ANC's "discursive practice", cited above, in order to breathe new life into the movement's time-honoured distinction between the "national democratic" and the "socialist" phases/moments of struggle. And they may also be quite happy to cede to the union movement and the SACP the role of safe-guarding that socialist moment in the struggle – the better to insulate the ANC from any such requirement! For background on this subject see the present author's "South Africa: The Question of Strategy", *New Left Review*, #160 (November/December, 1986).
29. Pallo Jordan, "Strategic Debate in the ANC" (mimeo, October, 1992); an abbreviated version of this paper appears as "Committing suicide by concession," *The Weekly Mail* (November 13 to 19, 1992).
30. Jeremy Cronin, "Nothing to gain from all-or-nothing tactics", *The Weekly Mail* (*ibid.*), p. 9; in Cronin's view. "Slovo reminds us we are dealing with a chastened, crisis-ridden but still powerful opponent. Both sides find themselves locked in a reciprocal siege. From our side the objective remains the total dismantling of apartheid. But we simply cannot will this objective into being. So how do we move from here to our longer term goals? Slovo suggests principled compromises . . ."
31. See Jeremy Cronin, "The boat, the tap and the Leipzig way", *The African lCommunist*, #130 (3rd Quarter, 1992). Note also Joe Slovo's own acknowledgement of this "short-coming" of the negotiations process: "The balance between negotiations and mass struggle was not always perfect. We were not always clear of what we were trying to achieve with mass action. Remember the debate about the 'tap', our tendency to turn mass action on and off in a very instrumentalist way?" (in his "The Negotiations Victory: a political overview", *op. cit.*, p. 10).
32. Cronin, "In Search of a Relevant Strategy", *Work in Progress*, #84 (September, 1992), p. 20.
33. Suttner's comments appears a part of the account of the "Central Committee discussion of Joe Slovo's presentation" in *The African Communist*, #135 (Fourth Quarter, 1993), p. 14.
34. Henry Bernstein, "South Africa: Agrarian Questions", *Southern Africa Report*, 9, #3 (January, 1994), p. 7.
35. Joe Slovo, "The Negotiations Victory: A political overview", *op. cit.*, p. 7.
36. There are also some grounds for viewing this effort quite critically, however; thus Roger Etkind and Suzanna Harvey, two NUMSA organisers, are particularly scathing about the moderate terms in which the Accord is being cast, suggesting that "the roles and interests of COSATU and the ANC are clearly opposed" and that the workers "must not adapt to a 'realism' dictated by leadership" (see their article, "The workers cease fire", *South African Labour Bulletin/SALB*, 17, #5 (September–October 1993), p. 85.
37. In the event, however, the ANC placed many fewer of the twenty COSATU nominees in the upper part of its electoral list than had been originally anticipated. This is a recent move that may prove to have been of some importance but its full implications are as yet difficult to decipher.

38. For a particularly effective statement of such concerns see Adrienne Bird and Geoff Schreiner, "COSATU at the Crossroads: towards tripartite corporatism or democratic socialism", *SALB*, 16, #6 (July/August, 1992). At least for the moment, however, it is difficult to avoid the conclusion that the trade unions remain the most progressive of actors within the new South Africa-in-the-making.

39. For a closely-related account of the positioning of gender-related struggles within an overall process of "democratization", see the important paper by Linzi Manicom, entitled "Women for Democracy, Democracy for Women? Gender and Political Transition in South Africa" and presented to the annual meeting of the (American) African Studies Association, Boston, December, 1993. See also Shireen Hassim, "The Gender Agenda: Transforming the ANC", *Southern Africa Report/SAR* 7, #5 (May, 1992) and Sheila Meintjes, "Chartering Women's Future", *SAR*, 9, #2 (November, 1993).

40. Nelson Mandela, quoted in Karl von Holdt, "COSATU Special Congress: The uncertain new era", *SALB*, 17, #5 (September–October, 1993), p. 19; Mandela is also quoted there as saying that "the SA Communist Party must also not be complacent. With our background I do not think it would be possible for the ANC to betray the SACP. But it would be foolhardy for the SACP to be complacent and rely on the goodwill of the ANC".

41. Friedman, *op. cit.*, p. 58.

42. *Ibid.*, p. 67.

43. Karl Marx, "On the Jewish Question", Robert Tucker (ed.), *The Marx-Engels Reader* (New York: Norton, 1978), pp. 26–46. See also the remarkable introduction by Lucio Colletti to *Marx: Early Writings* (Harmondsworth: Penguin, 1975), an edition which includes a different translation of "On the Jewish Question".

44. John Keane, "Democracy and the Idea of the Left", in David McLellan and Sean Sayers, *Socialism and Democracy* (London: MacMillan, 1991), pp. 16–17.

45. Andrew Gamble, "Socialism, Radical Democracy and Class Politics", in McLellan and Sayers, *op. cit.*, p. 29. Of course, it is also true (as Gamble concludes) that "socialists cannot assume any longer that socialism and democracy go hand in hand. It has to be demonstrated. The really testing time for the relevance of socialism to the modern world may only just be beginning".

46. Perry Anderson, *op. cit.*, pp. 361–3.

47. Anderson, *ibid.*, p. 366–7. This is suggestively phrased, although one might wonder about the pertinence to the efforts of South African socialists on their own turf of a vision of struggle cast so exclusively in terms of contestation at the global level (whatever that might mean).

48. Przeworski, *op. cit.*, p. 122.

49. Is Larry Diamond, for example, merely being disingenuous when he deals with the new global realities – significantly enough, as a kind of unproblematic aside – with the thought that "the new democracies will also need economic assistance, access to Western markets, and debt relief if they are to show that democracy can work to solve the staggering economic and social problems they face. The international system can play a crucial role in creating the economic space for struggling democracies to undertake badly needed economic transformation with a social safety net and a human face, thereby making them politically sustainable" (in his "The Globalization of Democracy" in Robert O. Slater, Barry M. Schutz and Steven R. Dorr [eds.], *Global Transformation and the Third World* [Boulder: Lynne Reiner, 1993], p. 61.

50. From an interview with Mbeki in the ANC journal, *Mayibuye* (March, 1991), p. 2.

51. *Business Day*, January 13, 1993.

52. Thus, in a recent speech – delivered at the University of the North (January 20, 1994) – Mandela spoke in praise of Investec's sponsorship of a new Business School there, citing "the skilling of Black prospective business-persons . . . [as] a solid investment in the future of our country": "Up until now Black business persons have been restricted to the role of taxi owners, shebeeners, tuckshop owners and the like. Notwithstanding, they have performed with remarkable aplomb. [But now] we can have the kinds of candidates for senior position in South Africa's financial and industrial world. *Now we can begin to talk about empowerment far more convincingly*" (emphasis added). As it happens – as part of a process that is not problematised by Mandela here – the speed with which this "financial

and industrial world" is snapping up such "candidates for senior position" is, presently, one of the most crucial processes redefining the South African class structure.

53. See my essays "South Africa: Between 'Barbarism' and 'Structural Reform'", *op. cit.* and "Structural Reform: A Model for the Revolutionary Transformation of South Africa?", *Transformation*, #20 (1992); these two essays are also published, in revised form, as chapters in John S. Saul, *Recolonization and Resistance: Southern Africa in the 1990s* (Trenton: Africa World Press, 1993). See also André Gorz, "Reform and Revolution" in *The Socialist Register 1968* (London: Merlin Press, 1968) and Boris Kagarlitsky, *The Dialectic of Change* (London: Verso, 1990).

54. See, for example, Eddie Webster and Karl von Holdt, "Towards a socialist theory of radical reform: from resistance to reconstruction in the labour movement", paper presented to the Ruth First Memorial Colloquium held at the University of the Western Cape in August, 1992, and also the thoughtful evocation of related themes by Jeremy Cronin in his contribution to the debate on "Social democracy or democratic socialism" in *SALB*, 17, #6 (November–December, 1993).

55. Enoch Godongwana in his own contribution to the debate on "Social democracy or democratic socialism" (*ibid.*), p. 86.

56. Pallo Jordan, *ibid.*, p. 92; Jordan does suggest, however, that there may be limitations to a perspective on the transition to socialism that underplays the importance of a "decisive rupture" (a "decisive transformative moment", as he also puts it) in the movement from the old society to the new.

57. Patti Waldmeir, "Mandela warns of need for change", *Financial Times*, February 15, 1994. Note, too, that even Archbishop Tutu is quoted to the effect that, "After sanctions are lifted, it must not be business as usual. There has got to be a code of conduct for business in South Africa for a kind of investment that seeks to turn around the dispossession of power and empower the dispossessed" (cited in Linda Freeman, "The New Rules of the Game", *SAR*, 9, #4 [March–April, 1994]).

58. Dave Lewis, *ibid.*, p. 86–87, but see also, *inter alia*, the paper prepared by ISP Co-Directors Avril Joffe, David Kaplan, Raphael Kaplinsky and David Lewis, "Meeting the Global Challenge: A Framework for Industrial Revival in South Africa" and presented to the IDASA meeting on South Africa's International Economic Relations in the 1990s, April 27–30, 1993.

59. "'Mutually searching': Trade Union Strategies, South Africa and Canada" (an interview with Sam Gindin) in *Southern Africa Report (SAR)*, 8, #5 (1 May, 1993) and "Trade Union Strategies: The Debate Continues" (an exchange between Gindin and the ISP's Avril Joffe), *SAR*, 9, #3 (January, 1994). This debate also surfaced provocatively at a workshop held in Toronto between delegations of South African and Canadian unionists; for a report on this workshop see "Workers of the World, Debate", *SAR*, 9, 1 (July, 1993).

60. Surveying the ISP and MERG undertakings, as well as the ANC's broader reconstruction and development programme (RDP), Jenny Cargill (in her article, "Superman State: Nothing less is needed to implement ANC 'reconstruction' proposals", *Finance Week*, December 9–15, 1993) suggests there to be "an underlying assumption among the ANC and its alliance partners that they have the capacity to organise a thoroughgoing reconstruction of a new society for South Africa." "At issue", she suggests, "is not state intervention per se, but the faith placed in the deitised 'democratic state' to fix everything . . ." However, substantively (in Cargill's judgement), the various proposals are actually not so very radical, seeking, in practice, to bend the existing production very little and implying, centrally, the need for "a more rigorous search for incentives to pull in the private sector"! Indeed, she argues, the RDP is likely to involve such a range of compromises vis-à-vis capital and the presumed imperatives of the global economy as to risk the ANC's alienating its popular constituency.

61. See, for example, Stephen Gelb, "Democratising Economic Growth: Alternative Growth Models for the Future", *Transformation*, #12 (1990) and subsequent writings by the same author.

62. Etkind and Harvey, *op. cit.*, pp. 86–7. Compare, however, the rather more modest, though still critical, tone in a second article on COSATU and its Reconstruction Accord with the ANC in the same edition of SALB. Thus, for Jenny Cargill, COSATU's "challenge is how

to tailor strategies to political and economic realities on the one hand, but avoid abdicating to the status quo on the other"!

63. See Lawrence Harris, "Building the Mixed Economy" and "How are we going to Pay for Economic Reconstruction", papers presented to the seminar held by the ANC's Department of Economic Planning, Harare, April–May, 1990.

64. Lawrence Harris, "South Africa's Economic and Social Transformation: from 'No Middle Road' to 'No Alternative'", *Review of African Political Economy*, #57 (1993), pp. 91–103.

65. I have noted some of Harris' distortions of my own position in my *Recolonization and Resistance*, (*op. cit.*), pp. 183–4.

66. Nicoli Nattrass, "Economic Restructuring in South Africa: What it is and how can it be managed", paper presented to the Annual Research Workshop of the Canadian Research Consortium on Southern Africa, Kingston, January 23, 1994.

67. As it happens, Nattrass cannot quite decide whether authoritarian or democratic structures are more conducive to capitalist development. She is, in any case, even more preoccupied with the likely capacities of the South African bureaucracy to play the "rational" role required of it than she is with the class character of the state itself.

68. The danger of such an outcome was amongst the possibilities discussed in an illuminating paper presented by Stephen Gelb to the "Political Economy Seminar" series at York University, February 14, 1994 and entitled "Democracy and Development in South Africa".

69. Colin Bundy, "Problems and Prospects for South African Socialists," paper presented to the Political Science Seminar, York University, October, 1992, p. 20.

70. Robert D. Kaplan, "The Coming Anarchy", *The Atlantic Monthly* (February, 1994).

71. Gamble, *op. cit.*, pp. 29–30.

72. Thus Ms. Mandela, so deeply compromised by the excesses of her own political practice, nonetheless struck a potentially powerful note – one that may well be heard again – when, in the wake of the ANC's "Strategic Perspective" document (cited above), she criticized the "so-called power sharing deal between the elite of the oppressed and the oppressors" and spoke of the "looming disaster in this country which will result from the distortion of a noble goal in favour of a shortcut to parliament by a handful of individuals" (Winnie Mandela as quoted in "Swinging attack by Winnie indicates populist dissent," *Southscan*, 8, #2 (15 January, 1993).

73. Roger Murray, "Second Thoughts on Ghana", *New Left Review*, #42 (March–April, 1967), p. 39.

THE DEVELOPMENT OF CAPITALISM IN VIETNAM

Gerard Greenfield

Only a generation ago, Vietnam's social revolution played a critical role in the revival of the Western Left. Protest movements in every major city in the West not only offered international solidarity but expressed a rekindling of interest in socialist ideas and a renewed capacity for mass political action. It is an important and unfortunate symptom of the generality of the crisis of the Left today that Vietnamese intellectuals, like many of their counterparts in the West, are abandoning the socialist project. Most are doing so not through disillusionment or the (re)discovery of alternative intellectual paradigms alone, but because a commitment to socialism denies access to the material rewards of alignment with, or a non-antagonistic stance towards, the interests of the state and capital. Ultimately this retreat provides the ideological basis for the exercise of state power against the working class in the interests of the new bourgeoisie emerging from within the ranks of incumbent state enterprise managers and the most powerful segments of the party-state bureaucracy. Dismantling the socialist project is central to the agenda of the new policy orthodoxy in Vietnam.

The removal of Ho Chi Minh's portrait from the roof of the State Bank for "structural reasons" – architectural, not social – coincides with the removal of statues from parks and other public places, apparently because "prostitutes and drug addicts were leaning on them". They were not torn down by crowds celebrating the collapse of Communist regimes and the (somewhat brief) advent of democracy as in Eastern Europe. But a change is taking place: an ideological transformation in which the ruling political class is consolidating itself in a new social order. The dominant discourse has not abandoned Ho Chi Minh, but reinterprets his intentions: more a nationalist than a communist. In the same way that the search for the tomb of Genghis Khan can be interpreted as a search for a nationalist identity by the communists-turned-nationalists in Mongolia, there is here the restoration of old identities, repetition, and ultimately reinterpretation. This involves a re-mystification of the nationalist revolutionary and hence the removal of the Stalinist iconography. The recent discovery of Ho Chi

Minh's will at least establishes the pretext for the removal of the mausoleum, given that he had asked to be cremated. And since Ho Chi Minh isn't around to say, as Deng in China, "To get rich is glorious!", they are saying it for him: Uncle Ho had sought national liberation for the purpose of building national wealth. Socialism becomes peripheral, subordinate to this national wealth.

This renewal of national consciousness is central to the ideological transformation taking place as the Vietnamese people face the development of capitalism under a single-party authoritarian regime. Vietnam's leading economic advisor, Le Dang Doanh, a proponent of the "Taiwanese model", stated unequivocally, "The Vietnamese people are nationalistic. When they're told something's in the national interest, they'll do it."[1] Inherent in this national interest is the legitimation of the rise of military-owned fractions of capital, and a group of powerful state conglomerates that will differ little from the bureaucratic bourgeoisie which prospered under the authoritarian-capitalist regime in the South before 1975.[2]

The mobilizing basis of the present reform process is precisely to replace class consciousness with a new economic nationalism. The adoption of the Asian NICs as the model for Vietnam's development is premised on the view expressed by Vietnamese intellectuals and policy-makers that state-led industrialization was based on a partnership between the proletariat and bourgeoisie in the interests of the nation-state. Ironically the statist analyses of East Asian development undertaken by analytical Marxists and the progressive Left in the West now inform an agenda where the crushing of working class struggle and repression of the labour movement is implicit in this model for growth. The trade union leadership itself has adopted the Singaporean model of trade unionism: business unionism and peaceful co-existence with an authoritarian-capitalist regime – a strategy by which they seek the political marginalisation of the working class.

There is a strong belief amongst the Western Left that the reform agenda is being thrashed out in debates over the merits of capitalism and socialism. Despite the zeal with which political economists and political scientists in Vietnam and abroad have described this 'public debate' it simply does not exist. When two hundred peasants arrived in Hanoi from Ha Bac province to protest against the theft of rice and land by local party officials, they were dispersed by police and within an hour had fled or been arrested.[3] It is the same problem we have with 'human rights': people seem to have different conceptions of who the humans are. Those who describe this public debate appear to be referring to the Vietnamese intelligentsia and state officials as the 'public'. But even when one of Vietnam's leading social scientists, Hoang Chi Bao, published a monograph earlier this year which attempted to outline the crisis of "real socialism" and criticize the neglect of the present social crisis by policy-makers, it was banned under the new press laws and he was forced to write a statement of self-criticism.

Unfortunately, the remnants of the Vietnamese Left who are committed to democratic socialism are confronted by a newly pragmatic Western Left all too ready to accept the term 'market economy' or even 'market socialism' as a euphemism for disguising the transition to capitalism. Many on the Left exhibit a fascination with entrepreneurial forces, the lifestyles of the new rich and the machinations of business in the new Vietnam. It is assumed that workers are benefitting from higher wages and the availability of more consumer goods, and that the peasantry are responding to incentives free of the constraints of cooperatives, as indicated by thriving rural markets. Massive increases in exports of food are cited by intellectuals and policy-makers alike as the great pay-off for years of market reform. Western observers – including those on the Left – talk in terms of the responsiveness to market incentives, the restoration of farmers' interests in output and profit, and the economic democracy embodied in agricultural reform. Yet the National Institute for Nutrition has pointed out the costs involved to these same beneficiaries of reform. Record rice exports by state trading companies have coincided with 2.5 million people going hungry each year, and over 6 million people suffer from an inadequate calorie intake.[4]

The health and education programmes freely available to the mass of the people regardless of the distribution of property and income is often considered as evidence of the ongoing commitment to social equality in Vietnam today. In fact, while free health and education was certainly a very important element in Vietnam's socialist project, it no longer exists outside a handful of foreign NGO programmes. Of the state-run primary and secondary schools that remain open – and the number is rapidly declining – informal fees have reduced class attendance of the children of workers and peasants to a four-hour week and of the 600,000 that graduate from primary school every year as many as half cannot afford to go on to secondary school. Even then public classes are hollowed out and real learning only begins after classes for the few whose parents can afford private tuition fees. This coincides with increased exploitation of child-labour, with the number of children working full-time in their millions.[5] Compulsory tuition fees introduced earlier this year have put tertiary education beyond the reach of the majority of those who finish secondary school.[6] Faced with these fees, students of poor families are forced to quit or to work. Students from the provinces prostitute themselves in dormitories of colleges to pay their fees. This privatization of social welfare has also spread throughout the health system, with informal fees charged for the staff's time, beds, medication, and even the right to visit patients. Finally, the number of unemployed has reached seven million, and, far from receiving welfare payments, the unemployed have to pay to register as being unemployed or buy their way into a private sector job.[7] Where money has been allocated to create jobs most of it has been misallocated or stolen by state officials.[8]

Melanie Beresford has articulated a view predominant amongst the Western Left and Vietnamese policy-makers concerning the decline of social welfare:

> Some Western critics have complained that the introduction of market reforms in Vietnam and elsewhere has led to the abandonment of social welfare programs. What is abundantly clear, however, is that it is not the market reforms that are responsible, but the severe fiscal crisis of the Vietnamese state, brought about by the massive budget deficits required to maintain an inefficient public sector. Maintenance of health, education and welfare systems, the past achievements of which the Vietnamese are justifiably proud, will therefore be dependent upon continued reform of the state sector enterprises.[9]

There can be no doubt that the fiscal crisis of the state is important in this respect. But the reform of state sector enterprises has intensified rather than resolved this crisis. It is characterized by the private appropriation of public resources on a massive scale, where the state acts as the instrument of this appropriation. The dismantling of the "bureaucratic centralism and subsidy system" has concentrated power in the hands of incumbent state enterprise managers and the most powerful segments of the party-state bureaucracy, including the military. The theft of state assets and the sacking of the state budget by those with political power and connections is the outcome of the unrestrained search for profit and the accumulation of private wealth under the liberalizing effect of market reforms and is a far greater leakage of wealth from the state budget than the system of state sector subsidies.[10]

The New Agenda

Variants of neo-liberalism, neo-conservatism and statism inform the economic reform agenda, not socialism. The policy discourse is informed by a 'new right': that group of state officials, policy advisors, economists, and officially endorsed intellectuals who are intent on imposing the disciplinary power of market forces on workers and peasants and demolishing what remains of the public sector. The new right has been institutionalized as an advisory body to the Council of Ministers and the Party's Central Political Bureau, in order to bypass bureaucratic obstacles and institutional constraints. This includes bypassing the National Assembly which, having been made more democratic under the 1992 constitutional reforms, is prone to take the notion of debate more seriously, slowing down the process of reform.[11] This elite advisory body includes state enterprise managers, private business managers, and overseas Vietnamese entrepreneurs, as well as reformist intellectuals and technocrats. The tasks of the advisory body include setting the agenda for reform and drafting legislation to be passed on to the National Assembly for its approval.

Divisions within the new right technocrats over economic reform concern the degree of state management of the market. Although these differences are important it should be recognised that the debate over the degree and type of state intervention is inextricably tied to their own interests and political power base. Policy advisors, consultants and bureaucrats from different ministries and state agencies are framing these opposing models of the state in terms of increasing their own power and influence. It is not over economic theory alone that central banks and finance ministries are pitted against each other the world over, and Vietnam is no different.

With support from the World Bank and UNDP, fiscal austerity, macroeconomic stabilization, the expansion of the private sector, and export-led industrialization founded on exploitation of passive, cheap labour are central elements of the new agenda. From within the ranks of trade unions it has been argued that legal recognition of the right to strike must not conflict with the interests of foreign capital.[12] The reform of state enterprises is not simply a matter of reorganization of authority and accountability, but recreating the structures of power and control over industry that exists in the private sectors of capitalist economies. This was the primary objective of economic decentralization and managerial autonomy introduced under the rubric of market reform policies. Although these policies were a *post facto* recognition by the state of the changes which had already been imposed by managers at the level of the firm, it nonetheless provided the impetus for the expansion of absolute managerial power on a larger scale, and legitimized the concentration of power in the new factory regime.

Official recognition of the "state capitalist sector" is a reflection of the contradictions inherent in the new right dialogue on reform, which must be carried out within the (fast diminishing) constraints of the Marxist-Leninist *political* discourse. The authoritarian political regime, with its ideological basis in democratic centralism, is critical for these intellectuals to maintain exclusive access to policy-makers and to free themselves from the constraints of public debate or mass political participation.

In 1990 and 1991 the Party daily *Nhan Dan* (The People) ran a number of articles which criticized party cadres and state officials for corruption. In the same newspaper a tight circle of academics and journalists raised the issue of the involvement of party cadres in private business and discussed the notion of democracy. But even this limited debate saw an official backlash against the deputy editor and led to his overseas exile. The new press laws introduced this year forbid criticism of the Party and of the "falsification of history through denial of the gains of the socialist revolution."[13] Clearly there can be no genuine public debate – not in the sense of genuine democratic participation – if it must be premised on the assumption that workers and peasants constitute the ruling class and social relations of exploitation and surplus extraction by the state do not exist.

A critical press does exist. The newspapers *Lao Dong* (Labour) and *Tuoi Tre* (Youth) have provided an ongoing critique of the social problems arising from market reforms. Unemployment, prostitution, child-labour, the failures of the trade unions and the corruption of state officials are issues that are regularly reported. But where political interests are threatened and the interests of the state bourgeoisie directly challenged, censorship laws close the doors on this debate.[14] More importantly, the destruction of social safety nets and welfare services, and the further impoverishment of millions is portrayed as the negative side-effect of the transition to a market economy, not an element of the market economy itself. Criticism can be directed at "the market mechanism" because, as with the anthropomorphized "economy" in advanced capitalist countries, it implies an autonomous force free of political interests and beyond the control of political power-holders.

In the early years of building socialism in North Vietnam, increased managerial control was argued to be a tactical necessity, shifting the structure of power in the factory regime against the workers. Unpaid overtime, the recruitment of extra workers at lower wages and the intensification of shift-work characterized the rush to meet plan targets. Under pressure to meet these targets, managers freely hired and fired workers. When workers' everyday forms of resistance manifested themselves in absenteeism, idleness and low labour productivity, the Party demanded that labour discipline be improved. Ken Post has concluded that: "This emphasis was most important for the future of the working class, because it put stress on management as the control of labour, implicitly shifting the balance against democratic participation."[15]

This shift against democratic participation and towards increased managerial control has been consolidated and expanded under the current reforms. Reforms introduced at the level of production which increase managerial control over the labour process and the redistribution of surplus are intended to "break the negative power of the working class which is seen as the ultimate source of inflexibility of the economic system."[16] Previously, the power of state sector managers over workers had been constrained by the Marxist-Leninist discourse which framed the labour-power of workers as their politically constituted property. One of the key effects of market reforms is to create the compulsion for workers to sell their labour-power, breaking down this "socialist fetter", and imposing the whip of capitalism.[17] Since exploitation occurred in redistribution rather than production, the state apparatus became the target of the struggle against surplus extraction. The struggle of the peasantry against the extractive mechanisms of the state was pivotal in the crisis which generated pressures for reform. But I will only deal here with the transformation of the state sector to examine the way in which state power has been exercised against the industrial proletariat, and discuss certain aspects of working class struggle in the transition to capitalism.

According to a senior Ministry of Labour official market reforms have freed managers from the constraints imposed on them by the state on the behalf of workers. Under a market economy, "industrial relations" are reconstituted as "the efficient utilization of labour in a relationship that is better understood by managers than workers".[18] The following is indicative of the centrality of this to the reform agenda of the new right intellectuals:

[I]n the socialist-oriented multi-sector commodity economy the labour force is also a commodity. Emoluments in general and wages in particular are the monetary expression of the value of labour. As such wages should in principle also be determined on the labour market.[19]

The same economists go on to claim that the labour market is constrained from allocating labour efficiently where the rise of the autarkic household economy has inhibited the commodification of the rural workforce. Market forces are also inhibited by the system of recruitment, guaranteed employment and fixed wages in the state sector.[20] It is on this basis that the 'surplus labour redistribution' programme was initiated: to massively reduce the state sector workforce and expand the pool of 'free' workers that indigenous and foreign fractions of capital could readily draw on. At present just over a million workers have been laid off from the state sector. According to the Ministry of Labour,the reform of the "economic managerial structure" had revealed the extent of "surplus labour" in state enterprises. In the first few months of 1989, the managers of some state sector production units laid off 80–90% of their workforce. In the early years of reform this mainly affected the bulk of the administrative staff and middle managers, and only later spread to the direct producers themselves. The decree on the redistribution of the workforce in state economic units created the premise for a more widespread and systematic application of what had long been a *de facto* reform – laying off workers to reduce production costs. State officials themselves recognize that this process was "lacking democracy, lacking openness."[21]

The second step was to reform wages under a new flexible structure that allowed a 13:1 differential between the highest and lowest wages. The reality, however, was that by this stage enterprise directors had already transformed the factory regime, enforcing competition between workers by hiring younger workers and first generation workers from within the peasantry. Tens of thousands of day labourers gather in the twenty so-called "open-air labour markets" in Hanoi everyday in search of work.[22] Day labourers gather on the fringes of Ho Chi Minh City and in the nearby industrial centre of Bien Hoa, Dong Nai province, in the sweatshop belt of small- and medium-scale factories that take up the production of state enterprises increasingly hollowed out through diversification, subcontracting and the private subsidiaries established by enterprise managers with state money. The collapse of rural cooperatives and *de facto* land reforms which saw the appropriation of land and its accumulation in private hands (usually local party and state cadres or their relatives) has provided enterprise managers with a pool of first generation workers willing to work for low wages under any conditions. The culture of resistance of these workers drawn from the peasantry is individualized and sporadic, unlike the sustained collective struggle of the industrial workers who had developed a high level of class consciousness under the socialist project.

The shedding of the state workforce and lower-level bureaucrats has given rise to a massive social class of petty traders and shopkeepers. The petty-embourgeoisement of the lower ranks of the party-state bureaucracy and workers and middle managers made redundant under state enterprise reforms is not simply an outcome of the fiscal crisis of the state but is a reaction of the ruling class and the middle strata to the struggle against the state. Individual ability, personal relations, thrift, and market forces are supposed to determine the fate of this rapidly increasing class of street traders, artisans, shopkeepers, bicycle repairers, and household petty commodity producers. The struggle against the state disintegrates into the struggle for survival, where market compulsion, indebtedness and intense competition create working and living conditions that fall well short of the glorified small entrepreneur that pioneers market opportunities. Petty street traders and household producers are subject to police raids, extortion, arbitrary state taxes and charges, and indebtedness to the state-sponsored credit schemes, banks and money-lenders. Surplus extraction may not occur through the social relations of exchange, but profits of the petty commodity traders and producers are whittled away by these extra-economic modes of extraction.

Massive unemployment and increasing social inequality is integral to the logic of the 'market economy'. Under-classes and the threat of falling amongst them is the whip of capitalism. But in the dominant discourse of 'market transition', social inequality is the inevitable social stratification arising from differences in the personal ability of individuals to exploit market opportunities and compete.[23] Inequality arising from the structure of power and control over the means of production have become peripheral issues, as equitable tax regimes become the radical edge of the 'socialist orientation':

> Acceptance of all the elements of the market and the regulating mechanisms of the market in accordance with the law of value and of supply and demand will inevitably lead to a polarization between the rich and the poor and to disparities in incomes. In order to ensure social justice, there should therefore be a policy for income redistribution through income taxes.[24]

Under the guise of a new national struggle, a 'social partnership' between workers and managers and owners emerges as a central tenet of the dominant discourse. As with the 'social contract' imposed on workers in advanced capitalist societies, workers are promised future rewards in return for accepting intensified exploitation and exclusion from control over the conditions and organization of production in a period of adjustment. The politics of 'social partnership' arises from intellectuals and state officials legitimizing their own partnership of interests with capital. Nearly all ministries, government departments and research institutes are involved in various types of profit-making activities ranging from the sale of information and skills to foreign capital to the export of unskilled workers and sex labour (brides and prostitutes), and theft of state funds through budgetary allocations for employment generation, research programmes and investment in buildings and equipment.[25] There are also cases where aid money from non-government organisations (NGOs) and foreign governments is used to finance lending in informal financial markets, personal consumption, smuggling, and the purchase of greater access to the state budget.

The intellectuals and technocrats of the party-state apparatus use their political authority, personal contacts and influence, control over information and inside knowledge to combine their position within the state apparatus with consultancies for foreign business interests and in many cases engage directly in private business activities. It is these intellectuals who dominate the discourse on reform, informing the work of foreign observers and receiving legitimation from them. Financial support from foreign governments, the World Bank and the UNDP rewards the pursuit of pragmatic neoliberal policy solutions by this segment of the intelligentsia, as well as preparing the next generation of technocrats through courses in business administration and orthodox economics. Show-case conferences and the mutual recognition and legitimation of each other's work is as much a part of intellectual life in Vietnam as it is in Western capitalist countries. As in China, the programme for financial and banking reform incorporates consultants from global financial corporations into that body of the technocratic elite that will make the tough decisions on what must be done.

Power and Capital: The Transformation of the State Sector

The coal mines in Quang Ninh, a northern province bordering China, are often cited as a branch of the state sector which has failed to respond to reform. A government directive issued in 1991 ordered the reorganization of production to reduce waste and inefficiency. Earlier directives on consolidation and reorganization had been ignored.[26] Yet the initial pressure for reform had come from the miners themselves. Quang Ninh was an extremely poor region with widespread underemployment and the predominance of seasonal workers, insecure and without the social welfare benefits of full-time employment in the state sector. The miners' struggle against the bureaucratic strata, particularly the provincial people's committee, manifested itself in tension over wages in the mid-1980s. This continued up until 1991 when lay-offs under the redistribution of labour surplus programme and the consolidation of the military's ownership of a number of the larger mines undermined workers' solidarity and ability to oppose the extractive mechanisms of the state.

The threat of competition for employment and the removal of the constraints on managers to fire workers did not have its full effect until the spread of over a thousand 'bandit' mines saw the disintegration of state production units. Contracting out and cooperation with the private sector by state mine managers saw workers forced into the unregulated small-scale private mines where intense competition and unrestrained profit maximization combined with the fracturing of workers into smaller groups. Economic decentralization and the release of 'market forces' resulted in the rapid expansion of smuggling from China, shifting the interests of local state officials away from coal mining to illegal trade. It is this illegal cross-border trade which accounts for the increased wealth and higher standards of living visible in parts of Quang Ninh. The proliferation of bandit mines occurred as state regulation collapsed altogether.

The gamble that many on the Left take with workers' lives in the hope that friendly capitalists or an unleashed state sector will observe the rights and interests of workers has not paid off. Changes in the nature and intensity of exploitation have seen extended working hours, environmental pollution, and increased accidents and occupational diseases. Lung and skin diseases have spread to the residential areas near the mines and silicosis afflicts over three-quarters of the miners.[27] Ironically, the government directives to reduce air pollution in the coal mining towns of Hong Gai and Cam Pha were concerned with cleaning up the area for the development of the tourism industry, not the health of miners and their families. This coincides with the shift in state wealth out of coal production into the tourism industry, forcing miners into the private mines or into petty trade and services. In the bandit mines hundreds die or suffer serious injuries every year. The exact figures are not available because the Vietnam General Confederation of Labour's (VGCL) Institute for Labour Protection does not have access to private firms. Miners have died from lack of oxygen only 16 metres down and floods and cave-ins occur regularly since the mines lack basic infrastructure. Children and female workers are targeted for the more dangerous night-shifts and are paid less. Even in state mines where millions of dollars have been earned in exports – cited by both the Right and Left as evidence of the success of the market economy – female workers replace the outdated technology, carrying baskets of coal on their heads.[28]

Hoang Chi Bao and Nguyen Thanh Tuan argue that as trade union cadres, enterprise managers and state officials plunder state assets and 'degenerate into thieves', workers are reacting against this by stealing from the shop floor.[29] The transparent increase in the private wealth of enterprise managers and cadres combined with increased exploitation and deteriorating living and working conditions has generated a culture of resistance which manifests itself in lax attitudes towards work and theft from the work-place. But this increasing idleness, petty theft, and lack of labour discipline amongst workers is interpreted by market reformers as the cause of the inefficiency of state enterprises – hence the need to increase the power of managers and subject workers to the whip of market forces – using trade unions to ensure workers' compliance.

The claim that the leading role of the state-owned enterprise sector constitutes the mainstay of the 'socialist orientation' is discredited by the loss of control over state enterprises and the effective economic ownership exercised by incumbent managers. In contrast to Russia where this loss of state control is argued to have consolidated the power of the workers' collective within the enterprise, the massive lay-offs, destruction of social welfare programmes, deteriorating working conditions, extension of the working day (well beyond the eight hours that over a century of international working class struggle has won as a human right), and the decline in workers' control over the production process, suggests that state ownership as it exists in Vietnam today has very little to do with socialism.[30] Vietnamese policy-makers and the new right intellectuals point to juridical property relations and legal-institutional arrangements to define this state ownership. This is readily informed by the revived bourgeois paradigms of neoliberalism and post-Marxism, particularly neo-institutionalism, where actual social relations are assumed to comply with these legal-institutional arrangements. Such a view is articulated in the Party's *Communist Review*, where the constitutional reforms of 1992 are argued to have raised the National Assembly above conflicting political and social interests, enabling it to carry out its 'fundamental activity' of 'changing social relations'.[31]

In two years, the number of state enterprises has declined from 12,500 to 6,450. Of this, another 500 local state enterprises have disappeared since the beginning of 1993. The state sector is now comprised of just under 6,000 enterprises, yet only two state enterprises have been officially privatised in the whole country to date. Another nineteen are scheduled to be privatised in 1994.[32] Market socialists and economic reformers would probably argue that this is the result of the dissolution of loss-making, inefficient enterprises, and the consolidation of the rest through mergers. But this sell-off of plant and equipment, buildings, and the illegal sale of land has not led to any payments to the state. Instead, virtually all of these enterprises borrowed heavily both from within the state sector and from overseas financial institutions leaving massive accumulated debts which must now be met by the state. This represents a stage of primitive accumulation in which the state budget and the accumulation of national debt are the source of capital for the private and quasi-private factories and businesses which have emerged out of the state sector.[33]

The state enterprise managers who initiated grassroots reforms in the early 1980s prior to the era of market reform illustrate precisely what Bao and Tuan are referring to. Yet, these have become models for enterprise reform for Vietnamese and Western economists and political economists.

It is a familiar model: increased efficiency; improved competitiveness and exports; higher labour productivity and output; and financial autonomy. The reforms introduced by enterprise directors were based on the reduction of the workforce to cut production costs, the intensification of exploitation through shift-work and incentive schemes, increased managerial control, closer linkages with the private sector, particularly the merchant capitalist class, and overseas borrowing. The transformation of the factory regime also saw exclusive control over the financial resources of the state enterprise shift to managers. Workers do not have access to the accounts of the enterprise and have no knowledge of the financial structure of the firm, not even the size of the wage bill or profits. This restricts the ability of workers to monitor collectively the financial assets of the firm which are effectively controlled by the director and the chief accountant. A practice common in most state enterprises is to exploit this exclusive access to financial information by undervaluing the wage fund and paying the amount withheld as bonuses and productivity incentives.

An example may give some substance to this. HCMC Food Corp. has long been considered a model of successful reform. The director, Nguyen Thi Thi, had close connections with Party leaders in southern Vietnam, including Nguyen Van Linh and Vo Van Kiet, when she reformed the enterprise in 1983. Thi reduced the administrative staff from 4,200 to 30, replaced middle managers with former capitalist entrepreneurs of the pre-1975 era, and placed workers on piece-rate wages. Retained profits and foreign loans were used to diversify the company's activities.[34] In 1987, the first joint-stock commercial bank was established, institutionalizing the informal banking and trading capital that had emerged from within a group of state enterprises in the South operated by reformist managers. The director of HCMC Food Corp. headed this group. By 1985 Vo Van Kiet claimed that Thi had succeeded in bringing merchant capital under the control of the state through the expansion of linkages with the private sector under a form of 'state capitalism'.[35] But Kiet had misunderstood the direction in which power and wealth was being transferred. Increasing dependence on the networks and business practices of private merchant capital and the transfer of state assets and parts of the production process to the private businesses owned by state managers and their relatives in fact brought these state factories and trading companies into the orbit of private capital. HCMC Food Corp. was gradually being hollowed out.

By early 1993, Thi was forced into retirement when it was revealed that the company had accumulated hundreds of millions of dollars in overseas debts and had misallocated millions more. Of course, these debts have been added to the national debt and will be met by the state, not the constellation of private business interests that arose out of it. In total US$60 million has been stolen from the enterprise, including US$4 million worth of machinery which was moved to private factories. In a related case a subsidiary of HCMC Food Corp., Miliket, was established in 1987 with money from the state budget. In 1990, the state enterprise director sold to himself the trademark, factory, warehouses and all of the physical assets of Miliket, paying for it by using funds from the state budget. Two years later, the HCMC People's Committee licensed Miliket Co. Ltd. as a private enterprise. In addition to the theft of the entire enterprise, the director accumulated millions in overseas loans which also have to be met by the state. This is only one of hundreds of illegal privatisations each year.[36]

What is clear from this is that corruption on this scale cannot be seen as the continuation of past practices or simply as the negative side effects of the market mechanism. Liberals and some on the Left have become obsessed with the phenomenon of corruption in itself, using it to measure the relative degree of democracy or to attack the individuals involved. And as far as the academics-turned-consultants working on Vietnam and China are concerned, there is no shortage of fascination with the methods of corruption and with the ingenuity of state officials. Despite the liberal rhetoric on political reform, this is not a peripheral phenomenon to be resolved by the 'rule of law' and the development of 'civil society'. The theft of state assets, pillaging of the state budget, the transfer of state-owned land, factories, buildings and other assets into private hands, and the involvement of segments of the party-state bureaucracy in the interests of indigenous and foreign fractions of capital are not simply aberrations of an imperfect transition, but the very foundations of the new social order itself: the beginnings of civil society. This is not to say that 'property is theft', but to identify the mechanisms by which material wealth is shifted outside the state, creating a sphere of social power in which the exploitation of those free to sell their labour-power by those who have effective private possession of the means of production is a dominant social relation. Marx showed that the rise of merchant capital is contingent upon its links to the state. State power is exercised in this process of primitive accumulation, in the form of state-sponsored monopolies and government contracts gained through bribery and corruption. The most critical source of merchant wealth is the accumulation of national debt, where 'a good part of every national loan performs the service of a capital fallen from heaven'.[37]

The link between corruption and the involvement of the relatives, particularly the children, of party and state officials in private business is critical to understanding this transfer of wealth from the state to the autonomous social sphere in which capital is emerging. Whereas previously, political authority and privilege had provided the means to transfer status and power from one generation to the next, the decline in the attractiveness of careers in the state bureaucracy relative to the potential wealth and power of private entrepreneurs, and the restructuring of the state apparatus, generates pressure on state officials at all levels to use their political authority to help their children set themselves up in private businesses. Although difficult to conceptualize, this personal interest in ensuring the well-being of their children, defined increasingly in terms of capitalist-entrepreneurship, is possibly the most powerful motivation of all for the private appropriation of public resources. In the case of both HCMC Food Corp. and Miliket, it was a network of family relations that underlay the process of privatisation.

The shift in state wealth out of production and the formation of direct links to the indigenous bourgeoisie and foreign capital characterises this privatisation process. It is exemplified by the transformation of the state enterprises controlled by the HCMC People's Committee where the retreat from production (manifested in factory closures and the reduction of the industrial workforce) coincides with the creation of the HCMC State Financial Holding Company which institutionalises the financial interests and nominal ownership rights of the local state apparatus. In the textiles industry, the creation of close relations with private capitalist entrepreneurs has effectively transferred control over production to private interests. The most powerful of these private interests is Minh Phung, who emerged from within the ranks of the ethnic Chinese merchant capitalist class. Close ties with local party and state officials saw the emergence of the Minh Phung Production Company (originally established as a 'collective economic production team' in 1991) as one of the largest private textiles conglomerates; subsuming state textiles production units as the HCMC People's Committee retreated into trade and finance. The nature of Minh Phung's ties to political power-holders was revealed in a recent investigation into his illegal banking and real estate activities in which he was shown to be providing city officials and their relatives with interest-free loans and new cars. Despite this investigation, state officials have indicated that policies to facilitate the expansion of Minh Phung's production and export activities will be implemented in 1994.[38]

The formation of merchant capital from within the state enterprise sector is not simply a response to higher returns or the inability to reform industrial production. It is the outcome of class struggle where the assets of the enterprises are moved beyond the workers' sphere of interests, and beyond their control. Just as de-industrialization and the casualization of work in the advanced capitalist countries has undermined the social power of the working class by shifting industrial production offshore or dissolving it into finance capital, the rise of merchant capital in Vietnam as the dominant form of wealth has created a sphere of accumulation outside of the direct participation of the industrial proletariat. Sub-contracting and the relocation of production into small- and medium-scale private subsidiaries undermines the social power of the industrial proletariat through disintegrating the production process, with workers gathered in fewer numbers and in conditions where their interests are atomized. Workers are exposed to the competition of the labour market and their ranks are filled with first generation workers and children who lack a sense of common interests that extend beyond mere survival, let alone a class consciousness.

It has been argued that in Russia the rise of merchant capital has not affected the social relations of production. In fact workers' control on the factory floor has increased.[39] There are critical differences in the historical development of class relations and the nature of the state sector which prevent any serious comparison with the case of Vietnam. However, where wealth is shifted out of the sphere of production into the sphere of circulation in the form of merchant capital, it cannot be argued that the social relations of production remain unchanged. And if social conditions beyond the enterprise (such as massive unemployment, poor housing conditions, and the collapse of social welfare programmes) are recognized as affecting workers as a social force, then the argument that workers have recaptured control of the factory floor must be treated with caution. Particularly for workers no longer on the factory floor.

While the bulk of the state enterprise sector is slipping into oblivion, a new group of enterprises is emerging from within the non-economic institutions of the state apparatus. The most prolific growth has been in the businesses and production units owned by sections of the military. Although around 300 enterprises in construction, mining and transport are recognized as belonging to the Ministry of Defence, there are over two thousand enterprises which have been established using state resources but which are not state enterprises.[40] The political power and influence of the high-ranking military officers that run these enterprises allows this entire sector to escape state control, while at the same time forging organic links with state trading companies and commercial banks, and channelling funds from the state budget. Both soldiers and civilian workers are employed in these factories, offices, hotels, and construction teams, although soldiers are only paid extra wages for this 'private' work in kind. Surplus extraction is not mediated by redistribution as in the pre-reform state enterprises, but is based on exploitation for private profit. But clearly, for these military workers extra-economic modes of appropriation remain important.

The significance of military involvement in private business on such a large scale should not be underestimated. The environmental protection laws due to be passed next year are irrelevant as long as logging and mining is carried out by military-run companies. The proposed labour laws are just as irrelevant. Mines owned and operated by the military have already shown that the safety and health of workers (let alone minimum wages or a limit to the working day) are interests suppressed by this combination of political power and capital, where the coercive power of the state extends into the factory regime itself. The murder of labour activists and the political repression of workers' rights and interests by the military in Indonesia gives us some insight into the possible dangers posed by military-owned fractions of capital. Obviously, there are differences: the People's Army cannot justify the repression of workers' movements on the grounds that it gives rise to the threat of communist insurgency, as the Indonesian military does. But the threat posed to political stability and economic growth by strikes has already been conceived as a matter of national security.[41]

Privatization: The Politics of Exclusion

In the opening session of the Seventh National Congress of Vietnamese Trade Unions, Communist Party General Secretary, Do Muoi, railed against corruption and mismanagement in the state sector. The solution was clear:

> Only through ownership of shares by the workers can they become the masters of their enterprises and through this rid the system of the disease of bribery and corruption.[42]

Socialists could interpret this as the reversal of a reform agenda intent on ridding the system of what is Left. But in his advocacy of workers' ownership, Do Muoi had deviated from his prepared speech and government policy, contradicting the agenda of policy-makers and their entourage of new right technocrats. The Prime Minister, Vo Van Kiet, stayed away from the congress on the second day, sending a telegram instead which stipulated that the government would certainly allow workers to participate in shareholdings – as members of the public. In other words, they could buy them if they could afford them. It is a reminder that for the new right technocrats, privatization is about resolving the fiscal crisis of the state, and they are well aware that the same workers impoverished and excluded under market reforms are unlikely to have all that much money stashed away under their beds.

As mentioned earlier, amidst the 6,000 state enterprises, two have been privatised. The first of these, Legamex International Corporation, was 'corporatised' in mid-1993. The Legamex conglomerate – combining nine subsidiaries, seven 'cooperation production businesses' and four joint ventures – employed 6,485 workers and had total assets valued at US$13 million. Its accumulated offshore loans nearly matched this at US$12.6 million. To reassure potential shareholders, the State Bank guaranteed these existing loans, shifting the burden yet again to the national debt. Despite the rhetoric that these shares were open to all, at least 100 shares (just under US$1,000) were needed to have the right to vote, and 1,000 shares (around US$9,500) to run form membership on the management board.[43] The first point then is the exclusion of workers from control over the enterprise even if they own a few shares, since access to the board would require them to spend anywhere between 250 and 700 times their monthly wage. Secondly, it exemplifies the creation of capital in the private sphere out of national debt. The fact that Legamex is only now under investigation for financial mismanagement and that the State Bank will have to cover its overseas debts comes as no surprise.

A programme for workers' shareholdings in the state sector had already been initiated by the government prior to Do Muoi's speech. Its aim is 'to create conditions for the workers to become the real masters of their respective enterprises by linking their interests with that of their enterprise.'[44] However, where shares have been issued to workers they have been to mobilize funds to finance the firm's operations, not to increase their participation in the control of the firm. In some cases workers have been issued shares instead of wages because another use had been found for the wages fund. In this sense their interests *have* been linked to the well-being of the enterprise.

Earlier Vo Van Kiet had ordered that funds be set aside for workers to borrow in order to buy shares. Initially announced as interest-free five year loans, workers are charged 4.8% per annum on amounts of US$300 to US$500, which are only lent on a one-to-one basis, where they are required to buy one share with their own money for every share borrowed funds are made available for. The funds loaned are taken from the social welfare fund of the enterprise. Every year the joint-stock corporation will use profits to pay back the debt to the state and the shareholders will then be responsible for paying this amount back to the corporation. After five years the debt to the state would have been paid off and the shares will become transferable. In effect these are not shares, but long-term fixed interest bonds which – as with all bonds – do not carry ownership rights.[45]

Where shares carrying ownership rights have been issued, workers have only been allowed to purchase just under 5% of the total shares and in other cases have been excluded altogether.[46] In one case workers in the Refrigeration Engineering Enterprise (REE) were able to acquire effective economic possession of the firm when it was equitised, collectively buying over 50% of the shares and gaining control of 30% of the shares held by the state. But far from constituting a model for workers' participation in state enterprise reform, the head of the privatisation bureau, Nguyen Van Tuong, has warned workers against following the example of REE, recommending that they limit themselves to 10% of the shares issued by an enterprise.[47] Another scheme often misinterpreted as a form of workers' shareholding is where workers are required to pay a fixed sum to owners of private enterprises to secure employment.[48] This is not a capital contribution but a way of buying your way out of the state sector or the ranks of the millions of unemployed.

In an indirect critique of the new orthodoxy, Nguyen The Kiet criticized the view that the working class has 'fallen into line with capitalism' in advanced capitalist countries. In stating that workers' ascent to middle class status through public share ownership underpins such a view, Kiet confronts the new right's attempt to collapse 'people's capitalism' with socialism. Kiet argues that the exclusion of workers from ownership of the means of production is in no way altered by workers holding shares, given that ownership of a few shares and dividends which supplement workers' wages cannot be compared to the power of the bourgeoisie. And it does not alter the fact that workers are compelled to sell their labour-power to live. Despite the rhetoric of 'people's capitalism', the exploitation of workers does not disappear. Rather, 'they are exploited by more subtle methods.' Ultimately the view that the working class has somehow been absorbed into the middle class attempts to conceptualize away the very notion of class, class antagonism and the exploitative relationships that underlie it.[49] It seems that this is precisely the objective of the discourse on 'corporatisation' constructed by the reformist technocrats.

Trade Unions and the Working Class: The Politics of Inclusion

The dismantling of the socialist project under state policies which attempt to break the power of the working class generates contradictions within Vietnamese trade union organizations which are themselves embedded in the structures of state power. According to Ken Post, the 'role of trade unions in state enterprises from the very beginning has been to settle internal problems, popularize labour discipline and mobilize workers to achieve State objectives.'[50] To a large extent, this role has been reinforced under the transformation of state enterprises described above where enterprise managers have been able to use this as a form of extra-economic coercion.

The extent of the crisis within the trade unions was revealed in the lead-up to the recent Seventh National Congress of Vietnamese Trade Unions. What began as the usual pre-congress 'mass mobilization' campaign in which national branch unions, local unions and primary unions held their own congresses, turned into open conflict between trade union members and their representatives in which public criticism of the failures of the trade union movement was unleashed. The national congress, planned for October, was postponed until November as the VGCL executive committee met in Hanoi in an attempt to resolve the crisis. It was at this meeting that critical differences within the trade union leadership were resolved and the political report that had been submitted to the sub-national congresses was redrafted. Internal struggles within the trade union leadership were resolved with the appointment of three new vice-presidents and changes in the membership of the secretariat. There has also been a further centralization of power within the VGCL which marginalizes the voices of dissent. The powers of the executive committee and secretariat were reduced and a more powerful presidential committee created. The outcome of this meeting set the agenda for the national congress a month later. Each of the six hundred elected delegates was given a list of issues and resolutions and instructed not to diverge from them as a way of preventing another outburst of public criticism at the congress itself.

From the very beginning of the pre-congress meetings workers accused trade union cadres of forcing the agenda away from the most critical issues. It was argued that trade union cadres were only interested in their own wages, trade union control over the social insurance fund, the selection of delegates and staff for the congress based on political alliances and personal contacts, and the preparation of documents praising the achievements of the trade union movement. Trade union members at the grassroots level began demanding that the failures of the trade union to protect the interests of workers be addressed. The trade union's own newspaper argued that the interests of trade union cadres are not aligned with those of the working class because cadres do not share the living and working conditions of workers and have no training in protecting workers' rights. The author concluded that they are not members of the working class but a middle stratum of bureaucrats with interests lying elsewhere.[51] In local and primary trade unions, it was argued that national trade unions are inclined to support the policies of the Party and the state regardless of the effects on the interests and rights of workers. This is reinforced by the fact that trade union leaders are chosen by the VGCL secretariat subject to the approval of the Party, with workers voting only to formalize this decision.

The most significant criticism was directed at the failure to abandon the trade union's role as a transmission-belt of the party-state in which trade union organizations 'neglect or nearly forget their function of protecting workers' legitimate interests, because it was assumed that all the interests of workers could not be separated from the common interests of the entire people for which the state is held fully responsible.'[52] As Xuang Cang has argued, by 'participating in state management' trade unions had gone against workers' interests, alienating their own constituency. The VGCL's current 'socialization' programme is intended to shift its social power base from the party-state bureaucracy to workers. But this has had little effect in resolving the basic contradictions within the structure of power that governs the existing trade unions. Cang argues that: 'There is a paradox in the trade union's activities: the popular movements which take place without the trade union's participation are more active than the movements organized by the union.'[53] The reasons for this are clear. According to Cang, the commodification of labour-power, the release of workers from the state and cooperative sectors in their millions, the impact of 'business criteria' on shop-floor participation, the absence of unions for workers in the private sector, and workers' critical awareness of 'private interests' (presumably meaning in the state sector) have widened the abyss between trade unions locked into the party-state apparatus and workers' interests, especially where these interests include social equality and the right of democratic participation in the control of industry.[54]

As an outgoing member of the now defunct secretariat, Xuan Cang's views differ remarkably from VGCL policy. In addressing the national trade union congress, the head of the Ho Chi Minh City Federation of Labour, Hoang Thi Khanh, argued that under the commodification of labour-power, workers have the right to sell their labour 'at the right price' whilst 'enterprise owners also have the right to buy what they need'. The degree to which the labour movement has retreated is reflected in the fact that workers' rights were defined as: 'the right to work, the right to get paid corresponding to the quality of their labour, and the right to social welfare'.[55] A democratic factory regime is not a right.

Criticism of the relationship between the trade union and the state included a demand for a restructuring of primary trade union committees to remove state enterprise managers. It was argued that the trade union committee could not be responsible for representing workers in collective labour agreements as long as managers represented both sides. The primary unions, organized within each enterprise, are emerging as mechanisms for organizing workers in the interests of the management (similar to enterprise-based unionism in Japan). It was in the context of the control of trade unions by managers that the issue of corruption and financial mismanagement was raised. Not only were trade union committees headed by directors or vice-directors but trade union officials were often involved in cases of corruption and theft of state assets. It was argued that workers' interests and rights could not be protected by the same people who were diverting state resources into private businesses of their own.[56] In those joint ventures between state enterprises and foreign companies where trade unions have been permitted, trade union cadres have become part of the middle management, receiving as much as US$600 per month – 20 times more than the average worker. In return they guarantee the foreign investors industrial peace.[57]

The low unionization rate in the private sector was an issue raised repeatedly in the lead-up to the national trade union congress, reinforced by the seven strikes which occurred in 1993, but was removed from the agenda by the VGCL executive committee. It is characteristic of 'business unionism' that the trade union operates as an organisation which delivers services to fee-paying members. The constituency is its clients – in this case the three million members of the VGCL – not the working class.[58] The VGCL is not concerned that only 20% of foreign companies have signed labour contracts with workers, and only 15% have allowed the formation of labour unions. Only 14% of private Vietnamese enterprises have unions. As a result there are 2.2 million workers in the private sector of whom only 43,700 are union members.[59] The trade unionists who have campaigned for the VGCL to recognize the need for unions in the private sector are aware of the limited capacity of workers to organize themselves. As To Tham has pointed out, 'the labourers themselves are not willing to join the trade union as they are concerned only with having a job while the enterprise owners do not want such an organization in their enterprise'.[60] Although it is illegal to sack workers for trying to form a union, they are well aware that employers would find another reason for firing them. Given that the number of unemployed has reached seven million and the number of 'underemployed' on starvation wages is ten million, the threat of unemployment as a result of demanding the right to unionize is very real.

Antagonism does not just exist between the VGCL and its nominal constituency. There are internal divisions, particularly between the different levels of the trade union hierarchy. Particularly within the lower ranks of the trade union, cadres' interests are aligned to the interests of workers. Part-time trade union cadres have always had stronger ties with workers, being workers themselves. It is likely that the agitation for improved conditions, better wages and investigation of financial mismanagement in the 1980s found expression through these part-time trade unionists, rather than the permanent trade union members. However, the reform strategy directed against workers in state enterprises was replicated in the trade union movement, with part-time trade union cadres laid-off and the position of managers within the VGCL consolidated. One outcome of this has been to release former trade unionists into the private sector, where they have continued to demonstrate a commitment to the collective expression of workers' interests. A strike in a foreign joint venture clothing factory in Ho Chi Minh City earlier this year was organized by a former trade union cadre who had left the state sector under the labour surplus redistribution programme.[61]

Although it is evident that there are political interests within the VGCL which support a radical transformation of the trade union in the direction of a genuine workers' movement, the domination of the trade union by the Party and state at all levels would pit the proponents of left unionism against the authoritarian Communist regime itself. The increased involvement of the military in capitalist enterprise and the rise of merchant capital from within the party-state bureaucracy has created the conditions for conflict between this movement and a nascent bourgeoisie whose power remains symbiotic with the structures of state power. It is not simply a matter of redefining the trade union agenda.

Recapturing this agenda is made all the more difficult by the material interests of fractions of the trade union bureaucracy embedded in it. This includes the interests arising from the diversion of trade union and state funds into business activities, particularly in the services sector. It can be argued that the profit-making business activities of the trade union increases the relative financial autonomy of workers' organizations and generates a source of funds for workers themselves. But these activities are based on channelling funds from the state budget, access to which is gained through political concessions; the main one being to deliver industrial peace to the state and foreign capital.

The export of workers to foreign countries for profit is the central business activity of the VGCL. The main agency for this is the Labour Centre of Vietnam Trade Unions (LACETU) and its provincial and city branches. Established by the VGCL with state funds in 1991, the function of LACETU was to provide training for unskilled workers and to assist in job creation. LACETU collects fees from workers who apply for training courses or register themselves as unemployed. There are discounts for the poor. Recently the Centre has introduced exclusive training courses – including business management – for high-ranking cadres and leaders of national branch unions.[62] LACETU sent 1,500 unskilled workers to Saudi Arabia in early 1993, and will send another 5,000 workers to the Middle East before the end of the year.[63]

Despite the fact that as few as 5,000 of the 80–90,000 Vietnamese workers in the CIS countries have regular employment (receiving wages which fall well below the US$35/month minimum set by Vietnam's law on employment in foreign enterprises), LACETU plans to increase the number of workers exported to the CIS countries.[63a] More recently, the VGCL executive committee approved a plan to establish direct links with foreign companies to export workers to the Asian NICs, in effect competing with the Ministry of Labour which monopolizes these markets. The Labour and Specialist Export Service (LSES), established by the Ho Chi Minh City Office of Labour, War Invalids and Social Affairs, has been successful in this respect, exporting workers to South Korea and Taiwan. In a report on the activities of the LSES, Phuc Tien revealed that workers sent to South Korea were not trained but were exploited as cheap labour, replacing Korean workers who were laid off as soon as the Vietnamese workers arrived. They were forced to work a twelve hour day, with unpaid overtime, and were subject to beating and humiliation by the managers.[64] When I raised the issue of poor working conditions, violation of workers' rights, and forced unpaid overtime as evidenced in the experience of Vietnamese workers in Taiwan and South Korea with the VGCL, I was told that the non-interference of Vietnamese trade unions is guaranteed in the labour export contracts.

The export of labour is justified on the basis that it creates employment. For the state officials and trade union cadres involved in this trade, it legitimizes intense exploitation and harsh working conditions as being better than nothing. It also gives exporting agencies access to the National Employment Fund provided by the state to reduce unemployment. However, in some cases the workers sent overseas already have jobs in the state sector and are hired out by state enterprise directors.[65] To argue that this is a conspiracy of some sort is to oversimplify the issue: there is a strong belief that workers who are sent overseas will be trained and experience better working conditions, particularly amongst trade unionists. Foreign conservative and centrist trade unions have played a critical role in shaping this discourse on the new global labour market and the necessity of integration. But the material interests of the exporters of labour reflect something more than a commitment to training. In one case where Vietnamese workers are earning wages of US$100–120 per month (prior to contributions to the Vietnamese government and transfer fees) the LSES official who travelled with them is being paid US$980 per month. In the case of the workers contracted to Sun Sports in South Korea, 20% of their wages were allocated to the LSES.[66]

The Vietnamese government and VGCL are currently negotiating labour export contracts with Finland, Lebanon, the Czech Republic, Japan, Poland and Malaysia. In marketing Vietnamese workers, the Ministry of Labour and trade union organizations promote their passivity, low wages, and 'unconditional sale'. The contracts for 2,000 workers supplied to Prince International and Thaico by the Vietnamese Government in 1993 included a clause which states that: '. . . workers are absolutely forbidden to strike, leave jobs, or disturb the peace wherever they work or live'.[67] On the domestic front, this reinforces the trade union's commitment to the suppression of workers' interests to maintain industrial peace.

International labour organizations have achieved much in promoting workers' rights, but the predominance of conservative and centrist trade unions in the formation of global links that parallel the globalization of capital has transformed a labour movement born from revolutionary socialism into a mere appendage of capital. It is business unionism which has internationalized, not labour unionism. In their commitment to employment and training, we find international cooperation between labour organizations facilitating the export of labour and the preparation of workers as 'human resources', regardless of the exploitation that they will face.

The Vietnamese trade union movement as it is presently constituted cannot represent the interests of workers or effectively defend their rights. Delivering industrial peace to the state and capital is its overriding objective. And as organizations within the VGCL extend their business activities further into banking, finance and trade, this industrial peace will become its own prerogative and the organized labour movement will be incorporated into the capitalist project itself.

In a critique of the failure of trade unions to protect the rights and interests of workers as they are forced into a labour market, Hoang Chi Bao and Nguyen Thanh Tuan argue that trade union cadres, managers and state officials have 'degenerated into thieves'. Thriving on corruption and shifting state assets into the private sector, 'they have betrayed their class', turning against the working class which brought them to power.[68] But the roots of this betrayal lay in the formation of the post-revolutionary state which established a structure of power that – through crisis and reform –

gives rise to the embourgeoisement of the staff of the state. To argue that these segments of the Party and state bureaucracy are betraying their class origins is problematic given that the petty bourgeoisie, rich peasants, landlords and the national bourgeoisie were incorporated into the formation of the state apparatus in the nationalist struggle.[69] Incorporation into the Party apparatus itself became a determinant of class identity. As the leading party ideologue, Truong Chinh, explained, '. . . because the Party is a party of the working class, once people, regardless of their social background, join the Party they already become a member of the working class'.[70]

Class Struggle and Collective Action

The extent to which the VGCL remains a mechanism for the suppression of workers' interests is evident in its policy towards strikes – the clearest expression of workers' solidarity and commitment to collective struggle in the face of the challenge of market reforms. How many strikes have occurred since market reforms were introduced is not clear. According to the VGCL executive committee's report to the national congress, there have been 'dozens of collective reactions against the misconduct of the management accompanied with claims for pay rises and democratic behaviour from the employees at private businesses, joint ventures with foreigners, and even at some state enterprises'.[71] Other sources put this figure at 54 strikes since 1992, with 70 'conflicts' in all. An article in the newspaper, *Labour*, addressed the issue of strikes in the lead-up to the national trade union congress, arguing that 'the unions have lost interest in workers and do nothing to protect the rights and interests of workers. Most of the workers' collective strikes occurred before the trade union cadres were aware of it'.[72] The main causes of these strikes were the fall in wages below the legal minimum, increased work intensity, including an increase in the working day to 10–12 hours without compensation, poor working conditions, and mistreatment by managers. Workers have never gone on strike to demand wage increases. They have only ever demanded that they be paid the legal minimum wage.

What is evident in these strikes is that workers have responded to changes in the factory regime where power has shifted to managers under market reforms. Virtually all of these strikes have involved criticism of management practices and demands for greater 'democracy' in the workplace. This is not limited to the foreign joint ventures where absolutist managerial control is introduced from the start as the way things are done. In 1990, 200 workers in a state rubber enterprise went on strike for thirteen days. The strike committee dismissed the manager for abuse of power and protested to higher authorities about the 'lack of democracy'. But the policy of the VGCL on strikes is clear. Strikes are viewed as 'an unavoidable phenomenon in a market economy', given that 'business profit is the primary aim of the employer, so it is necessary to increase productivity, reduce expenditure, increase labour intensity, and minimize wages'.[73] Where strikes occur 'the trade union must take measures in time to protect the legitimate interests of workers and employees *without affecting economic growth and political stability*'. (Emphasis added).[74]

In the textiles and clothing industry where workers have expressed a high level of class consciousness and solidarity through collective action since the 1930s, they now face a declining state sector which is forcing them into small-scale private enterprises and foreign joint ventures where conditions are much worse despite the higher wages. Textiles factories owned by the Ho Chi Minh City people's committee are laying off half their workers, and across the country 20% of workers in state textiles factories are out of work.[75] Thousands of workers in spinning factories throughout the country work only three weeks per month and receive 70% of their monthly wages.[76] Strikes had begun as early as 1989, when 170 female workers went on strike in a state-owned factory. The main issue had been the authoritarian system of management and deteriorating working conditions. More recent strikes have concerned the extension of working hours of up to 12 hours per day without additional pay, and the failure of the management to pay the legal minimum wage. In November 1992, workers in a Taiwanese joint venture factory in HCMC went on strike to demand full wages, where wages had fallen from US$15 to US$12 per month. In February 1993, 650 workers in a foreign joint venture clothing factory, Ree Young, went on strike and after two days had forced concessions: the full wage of US$35; overtime pay; a limit on night shifts per week; and the right to form a labour union. In making these concessions, the director said, 'I also told the Korean technicians not to hit the workers, even if they had explained something many times.'[77]

Despite the view expressed by the VGCL leadership that 'strikes are the last weapon of workers for defending their rights in worker-management relations', the trade union will support the new labour laws to be passed in July, 1994, which – despite the legal recognition of the right to strike – will criminalize strikes. According to the draft law industrial disputes will be settled by arbitration committees established at provincial and city levels. If the dispute has not been resolved within 20 days, it is passed on to the state committee of labour arbitrators. But the state committee of labour arbitrators 'only settle serious disputes in the most important enterprises'. If the matter is not resolved within 30 days and there is no other way of resolving the problem, 'a strike is acceptable' on the condition that it is agreed to by over two-thirds of the workers. On each strike day, the strike leaders must provide written documentation (concerning the content of demands, a list of strike leaders on each strike day, the time limit of the strike) to the state officials concerned. The prime minister is empowered to delay strikes at any given time, and the president can forbid or halt strikes in the interests of the state. Finally, 'Strikes which do not pass through the stages of conciliation and arbitration procedures are forbidden.'[78] The Minister of Justice, Nguyen Duc Loi, justified the legal recognition of strikes in a revealing admission: 'The world working class has fought for this decision for hundreds of years and the capitalist class has allowed it. And so we can't abolish this clause.'[79]

It is clear that the legal recognition of the right to strike amounts to its criminalization. The law will establish mechanisms for conciliation and arbitration built upon the notion of the partnership between workers and enterprise managers. By setting out the necessary steps to be taken in the event of a dispute between workers and employers, it is explicitly stated that these mechanisms must be resorted to and the verdict given must be adhered to. Strike action which takes place prior to, during, or in spite of formal arbitration procedures is considered a violation of the labour law. The impact of these mechanisms for arbitration enforced by the state and weighted in favour of political stability and economic growth should not be underestimated. Intimidation by managers and officials and direct confrontation with the state bureaucracy can undermine workers' solidarity and force them into compromise or retreat. Gender and race relations are another sphere of domination and intimidation. The female workers in the Ree Young factory strike found it extremely difficult to confront managers, which led the Korean manager to commend them on the 'passivity' of their strike action. Although collective struggle often makes workers aware of other issues that they should be fighting for, the confrontation with officials on the state arbitration committees, the time constraints imposed by law and the pressure by bureaucrats to simplify their demands may push more abstract demands (such as greater democracy on the shop-floor) lower on the agenda.[80]

The draft law also stipulates that, 'strikes are illegal if they do not concern issues relating to workers in the enterprise' and are only permitted if they deal with 'labour problems'.[81] Not only does this restrict political articulation of the economic struggle within the enterprise, but it also prevents workers from expressing class solidarity. This is a serious problem for those intent on describing the transition as the reinvention of socialism or a socialized market economy. Revolutions are not made by laws, but the labour laws crafted by the new right are indicative of changes in the structure of power. When the new constitution was passed in 1992, Do Muoi (somewhat ironically) quoted Ho Chi Minh as saying in 1956: 'In whose hands is political power and whose interests does it serve? This will determine the whole content of the Constitution.'[82] Few would disagree. The spontaneous workers' strikes which gave rise to the 'soviet movement' in Nghe An in the 1930s would today be illegal.

What is Left?

Whether or not workers consider minimum wages, basic health and safety standards, access to housing, decent working conditions, and participation in the control of production as having their origins in socialist ideas, these ideas remain, particularly amongst second and third generation workers. And as Richard Levins suggests, these ideas may be embedded in the popular consciousness (even amongst those who are bitter about their experiences under 'real socialism') and as such have come to be considered as elementary human rights.[83] A low-ranking trade union cadre who had spent ten years working in a northern textiles factory declared herself as being 'against socialism', arguing that, 'the socialist system only remembers workers when there's work to be done and forgets about them when the benefits are handed out'. The next time I met her she railed against the trade union leadership for failing to support the strikes in Ho Chi Minh City where workers were fighting for their rights. This consciousness of collective interests and critical awareness of workers' rights has seen increasing articulation of working class struggle. This is where the state runs up against its own socialist rhetoric. Usurping power is one thing, undoing the collective struggle of the workers and taking back what little they've gained is quite another.

Four decades ago the drive by the revolutionary state to shift popular struggle from national consciousness to a higher level of class consciousness in the period of radical land reform laid the basis for class struggle against the post-revolutionary state itself. The system of centralized administrative planning collapsed partly due to the struggle of peasants and workers against surplus extraction and exploitation by the state. The fact that the reform process itself is an attack on the class consciousness of the rural and industrial workers lays bare the crisis. We are also witnessing the attempt at the reconstruction of non-class alignments and divisions, with the new right intellectuals undermining the very consciousness of social conflict itself.

It could be argued that as the socialist project is dismantled and state power is withdrawn from the sphere of production, the working class is free to engage in collective struggle against the new capitalist social order. But the effects of alienation from political power and the meaningless forms of mass political participation that the Vietnamese people have been subjected to under an authoritarian regime should not be underestimated. Neither can the revival of a radical working class politics rest on the hope that a high literacy rate and a critical press will facilitate collective action, even if the fact that both are in decline is ignored. The experience of advanced capitalist countries has demonstrated that we have become more literate and less articulate. And as suggested in *Critique*, 'The commercialisation and bureaucratization of knowledge has permitted a vast expansion in information and a decline in understanding.'[84]

In Vietnam the radical discourse on capitalism and socialism faces a critical challenge: the language of revolutionary socialism remains discredited, having been hijacked and used to legitimate the usurpation of power by the party-state bureaucracy and the denial of socialist democracy. Even where there has been a shift from 'bullshit Marxism to bullshit liberalism', as Richard Levins has pointed out, this leaves behind bitter cynicism and an aversion to the language of Marxism amongst workers. To talk of 'socialist democracy', 'exploitation', 'working class struggle' or 'historical materialism' is to be reviving the Marxist-Leninist propaganda that workers have grown sick of hearing. To make things worse, the orthodox Marxist intellectuals who frame the current transformation in terms of constructing socialism, consolidating the dictatorship of the proletariat, and the Party's role as the vanguard of the working class, democratic centralism, and so on, further discredit the language of radical politics.[85]

The concept of a new partnership between the bourgeoisie and the proletariat which underlies business unionism and the denial of class antagonism in the post-radical politics of the Left, offers us what the new Vietnamese policy orthodoxy and Western intellectuals and trade unionists conceive as a market economy with a humane face or a friendlier sort of capitalism. In this abandonment of radical alternatives to capitalism, the working class is to make more concessions and compromises for the sake of the national or societal interest, which then legitimates the subversion or suppression of working class struggle. Yet every aspect of workers' rights, relative improvements in standards of living, minimal health and safety standards, the right to an education, social welfare and mass political participation, is the result of working class struggle against the very logic of capitalism itself. This was not achieved through concessions and compromise. It was certainly not achieved through retreat.

Yet this retreat is very real. In Vietnam today, we are witnessing the exercise of state power against what remains of the socialist project under the rubric of 'market reform'. The defeat for the socialist Left did not come with the collapse of Communist regimes in Eastern Europe or even with the adoption of capitalist projects by Communist regimes in China and Vietnam, but in the immediate aftermath of the socialist revolutions, in the years when the Communist leadership located its social power base within the party-state bureaucracy itself, alienating the workers and peasants from political power. It seems that the working class is only brought back on the scene where the collapse of Communism – this usurpation of political power by the party-state bureaucracy – and Social Democracy – the subversion of labour movements away from radical opposition to capitalism – is presented as evidence of its own retreat from radicalism. But is the *intellectual* Left and radical trade unionism that is in decline, as much in Vietnam as in the advanced capitalist countries.

NOTES

1. This is based on private discussions with Le Dang Doanh in Hanoi, October 11, 1993.
2. See L.D. Musolf, 'Public enterprise and development perspectives in South Vietnam', *Asian Survey*, 3, 8, 1963; and M.N. Trued, 'South Viet Nam's Industrial Development Center', *Pacific Affairs*, 33, 3, 1960.
3. This is based on interviews with witnesses to the incident on December 10, 1993. There have been no media reports.
4. 'Rice exported despite food problems', *Vietnam Insight*, March 10, 1993.
5. According to Vu Ngoc Binh, 'There is no official data available on child labour. The estimates in Vietnam could mount up to millions. . . . Many rural children are handed over by their parents to perform household chores in urban families. "Child catchers" roam rural areas, buying or taking children from poor families and selling them to private households, restaurants, workshops and brothels.' Binh describes the working conditions of child-labourers:

   > [L]ong hours of work; no wages or wages below the minimum rate; no weekly or annual holidays; lack of facilities in the work place such as light, water, space, rest rooms, bath rooms, urinals and medical facilities for growth and development; inhuman treatment, including physical and mental abuse; and health hazards.

   Vu Ngoc Binh, 'Child labour in Vietnam', *Vietnam News*, October 3, 1993, pp.4; 8.
6. Tran Kim Giang, 'New school tuition fees may threaten education system', *Vietnam Investment Review*, October 4–10, 1993.
7. Although the Ministry of Labour's Centre for Employment Promotion places the number of unemployed at 2.1 million, and the Institute of Labour Science and Social Affairs at 2.9 million, this is based on unemployment in the major cities and as such does not include the rural workforce which accounts for 75% of the total number of workers. The rationale for this view is that there cannot be unemployment in rural areas due to the nature of agrarian life. However, the people's army newspaper, *Quan Doi Nhan Dan*, has placed this at seven million, which accords with the Asian Development Bank's figure of 6.8 million.
   All employment centres charge unemployed workers to register as being unemployed. On the practice of workers buying their way into jobs, see Per Ronnas, *Employment generation through private entrepreneurship in Vietnam*. Geneva: International Labour Organisation, 1992, pp.120–121.
8. In April 1992 the National Employment Fund was established to create jobs for 1.3 million unemployed, a total of US$83 million, of which US$25 million was provided as interest-bearing loans. Of this amount 20% was misallocated and US$18.4 million used to create 161,535 mostly temporary jobs and the rest used by ministries, the VGCL, and provincial people's committees to finance the export of labour and other business activities. The money allocated to provincial people's committees for job creation projects remains in the hands of local cadres. Bui Ngoc Thanh, 'How the 250 million dong fund for job creation was used', *Nhan Dan*, August 5, 1993; 'Employment, still an uphill battle', *Vietnam News*, June 6, 1993.
9. Melanie Beresford, 'The political economy of dismantling the "bureaucratic centralism and subsidy system" in Vietnam', in Kevin Hewison, Richard Robison and Garry Rodan (eds), *Southeast Asia in the 1990s*. Sydney: Allen and Unwin, 1993, p.229.
10. For example, the largest allocations from the state budget is to finance 'investment in fundamental construction'. This money is accumulated by state authorities and diverted to other activities. Only 12% had been spent on the projects the money was allocated for and between 20–30% of total state investment was leaked 'due to loosened management'. Le Van Toan, *Viet Nam: Socio-economy 1991–1992 and the first half of 1993*. Hanoi: Statistical Publishing House, 1993, pp.34–35.
11. This was amply demonstrated by the struggle over the law on land where the fear of delegates from northern provinces of the resurgence of landlordism generated a drawn-out debate. Yen Hung, 'Parliamentarians simmer over land debate', *Vietnam Investment Review*, July 12–18, 1993, p.9.
12. 'Opinions for the 7th national congress of Vietnamese trade unions', *Lao Dong & Cong Doan* (Labour and Trade Union Review), 150, September, 1993, p.12.

13. 'Directive issued to restore order in booming media', *Vietnam Investment Review*, November 1–7, 1993.
14. For example, an article on the theft of electricity by the residents of Hai Phong City was published in *Lao Dong*, and an article on the theft of US$1 million worth of cement by the management of the Vietnam Union of Cement Enterprises was rejected by the editor, apparently because of the protective political 'umbrella' of those involved. Huyen An, 'Hai Phong: 59% of electric power, about 15.3 million KWH, is stolen every month', *Lao Dong* (Labour), July 25, 1993; Nguyen Anh Thi, 'Where is 120 billion dong?' (unpublished).
15. Ken Post, 'The working class in North Viet Nam and the launching of the building of socialism', *Journal of Asian and African Studies*, 23, 1–2, 1988, p.150.
16. Simon Clarke, 'Crisis of socialism or crisis of the state', *Capital and Class*, 42, 1990, p.24.
17. Michael Lebowitz, 'The socialist fetter', pp.362–363, and Ernest Mandel, 'The roots of the present crisis in the Soviet economy', *The Socialist Register 1991*. Merlin Press, 1991, p.204; 206.
18. Interview with Do Minh Cuong, director of the Institute for Labour Science and Social Affairs, Ministry of Labour, War Invalids and Social Affairs, September 28, 1993.
19. Nguyen Tuong Lai and Nguyen Thanh Bang, 'A development policy for human resources within the socio-economic strategy of Vietnam up to the year 2000', in Per Ronnas and Orjan Sjoberg (eds) *Socio-economic development in Vietnam*, Stockholm: SIDA, 1991, p.90.
20. *ibid.*
21. Speech by the head of the Department of Labour Policy, Ministry of Labour, War Invalids and Social Affairs, 'About the redistribution of the workforce in state economic units, and the role of the government in solving the problem of surplus labour', presented at the *Seminar on the Role of Labour Administration*, Hai Phong, 1990.
22. Vu Hung, '"Open-air" labour markets', *Thoi Bao Kinh Te Sai Gon* (Saigon Economic Times), July 22–28, 1993, p.13.
23. 'Polarisation of wealth widens in Nam Dinh City', *Vietnam News*, June 6, 1993, p.4; Ngo Manh Ha, 'On the present phenomenon of differences in the income and living standards in the countryside', *Nghien Cuu Ly Luan* (Theoretical Review), 3, 1993, pp.17–19.
24 Nguyen Tuong Lai and Nguyen Thanh Bang, *op.cit.*
25. Officials from the Institute of State and Law, the Ministry of Justice and the International Labour Cooperation Department of the Ministry of Labour are involved with a group of Japanese businessmen in plans to export sex labour to Japan. This is based on a meeting with one of the Japanese involved in the project. For a similar case see the article on a traditional dance troupe sent to Japan under the guise of 'cultural exchange' and forced into prostitution for three months. Do Quang Hanh, 'An artistic ethnic dance troupe performs in Japan', *Lao Dong* (Labour), October 12, 1993, pp.5–6.
26. BBC Summary of World Broadcasts, Far East, FE/1012 B/7, March 5, 1991; FE/1068 B/4, May 10, 1991.
27. See my article, 'Disaster for Quang Ninh coal miners', *Asian Labour Update*, 13, October 1993, p.20.
28. Dan Tam, 'A glimpse at Quang Ninh', *Bao Ho Lao Dong* (Labour Protection Review), 1, 1993, pp.22–23.
29. Hoang Chi Bao and Nguyen Thanh Tuan, 'The role of unions under the market mechanism', *Lao Dong & Cong Doan* (Labour and Trade Union Review), 150, September, 1993, p.9.
30. Simon Clarke, 'Privatization and the development of capitalism in Russia', *New Left Review*, 196, 1992, pp.3–27.
31. Nguyen Van Thao, 'About the executive, legislative and juridical machinery', *Tap Chi Cong San* (Communist Review), 8, 1993, pp.37–40.
32. This is based on discussions with Do Hoai Nam, deputy director of the Institute of Economics, who is a member of the special working group on state enterprise sector reform.
33. The outstanding debt in the state enterprise sector was over US$41 billion in 1991. This doesn't include overseas debt which has grown rapidly since 1989. The debt level is unclear

since only 64% of managers in state enterprises in the South and 45% in the North responded to a directive requesting information on debts owed or owing. BBC Summary of World Broadcasts, Far East, FE/1127 B/2, July 18, 1991; *Far Eastern Economic Review*, September 26, 1991, p.57. The accumulation of debt through overseas borrowing by local governments and state enterprises that must be borne by the state is discussed by Le Van Toan, *op.cit.*, pp.33–34.

34. Melanie Beresford, *National Unification and Economic Development*. London: Macmillan, 1989, p.207; Murray Hiebert, 'Enterprise encouraged to invigorate the economy', *Far East Economic Review*, July 23, 1987, p.28.
35. Vo Van Kiet, 'Transformation of private industry and trade in South Vietnam – some practical problems', *Viet Nam Social Sciences, 2, 1985, pp.55–56; 59.*
36. This is based on a series of articles in *Tien Phong*, March 23, April 6, and July 6, 1993; and 'The trial of Miliket', *Kinh Te Viet Nam* (Viet Nam Economic Times), 6, 2–1993, p.18.
37. Karl Marx, *Capital* (volume 1). London: Penguin, 1990, ch.31, pp.918–919.
38. Tran Kim Giang, 'Garment producer involved in illegal land deals', *Vietnam Investment Review*, December 13–19, 1993, p.7.
39. Michael Burawoy and Pavel Krotov, 'The economic basis of Russia's political crisis', *New Left Review*, 198, 1993, pp.52–55.
40. Nguyen Quoc Thuoc, 'The fourth military region', *Nhan Dan*, August 5, 1993; 'Organizing labour in military units engaged in business activities', *Kinh Te Doanh Nghiep*, 12, 1992, pp.20–21; Pham Van Tra, 'The third military region combines economic construction with national defence in the new economic mechanism', *Tap Chi Cong San* (Communist Review), 12, 1992, pp.27–30. See also, BBC Summary of World Broadcasts, Far East, FE/W0219 A/7, February 26, 1992.
41. The creation of the National Branch Union of Defence Industry Workers in mid-1993 follows the rise of the military bourgeoisie. It is difficult to ascertain where pressure for unionization came from. Whether the workers themselves demanded it is not clear. It is also not clear whether the union will represent workers in private military-run factories or only those officially recognized as belonging to the Ministry of Defence. But the role of the defence industry workers' union is clear. Although nominally under the control of the VGCL, it in effect operates as a 'mass mobilizing' organization that functions as part of the Ministry of Defence. The main concerns are labour discipline, recruitment and training, and delivering industrial peace to the new fractions of military-owned capital.
42. Speech to the Seventh National Congress of Vietnamese Trade Unions, Hanoi, November 10, 1993.
43. Nguyen Ngoc Chinh, 'Legamex equitisation showing early success', *Vietnam Investment Review*, July 12–18, 1993.
44. Thanh Phong, 'Business undertaking a motive force of production', *Vietnamese Trade Unions*, 2, 1993, p.11; Ngoc Anh, 'Government grappling with problems of privatization', *Vietnam Investment Review*, May 3–9, 1993, p.8.
45. Duc Thinh, 'The shareholding group', *Vietnamese Trade Unions*, 2, 1993, p.12.
46. 'Trade union and workers' rights', *Vietnam News*, November 28, 1993, p.2.
47. 'Equitisation chief calls for more state involvement', *Vietnam Investment Review*, December 13–19, 1993, p.14.
48. Per Ronnas, *op.cit.*, pp.120–121.
49. Nguyen The Kiet, 'Some thoughts on the modern working class', *Nghien Cuu Ly Luan* (Theoretical Research), 4, 1993, pp.1–5.
50. Post, *op.cit.*, p.145.
51. 'Does the Trade Union take care of workers?', *Lao Dong* (Labour), July 22–28, 1993.
52. Xuan Cang, 'The real situation of the working class and options for the Trade Union', *Tap Chi Cong San* (Communist Review), 10, 1992, pp.38–42.
53. *ibid.*
54. *ibid.*
55. 'Trade union and workers' rights', *Vietnam News*, November 28, 1993, p.2.
56. Hoang Chi Bao and Nguyen Thanh Tuan, *op.cit.*
57. Interview with an official of the Socio-Economic Department of the VGCL, Hanoi, October 16, 1993.

58. David Mandel, 'The AFL-CIO goes to the CIS', mimeo p.3.
59. Dang Ngoc Chien, 'The primary duty of the trade union in a market economy', *Vietnamese Trade Unions*, 5, 1993, p.11.
60. To Tham, 'For the benefits of labourers in all economic sectors', *Vietnamese Trade Unions*, 2, 1993, pp.7–8.
61. This is based on discussions with Phil Drew of the Australian Trade Union Training Authority after visiting Ho Chi Minh City.
62. *Vietnamese Trade Unions*, 4, 1993, p.15. The brochure advertising LACETU produced in 1993 states: 'LACETU is ready to supply technical workers for production establishments of various economic sectors and for foreign capitalists' enterprises or companies which are in want of such workers.'
63. *Thoi Bao Kinh Te Sai Gon* (Saigon Economic Times), May 20, 1993.
63a.'Most Vietnamese workers in CIS are unemployed', *Vietnam Investment Review*, November 22–28, 1993, p.6.
64. Phuc Tien, 'Skilling or selling our labour for peanuts?', *Tuoi Tre* (Youth), March 27, 1993. Translated by Hanh Tran in *Vietnam Today*, 65, May Quarter, 1993, pp.11; 15.
65. In the case of a state enterprise in Hai Phong, workers were sent to Japan after being 'sold' to the International Cooperation Department of the Ministry of Labour, by the enterprise director. This is based on research carried out in Hanoi and Hai Phong in October, 1993.
66. Phuc Tien, *op.cit.*
67. *ibid*.
68. Hoang Chi Bao and Nguyen Thanh Tuan, *op.cit.*, p.9.
69. Pham Van Dong, 'Revolutionary tasks, class composition and forms of the people's democratic power in Vietnam', in *On the problem of the State*. Hanoi: Foreign Languages Publishing House, 1983, pp.11–17.
70. Cited in Post, *op.cit.*, p.143.
71. Report of the Executive Committee of the Vietnam General Confederation of Labour to the Seventh National Congress of Vietnamese Trade Unions, Hanoi, November 10, 1993, p.8.
72. 'Does the Trade Union take care of workers?', *Lao Dong* (Labour), July 22–28, 1993.
73. President of the Ho Chi Minh City Federation of Labour, quoted in Murray Hiebert, 'Industrial disease', *Far Eastern Economic Review*, September 2, 1993, pp.16–17.
74. Report of the Executive Committee of the VGCL, *op.cit.*, p.8.
75. *Sai Gon Giai Phong* (Saigon Liberation), May 22, 1993.
76. *Vietnam Investment Review*, July 12–18, 1993.
77. Hiebert, 'Industrial disease', *op.cit.*, pp.16–17.
78. 'The problem of strikes', *Lao Dong Xa Hoi* (Labour and Society), September 10–25, 1993.
79. Quoted in *ibid*.
80. This is revealed very clearly in Li Meng-Zhe and Luo Xing-Jie's *Professor Chu's Summer Work*, a documentary which follows the struggle of women workers in a clothing factory in Taiwan.
81. 'The problem of strikes', *op.cit.*
82. Ho Chi Minh, *Selected Works*, volume 2, p.127, cited in Do Muoi, 'Towards a state based on the rule of law', in *Vietnam: One year after the 7th National Party Congress*. Hanoi: The Gioi, 1992, p.12.
83. Richard Levins, 'Eulogy beside an empty grave', *The Socialist Register 1990*. Merlin Press, 1990, p.341.
84. 'Critique notes', *Critique*, 25, 1993, p.4.
85. Anita Chan has noted this phenomenon in China where the Marxist terminology used by those aligned to the interests of the working class ('workers' advocates') has been undermined and discredited by the reformers. Anita Chan, 'Revolution or corporatism? Workers and trade unions in post-Mao China', *Australian Journal of Chinese Affairs*, 29, January, 1993, p.51.

THE DECLINE OF THE LEFT IN SOUTHEAST ASIA

Kevin Hewison & Garry Rodan*

A famous, but now defunct, Australian pop group of the 1970s once asked, 'Whatever happened to the revolution?'[1] If the late 1960s and early 1970s seemed like an opportunity lost in the West, then it is doubly so for much of Southeast Asia. For many, the prospects for socialism in Southeast Asia had often looked promising. In fact, in Southeast Asia, communist and socialist movements enjoyed their greatest influence during the anti-colonialist and nationalist struggles following World War II. The organisational strengths of these movements, embodying coalitions of workers, peasants and nationalists, made them indispensable to political strategies for self-government. Indeed, as will be indicated below, the Left played a pivotal role in the development of civil society in these years.[2] Socialists and communists also earned the respect of the masses for the often courageous roles played in confronting colonial forces in this process. Even so, the achievements of the Southeast Asian Left should be kept in perspective, noting that its ideological appeal was confined to strategic sites rather than being embraced by the masses.

Today, few commentators would suggest that the Left, especially in its revolutionary form, has much future at all in Southeast Asia. With the exception of the Philippines, few genuine armed struggles remain. Outside the Philippines, self-proclaimed leftist political movements barely exist and where Communist parties remain in power, in Vietnam and Laos, capitalist production dominates while authoritarian political structures are kept in place. And capitalist economic development continues at a hectic pace throughout Southeast Asia. For the Left, the situation appears more bleak than at any time this century.

At least this is the general impression. But it just might be that this view masks a wide and important struggle in contemporary Southeast Asia in which the Left may yet be an important participant. We refer to the struggle for the extension of civil society. Certainly, as we will indicate

*The authors thank John Girling, Andrew Brown and Jane Hutchison for their comments and criticisms. We are also grateful for research assistance provided by Damen Keevers.

below, the Left's role is being overshadowed by a range of other contending political forces. Nevertheless, opportunities do exist for the Left, providing it can link with other progressive groups now challenging the state's political domain.

In this essay we intend to examine the decline of socialism and communism (for convenience, we will sometimes refer to 'the Left') in Southeast Asia and, for the purposes of this discussion, we will focus on the modern countries of Singapore, Malaysia, Thailand, Indonesia and the Philippines, and their previous incarnations as colonies, with Thailand (previously, Siam) being the non-colonial exception.

In brief, our argument is that socialism and communism (as closely related political movements) have, in recent times, lost much of their political and economic attractiveness. However, we will show that the Left has been significant, giving much momentum to the development of non-state political space (what we will term civil society) in these countries. We suggest that this was particularly the case in three periods: 1920s–1930s, 1940s–1950s, and the 1970s, when the Left played a pivotal role in expanding the arena of political activity. The defeat of non-state movements saw civil society greatly reduced or even expunged by authoritarian governments, which especially targeted socialists, communists and labour and peasant organisations.

We will go on to suggest that in the contemporary period, the political space associated with civil society is again being created in the societies of Southeast Asia. However, for reasons to be set out below, it is no longer socialists and communists who are leading this movement. Rather, a range of other non-state groups (independent unions, non-governmental organisations, religious groups, women's groups, business and professional organisations, and the like) are playing the leading roles in establishing civil society.[3]

Finally, we contend that the contemporary situation is not all gloom for those on the Left. Indeed, for a number of reasons to be explained below, the political space created for non-state organisation is available to a range of groups, and the Left can utilise this space to develop new strategies of opposition to authoritarian regimes, non-representative government, the tyranny of the market, and capitalist exploitation and repression.

In taking these positions, we are challenging the increasingly common view that the development of civil society in Southeast Asia is recent. This position discounts the political struggles of earlier decades. We will contend that the earlier development of non-state political space was closed through the action of repressive governments, both colonial and post-colonial. In other words, we believe that the current deepening of civil society in many parts of Southeast Asia is not a new phenomenon and does not represent an evolutionary transition from authoritarianism to democracy.

The political movements of the Left have made an important, usually unacknowledged, contribution to the deepening and expansion of civil society in all of the countries of Southeast Asia. This contribution has not been acknowledged in the emerging literature on democratisation and regime change. Indeed, these works adopt definitions of political or regime change and democracy which direct attention only to the most recent round of jockeying between the state and civil society.

One of the reasons for this emphasis on recent events is the search for a relationship between economic development and political change. Political theorists from the modernisation school have staged a comeback on the strength of recent economic growth in parts of the developing world, prophesying the inevitable breakdown of authoritarian rule as growth and modernisation inexorably expand civil society and come into contradiction with the centralised political structures of authoritarianism. From this perspective, social pluralism is all too neatly translated into political pluralism, hence democracy. The emergence of a middle class and a technically-educated population is especially important in this analysis, creating new centres of power and greater exposure and receptiveness to liberal democratic ideals.[4] This interest in establishing a link between economic growth and political structure may appear odd, as economic determinism was used by these theorists as a damning charge against Marxists.

Indeed, in Marxist theory, the equation of capitalist development with a more advanced civil society is also present, especially in Gramsci's understanding of the way in which bourgeois 'consensus', or ideological hegemony, is either maintained or challenged. In his attempt to work within this tradition, Girling refers to economic growth leading to a corresponding expansion in 'intermediate' forces of civil society (professionals, intellectuals and organisers) who form a new layer of society and effectively 'prise society apart from the direct weight of a powerful elite and a powerless peasantry'. But consider the following proposition by Girling:

> . . . economic development gives rise to 'civil society' i.e. *new* intermediate groups ranging from middle class professionals to labour organisers and party officials – which in turn creates pressure for the development of representative institutions enabling the 'new social forces' to take part in decisions affecting them.

To reinforce this, he adds that civil society and democracy require significant economic development, where the state is powerful, and where officials and the private sector can co-operate.[5] In other words, a strong capitalism seems to be theorised as a necessary prerequisite for the emergence of civil society and democracy, even if the direction of political change is viewed in much more problematic terms than is the case for liberal theorists.

Marxists have also noted the structural contradictions between advancing capitalist industrialisation, the attendant class structures, and authoritarian rule. Here accountability, mediation and conciliation are seen as functional requirements of a sophisticated market economy. Unresolved competition between emerging social forces – including different fractions of capital – also threatens political stability and thus the climate for capital investment.[6] Such circumstances also facilitate a measure of tolerance of, and even dependence on, a more expansive civil society.

The presumed link between capitalist economic development and the emergence of civil society is taken further when the focus falls on democracy. There is often a normative assumption in both liberal and Marxist-influenced theory that equates democracy and parliaments, voting and consent.[7] This is taken furthest by pluralist writers in the identification of political opposition with political parties and constitutionality; that is the existence of loyal oppositions as the only legitimate political opposition.[8] This position means that the parliamentary form in capitalist society is idealised as the most appropriate model of democracy, especially as it is seen to divert political conflict into an arena where physical coercion or violence is replaced by discussion, argument and the rule of law.

A problem with these perspectives is that they tend to ignore the struggles involved in the emergence of civil society. Many of these struggles have taken place outside the confines of parliaments, constitutions, and legal political parties. In the case of Southeast Asia, for example, Girling identifies instances of democratic regression without any serious acknowledgment of the preceding gains. By implication, they are an aberration.[9] Interestingly, van der Kroef utilises a far wider definition when discussing political opposition in Southeast Asia, noting that there were at least three categories: constitutional-reformist; ideological-totalitarian; and secessionist.[10] While one might quibble about the terminology, his categorisation is important for recognising that political opposition is not limited to the formal institutions of government.

Such views also tend to confirm the perspective that economic development leads to the inevitable expansion of civil society and, hence, a pluralist political system. But, as we will note below, the emergence of civil society is not an historical end-point, but may be seen as a product of the ebbing and flowing of opposition. Indeed, while the emergence of civil society is significant to the development of democracy, the space of civil society can expand and has expanded even under unrepresentative regimes. As will be indicated below, this has certainly been the case in Southeast Asia. It is appropriate, then, to define briefly what we mean when we refer to civil society.

Civil society refers to an autonomous sphere '. . . from which political forces representing constellations of interests in society have contested state power'.[11] The range of organisations in society may be enormous, but not all engage in overtly political activity. For example, seemingly apolitical groups can include sporting clubs as well as charitable and welfare-oriented associations – these might be considered as civic organisations.[12] Politically active groups include political parties, trade unions, employer and professional associations, women's groups, student organisations, peasant and ethnic associations, an increasingly expansive group of politically activist non-government organisations (NGOs), and a range of social movements. These groups are regularly involved in political actions which attempt to advance the interests of people, ranging from their members to a more general interest of wider groups in society.

However, and contrary to the influential liberal view, civil society is not the natural opposite to the oppressive state, nor separate from capitalist relations of exploitation and domination.[13] Hence, the existence of activist organisations does not guarantee parliamentary democracy. Rather, as has been shown for Eastern Europe, and will be demonstrated for Southeast Asia in this essay, civil society can in fact co-exist with an authoritarian regime.[14] Nevertheless, it is clear that the existence of such organisations can widen political contestation beyond the narrow base in parties and parliaments. This possibility is contingent upon class power. As Rueschemeyer and his colleagues observe, where 'powerful and cohesive upper classes' dominate the organisations of civil society, they may 'serve as conduits of authoritarian ideologies, thus weakening democracy'. Employer organisations, for example, may agitate for the right to represent independently their members' interests in policy deliberation but, at the same time, encourage the suppression or prohibition of worker and consumer organisations. Nevertheless, the autonomy of such organisations is fundamental, even if the class interests of a particular organisation may vary widely and, in some cases, may serve to consolidate the hegemony of dominant classes. Only through autonomous organisations can the numerical strength of subordinate classes be realised; only through them can they be protected from the hegemony of dominant classes.[15]

However, this need for autonomy involves the state. Bernhard points out that, for an organisation to qualify as part of civil society, its autonomy must eventually be legally sanctioned by the state. Through struggle, the state will be compelled to recognise a political space where autonomous self-organisation can occur outside the sphere of official politics.[16] This autonomy is used to place civil society in a position to have an institutionalised influence over the official political sphere. In other words, the state must itself establish boundaries to define that autonomous space and protect it from its own interference. In essence, then, the state must define what is to be considered 'political' and 'legitimate'.

In return for the granting of political space, the organisations and associations occupying it are expected to engage in self-discipline in return for the protection afforded them. Thus, it is not the emergence of organisations that is the measure of an expanded civil society. Rather, state actors must effectively legitimate the rights of such bodies to engage in political activity and even to challenge the exercise of state power before civil society can be said to be established. Thus, civic organisations may exist in the most authoritarian polities, but they do not then have the right to be politically activist. It can thus be seen that social pluralism does not always translate into political pluralism, as many liberal theorists would have it.

For the purposes of this essay, we can now summarise our picture of civil society. We begin by differentiating our position from those who see economic development as necessarily leading to the emergence of civil society. Social pluralism, we suggest, does not necessarily translate into political pluralism and democracy. Certainly, capitalism does not require political pluralism or democratic forms. Thus, the extension of the political space which constitutes civil society is not seen as an end-point to political development. Rather, we argue that the space of civil society ebbs and flows, and can exist under a range of political regimes. More important for us is the activity of political oppositions. While we see oppositions as central to the emergence of democratic politics, we also see this as being shaped by class forces and through extended political and social struggle. In addition, opposition is not something which only takes place within parliament and political parties, and we argue for a wider perspective on opposition and civil society. Finally, we make the point that the extent of the political space of civil society and the definition of 'legitimate' or 'acceptable' political activity depends, in large measure, on state acceptance.

A Brief History of Civil Society in Southeast Asia[17]

Writing in 1947, Du Bois noted three 'European streams of thought' which she considered had had a marked impact on Southeast Asian societies. These were social humanism, nationalism, and Marxism. Social humanism was seen to involve education and trade unionism, and provided legal protection as well as introducing the ideal of the dignity of the individual. Nationalism was seen as being crucial as a powerful force against colonialism.[18] Marxism was clearly linked to the rise of nationalism and anticolonialism, and appealed to internationally-linked labour. It should be remembered that Lenin's contribution to the debate on imperialism was a powerful document for those opposing colonialism. Lenin had seen the potential for revolution in Asia, writing in 1913, for example, that in the Dutch East Indies there 'was no stopping the growth of the democratic movement'.[19] Du Bois explains the attractiveness of Marxism: '. . . its apparent reconciliation of social humanism and nationalism in colonial areas; . . . its appeal to . . . intellectuals and seamen; and . . . the practical efforts of Russia, which in the 1920s was still a revolutionary nation.'[20]

As will be indicated below, there is considerable insight in these observations. While historians have noted the impact of nationalism, little has been made of the contribution of Marxism, and the manner in which the Left took a leading role in linking anti-colonialism, nationalism and 'social humanism'. Du Bois was writing in one of the periods where civil society was expanding, and the Left was playing a central political role. This period was, however, just one of a number of such periods.

It is obviously not possible to provide a full account of the trials and tribulations of the relationships between civil society and the state in all of the countries of Southeast Asia over a period of some 70 years. Rather, we will take three broad slices through the modern history of Southeast Asia, when civil society did develop, indicate the crucial roles played by the Left, and show how governments were able to limit and close this space. We begin with the 1920s and 1930s, not a period usually considered to be a hotbed of Leftist activity in Southeast Asia.

The 1920s and 1930s

In the century up to the 1920s, the colonial governments (including the modernising Thai state) of Southeast Asia had seen and defeated numerous uprisings, most of them in the countryside. These millenarian reactions to colonial rule were, in part, a response to economic and political change. By this time, the various governments had instituted centralised and bureaucratised administrations, had marked out the geographic boundaries of colonies and nation-states, and had, by and large, established government-defined systems of law and order.[21] In addition, in this era of high colonialism in Southeast Asia, local economies had been reoriented to the demands of mercantilism, with trade in commodities dominating the economic relationship with the West. The focus of political activity perceptibly shifted to urban areas and civil society-state relations.

It is sometimes forgotten that the 1920s marked the beginning of a period of renaissance in Southeast Asia, and a significant change in the ideological climate and considerable political and social ferment. This ferment represented, in part, a struggle for the expansion of the political space we call civil society. The governments of the period were unrepresentative, either as an absolute monarchy as in Thailand, or as colonial administrations. The ferment was a struggle to gain greater political representation and national independence.[22]

It is noteworthy that, prior to the 1920s, non-state community (or civic) organisations were significant. Throughout Southeast Asia a large number of civic associations had emerged, especially in urban areas, to further the interests of local people and the large immigrant communities of particularly the Chinese, but also other immigrants like the Indians. These groups were not generally politically active, and were certainly not sanctioned to engage in oppositional politics, and their activities were usually social, cultural and apolitical. However, they were often utilised by the state in managing their community, acting as political compradors between the state and their constituents, who were usually non-citizens. However, there were times when these organisations became politicised and found themselves acting in opposition to the state. This often led to labour activism, which immediately pitted these organisations against the state. Where labour was involved, the state would quickly brand their activities as subversive, and the organisation risked being labelled as a 'secret society', which meant illegality.

In Singapore, while the British maintained social order through direct repression, their general neglect of the population's welfare had the effect of encouraging voluntary and independent organisations to fill the vacuum. Privately-funded vernacular-medium schools, usually operating as night schools, were amongst the most numerous and significant of such organisations in Singapore, prompting the colonial state to require registration of schools and teachers and giving the government the power to regulate school activities. Apart from education, the associations provided welfare, legal and minor infrastructural services.[23]

But some politically significant groups also emerged. These included debating clubs, literary and study groups, and the like, which were often the training ground for nationalists. Educated locals in such groups soon found themselves confronting many of the assumptions of colonial rule while organised as 'native' associations.[24]

Much of this growth of civic organisations took place in the period between 1890 and 1920; and by this latter date, many of them were moving beyond welfare and becoming politicised. For example, in British Burma, the Young Men's Buddhist Association became the General Council of Burmese Associations in 1920, and began agitation against the colonial government, including strikes and boycotts. In the Dutch East Indies (Indonesia), a plethora of associations had become politicised, especially student groups and religious, notably Muslim, organisations. Many of these religious groups in Indonesia and British Malaya were influenced by the anti-colonial sentiment of Islamic reform movements in Egypt.[25]

Chinese societies and guilds were in many cases transformed into separate employer and employee organisations as capitalism developed, and ethnic workers' organisations were often showing solidarity.[26] The response from administrators was, as Trocki notes, the creation of '. . . security forces, secret police organizations and spy networks to suppress political movements and labour unions.'[27] While unions were small and represented only a fraction of the population – most of the population were farmers – they were economically significant groups operating in strategic areas such as the ports, transport and other activities central to trade.[28]

Unions were clearly non-state centres of political activism, especially when linked to socialist, communist and oppositional movements as they were prone to do, seriously challenging state power.

The 1920s and 1930s saw significant labour organisation. For example, in Thailand, the earliest recorded labour activity dates from the 1880s, and by the 1920s labour activism led to the establishment of a workers' newspaper during a particularly vicious strike in 1923. The group behind the strike and the newspaper was to become a driving force organising both the industrial and wider political struggles of industrial workers against the absolute monarchy. This activism caused the state to confront the so-called 'labour problem.'[29]

Whilst the colonial and Thai states seemed prepared to tolerate, indeed, in some respects were relieved, that there were a range of non-government associations promoting the collective interests of different social and ethnic groups, they appear to have felt most threatened when the developing Left joined these organisations. For example, private, Chinese-language schools throughout the region were caught up in the political movements in China, especially after the 1911 Revolution, and became important recruiting grounds for leftist youth and student movements. A strong anti-imperialist and anti-colonial rhetoric began to emerge from these schools, and communists were seen to control many of them. The Communist Youth League in Singapore was established in 1926, with a strong base in such schools. A similar pattern was seen in Thailand and Malaya, and the authorities closed Chinese schools and attempted to control curricula.[30] But it was not just the Chinese groups which became a focus of left-wing activism. Indeed, from the early 1920s, socialist and communist organisations had formed in Southeast Asia. For example, the Communist Party of Indonesia (later, *Partai Kommunis Indonesia*, or PKI) was formed in 1920. Following this, and in concert with developments in Vietnam and China, communist organisations were founded throughout the region, and many of the nascent trades unions came under Left influence.[31]

Some of this early activity was clearly related to the establishment of the Third International (Comintern) in 1919 and developing Soviet foreign policy. The Comintern had seen significant debate, especially between M.N. Roy and Lenin, over the relationship between communist parties and anti-colonialism, with the latter favouring alliances with nationalist movements, while the former wanted an emphasis on developing the communist movement. While a later meeting agreed to a compromise, it was clear that local conditions also played a significant part in the strategy adopted. For example, in the Dutch East Indies the 1920s saw the strengthening of anti-colonialism and a nationalist movement, within which the PKI became a leading element, developing a revolutionary strategy which placed emphasis on the anti-colonial struggle. The PKI suffered a serious setback in 1926–27 following an abortive uprising, but its influence was soon to be restored. In Thailand, where anti-colonialism was not an issue, the nascent Left was able to develop, from its origins in the Chinese community, as the absolutism of the monarchy was questioned.[32]

A major boost to the Left came with the Great Depression, when economic and social conditions deteriorated, paving the way for more concerted action. In Singapore, the Comintern-inspired South Seas General Labour Union (GLU), which was established in 1926, had been unable to make any headway. By 1930, however, organised labour and the Left advanced. The Malayan Communist Party (MCP) was established in 1930, with Singapore as its base. The economic downturn in the rubber plantations and tin mines gave considerable impetus to the MCP and its associated unions. A concerted campaign to mobilise labour, which included the formation of the Malayan General Labour Union in 1934, saw the unions become a strong base for left activism.[33]

In the Philippines, the Depression saw the expansion of the opposition and independence movement and, in 1929, the founding of the Socialist Party, which had its own labour organisation. Supporting peasants, tenant farmers and workers and taking a nationalist stand, the Party ran in elections as the Popular Front, and increased its support between 1933 and 1937. The Communist Party (*Partido Komunista ng Pilipinas* or PKP) was officially established in 1930, but banned a year later, and went underground. The Socialists merged with the Communist Party in 1938 to establish an anti-fascist front.[34]

It is usually said that the Communist Party of Thailand (CPT) did not establish itself until 1942, but reports from the 1930s indicate that a variety of communist organisations existed, particularly within the Chinese and Vietnamese communities, but also including ethnic Thais. More importantly, however, following the overthrow of the absolute monarchy in 1932, one faction of the People's Party was accused of 'Bolshevist' tendencies, especially in its relations with labour and students and in its economic policies. The government banned communism in 1933.[35]

By the late 1930s, communist and socialist movements had emerged throughout Southeast Asia, both linked and divided by ethnicity and all influenced by the nationalist, anti-colonial and anti-imperialist movements. Even where the anti-colonial struggle was emphasised, this did not diminish an element of internationalism on the Left, evidenced by the activities of revolutionaries like Tan Malaka and Ho Chi Minh who travelled the region. An element that linked these groups was a shared distrust of Western liberalism and capitalism. Certainly, the colonial experience had discredited capitalism for many locals.[36]

It is apparent that the Left in Southeast Asia had been able to capitalise on these suspicions, and utilise the political space which developed in the 1920s and 1930s. Indeed, the Left was a driving force for the extension of this space. However, as World War II approached, there was a move to curtail some of the resultant political activity, which was seen by governments as a measure of rebellion. In Thailand, the military had established its control over government and moved closer to fascist regimes in Europe and Japan. In Singapore and Malaya, the colonial state felt threatened by communism, crushed the Party in 1931, but again faced strong communist-led worker opposition in the mid-1930s.[37] This coalition of workers and communists was seen as a major challenge throughout the region.

The 1940s and 1950s

Immediately following World War II there was another period of relative political openness. While this period was sometimes short, as in Malaya, and intermittent, as in Thailand, this was a time that saw considerable political change in the region. However, the dynamic force of the period was not socialism or communism, but nationalism. Nationalists and the Left linked to challenge colonialism and expand political space outside the state.

During the Pacific War, the early defeats inflicted on Western colonialists by the Japanese gave strength to the various anti-colonial movements, and clearly showed that loyalty had not been strongly established amongst the subject peoples. The Japanese reinforced this through their propaganda attacking Western colonialism. While Southeast Asians were far from enamoured with Japanese colonialism, and many took up arms to oppose them, the Japanese interregnum set the wheels of decolonisation in motion.[38]

After the defeat of Japan, the colonial powers were slow in re-establishing their administrations, which meant that the Western colonialists were seen to be replacing nationalist administrations. Not only this, but the re-ensconced colonial regimes presided over severely damaged economies. The destruction wrought on Europe meant that the colonies could not be supported, and nationalists and communists were concerned that Southeast Asian colonies would be heavily exploited, but it was clear that any colonial re-establishment would require a greater effort than anything prior to the war. In Thailand, it was felt that the British wanted to establish a neo-colony.[39] In other words, not only was much of the economic infrastructure severely damaged, but so were the political and social structures of colonial Asia, and social change was accelerating.

Nationalists saw that the historical tide was running to their advantage. For example, the establishment of the United Nations clearly implied that decolonisation would be on the international agenda. Indeed, moves to decolonisation in the Philippines and India and Pakistan suggested cause for optimism. Interestingly, while the British were leaving South Asia, they appeared keenest to re-establish the colonial regimes of Southeast Asia. Not only did they do this in their own colonies, but they were

instrumental in the reinstitution of colonialism in Indochina and Indonesia.[40] For nationalists, and this included most on the Left, anti-
colonialism became the major political issue. Thus, much of the political
rhetoric exhibited a strong anti-Western tone.

World War II also saw communists gain considerable credibility through
their leading role in anti-Japanese resistance movements. Like their
Western predecessors, the Japanese were anti-communists, and vigorously suppressed communist movements, forcing them underground.
Yet in Malaya, Singapore, Indochina and the Philippines, communists led
or were major elements of the anti-Japanese movement.[41] At the end of the
war these movements were in a strong and popular position, and the link
between nationalism and communism was well-established.

In addition, the increased international influence of the USSR, based on
its role in the European theatre of war, gave the communists considerable
cause for optimism. As a founding power in the United Nations, the USSR
was able to provide some support for local communists. For example,
Thailand wanted to join the UN and required Soviet support, and for this,
the USSR sought and received the repeal of Thailand's anti-Communist
law in 1946.[42]

One of the many links drawn between nationalists and the left was in the
area of economic development. The example of the Marshall Plan for the
reconstruction of Western Europe gave an impetus to the idea of economic
planning, suggesting that benefits could be obtained from centralised
planning. Nationalists argued that modernisation could only be achieved
in the Southeast Asian countries through government investments and
planning, thereby strengthening the position of the Left which had long
argued for this kind of economic intervention.[43] Economic nationalism
became a solid stream of Left and nationalist programmes. In the words of
one commentator:

> Indigenism is also influenced by the extent to which the ideology of nationalism is socialist.
> Independence movements in Southeast Asia, to a substantial degree, were recruited from
> elements uncommitted by ownership of property or job security. Furthermore, because
> socialism is identified with social and economic reform in the industrial West, it appeals to
> nationalist elements whether evolutionary or revolutionary. This appeal is reinforced . . .
> by the Western socialist tradition of opposition to colonialism.[44]

This was clear in Burma, Indonesia and, in a more limited way,
Thailand, Malaya and the Philippines. In Indonesia, for example, most of
the political parties were strongly nationalist and anti-colonialist, and this
was reflected in an anti-foreign capital stance. The PKI was opposed to
foreign investment, but it tended to be supportive of the role of national
capital, while the PSI (Socialist Party) opposed extreme nationalism.[45]
Many communists were also greatly heartened by the progress made by the
communist parties in Indochina and China.

By 1950, both nationalists and the Left in Southeast Asia must have felt
that the tide of history was changing. The Philippines and Indonesia had

gained their independence, albeit by very different routes; Thailand had remained independent; the Chinese communists were in power; the situation in Indochina was in the balance; communists had launched armed struggles in Malaya and Singapore, the Philippines (the Hukbalahap rebellion), Indonesia (the Madiun affair), and Burma.[46]

The history of the Left in Southeast Asia often ignores the contribution made by the legal socialist movement. This ignorance stems from the fact that, by the early 1950s, most socialists had taken an anti-communist stance, even amongst those who were at the forefront of the Asian socialist movement. Many presented an unusual position by supporting the Chinese Revolution while opposing communists in Southeast Asia. This group adopted what the then Burmese Prime Minister U Ba Swe called 'revolutionary democratic Socialist methods to improve the standard of living of the masses . . .'. For Josey, 'Asian socialism' was about easing the underdevelopment of the region and the poverty of millions through some form of collectivism. It was interested in social welfare, and socialists 'were nationalists first', opposing colonialism and imperialism by 'democratic, egalitarian and fraternal' methods. Significantly, Asian socialism was opposed to capitalism *because* of its links with colonialism, but opposed to communism, which it saw as totalitarian.[47]

The connection emphasised here, between nationalism, anti-colonialism and socialist and communist movements, was crucial. Of course, the relationship between each of these political elements varied according to local conditions. For example, the PKI, which became the largest communist party in the non-communist world, came to see that:

> the nationalist movement, and later the national state, might be captured by Marxism through peaceful means and, having been captured ideologically, would naturally admit Marxists to positions of power.[48]

However, in Malaya, the communists had abandoned peaceful and constitutional opposition to the reinstitution of colonialism, and had embarked on an armed struggle. The MCP was unable, though, to establish fully its struggle as a national movement.

Given the united front tactics commonly used against colonial powers, left-wing influence can easily be exaggerated by conflating it with nationalism and anti-colonialism. However, if socialist revolutions elsewhere have occurred with little or no consent amongst the population to socialist values [49], and created problems thereafter, then the successful conclusion of nationalist struggles in Southeast Asia certainly did not leave socialist ideas in any better position. The Left was soon moved off the legal political stage. The reason for this had little to do with the success of Left ideology or values, but with the ability of the Left to build links with labour, and in some cases the peasantry, and the West's perception of the success of International Communism.

Working and living conditions had deteriorated during the war, with food and commodity shortages and inflation common. Under such conditions worker unrest increased, with the Left and the anti-colonial movement able to capitalise on this. By 1947, for example, the MCP-dominated Singapore GLU controlled three-quarters of the organised work force. In Thailand, labour organisation increased, and a major labour confederation, the Central Labour Union (CLU) was formed. A new generation of labour leaders, much influenced by Marxism and close to the CPT, emerged to lead the Thai labour unions. Their approach was attractive, and by early 1949, CLU membership was 60,000. In Indonesia, the PKI also had strong links with labour which supported its programme.[50]

The radical wing of the labour movement can be seen as a part of the rise of a more generalised Left discourse. As Reynolds observed for Thailand, '. . . there was a distinctly Left orientation in Bangkok public discourse for a decade or so after World War II.'[51] This was common throughout the region. For example, in Malaya and Singapore, while the colonial state attempted to repress labour after 1948, this was temporary. The fundamental grievances of students and workers, when combined with the unprecedented strength of anti-colonial feeling, were manifested in a new phase in the development of independent organisations. This involved labour, students and, for the first time, formal political parties which geared-up for the achievement of self-government. The radical unions played a critical role in mobilising the masses in this broad movement. Most of the strikes in Singapore involved demands for the release of imprisoned union officials, or were part of the broader Left strategy of keeping pressure up for full self-government.[52]

Throughout the region, a feature of this period was the linking of a range of politically active groups within civil society. Leftist discourse, especially in labour circles, employed concepts of class, class struggle, and exploitation, seriously challenging colonialist and nationalist rhetoric which emphasised capitalist development. Significantly, whilst the authorities readily employed internal security forces and legislation to detain labour leaders and proscribe cultural and social organisations in which the Left was influential, these moves were not initially successful. Far more repressive measures were required. As labour conflicts continued, governments soon defined these actions as unlawful and as constituting 'revolt', and anti-communist laws were made increasingly draconian. For example, in Thailand, the 1952 Act prevented attacks on the private enterprise system and outlawed acts defined as 'creating instability, disunity, or hatred among the people, and taking part in acts of terrorism or sabotage'.[53] This did not end labour disputes, but it did restrict Left-wing influence in the labour movement. In the Philippines, once the Left's influence had been reduced, collective bargaining was expanded after 1951.

The seemingly bright prospects for the Left after World War II were tarnished by the Cold War and the rise of US-sponsored anti-communism and anti-neutralism. As is well-known, the US and other Western powers, shocked by the 'loss' of China and Eastern Europe, and an apparent threat in Korea, moved quickly into the Cold War. Of course, Southeast Asia was not immune from this, being seen to be in the path of a southward movement of communism. As one US policy document explained:

> [S]outh of the ominous mass that is Red China, Thailand, along with her embattled but still free neighbours, shares a peninsula. The Communists want it. They covet its riches. . . . They consider it [Thailand] a prize base, for like an oriental scimitar, the peninsula's tip is pointed at the throat of Indonesia. . . . In Malaya, Burma and Indo-China, Communist-led rebels plunder, kill and burn.[54]

This Cold War mentality translated to support for actively pro-Western and pro-business governments. In Thailand, for example, the US supported, with the help of the CIA, generals in the police and army who were opposed to the Left. There is no doubt that this support for repressive political structures (the military, police and internal security) was crucial in narrowing the political space, even for democrats and nationalists. Throughout Southeast Asia the US supported anti-communists: in Indo-china, supporting the French, and then becoming directly involved; against Sukarno and the PKI in Indonesia, championing the military; supporting Magsaysay in the Philippines, against the Huk rebellion; in Burma and Cambodia against leaders defined as 'dangerously neutral'; and in Malaya, supporting the British in their anti-Communist war.

This anti-communism fitted well the domestic agendas of increasingly authoritarian regimes whose repression was justified on the basis of developmental imperatives. The Left was increasingly identified as 'alien' and as a 'fifth column' movement, and this perspective was supported by Western powers. It also found itself having to defend its political organisations, developed in the nationalist campaigns, as others moved to marginalise them from the political process and weaken their bases in civil society, most notably in trade unions. This absorbed much of the creative energy of socialist and communist movements. Externally, the Cold War climate necessarily meant various pressures would be exerted to undermine socialist economic experiments and shore up market-oriented economies. Thus, by the mid- to late-1950s, throughout Southeast Asia, the Left, including anti-Communist socialists who had supported constitutional opposition, was being repressed or forced underground. In many places, repression resulted in an intensification of armed struggles.

The 1970s

During the 1970s, while not as regionally widespread as during the earlier periods discussed above, there were significant attempts to expand civil society. This took place in a quite different environment from that in earlier epochs: all of the countries of the region were ruled by post-colonial regimes; communist-led armed struggles in the Philippines and Thailand appeared to be gaining strength; and the US intervention in Indochina was coming to an end, on a wave of opposition in the West. The eventual victories for the communist movements in Indochina initially gave considerable impetus to the Left in Southeast Asia. Again, it should be emphasised that much of the opposition which developed was related to conceptions of anti-imperialism and economic stagnation or decline, associated with the first oil shocks.

For example, the extreme dependence of the Singapore economy on external demand meant that the mid-1970s recession hit hard, with heavy job losses in manufacturing industries, with official unemployment reaching 4.6% in 1975. The ruling People's Action Party's (PAP) tame union organisation was unable to effectively represent worker interests, presenting an opportunity for a short-lived revival in the student movement. The students had widened their agenda to include the promotion of civil liberties and links with workers. The latter prompted a swift reaction from the government, resulting in the conviction of student leaders for 'unlawful assembly' and 'rioting' and the student union having its funds placed under the control of the university administration and Ministry of Education. The student union was barred from engaging in or making pronouncements on matters of a political nature.[55]

The role of students in Singapore was seemingly part of a pattern throughout the region. Between the late sixties and 1975, students were active in most of the countries of the region: in Indonesia, students protested Japanese economic domination; in the Philippines, students were active until martial law was introduced in late 1972, with the breakaway Maoist Communist Party of the Philippines formed by student leaders and intellectuals in 1968; and in Malaysia, students demonstrated in 1974. The most remarkable student activism was, however, in Thailand in 1973, where students and intellectuals brought thousands of people into the streets to overthrow a military dictatorship.

Such student activism grew, in part, out of a massive expansion of tertiary education, but also out of the changes taking place in social structures through the growth of import-substituting industrialisation. Regional governments, however, having observed Western students challenging their own governments in the late 1960s, were decidedly uncomfortable with the prospect of student radicalism which they saw as subversive and manipulated by the Left. The result was that many took the Singapore road, introducing repressive measures.

These student activists did not operate in a vacuum, and the example of Thailand showed that students and intellectuals could be powerful forces for the expansion of political space. Indeed, the growth of solidarity movements between students, workers, peasants and the downtrodden was greatly feared by the governments of the region, especially as students were seen as allies of the communists. But, by the late 1970s, authoritarian governments had again moved to close the political opening, and repres-

sive regimes dominated the political stage throughout the late 1970s and
into the 1980s: the Marcos dynasty and its lackeys kept the pressure on
through martial law, although some concessions were made; Thailand had
a military government again, although limited elections were reintroduced
in the early 1980s; New Order Indonesia was still under a military-
dominated government, and Suharto appeared stronger than ever; Lee
and the PAP had further entrenched themselves in Singapore, having
arrested more than 100 'communists' and harassed all legal opposition;
and the Malaysian government had cracked down on opposition groups.

For the Left, the only glimmer of hope in this political gloom might have
been the establishment of self-declared socialist governments in Laos,
Vietnam and Cambodia and the expansion of communist-led rebellions in
Thailand and the Philippines. But this came to nothing. In Cambodia, the
Pol Pot regime embarked on a reign of terror and hyper-nationalism
which, while initially supported by many on the Left, was only concluded
when Vietnam invaded. The result of this was a brief but bloody war
between China and Vietnam, which threw most of the Left in Southeast
Asia into confusion.[56] This confusion was amplified by the strange sight of
the US and ASEAN supporting their former enemy, the murderous
Khmer Rouge.

These strange events also had much to do with the implosion of the CPT.
In 1977 the CPT could claim more than 15,000 under its banner, and was
waging an armed struggle, apparently with considerable success, reinforced by thousands who had fled right-wing repression after the 1976
coup. However, the CPT, dominated by a leadership allied to China, had
been unable to incorporate the young and idealistic revolutionaries from
urban areas. In supporting the Khmer Rouge and China, the CPT lost its
bases in Vietnam and Laos, and then 'lost' its internal debate with students
and intellectuals who willingly accepted a government amnesty. By the
early 1980s, the CPT was dead. Only in the Philippines, where antagonism
to Marcos united the opposition in a way not seen since the War, did an
armed struggle continue and grow. Even here, however, there were splits
within the Party.[57]

It should also be noted that the changing nature of international
production had a major impact in the region. The tendency of international capital, beginning in the 1960s, was to transfer labour-intensive
manufacturing production to the developing world to exploit lower labour
costs. Not only did this boost economic growth in East Asia (Hong Kong,
Taiwan and South Korea), but it also proved timely for Southeast Asia. For
example, following the mid-1960s failure of the political merger with
Malaysia, Singapore's policy-makers realised that with no prospect for a
larger market for manufactured goods – the basis of Singapore's import-
substitution industrialisation (ISI) strategy – a different strategy was
required. Singapore led the way, to be followed by Malaysia, Thailand

and, to a lesser extent, Indonesia and the Philippines, in moving to a more export-oriented industrialisation (EOI) strategy.

Such a move in production did not cause any decline of the Left; indeed, since the move from ISI to EOI actually expanded the industrial work force, it might have been expected this would enhance the Left's political potential. However, as the region's states moved to create their comparative advantage as low wage manufacturing sites, independent unions were smashed, seriously weakening the Left.[58]

At the same time, three other nails appeared poised to be driven into the coffin of the Left in Southeast Asia: first, the move to 'market socialism' in China; second, the political and economic collapse in Eastern Europe; and third, the amazing economic success of the capitalist Southeast Asian countries (with the Philippines the exception), in stark contrast to the stagnation of the Indochina countries. But, as we have already suggested, this is not the end of history, and there is reason to embark on a deeper analysis of political and economic change and the opportunities this provides for the Left.

The Left and Contemporary Southeast Asia

As noted at the beginning of this essay, the 1980s and 1990s appear bleak for the Left in Southeast Asia. This is a paradox; think about the most enduring of Left strategies – support of labour. As we have noted, this area of activism has been seen by various kinds of regimes as a powerful threat. If, however, we examine the rapid economic development of Southeast Asia, driven by strong, local, capitalist classes, then the current epoch *should* suggest an *opportunity* for the Left, organising among the growing working class. As yet, this has not been the case. Why?

An important point to emphasise is that changes to the global political economy have facilitated a positive capitalist alternative for developing countries which has greatly undercut socialism's potential appeal in the region. One of these was, of course, the search by international capital for the low-cost manufacturing export bases which began in the 1960s. More recently, the conceptualisation by international capital of the global economy in terms of three economic regions – Europe, North America, and the Asia-Pacific – has meant a 'regional focus'.[59] This emphasises the importance of honing operations to the peculiarities of local markets and affords more autonomy to transnational corporations (TNC) subsidiaries. Consequently, Asia is elevated from the status of a site for low-cost production to be exported to consumer markets elsewhere to a crucial set of markets in its own right. Commensurate with this is a preparedness by transnational corporations (TNC) to invest in higher value-added products and processes – both within and beyond the manufacturing sector – than was previously the case. In conjunction with the internationalisation of capital emanating from the region and the forging of structural linkages between the different regional economies, this investment pattern further bolsters capitalism in the region.

This process appears to be deepening capitalist accumulation, giving rise to a capital development alternative in Southeast Asia.[60] For the argument here, the significant issue is that remarkable capitalist economic development (with the exception of the Philippines) has been achieved with associated authoritarianism. Indeed, Southeast Asian leaders have used economic success to boost their political legitimacy and to justify authoritarian regimes in Thailand, Singapore and Indonesia.

So it is not just the negative example of state-led socialist experiments around the world that has reduced the appeal of socialism in Southeast Asia, but the demonstrable achievements of capitalism in Asia and the seemingly bright prospects it holds for the future. This has been especially noticeable in Thailand. Many of those who joined the CPT in the 1970s and 1980s have returned to urban life to become successful business people, suggesting that communism was a dead-end. They argue that the best they can now hope for is a capitalism with some heart, meaning that some of its rough, exploitative edges are taken off. In essence, 'socialism as collectivism' is no longer a supportable goal, even for some on the Left, and has been replaced by a growing interest in more limited but laudable political goals including human rights, liberty, constitutions, and representative forms.

Paradoxically, it is the success of capitalist revolutions and the decline of socialist models which have raised the prospect of political change. The social transformations in Southeast Asian societies have not only involved the expansion of capitalist and working classes, but the emergence of sizeable middle classes, with each of these classes being segmented.[61] The social, political and cultural manifestations of this process are complex, and there is a literature which sees pressures for new organisational forms to protect and advance the particular interests of these strata as an unavoidable byproduct of economic development.

As we have already argued, the historical evidence contradicts the assumption that the development of civil society in capitalist societies is a progressive and incremental outcome of economic growth. Rather, civil society has ebbed and flowed in the region throughout this century. For us, the significance of the current social transformations brought by advanced forms of capitalist accumulation lies in the nature of new social groups. As we have seen, at different periods in the respective histories of Southeast Asian societies, a range of social groups have succeeded in expanding the political space outside the state, even if this space has subsequently been closed as authoritarian regimes have reasserted their dominance.

Whereas independent labour organisations have been central to this periodic reconstitution of civil society in the past, what is significant in the current expansion of civil society is the greater social differentiation characterising the groups involved. It is important to acknowledge the expanding complexity of Southeast Asian social structures. The increasingly numerous and differentiated middle class, encompasses a range of professionals, public and private bureaucrats and the self-employed. The growth of this class is generated out of expanded capitalist development, which also sees an ever more complex bourgeois class engaged in diverse domestic and global accumulation strategies. Not surprisingly, these processes generate new political aspirations and demands, some of which reflect the new material conditions. Hence, environmental and consumer organisations have joined professional and employer associations to establish their identity in civil society.

From the mid-1980s, there has been a rapid expansion of business and professional organisations in many parts of Southeast Asia. In Indonesia and Thailand at least, some of these groups have achieved considerable power. A new literature, much of it placing a heavy emphasis on instrumental relationships between business and government, has emerged in recent years. MacIntyre has demonstrated that industry associations and business groups have been able to use the Indonesian state's corporatist structures to derive benefits which are for their members, and not for the state. This, he argues, involves an expansion of political representation. For Thailand, MacIntyre suggests that the representation of organised business on joint government bodies has allowed it to deal directly and independently with government and shape policy. Anek, also writing on Thailand, argues that business associations have become autonomous of the state, acting as interest groups, that organised business has had a significant influence on the pattern of economic development, and that like '. . . South Korea, Taiwan and Singapore', there are '. . . close and supportive relations between the government and organized business . . .'.[62]

Even in Singapore, and despite the government's brusque treatment of non-state groups in the 1980s, notably the Law Society and lay religious organisations [63], some middle-class and professional organisations have emerged or become more active in recent years. The most notable of these have been the Nature Society of Singapore, the Association of Women for Action and Research, and the Association of Muslim Professionals (AMP). The evolution of these three groups reflects a perception that existing political structures inadequately accommodate distinctive views and interests.

As we stressed earlier, following Bernhard, the existence of autonomous organisations requires the sanction of the state. This means that the existence of some of these organisations can be highly conditional: as soon as the state defines their activities as political, they are in trouble. This is especially so in the Singapore case, where legislation means they face the threat of de-registration should they be seen to pose a challenge to the

PAP's authority by acting 'politically'. Equally, the threat of being co-opted by the government is real, as the AMP in Singapore demonstrates. The threat of co-option and corporatism has meant that it is sometimes difficult to distinguish between state and non-state organisations. For example, in Thailand, the government ordered the establishment of provincial chambers of commerce, while claiming that they are private and voluntary.

Nevertheless, and despite the moderate political objectives of many of these organisations, some do represent attempts to negotiate increased political space, separate from the state's extensive bureaucratic structures. Through the demarcation of this non-state space, some form of political contestation becomes possible. This is true even if, in order to avoid proscription and co-optation, contestation can neither be confrontational nor particularly public. Even so, owing to the class nature of the constituencies and leaderships of these organisations, being disproportionately middle class, contestation will inevitably be circumspect. Many of them also proclaim, as they must, a non-ideological position, and it is fair to say that they see themselves in this light.

At the same time, the position of independent labour organisations has substantially altered. In the past, linkages between labour and political opposition movements have posed a challenge to authoritarian regimes, both colonial and post-colonial. But the legacy of decades of authoritarian rule has been seriously destabilising for labour. The institutionalised incorporation of labour into the structures of the state is now well advanced throughout the region, and the existence of independent labour organisations is everywhere threatened.

Today, the under-privileged, who are not often wage labourers, find their interests being represented by groups outside labour movements. NGOs are not only leading this, but are also critical avenues for expanding the political space of civil society. Significantly, though, the agendas and constituencies of such independent organisations do not afford labour the control and influence offered by trade unions. None of this rules out the possibility of the Left shaping politics in contemporary Southeast Asia, but it does suggest that the sites of struggle will be varied, as will the political alliances involving the Left. Neither are the sites of struggle necessarily going to be the constitutional oppositions and political parties. After all, the experience in Southeast Asia has been that parliaments and elections do not necessarily mean increased popular representation. The rise of capitalism, middle classes and electoral politics can increase representation for some classes, but not necessarily for the masses.[64]

In Southeast Asia there are various opposition groups and movements outside this narrow, party political focus, and many of these operate in a manner which distinguishes them from the influence or lobby groups so central in liberal-pluralist democratic theory. Specifically, they are activist and do not appear to act as more or less narrow advocacy groups, for they marshall support from a range of groups and classes in society. Good examples of this kind of non-state group are the activist development NGOs which have become important political actors since the early 1980s.

There has been considerable enthusiasm concerning the political potential of NGOs. For example Jones, writing of Southeast Asia, argues that:

> . . . NGOs . . . have been chipping away at entrenched power structures. . . . [T]hey have played a critical role in forcing governments to listen to the demands of the poor, the marginalised and the abused.[65]

Not all analysts are so enthusiastic, pointing out that many NGOs are not non-governmental at all, having been co-opted by government, and noting that many are self-interested and self-promoting.[66] Indeed, the roles of NGOs in Southeast Asia vary, from the high profile activism of NGOs in the Philippines and Thailand, to a more moderate role in Indonesia and Malaysia, very limited in Singapore, to virtual non-existence in Burma and Laos. Even allowing for this, the political role of NGOs has been remarkable.

In theory, NGOs are defined as voluntary and non-profit associations with development-oriented goals. Therefore, NGOs are not necessarily defined as political opposition by governments, at least initially. Indeed, NGOs often shy away from institutionalised relationships with political parties, arguing that political parties can be no more than allies of NGOs, not their leaders.[67] However, as NGOs have matured and so-called grassroots development strategies have emerged, so their political role has been delineated. While not all NGOs are politically radical, in Southeast Asia, many have experienced a degree of radicalisation.

It is often argued that this radicalisation is due to the nature of their development activities. Sasono points out that most NGOs are not 'the grassroots', and in fact are most often drawn from 'urban intellectuals and middle class groups', and the NGOs are certainly not social movements. Despite this, he argues that they act in a *class-biased* manner, working for the poor, and taking risks, knowing the economic and political costs involved.[68]

A new development NGO ideology has evolved out of their work. Many have learnt that development practice cannot be neutral and that *empowerment* of the poor, disorganised and disenfranchised is the key to 'real' development. In addition, poverty has been defined as a political issue, as poverty has a lot to do with powerlessness. NGOs have learnt that development projects are more successful '. . . if they are based on people's own analysis of the problems they face and their solutions'.[69] In essence, this suggests an approach to participation, representation and collective action, where political action on a national or even international stage is necessary.

In other words, their ideology and methodologies create an imperative for NGOs to expand the political space at all levels of their operations. As has been demonstrated in all of the countries of Southeast Asia, this can involve the building of oppositional coalitions between unions, development groups, women, religious groups, and environmentalists. Most importantly, and like the Left in earlier periods, NGOs assist dissidents by maintaining an intellectual life, providing space for ideological debate.[70]

The oppositional status of NGOs is demonstrated where authoritarian regimes have been replaced by more representative forms, such as in Thailand, the Philippines. In Thailand, NGOs played leading and co-ordinating roles in the events of 1991 and 1992 which eventually led to the demise of a military government. Earlier, in 1986, NGOs played a similar role in overthrowing the Marcos regime.[71] Significantly, following these events, many of the NGOs still find themselves having to challenge government at all levels, supporting the poor and arguing for greater representation and participation in policy-making at all levels. Much of this tension between NGOs and governments arises from differing approaches to development.

Concluding Remarks

In Southeast Asia, as elsewhere, capitalism has not had a complete victory. Rather, with the rapid maturation of capitalism, the social shortcomings and contradictions of market relations increasingly manifest themselves in political problems for governments in the region. Many of the existing conflicts and disputes in Southeast Asia are fundamentally about the naked exploitation and oppression of capitalism, both in the human and environmental dimensions. Where economic development is most advanced, increased conspicuous consumption only highlights material inequalities. Heightened resentment of authoritarian political structures amongst the relatively-privileged classes is also evident. Indeed, the demands people are making are not for socialism, but for representation in policy-making. It is this dynamic which underlies the recent development of independent organisations and the push for an expanded civil society. Socialism, of course, has much to say about issues of representation and participation, and these concepts are not necessarily linked in the public mind to capitalism.

Current attempts in Southeast Asia to create an expanded sphere of public political space thus have a special significance for the Left. At this point in time, such a development offers the best avenue for mounting a challenge to the values of capitalism and, most importantly, contesting the power structures in support of that system. The extension of non-state political space is a necessary precondition for any such challenge to be effective, though not in itself indicative of it. It still remains that struggle within non-state organisations is required to ensure Left values and agenda are advanced, and certainly some organisations are more favourable arenas for the Left than others.

As we have seen in this discussion, there are some emerging non-state organisations whose class composition predisposes them toward rather limited forms of contestation over state power. They are jockeying within the political system to operate as interest or lobby groups and are vulnerable to co-optation. Others, namely the activist NGOs, demonstrate broader objectives and are more removed from the constitutional political process. To the extent that the latter exploit their location in civil society to agitate for an empowerment of underprivileged classes, they represent a force for substantive democracy, and one through which left values can be promoted. Whilst these organisations do not constitute social or political movements, they have the potential to precipitate them through the legitimation of class-based action. In this sense, they are not so much alternatives to more traditional Left organisations, such as trade unions, as complements to them.

The economic triumph of capitalism in Southeast Asia, then, does not close off democratic possibilities; nor, however, does it set in train an inexorable, even if protracted, force for political pluralism. Rather, it represents another historical opportunity for the establishment of a more expansive civil society. This, in turn, creates the possibility of politically contesting the exercise of state power from outside the formal political structures of the state itself. Certainly we are a long way short of realising that possibility, but if this is a priority of the Left, current political developments in Southeast Asia are nowhere near as depressing as their surface appearances suggest.

It might be that on this occasion the political space will be more resilient and less vulnerable to repression than it has been in the past. A possible reason for this is that important elements within the capitalist and middle classes appear to be supportive of the current expansion of political space and increased representation for their interests. This is an added dimension, because in the past the dominant classes were often supportive of authoritarian reversals, since they perceived the push for increased political space as being led by working class organisations, supported by communists and socialists.

We believe that these political changes offer great potential for the Left in Southeast Asia. Like Wood, we feel that the time is ripe for those on the Left to provide the definitive critique of capitalism.[72] At present, however, the Left is not doing this. Rather, the expanded political space is being dominated by organisations of the middle class and capitalists. The Left should present its critique of capitalism and its class analysis by forming alliances with the progressive elements of Southeast Asian politics. This might be achieved if those on the Left bring their skills and analysis to the membership of many progressive groups – quite a different strategy from that in previous epochs, when the communist and socialist parties were in the progressive vanguard.

NOTES

1. One of their answers was, 'We all got stoned and it drifted away.' Greg Macainsh wrote 'Whatever Happened to the Revolution for Skyhooks, *Living in the 70s* Sydney, Mushroom Records, 1974.
2. The use of 'Left' is not meant to submerge the very real differences between communists and socialists in Southeast Asia. Aspects of this will be discussed below.
3. We are not entering the debate on social movements. It remains to be assessed whether any of the groups discussed for Southeast Asia constitute social movements – see the definition in Alan Scott, *Ideology and the New Social Movements* London, Unwin Hyman, 1990, p. 6.
4. See Lucien Pye, 'Political Science and the Crisis of Authoritarianism', *American Political Science Review* 84 (1) 1990, pp. 3–19, and Samuel Huntington, *The Third Wave: Democratization in the Late Twentieth Century* Norman, University of Oklahoma Press, 1991.
5. John Girling, 'Development and Democracy in Southeast Asia', *The Pacific Review* 1 (4), 1988, pp. 332–6. The quotations are all drawn from p.332.
6. Richard Robison 'Authoritarian States, Capital-Owning Classes, and the Politics of Newly Industrializing Countries: the Case of Indonesia', *World Politics* 41 (1), 1988, pp. 52–74, and Nigel Harris, 'New Bourgeoisies', *The Journal of Development Studies* 24 (2), 1988, pp. 237–49.
7. Girling, p. 337.
8. Stephanie Lawson, 'Conceptual Issues in the Comparative Study of Regime Change and Democratization', *Comparative Politics* 25 (2), 1993, pp. 192–3.
9. Girling, pp.333–4.
10. Justus M. van der Kroef, 'Introduction: Structure and Theoretical Analysis of Opposition Movements in Southeast Asia', *Journal of Asian Affairs* 9 (Special Studies No. 154), 1984, p. 15.
11. Michael Bernhard, 'Civil Society and Democratic Transition in East Central Europe', *Political Science Quarterly* 108 (2), 1993, pp. 307, 326.
12. Civic groups may occasionally become politically active. For example, such associations might attempt to influence public policy in narrow ways, however removed from formal political processes they may be. It should also be noted that some civic organisations can often play important class functions. For example, sporting clubs might provide for solidarity among workers.
13. Ellen Meiksins Wood, 'The Uses and Abuses of "Civil Society"', in *Socialist Register 1990* London, The Merlin Press, 1990, p. 74.
14. Bernhard, p. 326.
15. Dietrich Rueschemeyer, et. al., *Capitalist Development and Democracy* Cambridge, Polity Press, 1992, p. 274. The quotation is from p. 49.
16. Bernhard, pp. 308–9.
17. We are very much aware that the interpretation we propose here is new, and requires far more research and documentation than we can provide in this essay. Here, we can only suggest some lines that further research might take up.
18. Cora Du Bois, *Social Forces in Southeast Asia* Cambridge, Harvard University Press, 1962, pp. 42–4.
19. B.G. Gafurov and G.F. Kim (eds.), *Lenin and National Liberation in the East* Moscow, Progress Publishers, 1978, p. 385.
20. Du Bois, p. 45.
21. See Reynaldo Ileto, 'Religion and Anti-Colonial Movements', in Nicholas Tarling (ed.), *The Cambridge History of Southeast Asia*, Volume 2 Cambridge, Cambridge University Press, 1992, pp. 197–248, and Carl A. Trocki, 'Political Structures in the Nineteenth and Early Twentieth Centuries', in Tarling (ed.) p. 85.

22. J.M. Pluvier, *South-East Asia from Colonialism to Independence* Kuala Lumpur, Oxford University Press, 1974, pp. 15–21, 72–91, and John Bastin and Harry J. Benda, *A History of Modern Southeast Asia* Sydney, Prentice-Hall, 1977, pp. 95–7. In the Philippines, the struggle was over the extension of voting and representation.

23. C.M. Turnbull, *A History of Singapore 1819–1975* Kuala Lumpur, Oxford University Press, 1982, p. 134, and Chua Beng Huat, 'The Changing Shape of Civil Society in Singapore', *Commentary* 11 (1), 1993, pp. 9–10.

24. David Joel Steinberg et. al., *In Search of Southeast Asia: A Modern History* New York, Praeger, 1971, p. 251.

25. Steinberg et. al., pp. 275–6, 290–8, 326.

26. See M.R. Stenson, *Industrial Conflict in Malaya* London, Oxford, 1970, p. 34, Andrew Brown, 'The Industrial Working Class and the State in Thailand: An Introductory Analysis', M.A. Thesis, The Australian National University, 1990.

27. Trocki, p. 85.

28. It is worth pointing out that the so-called 'intermediate groups' were not particularly significant in this period largely due to the nature of the economy. Trade and government service were the employers of these professional groups, but these sectors did not require large work forces, and many who did occupy these positions were expatriate professionals or privileged locals. This meant they were unlikely to fill the ranks of the anti-colonial movement, although there were some significant exceptions.

29. Brown, pp. 30–73.

30. See Turnbull, *passim*, and G. William Skinner, *Leadership and Power in the Chinese Community of Thailand* Ithaca, Cornell University Press, 1958.

31. Justus M. van der Kroef, *Communism in South-East Asia* Berkeley, University of California Press, 1980, pp. 4–7, and Robert Cribb, 'The Indonesian Marxist Tradition', in Colin Mackerras and Nick Knight (eds.), *Marxism in Asia* New York, St. Martin's Press, 1985, p. 251.

32. On the Comintern, see Nick Knight, 'Leninism, Stalinism and the Comintern', in Mackerras and Knight (eds.), pp. 53–59, and Frank Moraes, *Yonder One World. A Study of Asia and the West* New York, Macmillan, 1958, pp. 45–47. For Indonesia, see Cribb, pp. 253–6, while for Thailand, see Scot Barme, *Luang Wichit Wathakan and the Creation of a Thai Identity* Singapore, Institute of Southeast Asian Studies, 1993, Ch. 4.

33. Francis L. Starner, 'Communism in Malaysia. A Multifront Struggle', in Robert A. Scalapino (ed.), *The Communist Revolution in Asia. Tactics, Goals, and Achievements* Englewood Cliffs, Prentice-Hall, 1965, p. 223; van der Kroef, *Communism*, p. 13.

34. Paul Kratoska and Ben Batson, 'Nationalism and Modernist Reform', in Tarling (ed.), pp. 264–5, and Jim Richardson, 'Review Article: The Millenarian-Populist Aspects of Filipino Marxism', *Journal of Contemporary Asia* 23 (3), 1993, p. 386. See also Alfred W. McCoy and Ed. C. de Jesus (eds.) *Philippine Social History: Global Trade and Local Transformations*, Sydney, George Allen & Unwin, 1982, and B.J. Kerkvliet, *The Huk Rebellion: A Study of Peasant Revolt in the Philippines*, Berkeley, University of California Press, 1977, Chs. 1–2.

35. van der Kroef, *Communism*, p. 22, and Frank H. Golay et. al., *Underdevelopment and Economic Nationalism in Southeast Asia* Ithaca, Cornell University Press, 1969, p. 287.

36. Golay et. al., p. 18.

37. Starner, p. 237.

38. Bastin & Benda, p. 109, and Pluvier, pp. 195, 198.

39. Pluvier, pp. 334–59, Steinberg et. al., p. 348, and A.J. Stockwell, 'Southeast Asia in War and Peace: The End of European Colonial Empires', in Tarling (ed.), pp. 340–6, 351.

40. Bastin & Benda, p. 137, and Stockwell, p. 353.

41. Bastin & Benda, p. 116, and Pluvier, pp. 286–311.

42. D. Insor (pseud.), *Thailand. A Political, Social and Economic Analysis* London, George Allen and Unwin, 1963, p. 90.

43. On the planning imperative, see Alex Josey, *Socialism in Asia* Singapore, Donald Moore, 1957, pp. 5–6.

44. Golay et. al., p. 453.

45. Golay et. al, pp. 119–24.

46. van der Kroef, *Communism*, pp. 25–32, and Pluvier, Part VI.
47. The quotations are drawn from Josey, pp. ii, 2–5.
48. Cribb, p. 259.
49. Forrest D. Colburn and Dessalegn Rahmato, 'Rethinking Socialism in the Third World', *Third World Quarterly* 13 (1), 1992, pp. 159–173.
50. For Malaya and Singapore in this period, see Stenson, Chs. 2–4, while the Indonesia case is in Golay et. al., pp. 198–9. For Thailand, see Kevin Hewison and Andrew Brown, *Labour and Unions in an Industrialising Thailand: A Brief History* Perth, Asia Research Centre, Murdoch University, Working Paper No. 22, September 1993, pp. 12–4.
51. Craig J. Reynolds, *Thai Radical Discourse. The Real Face of Thai Feudalism Today* Ithaca, Studies on Southeast Asia, Cornell University, 1987, p. 25.
52. Turnbull, p. 262.
53. Reynolds, p. 28.
54. Akira Iriye, *The Cold War in Asia: A Historical Introduction* Englewood Cliffs, Prentice-Hall, 1974, pp. 130–91. The quotation is drawn from a US government document by the Mutual Security Agency, *East Meets West in Thailand* Washington D.C., n.d. [1952?], p. 1.
55. Chua Mui Hoong, 'Campus activism? What activism?', *The Straits Times Weekly Overseas Edition* 25 January 1992, p. 14.
56. For examples of Left support for Pol Pot, see Malcolm Caldwell, *The Wealth of Some Nations* London, Zed Press, 1977, pp. 169–72, and Samir Amin, *Imperialism and Unequal Development* New York, Monthly Review Press, 1977, pp. 147–52. Regarding the wars see Grant Evans and Kelvin Rowley, *Red Brotherhood at War. Indochina Since the Fall of Saigon* London, Verso, 1984. For the politics of Cambodia under Pol Pot see Michael Vickery, *Cambodia: 1975–1982* Boston, South End Press, 1984, and his *Kampuchea. Politics, Economics and Society* Sydney, Allen & Unwin, 1986.
57. A useful discussion of the Communist Party of Thailand can be found in Chai-Anan Samudavanija, Kusuma Snitwongse and Suchit Bunbongkarn, *From Armed Suppression to Political Offensive* Bangkok, Institute of Security and International Studies, Chulalongkorn University, 1990. The Philippines case is explained in Max Lane, 'Philippine Students and Peasants Reorganise', *Green Left*, 29 September 1993, p. 24.
58. Garry Rodan, *The Political Economy of Singapore's Industrialization: National State and International Capital* London, Macmillan, 1989; Frederic Deyo, *Dependent Development and Industrial Order: An Asian Case Study* New York, Praeger, 1981, and F. Frobel, H. Jurgen and O. Kreye, *The New International Division of Labour* Cambridge, Cambridge University Press, 1980.
59. C.Y. Ng and S. Sudo, *Development Trends in the Asia-Pacific* Singapore, Institute of Southeast Asian Studies, 1991.
60. It is not appropriate to embark on a long discussion of this development as we and others have done this extensively elsewhere. See Rodan, 1989; Richard Higgott and Richard Robison (eds.), *Southeast Asia. Essays in the Political Economy of Structural Change* London, Routledge and Kegan Paul, 1985; Richard Robison, *Indonesia: the Rise of Capital* Sydney, Allen & Unwin, 1986; Kevin Hewison, *Power and Politics in Thailand* Manila, JCA Press, 1989, and Ruth McVey (ed.), *Southeast Asian Capitalists* Ithaca, Southeast Asia Program, Cornell University, 1992.
61. See the special issue on middle classes in Asia of *The Pacific Review*, 5 (4), 1992.
62. Andrew MacIntyre's perspective on Indonesia is best explained in his *Business and Politics in Indonesia* Sydney, Allen & Unwin, 1991, pp. 246–7; on Thailand see his *Business-Government Relations in Industrialising East Asia: South Korea and Thailand* Nathan, Centre for the Study of Australia-Asia Relations, Griffith University, Australia-Asia Paper No. 53, 1990, pp. 32–3. The quotation is from Anek Laothamatas, *Business Associations and the New Political Economy of Thailand: From Bureaucratic Polity to Liberal Corporatism* Singapore, Institute of Southeast Asian Studies, 1992, pp. 12–5. For a critique of this genre, see Kevin Hewison, 'Liberal Corporatism and the Return of Pluralism in Thai Political Studies', *Asian Studies Review* 16 (2), 1992, pp. 261–5.
63. Garry Rodan, 'Preserving the One-Party State in Contemporary Singapore', in Kevin Hewison, Richard Robison and Garry Rodan (eds.), *Southeast Asia in the 1990s: Authoritarianism, Democracy and Capitalism* Sydney, Allen Unwin, 1993, pp. 75-108.

64. On oppositions as parties see Lawson, 'Conceptual Issue', and her 'Institutionalising Peaceful Conflict: Political Opposition and the Challenge of Democratisation in Asia', *Australian Journal of International Affairs* 47 (1), 1993, pp. 15–30. For a brief discussion of electoral politics and lack of representation, see Kevin Hewison, 'Of Regimes, State and Pluralities: Thai Politics Enters the 1990s', in Hewison, Robison and Rodan (eds.), pp. 159–89.

65. Sidney Jones, 'The Organic Growth. Asian NGOs Have Come Into Their Own', *Thai Development Newsletter* 22, 1993, p. 70.

66. For discussions of NGOs, see Rajni Kothari, 'The NGOs, the State and World Capitalism', *New Asian Visions* 6 (1), 1989, pp. 40–58; Adi Sasono, 'NGOs [sic] Roles and Social Movement in Developing Democracy: The South-East Asian Experiences', *New Asian Visions* 6 (1), 1989, pp. 14–26; Majid Rahnema, in 'Shifting [sic] the Wheat From the Chaff', *New Asian Visions* 6 (1), 1989, p. 9, makes an obvious point when he warns that there is a tendency to create a false view of NGOs, seeing them as implicitly 'good' because they are non-state. In the Philippines, NGOs have been incorporated within the structures of local government, and this co-option of NGOs by the state and international agencies like the World Bank has led to a debate concerning the independence of NGOs – see A.B. Brillantes, Jr., 'Local Government and NGOs [in] the Philippines: Development Issues and Challenges', paper presented to the 4th International Philippine Studies Conference, Canberra, July 1992.

67. Rahnema, p. 7. See also John Clark, *Democratising Development. The Role of Voluntary Organizations* London, Earthscan Publications, 1991, p. 18.

68. Sasono, p. 19.

69. Clark, p. 102.

70. Mario Padron, 'Non-governmental Development Organizations: From Development Aid to Development Co-operation', *World Development* 15 (Special Supplement), 1987, p. 75.

71. On Thailand in 1992 see Paisal Sricharatchanya et.al., *Uprising in May: Catalyst for Change* Bangkok, The Post Publishing Co., 1992, pp. 54–72. For the Philippines see Max Lane, *The Urban Mass Movement in the Philippines, 1983–1987* Canberra, Research School of Pacific Studies, The Australian National University, 1990.

72. Wood, p. 60.

THE LEFT IN RUSSIA

Poul Funder Larsen and David Mandel

I. Introduction

The central problem facing the democratic left in Russia is its failure to date to win mass support, in particular among the working class, its natural social base. An analysis of this failure must, therefore, form the background for any discussion of left Russian political parties and movements. Accordingly, the first part of this article will deal with the social and political situation in the working class and the ('non-political') labour movement. The second part will present an historical overview and analysis of the left.

First some definitions are in order. By 'working class' we mean that part of the population that depends mainly on wages or salaries for its subsistence and does not hold managerial positions. This includes also the 'toiling intelligentsia' (that is, people in non-managerial positions normally requiring diplomas of higher education), although for some purposes in this essay we will refer to the latter as a separate group. The social structure of Russia is in rapid flux, but the working class and their dependents (with or without the 'toiling intelligentsia') still make up the vast majority of the population.

A definition of the 'left' is somewhat more problematic. Strictly speaking, these are the democratic socialists (the word 'democratic' is, admittedly, redundant), that is, anti-capitalist political groups striving for the maximal extension of democracy (in the literal sense of popular power), not only in the narrowly defined political sphere but also – and perhaps especially – in economic and social life. This consistently democratic left objectively reflects the interests of the working class.

However, in this article we will also use an expanded definition of the 'left' that includes those anti-capitalist elements who refer to themselves as 'socialist' or 'communist' but whose practice and real programmes may have little to do with the extension of democracy. In Russia, these elements are mainly the various successor groups to the Communist Party of the Soviet Union (CPSU), outlawed by Yeltsin after August 1991. We will refer to these groups, for lack of a better term, as the 'nostalgic left' (though in their social and economic programmes, most of them actually tend more toward social democracy; the parties that call themselves 'social democratic', in turn, tend more to economic liberalism).

II. THE WORKING CLASS AND LABOUR MOVEMENT

1. The Working Class As It Emerged from Bureaucratic Rule

Until the late 1980s, there was a widespread assumption among the democratic left, both inside and outside the Soviet Union, that the anti-bureaucratic revolution would be socialist in content, that is, would lead to a genuine socialization of the nationalized economy. This has so far obviously turned out to be illusory. But the illusion (which itself may yet be overturned) did have some basis in reality. Workers played leading and independent roles in all the anti-bureaucratic movements in Eastern Europe in the four decades following World War II. These movements almost always gave rise to workers' councils and to demands for self-management, their participants often displaying remarkable solidarity and organization. Even in the Soviet Union, the centre of bureaucratic power, disillusionment with de-Stalinization in the early 1960s provoked a significant protest movement among workers, which was severely repressed.

In general, it was difficult to conceive that workers in these nationalized economies would tolerate the substitution of a capitalist class for their former bureaucratic overlords. The basic thrust of the labour movement since the very origins of modern capitalism has been to subordinate the market to social needs, when it was not completely to replace the market with a planned economy based upon production for use. It seemed reasonable to assume that workers in the bureaucratic states would oppose attempts to restore market relations to dominance in their economies.

That capitalism is now being restored, albeit in a confused and still far from complete manner, is primarily the result of the weakness of the working class as it emerged from decades of bureaucratic dictatorship. However, the extent of this weakness was not immediately evident in the Soviet Union. In particular, Perestroika, initiated from above under the banner of a return to socialist principles (a banner that soon proved false), gave rise to a growing, if uneven, social and political mobilization in the working class. This took the form of strikes, the formation of independent trade unions, of self-management movements, as well as active participation in electoral politics in support of anti-bureaucratic forces.

This activity played an important role in the gradual expansion of political freedoms under Perestroika that finally led to the fall of the 'Communist' bureaucratic regime. But the fruits of this mobilization, which in Russia itself never embraced more than a minority of the working class, were harvested with relative ease by liberal forces (in and outside the bureaucracy) hostile to the workers' interests. Despite their promises of democracy and Western-style living standards, the policies of the new/old elite have left workers much worse off both economically and even politically than under Brezhnev.

In retrospect, the weakness of the working class is not difficult to explain. The rapid collapse of bureaucratic rule left in its wake an atomized society. That regime had for over 60 years effectively prevented independent collective activity and organization (with the exception, under Brezhnev, of bureaucratic-mafia groupings). The relative ease with which some workers were able to mount collective actions during Perestroika – in the miners' case, this occurred on a very large scale – was largely due to the fact that the state itself provided a ready organizational framework for mobilization: the party-state bureaucracy organized society in order to control and administer it. When repression was relaxed in the first years of Perestroika, these structures – especially the state enterprises and their centralized ministries – were still intact, and economic protests quickly became politicized. The centralized, authoritarian state presented itself as the natural target of discontent. The goal – popular control – was self-evident.

The high point of this popular mobilization was reached in 1990, with the election of many liberals, running under democratic, anti-bureaucratic banners, to local and republican soviets. After that, activism steadily declined. (There were some, admittedly weak, signs of a resurgence in the fall of 1993 before Yeltsin's tanks gutted the Supreme Soviet.) In August 1991, the liberal forces around Yeltsin were able to defeat the attempted putsch by conservative forces with minimal popular mobilization. This development opened the way for a time to the unlimited dominance of the liberals and the launching of 'shock therapy', a massive assault on popular living standards and social and political rights.

By then, much of its old state structure had already been dismantled, especially in the economic sphere, and so it could no longer serve as an organizing element for popular discontent. In particular, enterprises, though still state-owned, had 'won' their autonomy. The resultant atomization was well reflected in the union movement, where decentralization was carried to the extreme. The national branch unions and federations lost their former dictatorial powers and most of their budgets to the enterprise-level unions and saw their roles reduced to mere co-ordinators and political lobbyists. In most of industry, sectorial collective agreements became almost irrelevant; it was increasingly every plant for itself. There is some reaction against this today, but the absence of solidarity in the union movement remains very striking.

At the same time, once democracy had been won – or, at least, appeared to have been won – and once the grandiose promises associated with market reform (which had been sold to the populace as the opposite of bureaucratic centralization, and so the natural economic counterpart of political democracy) had proved empty, it became much harder for workers to find positive common goals to unite their opposition to the policies of the new/old liberal/bureaucratic regime.

Another factor was the discrediting of socialism by the old regime, which made it difficult to conceive of a coherent, working class alternative. However, this problem played a more central role really in the final period of Perestroika, when people still took the promises of the market reformers seriously. Today, the majority of workers look back fondly at their economic security and living standards under the old system. Despite the government's continued propaganda efforts, the mention of socialism, at least as an idea, no longer provokes negative reactions in most people.

Today the basic factor preventing the emergence of a working-class alternative to capitalist restoration is the social and political demoralization of the working class against the background of an unprecedented peacetime economic crisis. According to one independent estimate, the gross domestic product at the end of 1993 was 38 per cent below the level at the end of 1990. The volume of industrial production, according to official figures, fell by 16 per cent in 1993 and by 18 per cent in 1992.[1] There is no sign of an end to the economic decline. Fear of mass protest has so far kept the government from allowing open mass unemployment. But shortened work weeks and forced extended leaves at a fraction of regular pay are very common. Without a major shift in policy, mass bankruptcies and dismissals cannot be far off.

The material and social distress experienced by the average Russian citizen is eloquently summed up in a few demographic figures. Infant mortality, already very high at the start of 'shock therapy' for an industrialized country, rose from 16.8 per thousand in 1991 to 19.1 in 1993. Life expectancy for men dropped in 1993 from 62 (already ten to thirteen years below Western figures) to 59 years (for women: from 73 to 71). Only one fifth of children upon graduation from high school are considered by medical authorities to be in full health. In 1993 alone, the population of Russia declined by over one million, with the gulf between births and deaths continuing to rise at a precipitous rate.[2] Government statistics put average real incomes at the end of 1993 at one third of the pre-'shock' level of the end of 1991.[3] The old social guarantees – full employment and job security, free health care and education, free housing and heavily subsidized communal services, transportation, and basic food products – are being rapidly dismantled.

In brief, Russian workers today find themselves in an entirely new situation of economic insecurity that is fast coming to resemble that of workers in Third World countries. The reactions to this social earthquake among workers, the great majority of whom have no experience of collective action, has been to retreat into the private struggle for survival, while clinging to the hope that somehow management and/or the state will defend them. This attitude comes naturally as a legacy of the past: though ultimately backed up by the threat of repression (made good whenever workers openly clashed with their masters), the relationship of management and the political authorities to workers for several decades was one of more-or-less benevolent paternalism. Today, in conditions of rapidly deepening crisis, few workers have any faith in their own collective ability to defend themselves.

Another crucial factor, one often overlooked, is the relative ease with which liberal forces hijacked the anti-bureaucratic revolution is because of the weakness of the labour movement on the international level. In a largely forgotten passage of the *Revolution Betrayed*, in the chapter significantly entitled 'The Inevitability of a New Revolution', Trotsky wrote in the mid 1930s that the fate of the October Revolution was inextricably tied to the fate of Europe and of the whole world and that if no revolution were victorious in the developed capitalist countries

> then a bourgeois counterrevolution [in the USSR] rather than an uprising of workers against the bureaucracy will most likely be on the agenda. But if, despite the joint sabotage of the reformers and the 'communist' leaders, the proletariat of Western Europe finds the way to power, a new chapter will be opened in the history of the Soviet Union. The very first victory of the revolution in Europe will flow like an electric current through the Soviet masses, straighten them up, raise their spirit of independence, awaken in them the traditions of 1905 and 1917. . . . Only in that way can the first workers' state be saved for the socialist future.[4]

Not only has there been no successful revolution, but the collapse of the bureaucratic regimes occurred at a very low point in the fortunes of the world labour and socialist movements. Almost everywhere, these movements are on the defensive and retreating. Except perhaps for the Workers' Party in Brazil, there is today no mass party anywhere that sees socialism as its immediate task, let alone does something to achieve it. In these circumstances, it is little wonder that Russian workers fell easy prey to liberal ideology. They were constantly reminded that 'the whole world has embraced the market'. Ideological, economic and political pressure from abroad played a key role in directing the anti-bureaucratic revolution onto a capitalist path. There was practically no countervailing pressure from the international labour and socialist movements.

Now, more than two years into 'shock therapy', Russian workers have been immunized against the siren songs of the liberals, but they still cannot practically conceive of an alternative to capitalist restoration. It is on this background of demobilization and despair that fascism in Russia can become a real potential (as evidenced in the recent electoral showing of Vladimir Zhirinovsky).

Indeed, if one considers the international context of the collapse of the bureaucratic regime (and it was more collapse than overthrow, the elite of the ruling caste itself having lost confidence in its system), the turn that events have taken no longer seems quite so predestined. If, for example, the collapse had occurred in 1968 (it was in progress in Czechoslovakia before the Soviet tanks rolled in), it is not hard to imagine the ensuing transformation taking an entirely different direction. This is not to deny that the crisis of the labour and socialist movements in the capitalist world and the collapse of the bureaucratic regimes are linked. But that link is much less direct than the coincidence of the two crises might lead one to think.

2. The Russian Labour Movement and the Collapse of the Old Regime

In this section we will look at the political responses of the main types of labour organizations to the collapse of the bureaucratic system and the process, still far from complete, of capitalist restoration. Perestroika gave rise to many workers' organizations, but most remained small and were short-lived. The three types of organization that displayed some staying power and significant memberships are the new trade unions, the work-collective councils (STKs) and their associations, and finally the old trade unions. We will deal with them in that order, since that is how they made themselves felt on the political scene.[5]

a. The New or Alternative Trade Unions

With their general strike in the summer of 1989, the miners became the vanguard of the movement for renewal of the labour movement, which except for brief, localized explosions, had been stamped out back in the late 1920s. That strike eventually gave rise to the Independent Miners' Union (NPG), the rival to the old Union of Employees of the Coal Industry. The founders of the NPG reproached the old union, among other things, with being conciliationist and including management in its ranks. They set out to organize a union exclusively of underground coal workers, unlike the old union which also included thousands of surface employees in the varied enterprises of the coal ministry. (The NPG eventually yielded on that point, but it still excludes anyone above the rank of foreman.)

Overall, the new union movement has made rather limited progress outside of the coal sector. Although exact numbers are hard to come by (all the unions tend to inflate their membership figures), today probably more than 90 per cent of organized workers still belong to the old unions, which include around 90 per cent of all wage and salary earners. Even among coalminers, probably less than ten per cent belong to the NPG, though the latter's influence, now on the decline, has in the past gone well beyond its formal membership. Outside of coal, the new movement has met with some success mainly in the transport sector (aside from the relatively few individual new unions in scattered enterprises and shops elsewhere): among air-traffic controllers, pilots, locomotive drivers, port workers, city transport drivers. These are strategic economic positions that give these relatively small groups of workers exceptional leverage.

In deciding to split off from the old unions, the organizers of the new ones argued that the old structures were unreformable. The obstacles to reform in 1990, when the NPG was founded, must indeed have seemed formidable. Even today, more than three years later, the main problems – the absence of democratic accountability of union leaders and their subordination to enterprise management – are still far from being resolved in the majority of enterprise-level unions, where the real power now lies.

Still, progress is being made, though at a very uneven and slow pace that may prove insufficient to save the organised labour movement, weak as it already is, from a definitive defeat by the forces of capitalist restoration. One example of reform at the national level is the old coal employees' union itself, which has no doubt benefitted from the competition provided by the rival NPG. Under a young president who rose from the ranks (rather than coming from the party apparatus, as was past tradition), this union has become increasingly militant in the defence of its members' interests, and its president's authority among miners today far surpasses that of the NPG's leaders. (In the recent national elections in a mining and heavy industrial region of Siberia, the Russian NPG's leader lost out to the director of a department store, generally one of the most hated economic figures in Russia.) Other unions that have undergone far-reaching reform at the national level are the Byelorussian Autoworkers' and Radio-electronic Workers' Unions.

These examples, unfortunately still quite rare, nevertheless demonstrate that reform of the old structures, however difficult, is possible. It is true that most of the old unions' new-found militancy has been directed at the state and not against enterprise management. Indeed, many of the collective actions organized by these unions have had the active or passive support of management, since their aim has been to force the state to live up to its commitments to pay subsidies, to provide credits, to lighten the tax burden on enterprises, and the like. These and similar issues, upon which the very survival of the enterprise hangs, represent interests still shared in common by workers and much of enterprise management. Privatization, at least in the large enterprises, has in most cases still not significantly affected worker-management relations, which retain much of their old paternalistic character.

Thus, if union reform has not gone very far at the level of the plant committees, it would be wrong to attribute this merely to corruption or to the allegedly unreformable nature of the old unions. There remains an objective basis for the close collaboration of management and the union. The problem is not the co-operation itself, but that the union rarely takes part in it as an equal and independent partner. But again, there are examples of old unions at the shop and plant levels that have become accountable to the membership and independent of management. This has occurred when the rank-and-file union members themselves mobilized against management to elect democratic leaders prepared to adopt independent positions.

That this is still rare is certainly in part due to managerial repression against activists, often with the co-operation of old union leaders. But the main reason, as argued above, is undoubtedly the prevailing demoralization and demobilization among the rank and file. The strategy adopted by some labour activists to form new unions alongside the old ones is, at least in part, a way of avoiding the difficult task of mobilizing the majority of still inert workers for union reform by concentrating efforts on the minority, who for one reason or another, are prepared to support more independent and accountable union organizations.

But if in the early stages of the new union movement, its activists adopted more solidary positions and made some efforts to reach the broader strata of workers (for example, by founding the now defunct, quasi-political Confederation of Labour in 1990), this movement has increasingly taken on a narrow craft character, to the point where many parts of it have become a sort of labour aristocracy in their attitudes and practice.

The 'aristocratic' outlook of the leaders of the NPG came to the fore in the spring of 1992, when they refused to support the strike movement – some even condemned it – among the health and education workers, the lowest paid workers in Russia, whose wages remain well below the poverty line. (The old miners' union supported this movement, though its support rarely went much farther than declarations.) The NPG has also come out in support of such non-solidary forms of social benefits as individual social security and health insurance accounts.

The support for Yeltsin and his neo-liberal policies among almost all of the new unions is closely linked to this 'aristocratic' outlook. On the one hand, the strategic economic positions of their members (as one old union activist put it: 'They sit on the golden tap') have allowed them to fare better than other workers under the liberal reforms. On the other, these unions try to compensate for their political isolation from the broader mass of workers by developing a special relationship with the government: their political loyalty has won them a certain degree of favoured treatment. All the major new unions supported Yeltsin to the hilt in his bloody confrontation with parliament in September–October 1993, while virtually all the old unions, to one degree or another, supported the parliament (whose majority had been shifting to the left (or rather centre) against Yeltsin's 'shock therapy').

This explains the major paradox of the organized labour scene in Russia: the new unions generally adopt militant, independent positions toward enterprise management but display touching loyalty to the government;

the old unions tend to do the opposite. The upshot of this is that the most active elements of the working class, those in the new unions, have been detached from, and to some degree even turned against, the basic mass of workers.

This, of course, is not unrelated to the ties that the AFL-CIO's U.S.-government-funded Russo-American Foundation has managed to develop with these new unions. This foundation openly professes a liberal ideology and supports the pro-Yeltsin forces, while decisively refusing any contact with the 'former Communist' organizations belonging to the old union federation.[6]

Despite all this, one has to doubt whether these new unions (at least, those of them that are real unions and organize the workers in entire enterprises, trades and/or sectors) can long maintain their 'aristocratic' orientations. In Russian conditions, to say that the material situation of these workers is privileged is only to say that they are less poor than most. In addition, the special relationship with the government is anything but secure and is certainly no protection against periodic efforts on the part of state enterprise management to break these unions through strong-arm tactics.

b. The STKs and the Self Management Movement

The STKs (work-collective councils) were created by order from above on the basis of Gorbachev's 1987 Law on the State Enterprise, adopted when Perestroika still paraded under the banner of a return to socialist ideals. Largely because of these origins and because little else had yet changed in the economic relations, the great majority of STKs remained subordinate to the enterprise administration. The STK movement as such only began to take off after the first miners' strike in 1989, and especially when Perestroika began to shift to an openly restorationist course. The new 1990 Enterprise Law, which virtually abolished the STKs, provided the major impulse for the creation of national and regional STK unions, with the first national congress taking place in Moscow at the end of 1990. Even so, the activists of this movement came disproportionately from the enterprise intelligentsia.

At its high point, this current of the labour movement came closest in its demands to a socialist programme for reform of property relations, calling for the full transfer of management in the state enterprises to the work collectives. This meant that the enterprise would enjoy economic autonomy, with the plant employees collectively deciding its basic policy and hiring the management. At some later time, the collectives would themselves decide what form of property the enterprise should take. This could range from full collective ownership to full state ownership, but the key point was that any change in property relations would be the voluntary decision of the collective.

The major weakness of this position was that it presented no macro-economic vision, that is, there was no attempt to deal with the nature of relations between the enterprises nor with the role of the state or of other political and collective institutions in the economy. That this critical issue was left open was no doubt due to a combination of a reaction against the old centralized, bureaucratic system of management as well as to the influence of liberal ideology, which painted any direct state role in the economy management as 'totalitarian' (whether that state was democratic or not was irrelevant to the liberals).

Nevertheless, the STKs' position was anathema to the reform-minded section of the nomenklatura, originally Gorbachev's main political base, which by this time was fast abandoning its attachment to 'socialism', hoping itself to appropriate privately the best parts of the nationalized economy. The STKs' demands were also strongly opposed by the liberal forces that dominated the elite intelligentsia and by their political allies abroad in the IMF and World Bank. They constantly cited the Yugoslav example as 'proof' that self-management does not work. But, in fact, they saw self-management and worker ownership as a major obstacle to rapid capitalist restoration.

This opposition to the STK movement was well-founded. It is true that the absence of an explicit macro-economic conception of reform, at least among the majority of activists, implied an essentially market-dominated view of the future economy. Nevertheless, worker self-management would have put a brake on rapid privatization (primitive accumulation), which (along with the creation of favourable conditions for foreign investment and trade – mostly, in practice, outright plundering) is the real main goal of 'shock therapy' (all the talk about restructuring and efficiency being mainly a smokescreen to hide the rapid formation of a bourgeoisie). Worker self-management would have left open the possibility that workers would be led by their practical experience to see that a genuinely demo-cratic state and other accountable collective institutions have a positive and necessary role to play in economic organization, since a purely market system of self-managed enterprises would spell sure bankruptcy for many enterprises and entail mass unemployment. In the summer of 1993, for example, after getting a taste of privatization in practice, despite a massive propaganda campaign (largely financed by the U.S. government), 72 per cent of the respondents in a national survey opposed privatization of large-scale enterprises.[7]

The major weakness of the movement was probably less ideological than political: it failed to mobilize mass worker support behind it. The great majority of workers apparently did not see the practical relevance of the property question for themselves. Back in 1990 and even 1991, few understood that privatization would eventually put an end to the prevailing paternalistic practices of management and the state, that it threatened workers with loss of key social benefits and especially with mass unemployment. Russian workers had no direct experience of capitalism and they typically reacted with disbelief when told that in capitalist economies productive, disciplined workers are regularly fired when their labour can no longer make a profit for the owners. On the contrary, many workers believed that a 'real owner' (the liberals insisted that under the old system 'no one' owned the enterprises) would introduce the latest technology and eliminate the semi-organized anarchy that characterized Soviet enterprises.

Worker indifference and even distrust toward the STKs were bolstered by their official origins and their widespread subordination to the plant administration. This problem was compounded by the tacit and often open hostility of most unions to the STKs. Union leaders tended to see them as rival organizations. Many believed that self-management and/or collective ownership would lead to the elimination of trade unions as unnecessary. Rather belatedly, toward the end of 1991, both the new and the old trade unions, at least formally, finally came around to supporting the original demands of the STK movement. Nevertheless, both union movements consistently refer to their main task as defending 'hired labour', a phrase that would seem to imply that they have, in fact, given up on defending the workers' claim as collective owners of the nationalized economy, built by their labour and that of previous generations.

But part of the responsibility for the failure of the movement lies with the movement's leadership itself, who did little to mobilize workers around its demands. Instead, they concentrated their efforts on political lobbying in the corridors of power. This choice of tactic was probably related, at least in part, to the predominance of the enterprise intelligentsia among the movement's activists. They tended to be less confrontational and more trusting of authorities than workers. In Russia, the national STK movement's leaders cast their lot with Yeltsin and his push for Russian sovereignty (this was at a time when the USSR still existed). No sooner had Yeltsin and his liberal supporters acquired the power they coveted than they openly turned against the self-management movement. (Kravchuk repeated the same trick on the Ukrainian movement.)

Under tremendous ideological and political pressure from above, and with little active support from below, the STK movement gradually retreated from its original demands and began to defend the workers' right to at least some share of the nationalized property. But the choices offered by Yeltsin's Law on Privatization included neither self-management nor collective worker ownership. Today, few STKs still exist. But despite the official self-congratulations on the progress of privatization, the issue of property is a long way from being resolved. As we have noted, worker-management relations in most enterprises that have formally been privatized have yet to change fundamentally. In some enterprises where conflicts over property have become acute, in the absence of STKs, the trade unions and other ad hoc organizations have taken up the battle for the workers. In a number of cases, workers have tried to circumvent the law by pooling individually-held shares. In a few instances, workers have openly revolted and de facto annulled the privatization of their enterprise, once they had understood what it meant in practice.

The real change in property relations in Russia will be marked by mass dismissals. It is difficult to predict how workers will react to that. A major labour upsurge would surely spell the end to the neo-liberal reforms. So far, there are few signs of such mobilization, but the contradictions – and the anger – are mounting.

3. The Old Unions.

The miners' strike in 1989, which saw the old miners' union sitting beside the government and ministry representatives across the table from the strikers, provided the first real impetus for change, albeit slow and tortuous, in the old unions. But probably more decisive than the competition from new worker organizations was the shift in government attitude toward the old unions. With the change in state policy to a liberal course, the old unions lost their status as junior, subordinate partners and became the objects of open government hostility.

The onslaught caught the old unions quite by surprise, as was demonstrated by the central slogan of the FNPR's (Federation of Independent Trade Unions) 'fall campaign' (a tactic mechanically adopted from the Japanese labour movement): 'market wages for market prices', a campaign that failed miserably. The unions had done next to nothing in the enterprises themselves to win the confidence of their members and were unable (many plant chairpersons were unwilling) to mobilize them around this essentially political slogan.

Between 1989 and Yeltsin's state coup in September–October 1993, the old unions gradually shifted to a position of open opposition to the government. But this evolution was halting and contradictory. They continued – and continue today – to embrace the slogan of 'social partnership', even though the government consistently violates its signed agreements. At the same time, the old unions mounted, or tried to mount, political pressure campaigns to force the government to live up to its commitments and to change an economic policy ruinous for their members. One such campaign was building up, with somewhat more success than usual, in the weeks preceding Yeltsin's decree that abolished the constitution and shut down the parliament. (Most of the new unions also embrace the slogan of 'social partnership', which is being pushed vigorously by the ILO and the AFL-CIO.)

In conditions of a collapsing economy, unions can achieve relatively little for their members through traditional 'trade-unionistic' actions. To be effective in Russia in today's situation, the main struggle has to be conducted on the political level. To a degree, this is understood in the old unions, since most of their militant actions have, as noted, been directed at the state. But the political action of the old unions suffers from two major and related weaknesses.

One of these is the failure of the plant unions clearly to demarcate themselves from enterprise management. This, of course, does not rule out co-operation when it is in the workers' interests, but it must be from independent, union positions. Unless unions can demonstrate to their members that they are something more than the tail of the administration, unless they clearly take up the defence of the workers' interests in the enterprise itself and win them at least some small, but real, victories, they have little hope of leading them into political action against the state. Today most workers do not even understand why they need a union (and most plant union chairpersons do not understand why they need an active, conscious rank and file).

The other major weakness of the old unions' political action has been its inconsistency. This, too, is related to the unions' refusal to assert their independence from management. The FNPR and its affiliated unions support a 'centrist' position on economic reform in a tacit alliance with the so-called 'directors' corps', those enterprise directors who have remained more-or-less 'red', that is, who have not totally given up on saving their enterprise and its work force. This position (which also characterized the majority of the old parliament in its latter days) accepts the 'inevitability' of capitalist restoration, but calls for a 'socially-oriented market' – a regulated transition to a capitalism oriented to national needs, with a strong state sector and social-welfare safety net: in other words – capitalism with a human face. But one has seriously to doubt the realism of such a programme, given the current crisis and restructuring of world capitalism and the subordinate place the Russian economy would inevitably occupy in it.

In this sense, the liberals' criticism of the 'centrist' programme as inconsistent has some merit. In effect, the old unions want it both ways: they accept capitalist restoration but reject its consequences. They are not opposed to privatization but it should be carried out 'in the interests of the work collectives', a vague and meaningless phrase. If they are serious about defending their members' interests, they have to opt for a clean break with the government and the 'directors' corps' (that is, abandon 'social partnership') and come out with a clear workers' alternative to capitalist restoration. In private conversations, many union leaders appear to understand that the defence of workers' interest in current conditions has to assume an anti-capitalist character, but most refuse to adopt that position in practice.

In the past, the old unions have toyed with the idea of forming their own labour party but have never decided to do it. (In Byelorussia, the Auto-workers' and Radio-electronics Workers' Unions created such a party at the end of 1993.) The idea is still in the air, but the new leadership that was elected to the FNPR after the October 1993 crisis has so far shown itself even more timid than the old.

This is partly a response to government repression: the unions lost their control of the social security administration at the end of September 1993 (a few days after the FNPR executive condemned Yeltsin's state coup), and the government made clear that if they are disloyal, they stand to lose their automatic dues check-off and their property, if not worse. At the same time, since the defeat of pro-'shock' forces in the December 1993 elections, there seems to have been some shift in government economic policy toward a more 'centrist' position. This has created an expectant mood among some of the union leaders.

But probably as important is the old union leaders' sense of isolation from their millions of members, who are not ready to support them in a confrontation with the government. This is really a magic circle that can only be broken by a labour upsurge from below or by the adoption by the union leadership of an independent, far-sighted, and consistent strategy that their members can come to believe in. Ideally, it would be a combina-tion of both. Whether any of these eventualities will happen and when is anyone's guess. The only thing that is sure at this point is that the immediate future is not bright for workers and the labour movement.

III. THE LEFT

A basic knowledge of the history of the left in Russia from the time of Perestroika is indispensable to understanding its present state. The real impact of the left on state policy has been small, but, at the same time, the left's manifestations and evolution have been extremely varied and com-plex. This poses real problems for an adequate treatment of the topic in so limited a space. We have tried to deal with this by combining an historical survey with elements of analysis that focus primarily on the obstacles (besides those 'objective' factors already treated in the first section) to the democratic left's acquiring a mass social base.

It would, of course, not be entirely correct to claim that the labour movement and the various left organizations and groups that emerged during and after Perestroika developed along totally separate paths. In fact, over the years, various attempts on the left have been made to forge links with the workers' movement. Following the miners' strike of 1989, these efforts met with some temporary success. In particular, there was considerable left influence at the founding of the Confederation of Labour in May 1990. But the Confederation itself never really got off the ground.

Since then, aside from a few regional political groupings consistently oriented toward workers (such as Rabochii, a socialist association of workers' clubs in the Volga and Urals regions), and some groups of socialist intellectuals (such as the Moscow-based KAS-KOR Bulletin on the Labour Movement and the Committee to Support the Labour Movement), most leftwing organizations gradually gave up systematic efforts directed toward workers.

In the first section, we tried to understand the isolation of the left by focusing on the politics of workers and their ('non-political') labour organizations. In this part, we will approach the problem from inside the left itself.

1. Before August 1991[9]

a. The 'Informal' Left[10]

For the sake of clarity, we will treat separately the early stages of the development of the 'informal' left from that of the left within the Communist Party of the Soviet Union. However, it should be kept in mind that these currents interacted to a large extent, both in their political dynamics as well as in a direct organizational sense, since the CPSU or Komsomol structures often gave tacit support (political and even material) to many of the 'informal' groups, whose members were themselves frequently recruited from these structures. Nevertheless, until 1991 open and direct collaboration between the 'informal' and the 'formal' structures was very limited, as the former feared manipulation and discrediting, while the latter were wary of encouraging potential competitors.

Many of the 'informal' left groups had their roots in the pre-Perestroika era, when discontent with the regime was growing in intellectual circles.[11] When Perestroika was put on the official political agenda in 1986–1987, many of these small groupings already had several years of discussion and even samizdat publication behind them. But for obvious reasons, their practical experience with political intervention and campaigning was next to nonexistent, and when liberalization made possible open political struggle, this lack of experience, especially in contest with the shrewd tacticians of the party apparatus, was very telling. (The average age in the 'informal' socialist clubs in 1986–1987 was probably less than 25 years.)

The multitude of clubs and currents that emerged in this period was the manifestation of a genuine, if limited in scope, anti-bureaucratic movement that posed vital social and political issues hitherto exclusively restricted to the jurisdiction of the bureaucratic authorities or else completely outside the bounds of legitimate political consideration.

The formation in August 1987 of the Federation of Socialist Clubs was a major breakthrough for the 'informal' democratic socialists. A key player in this was the Moscow Social Initiative Club, led, among others, by Boris Kagarlitsky, who had been arrested in 1982 as a leader of the Young Socialists, and Gleb Pavlovsky, a former samizdat journalist.[12] The Federation was founded under the formal banner of 'consolidating the left wing of Perestroika', a phrase obviously designed to calm the fears of the authorities, but which also reflected the political outlook of many of the 'informal' political activists of the 'first wave'. The declaration of the founding conference was carefully worded to avoid any head-on confrontation, but it nevertheless signalled the two concerns that would come to dominate the political struggles on the left in the following years: the struggle for democratic rights and the introduction of the market mechanism as a regulator in economic relations.

But if the Federation of Socialist Clubs was a step forward, both in terms of its own organizational ambitions and its winning of somewhat broader public recognition for the left, it soon became obsolete, due to its ideological and structural amorphousness in a period of extremely rapid political evolution and differentiation. Within less than a year, it had vanished from the political scene.

As the 'democratic movement' gained momentum, Popular Fronts, uniting very heterogeneous groups and organizations that professed a democratic orientation, were created, first in provincial centres (where the political scene was less factionalized) and then finally in Moscow in the spring of 1988, where socialists played an important leadership role. These Popular Fronts typically had broad democratic, social and environmental programmes, uniting substantial layers of activists. But they were unable to transcend their own nature as coalitions in the defence of a radical version of Perestroika. Consequently, when official Perestroika entered its terminal phase in the winter of 1989/90 against the background of the failure of Gorbachev's economic reform, and a series of alternative, mainly liberal, options, came to dominate the political debate, the underlying basis of the Popular Fronts disappeared.

Although the experiences of the Popular Fronts varied from region to region, some general statements can be made about the problems faced by the left in that period inside this type of broad coalition. The forces involved in these movements were of such a heterogeneous, sometimes even mutually contradictory, nature, that they could not possibly develop anything even resembling a clear political platform or ideology. This tended to restrict them to their 'lowest common denominator', which, in practice, was the goal of winning concessions from the more progressive elements of the party apparatus. As Kagarlitsky, then a prominent leader of the Moscow Popular Front, stated: 'We are realistic and don't demand the impossible. We make radical, but realizable demands.'[14] However, the movement did show some radicalism, and was undoubtedly successful in several cases in setting the political agenda, especially in its campaigns around single issues, for example, on the environment or for the truthful treatment of Soviet history.

The political incoherence of the Popular Fronts also helps to explain their inability to develop lasting organizational structures. And despite the significant level – especially in the Soviet historical context – of rank-and-file activity involved in these movements, there was never any effective control by the members of the leadership. As a result, when the ideological and political winds shifted in favour of liberalism, many of the 'informal' leaders aligned themselves with the liberal forces that were coming to dominate the state apparatus and took with them sizeable parts of their organizations.

The rapid succession of events, the constant internal struggles within the Popular Fronts and their permanent organizational flux left little political space, time or energy for the socialist currents inside them to organize themselves in an efficient way. Thus, for example, even though the Confederation of Anarcho-Syndicalists counted perhaps one thousand activists and the New Socialists several hundreds, neither of them could even begin to pose a real alternative to the liberals once the Popular Fronts fell apart, as they had neither the structure nor a regular press.

Despite attempts to link up with the emerging, new workers' organizations, the 'informal' movement remained largely confined to student and intellectual circles in the major urban centres. The links made with the miners after the 1989 strike soon disappeared, and the quite serious attempt to give the 'informal' movement a working class wing by creating Sotsprof, 'an association of socialist trade unions', ended with the left's ejection from Sotsprof and its national leadership aligning itself fully with the liberals.

b. The Left Within the CPSU

Contrary to the simplistic, latter-day liberal myth of a prolonged showdown, from 1987 onwards, between 'communists' and 'democrats', the real political process was far more complex and the relationship between the members of the party-state apparatus and the democratic movement was to a degree even symbiotic. Indeed, it was to a large extent initiatives originating in the party-state leadership that opened the political space for the rise of the 'informal' movement.

As the independent democratic organizations declined or became incorporated into the pro-Yeltsin Democratic Russia organization, the discussions of a socialist alternative continued mainly among the oppositional currents within the CPSU, although these discussions often remained within the framework set down by the apparatus, that was still paying lip service to a 'renewed socialism'.

The conservative wing of the apparatus, which itself was a very hetero-geneous entity, rallied around the so-called 'Leningrad Initiative' for a 'Russian Communist Party within the CPSU'.[15] This movement, whose key orientation (for a Russian CP) already gave a foretaste of the nationalist tendencies that would later come to dominate it, was to a large degree a movement from within the apparatus, with its stronghold in Leningrad as well as in some provincial centres. But it also attempted to organize its own 'independent' popular base, especially the United Front of Toilers, a conservative front organization that borrowed its methods from the 'infor-mals', organizing rallies, drafting petitions, distributing leaflets, etc.

But despite the real support the conservative opposition to Gorbachev enjoyed within the party apparatus and even among part of the rank and file, it failed to put forth a clear political programme. It tried to make up for this with nostalgia for the past and the promotion of traditional values of 'statehood' and 'recentralization of the economy". (This conservative orientation within the CPSU was bequeathed after its dissolution to its successor parties in what we have termed the 'nostalgic left'.) The lack of a concrete programme greatly facilitated the humiliation of this opposition, first by the Gorbachev leadership at the 28th Party Congress in the summer of 1990, despite the opposition's strong showing among the delegates there, and later by the liberal reformers who succeeded Gorbachev.

In the months leading up to that 28th Congress, two other opposition currents were formed within the party: the Democratic and the Marxist Platforms. The former united a broad range of supporters of a 'radical Perestroika', from Yeltsinites through social democrats to socialists. The latter was founded by Marxist social scientists from the Moscow University but soon came to be dominated by more conservative forces.[16]

Although the Democratic Platform had the support of tens of thousands of party members, it suffered from many of the same problems that had made the democratic 'informal' movement a dead-end for its leftwing participants. Its platform was formulated in very broad terms in order to reconcile the diverse tendencies that coexisted within it. In its programme, the perspective of a 'transition to democratic socialism' stood alongside the obviously utopian call to transform the thoroughly bureaucratized, os-sified CPSU 'into a modern democratic party'.[17] Such contradictions really ruled out the Democratic Platform's becoming much more than a discus-sion club that loosely united oppositional delegates to the upcoming 28th Party Congress. Once the major liberal figures in the Platform left the party in July 1990, its influence quickly declined.

The Marxist Platform clearly distanced itself from the liberals who tended to dominate the Democratic Platform (at that time, still parading as 'social democrats') and the party conservatives. It proposed a return to 'classical Marxism'. Most of the academic leftists in this group had actually joined the party only in the late 1980s. Before becoming active in the movement of Moscow party clubs, they had been organizing educational and research activity in the framework of the non-party Club of Marxist Researchers.

But soon after the publication of its manifesto, the Marxist Platform received a strong influx of activists with a very different background: rank-and-file party members as well as lower-level functionaries who saw the Platform as an avenue for voicing their more conservative opposition to Gorbachev's leadership of the party. While these new members strengthened the Platform numerically, they also rendered it useless as an instrument for crystallizing a principled Marxist current within the party. This was fully confirmed in August 1991, when a significant minority of the Platform endorsed the abortive, conservative putsch. Needless to say, the Platform subsequently split.

All the organizations that arose after the dissolution of the CPSU that openly profess a 'communist' orientation draw their membership overwhelmingly from the former conservative opposition within the CPSU. They identify, to one degree or other, with the bureaucratic past as essentially a socialist one, even if they admit that the system suffered from deformations. On the other hand, the democratic socialists inside the CPSU failed to rally any significant forces after its demise.

There are several reasons for this, the main one being that the CPSU was in many respects a microcosm of Soviet society, some of whose main traits we have discussed in the first section. The CPSU almost six decades before had ceased to be a living party. Until Gorbachev's Perestroika, it had been devoid of even the suspicion of democracy, with any independent rank-and-file activity totally out of the question. Even after Gorbachev relaxed the leadership's hold on the party, the rank and file, in its vast majority, remained passive. According to estimates made at the time, of the 4783 delegates to the 28th Party Congress, the Democratic Platform counted little more than a hundred, and the Marxist platform had only a handful of delegates.

The supporters of the two opposition platforms were by and large concentrated in Moscow, Leningrad and a few other major cities. Moreover, their social composition made it difficult for them to enter into a dialogue with the millions of mostly politically inert working class members of the party. By 1990, the CPSU had some nineteen million members, of whom approximately twenty per cent were manual workers, fifteen per cent peasants, and 40 per cent white-collar employees. The rest were pensioners and employees of the so-called 'power ministries' (the repressive apparatuses). At a joint conference of the Democratic and Marxist Platforms after the 28th Congress, 30 per cent of the delegates were university or institute teachers, twenty per cent were party functionaries, and only three per cent were workers.[19]

2. After August 1991

With the elimination of article six of the Soviet constitution[20] in the winter of 1990, the CPSU's claim to political monopoly officially ended. Dozens of new 'parties' were subsequently created, typically groups of a few hundred followers around a recognized leader. Almost all of them soon disappeared without a trace. The serious political players, after the decline of the popular democratic movement, remained the old nomenklatura cliques and their allied 'democratic' luminaries. It was to a large extent the emergence within the leading bureaucratic circles of a liberal consensus that really profoundly altered the framework and tone of the public debate.

For reasons mentioned earlier, the democratic left was ill-prepared for this quite rapid turn of events, which found its members isolated in small, more-or-less ideologically defined but badly organized groups. This was true both of those democratic left currents that came out of the 'informals', as well as of the opposition in the CPSU. None of these groups numbered more than a few hundred members and none had any organic links with the workers' movement.

Several attempts were made to establish a broader framework for leftwing co-operation but they did not get beyond common declarations. For example, a Moscow initiative group 'For People's Self Management' brought together in the fall of 1990 representatives of all major left groups – social democrats, socialists, anarchists, the CPSU opposition.[21] However, this meeting failed to take any decisions on united campaigns nor did it create an organizational framework for future discussions, and the initiative petered out within a few months.

Meanwhile, the political scene was polarizing between the liberals, on the one side, who were increasingly gaining the upper hand in the central party-state apparatus (though their mass popularity had already peaked and their Democratic Russia movement was on the decline), and, on the other, the conservative bureaucratic tendency that retained strongholds in various regions and levels of the apparatus and was trying to organize a mass movement.

The failure of the August 1991 'operetta putsch' gave a further impetus to this polarization: the 'centrists' of the apparatus of the Soviet Union (Gorbachev, Lukyanov, Pavlov) were rapidly outflanked by the liberals, led by Yeltsin. Yeltsin's suspension (later followed by formal outlawing) of the CPSU in Russia following the putsch left the party's Central Committee apparatus in a state of total paralysis. Not one prominent party leader came out with a call to create a new organization that could rally those party members who wanted to continue their political activity under the changed conditions. It was not until mid September that the Central Committee secretariat met anew, but according to one report, 'the only problems being discussed are those linked to the creation of jobs for former party officials'.[22]

It would be another eighteen months before any group originating from the former Central Committee leadership took an initiative toward recreating a Communist Party within the Russian Federation. By that time, a majority of the former party high officials had already migrated to the Russian state administration or to business (often to both) and they had little use for a party that still identified itself, at least in words, with 'communism'.

This breakdown of the old party leadership opened the way for the rise to prominence of formerly marginal forces and personalities. But only two structures managed to acquire a broad following: the Russian Communist Workers' Party (RKRP) and the Socialist Workers' Party (SPT). The former's supporters were recruited primarily from the conservative wing of the CPSU, while the latter attracted many former middle-level party functionaries around what could be termed a 'left-Perestroika' platform.

The RKRP, formally founded in November 1991, soon became the organizational expression of a narrow, but real enough mobilization of activists and former low-level party functionaries with neo-Stalinist and often strongly nationalist inclinations. This nationalism, which was to come subsequently to dominate all of the political groups that came out of the CPSU, draws on widespread values of 'statehood' (derzhanvnost'), (which traces its roots far back into pre-revolutionary times and was resurrected with a vengeance by the bureaucratic counterrevolution in the 1920s and 1930s) as well as on the reaction to the obviously comprador nature of the new Russian ruling circles, whose policies have led to the rapid decline of the country's economic and cultural wealth, not to mention its military might.

At its founding, the party had 5,000 registered members; by the spring of 1992, their numbers had reached 50,000, making the RKRP the most important of the post-CPSU formations. It was the driving force behind the creation of Toiling Russia, with affiliates in major cities. This front organization united the neo-Stalinist 'communist' organizations with the growing 'patriotic' movement. Although it lacked any positive political programme – except for the resurrection of the USSR, possibly in the form of a Greater Russia – Toiling Russia was able to bring tens of thousands of people into the streets in the aftermath of the dissolution of the USSR at the end of 1991 and the launching of 'shock therapy' in January 1992. With access to broad-circulation dailies like *Sovetskaya Rossiya*, as well as their own press (with a circulation of tens of thousands copies), it could reach broad layers of frustrated and embittered former party members.

In 1992, the RKRP claimed that 30 per cent of its members were workers. Its leaders put much effort into the creation of its own workers' organizations, like the Union of Workers of Moscow. But while the mass demonstrations of the winter and spring of 1992 undoubtedly had a certain working-class element (though the majority were pauperized white-collar employees and pensioners), the attempts to organize separate working-class structures were largely a failure. These organizations still exist in many places, but in any one place they count no more than a few hundred, albeit highly politicized, activists and command no real authority among the broad masses of workers, who have ignored their frequent calls for strike action.

Indeed, the virtual hegemony of the RKRP in the political protest movement against 'shock therapy' in 1991–92 probably played a role in dissuading the mass of workers from participating in such activity. The RKRP's predilection for abstract, patriotic slogans and the evident lack of seriousness on the part of its leaders (for example, the flamboyant Viktor Anpilov – former *Pravda* correspondent in Cuba – calling to overthrow the 'fascist' Yeltsin regime through a spontaneous uprising) did much to discredit the idea of a serious socialist alternative to 'shock therapy'. The RKRP's more concrete campaigns, such as the collection of a million signatures for a new 'Soviet Constitution', pointed to no way forward for the movement and left the mass of workers cold.

The SPT (Socialist Workers' Party) was also founded in the fall of 1991, but it had quite a different political and organizational profile. The Brezhnev-era dissident Roy Medvedev (who was semi-tolerated by the old regime) was among its founders, but the party was dominated by former middle-level party officials of the younger (35–50) generation who shared an orientation toward a regulated mixed economy, market reforms without 'shock therapy', and moderate nationalism. The new party adopted the last draft of the CPSU programme (which had been endorsed by Gorbachev and the Central Committee a month before the CPSU's demise).

The SPT had an official membership of 50,000–70,000, thirty deputies in the now dissolved Supreme Soviet of Russia (though they belonged to five or six different fractions!), regular access to *Pravda*, and its own bi-monthly with a circulation of about 15,000. Nevertheless, it could not count on any significant active support from its membership, which, in any case, it did not really try to mobilize, preferring to lobby in the corridors of power. Indeed, there was really little in this party to give its members a sense of identification with it, and so when the project for recreating a Communist Party of the Russian Federation was launched at the start of 1993 (by Valentin Kuptsov, former chairman of the Russian CP, created in 1990 and dissolved by Yeltsin after August 1991), over 80 per cent of the SPT's members (as well as most of the members of the smaller 'communist' organizations) left to join the new party.

This resurrected Communist Party of the Russian Federation (KPRF) immediately became the largest party in the country with half a million members and a network of regional organizations. This new/old party was from the outset a compromise between moderate reformist forces from the old Central Committee apparatus (led by Kuptsov, a Gorbachevite) and an increasingly assertive nationalist current that also originated in the old party apparatus but had close links with the entire spectrum of 'patriotic' organizations, as well as with 'nationally-oriented' businesses. In a clear sign of the shifting mood among the party's supporters, Gennadyi Zyuganov, a former Central Committee apparatchik who had become co-chairman of the ultra-nationalist Russian National Assembly and leader of the broad 'patriotic' alliance, the National Salvation Front, beat out Kuptsov in the elections to the leadership of the party's Central Committee.

Under Zyuganov's leadership, the KPRF actually adopted a rather conciliationist policy toward the liberal regime. It presented itself as a reform-oriented, but socially conscious opponent of 'shock therapy'. The party's leaders now claim to be 'left social democrats'. But it is much more around the issues of Russian 'statehood' that the party has kept a high profile. If one judges by Zyuganov's statements (and in the Russian context today, the leader generally *is* the party), it is hard to qualify the KPRF as socialist in any traditional sense of the term. For Zyuganov, the key concepts are not 'social justice' or 'popular democracy' but 'statehood' and (Russian) 'spirituality' (dukhovnost). His historical reference points are more Peter the Great and Stolypin than Marx or Lenin. This shift to the 'patriotic' wing of Russian politics has obviously not hurt the party's popularity: together with the closely allied Agrarian Party, the KPRF took about 25 per cent of the vote (in voting according to party slates) in the December 1993 elections to the Duma (the new parliament created by Yeltsin's constitution). (In assessing the electoral returns, it is important to keep in mind that, according to official figures, 48 per cent of the electorate did not participate in these elections. The real figure is probably even higher.)

While the KPRF and what was left of the SPT (after the mass defections to the KPRF) participated in these elections, most of the smaller 'communist' groups called for a boycott, arguing that participation would legitimate Yeltsin's state coup. This is one of the signs of a rapidly growing split between, on the one hand, those 'communist' groups oriented to parliamentary activity and reform, and, on the other, those who pose more radical goals and advocate more militant tactics. Moreover, although the 'patriotic' current clearly dominates in the 'communist' camp, there are today some signs that certain elements of its more radical wing are reconsidering the wisdom of their tactic of blocking with the nationalists.

3. The Crisis of the Democratic Left

While the organizations that came out of the CPSU could draw on inherited structures and networks, had access to a mass press ready to publicize their activities and positions and could rely on a pool of thousands of former party activists, the democratic socialists had no such resources. Faced with an official ideological climate that was completely hostile to any talk of democratic socialism or a 'third way' between an increasingly authoritarian liberalism and a potentially even more authoritarian nationalism (in official discourse, you are either 'for reform', i.e. the liberals, or 'against reform'), the small groups of the anti-Stalinist left reacted in various ways.

One tactic was to attempt to regroup their scattered forces within broader left-democratic coalitions. This tactic, which had already been tried in 1990-91 by anarchists when they founded the radical Green Party (which has no discernible presence today on the political scene), was chosen by socialists, anarchists as well as Marxist activists from the dissolved CPSU, who formed the Party of Labour (PT) in the aftermath of the August 1991 putsch. It was tried again in the fall of 1992 when a broad range of moderate and more radical leftists (from the SPT to small Trotskyist groups) assembled at the first Congress of Democratic Left Forces.

But although the Congress itself was a remarkable success in gathering more than a thousand participants, it failed subsequently to develop any real activity. At present, elements in the PT are attempting to form a Union of Labour, including parts of the old trade-union apparatus, as a moderate coalition of left forces. Its immediate function would be to run candidates in the upcoming regional and local elections.

To date, none of these attempts at a broad democratic left coalition have succeeded in their goals, that is, to win new adherents to their movement, to establish lasting structures, or to extend their influence beyond the essentially Moscow-based left-democratic intelligentsia. Their main contribution has been somewhat to raise the public profile of this current, which is still little known in the larger population.

A second tactic was to create small, ideologically well-defined propaganda groups. But it has hardly fared any better. Various anarchist and Marxist groups have been attempting to create their own small 'parties', complete with national leaderships, programmes and miniscule presses. But none have been able to reach out much beyond their original circle of founders. Most are actually on the decline, and none are a national factor even in Russian left politics, though some have relative strongholds in one or two regions.

A third tactic has been, in face of the failure to win a popular base, to try to win the support of more progressive elements in the old trade-union apparatus for what is termed a 'British-style labourist party'. At different times, there were hopeful signs of a favourable response to such overtures made by the PT, especially from the Moscow and Leningrad regional trade-union federations, but they came to nought, as the dominant circles in the union apparatus preferred more substantial, and less radical, partners, such as the Civic Union, or even different factions inside the ruling liberal elite. Thus, the head of the Moscow Federation of Trade Unions (and presently also of the FNPR), Mikhail Shmakov, was long seen as favouring a labour party but he has apparently now given this up in favour of developing a sort of working relationship with the Yeltsin regime, as he had done earlier with the Moscow government.

CONCLUSION

In reviewing the fate of the Russian left over the past seven or eight years, it is tempting to try to assign respective responsibilities to 'objective' factors (the 'masses', for reasons outlined in the first section, simply not being ready to respond to a left alternative) and to 'subjective' ones (the weaknesses and errors of the political left, some of which were mentioned in the second section). But while it may be useful to separate these types of factors for analytical purposes, in reality they are all part of the same totality and ultimately merge into one another. The Russian left could not easily transcend the nature of the society from which it emerged.

Despite the upsurge of popular activism in the 1987–90 period, almost no permanent, really popular democratic structures emerged. The impression, held at the time by many Western and Soviet observers, that the Glasnost era was fast creating an independent civil society, with genuine social movements and organizations and a lasting space for public, democratic debate, proved deceptive. As we noted earlier, sixty-odd years of Stalinism had bequeathed an atomized society, lacking any experience of self-organization and with deeply ingrained tendencies among the population to look to patrons and 'leaders' to act on their behalf. The quite sudden collapse of the old official ideology and almost as rapid loss of the old social guarantees left people deeply insecure and disoriented.

In these conditions, a socialist programme based upon self-organization and genuine popular democracy was unlikely to find many ready takers. Once liberalism had disappointed, nationalist appeals proved much more accessible to broad strata of the impoverished population. The bulk of the remaining active elements of the former CPSU readily embraced this nationalism, always a central feature of Stalinism, helping to further discredit socialism among workers as a real alternative and leaving the democratic socialists to explain in their isolation what socialism was really about. (In one bizarre, but very telling twist, the leadership of the SPT opted out of a joint leftwing slate with democratic socialist groups in the December 1993 Duma elections in favour of a moderate nationalist bloc that included, among others, the Cossack Union and managers in the oil industry! But this list failed to collect the required number of signatures to present candidates.)

The weakness of the democratic left was to a large degree a product of these external developments and pressures. But most activists of the democratic left, on their part, failed to appreciate fully these factors and to draw appropriate conclusions for a successful strategy, that in the circumstances, could only be a long-term one. The momentous developments of the Perestroika period stimulated a certain 'spontaneist' tendency in the thinking of the democratic left, the expectation that increasingly broad layers of the population would, following their objective interests and in the wake of the loosening grip of the old structures, come to embrace their cause. With a few exceptions, most of the democratic left suffered from a related 'vanguardism' that had its roots not only in its social and political isolation but also in inherited Soviet traditions.

This led to a very distorted view of the real correlation of forces and to a failure sufficiently to appreciate the need for a long-term strategy involving organic organizational and propaganda work among the general population, and particularly among workers. Such a strategy, of course, could not be very attractive to socialist activists in the rapidly evolving situation, since it could not hope to bear much fruit in the short term, for reasons we outlined in the first section.

Russia is in what will undoubtedly be a lengthy period of major social and economic upheaval, with no point of stabilization yet in sight. These processes are constantly deepening the contradictions in Russian society. But the latter have yet to find their adequate expression in the political sphere. As bleak as the picture now seems for the democratic left, many ordinary people have gained, and are gaining, valuable political experience, gradually shedding long-held illusions about the paternalism of state authorities and the role of political patrons and leaders. They are learning to distinguish between the promises of politicians and their actual practice.

The pent-up forces of popular discontent will eventually break through the present political demobilization. When this happens, new, broader possibilities should open for Russian socialism. But the struggle will necessarily be a long-term one.

NOTES

1. *Segodnya*, January 12, 1993, p. 2.
2. Moscow Radio broadcast in Russian, February 3, 1994; *Nezavisimaya gazeta*, February 6, 1994.
3. *Rabochaya tribuna*, January 18, 1994. This figure apparently refers to cash incomes only. In 1993, the decline of real incomes slowed down somewhat: while the price index rose by 1,000 per cent and the average wage rose by 800 per cent.
4. L. Trotskii, *Chto takoe SSSR i kuda on idet?*, Slovo, Paris, n.d., pp. 292–93.
5. For more detail on these organizations, see David Mandel: *Perestroika and Soviet Society*, Montreal, Black Rose Press, 1992, and *Rabotyagi: Perestroika and After, the View from Below*, New York, Monthly Review Press, 1994.
6. For example, the editors of the foundation's journal, who, incidentally, falsely claim that the foundation was created on the funds of American unions, state that they 'support a

policy directed at the consolidation in Russian democracy and a market economy'. (*Novoe rabochee i profsoyuznoe dvizhenie*, Moscow, no. 1, 1993, p. 3.) When these two goals are in conflict, the foundation opts for the second, for example, when it supported Yeltsin in his tearing up of the constitution in September 1993. For more on the AFL-CIO in Russia, see P. Bracegirdle and D. Seppo, 'The AFL-CIO in the Community of Independent States', *Socialist Alternatives* (Montreal), vol. II, no. 2, 1993.

7. *Financial Times*, October 6–7, 1993.

8. For one leader who is more explicit on this, see I. Yurgens, 'Listen, Worker!' *Socialist Alternatives*, vol. II, no. 2, 1993.

9. This date of the abortive conservative putsch marks the definitive ascendancy of Yeltsin and the liberals to power in Russia.

10. That is what the left outside the Communist Party called itself.

11. Among the left 'informal' groups tracing their roots back to the pre-Perestroika or early Gorbachev period, one can mention the Socialist Party (now inside the Party of Labour), the Confederation of Anarcho-Syndicalists (KAS), the Marxist Workers' Party, and Rabochii.

12. One of the major public activities of the Social Initiative Club in the winter of 1987/88 was a petition campaign in favour of Boris Yeltsin, who at the time was see as a progressive, left Communist leader, fighting against bureaucratic privilege and arbitrary power. Yeltsin had just been ousted as Moscow party boss.

13. This is how the movement referred to itself. In retrospect, many elements of this movement turned out to be merely economic liberals but far from democrats.

14. Interview with B. Kagarlitsky, *International Viewpoints* (Paris), no. 152, 1988, p. 26.

15. The Russian republic, unlike the other republics in the USSR, did not have its own party structures separate from the CPSU until 1990.

16. Roughly analogous currents emerged within the Komsomol.

17. *Pravda*, March 3, 1990.

18. *Pravda*, April 16, 1990. The story of the Marxist Platform has been told by one of its founders, Aleksander Buzgalin, in his *Belaya vorona* (White Raven), Moscow, 1993.

19. *Moskovskie novosti*, July 8 and 15, 1990; 'Report of the Mandate Commission to the Conference of Supporters of Democratic Movements within the CPSU, November 17–18, 1990'.

20. Consecrating the 'leading role' of the party.

21. For its platform, see *International Viewpoints*, November 12, 1990.

22. *Kommersant*, September 16, 1991.

WORKERS AND INTELLECTUALS IN THE GERMAN DEMOCRATIC REPUBLIC

Patty Lee Parmalee

It is supposed to be a goal of communism to achieve a classless society. The working class becomes the universal class: both because it has taken power in order to abolish private ownership of land and industry, which is the basis of class domination, and because now everyone will be a worker of one kind or another. Society may need to curtail some freedoms to achieve it, but the commitment to equality is unequivocal.

If socialist societies are in transition toward communism, we expect to find a deliberate process of gradual abolition of class difference; certainly we expect there to be less antagonism than in a capitalist society. But my experience of the GDR over the past 30 years was that despite rhetoric and impressive programmes designed to bring the classes together, social distinctions were quite rigid, more rigid than I was used to in the capitalist USA.

A few weeks after the wall 'came down', Christa Wolf, East Germany's best novelist, published a radical statement which might seem to confirm my perception, but raised many more questions. 'I see the policy of separating the "intelligentsia" and the "people" which was followed more or less consistently for decades still has its effect – perhaps not with many, but the effect is there. . . . I'd like to warn against a continuation of the unholy tradition in German history that so often drove producers of material vs. spiritual goods to different sides: this has never served revolutionary renewal well.'[1]

Presumably she meant the Socialist Unity (i.e. Communist) Party (SED), or the government – they were essentially the same thing – as the perpetrators of this deliberate policy of separation of the workers and the intellectuals. But how could that be? Hadn't the Party always spoken of the 'Intelligenz' as the allies of the workers? Hadn't there been well advertised programmes to bring them together, to upgrade the cultural and intellectual skills of the workers, 'break the bourgeoisie's monopoly on education', and acquaint writers with the world of manual labour? What about the classless society?

Ehrhart Neubert, a critical sociologist, wrote a few months later that if fundamental equality was not after all both the goal and the means, the socialist regime would lose its justification. 'The great value of the socialist state, its assertion of a historic mission, its security and defence needs were all grounded in the claim uniquely and for the first time to have made the principle of equality realizable.'[2]

Intrigued and a little disturbed by these accusations, I decided to go to the source, to try to find out whether the Party indeed had abandoned equality, specifically whether it had a conscious policy to separate rather than unite workers and intellectuals. After sifting through thousands of pages in the Socialist Unity Party's Central Archives in East Berlin during Spring 1993, my preliminary answer is still only a 'definite maybe'. But exploring the question involves opening the doors to many rooms, and a look inside them gives a composite inside picture of how this Party thought, how it ruled, and how it attempted to transform its populace into the kind of 'new man' it believed socialism should produce. In a sense, the Party's strategy really was to dissolve the people and elect another one – as Brecht sardonically recommended after the workers' uprising in 1953.[3]

What follows, then, is a progress report on my findings about the mind of the Party from its archives, as well as from conversations and other materials, with some tentative conclusions offered not as definitive answers but for discussion.

Why should we want to do this? The disaster that capitalism is perpetrating on the non-owning classes in the first, second, and third worlds alike is accelerating at such a rate, that the search for alternatives to barbarism will be on the agenda almost before socialists get around to placing it there again. If we don't use the suffering of both the victims and the perpetrators of recently-existing socialism to get it right, or at least more right, next time around, we consign their lives to meaninglessness, and the coming generations' lives to hopelessness. Whether we like it or not, understanding the past of socialism in preparation for its future is the task laid on those on the left fortunate or unfortunate enough to live through this period; if we don't learn from the past we doom others to repeat it.

The story of 'the other Germany's' attempt at socialism contains some good ideas and some sad perversions of the same. It viewed itself as the embodiment of the ideas of its own native son Karl Marx rather than the importer of a foreign doctrine; it contains some constraining historical circumstances, some missed chances, some heroic attempts to build socialism, and some personal failures. From all this we can learn, not least because its archives are more (teutonically) thorough and the access to them, thanks largely to the citizens' movement, more complete than the others.

Learning by reading Party or government archives is of course a tricky business. Suffice it to say here that everything in them is both revealing and misleading; there are no complete narratives, only pieces; the contexts must be either imagined or researched. Thus it will make a big difference who is doing the reading. My reading, though it may appear to be disgusted with the manipulations of the functionaries, is also informed by a basic sympathy for the project they were attempting.

What were they attempting in class relations? In order to know what we are talking about when we examine the relation of workers and intellectuals to each other, first we need to examine their respective definitions separately. That is not, however, simply a matter of looking them up in a Marxist-Leninist dictionary. Contrary to the image that there was only one line about everything in the GDR, there was (and is) actually quite a lot of debate about the structure of classes or 'strata' there. What did East Germans mean when they said 'worker' or 'intellectual'? And what was the respective relation of each to the Party?

Workers

Despite their long history of class division and class consciousness, both Western and Eastern Europe seem to be headed today more toward the American model of atomization of class communities into individuals. But according to one view of East German society, a kind of atomization or levelling had already taken place, the Party having replaced traditional horizontal working-class relations with vertical relations by individuals to itself, the Party, rather than to each other. Leisure time as well as work time were centred around mass organizations that were all organized by the Party, independent interest groups were to say the least discouraged (thus the importance of the Protestant Church as an autonomous centre of social life), and old working-class communities were broken up as the work force was shifted around to various massive construction and production facilities.[4] The proletariat's consciousness of itself as a class was both promoted and fractured.

How *do* you define classes in a society where the means of production are socially owned? One might have thought it would be enough simply to define people by what they actually do – clearly a teacher's work activity is different from a miner's is different from a petty bureaucrat's – but the infinite divisions got rather tricky.

One frequently comes across the formula 'workers and all working people' ['Arbeiter und alle Werktätige'], which suggests that in the narrowest sense the word 'Arbeiter' meant *industrial* worker, the traditional muscular, male, heavy-industry worker in the mine, the steel mill, the refinery, or construction. This narrow focus had its source both in the Marxist focus on production workers – those who transform raw materials from nature into commodities and create surplus value – and in the birth of the GDR in a ruined landscape requiring prodigious feats of construction and heavy industry. These were the workers celebrated in socialist realist novels and art, whose contribution to society is meant to be ever greater effort and efficiency in creating the wealth that will then provide them with the goods to make them happy. The other working people ('andere Werktätige'), those in services and higher up the ladder of qualification, such as professionals, existed in a kind of definitional limbo, as did the few self-employed or shopkeepers and private farmers. (Farmers were generally lumped together with workers if they were collectivized; private farmers, like petty bourgeois, just don't appear in the rhetoric.)

On the other hand, sometimes 'die Arbeiter' just seems to mean 'das Volk'. In this meaning it becomes insidious when intellectuals and workers are treated as a dichotomy: it suggests there is a kind of opposition by intellectuals to the people in general, or vice versa. Furthermore, in reading Party documents one often gets the sense that 'workers' really means the Party, as in various attempts at self-fulfilling propositions about what the workers think, feel and want. The Party speaks in the name of the workers, for the workers, and instead of the workers.[5]

The Party had to speak for the workers not only because the working class was allegedly the ruling class (but a whole class can't govern, only its delegates, whether self-appointed or elected); there is also the problem that it had been only a few years since many of these workers were Nazis. The rhetoric always announced that antifascist resistance could come only from the working class and its revolutionary Party; and working-class consciousness had to be aspostrophized as by definition correct (antifacist, for instance) consciousness, but in fact the leadership of the SED had the thankless task of building a socialist society with partially fascist raw material. This is not to be taken as an excuse, but it must be recognized as a genuine dilemma. Heiner Müller says Ulbricht's genius was that he never expected to be liked by the people he publicly had to praise. Privately he thought of them as still requiring re-education; and that was the basic attitude of the Party to the people throughout GDR history.

The workers' real role was not to rule or to think but to work, to produce. Stalin's economic theory adopted in the GDR (according to Sigrid Meuschel) was very simple: 1) The way to keep the populace content is to provide them with an increasing number of goods. 2) But it is they themselves who produce these goods. 3) Therefore if they want contentment they must be persuaded to produce ever more.[6] This is of course exactly the strategy that various left movements have accused capitalism of: convincing workers all their needs are material, and providing the goods (and incidentally of course profits) by exploiting alienated labour. Work is performed only for the wages, not for any intrinsic sense of creativity or belief that one is making a contribution; the wages are then used to fill leisure time, private life (in East Germany, called 'niches') with the satisfaction that is absent during the work day. Robert Havemann, the great socialist critic in East Germany, pointed out that this is capitalism's game, and if the only value 'really existing' socialist society intends to offer its workers is goods, then of course capitalism would win hands down.[7]

This is, however, selling the work arrangements in the GDR a little short. Although the content of the work may have been dreary, dirty, or dangerous, and although the ideology claiming to have its source in the working class while actually hardly consulting them was hypocritical, nevertheless there were many innovative methods of workplace organization that did make work more humane than it usually is in the hyper-disciplined work ethics of West Germany, Japan, or the USA. Absent the disciplining effect of fear of losing your job, you were free to work at a leisurely pace, with breaks, long vacations, sick leave, parental leave. (Whether this is a good thing or a bad thing is a complex debate.) Workers in large plants were organized into brigades, somewhere around ten people each, and the bonding within the brigades was very strong, sometimes lifelong. Your social life and an extensive cultural life were organized around the plant; your children were in day care there, you could shop and eat there and get theatre tickets or join a sports club. It is also important to realize that the very challenge of building up the country created a strong work ethic among the 'Aufbaugeneration' (both East and West), which included a certain proletarian pride in reality, not just in official statements.[8] Over the years though that motivation faded. It is always more stimulating to work hard for a cause than to find ways to avoid work.

The working-class consciousness of Marxism rests on the analysis that it is the workers who necessarily represent the force which opposes – and will eventually overthrow – capital. Even those Marxists who believe a vanguard party must rule derive its legitimacy from its working-class standpoint. What, however, happens when there is no more capital, no more bourgeoise? Does it even make sense any more to speak of a working-class standpoint, when everyone works, and the perceived boss or even enemy is now the government, the vanguard Party, itself?

In fact, in order to maintain the logic of the class position, the bourgeoisie, without whom the language of class conflict makes no sense, was now perceived as outside the borders. The class enemy was the Bundesrepublik, with its various ideologies that could undermine a secure communist position, such as social democracy. Anyone who published in the West – especially criticism – or was interested in those ideologies, was 'delivering arguments to the class enemy'. (One sees in Archive documents again and again how the Party destroyed itself partly through its obsession with West Germany.)

Belief that the 'socialist person' is a fundamentally different personality type, without whom socialist democracy is premature, implies the necessity of somehow producing this type. A genuine problem. The Party had a mistrust of unsupervised, spontaneous, self-organized activity, and one purpose of this system of organizing life and leisure around the workplace – organizing free time as well as work time – was to keep everyone in constant relationship to organs of control and education. Many of the programmes were valuable in their conception, and workers did participate enthusiastically; but the Party could never leave the programmes alone, everything had to be used to a 'constructive' purpose to try to develop loyalty and consciousness – and, not so incidentally, productivity. A structure designed to stimulate creativity and the full development of the personality turned into its opposite. In everything we look at in the GDR, we have to encourage ourselves to have this double vision: see how good ideas could be perverted – but also, by examining exactly where the perversions lay, see that in fact there were some good ideas. The GDR's failure is not necessarily socialism's failure. But it illustrates to us some temptations well-meaning socialism must avoid.

Most of these programmes were designed for workers, especially workers in that traditional sense. In this respect they were indeed privileged. Skilled workers were paid well, and all workers were encouraged to advance themselves through further education. There were special high schools (called Workers' and Farmers' Faculties) where workers such as older people returning from prisoner-of-war camps could meet the requirements for university admission; and the regime was serious about making education available to their children as well, breaking the German tradition of a Bildungsbourgeoisie, an hereditary educated class from which civil servants and government are drawn. The privileging of the working class of course caused disgruntlement among educated people whose children certainly did not want to go 'down' in the world – but determined young people from any background could usually manage to get into advanced study by one method or another (choosing a less popular field, or going to work and then being delegated to study from the workplace, or connections and personal petitions).

The policy was loosened anyway partly because after the early reconstruction period scientific and technical skills were recognized as an important productive force, and partly because after a generation of workers has gone to university it is hard to say whether their children are the children of workers. But what remained until the end was the ubiquitous demand for announcement of your class origin. Many years after joining the Party, perhaps even becoming powerful functionaries, members' occupations would be listed as what they were at the time of *entry*. In fact, the operational definition often went farther back, not to what did you do, but to what did your father do. On every form you filled out you had to state your parents' (or often only father's) occupation; every little biographical blurb would always say 'father worker' or 'bourgeois origin'; it was as much part of your identity as your eye colour, name and birthplace.

(After the fifties 'bourgeois', which no one wanted to admit to, would be replaced by the choice between 'employee, intelligentsia, or self-employed'.)

The GDR was the home of irony as much as repression, irony both in fact and in people's attitude. Call something by the name the Party gave it and you were often making a joke with no further comment necessary – as for instance when dissident writers were sent into production to be re-educated and said they were being 'transferred to the ruling class'. The irony here is, in the attempt to make people more equal, the old categories got rigidified and fluidity was more difficult rather than less; you were defined throughout your life by the accident of your birth status. (And woe if your parents were not just bourgeois intellectuals but churchpeople or small businessmen.) Like so many customs in the GDR, this one had a noble purpose – breaking the tendency of class status (culture, function, and income) to be inherited – but it turned into its opposite, branding people for life with the accident of their birth.

The tendency to define classes by the occupation of the parents also ipso facto leads to a conception of the nature of production and work which is inherited from previous generations; it is hard to adjust to the increasing importance of technical, information, and service jobs if those careers are still thought of as bourgeois, and the knowledge they require as dangerous because bourgeois consciousness is dangerous. It also doesn't help that the classical Marxist categories of class are grounded in an analysis of 19th-century capitalism.

Another privilege enjoyed by workers was the ironic result of their political powerlessness. Since their opinions had little chance to be heard publicly or to influence others, they enjoyed the 'Narrenfreiheit' of being able to say pretty much anything they wanted. The security police apparently had little interest in monitoring workers (except during rare periods like 1953 or 1968 when they flexed their oppositional potential). Party membership was notoriously low among rank and file, and of course the one umbrella trade union was strictly a Leninist organ for bringing directives from the top to the bottom, not for defending the interests of the workers (except in that long-range sense that the harder they work, the more goods they produce for themselves). Much of the anger expressed out loud in 1989 was directed at the union.

Meanwhile, although manual labour was praised as the salt of the earth, an opposing trend was encouraging moving up into technical skills as the Party economists became more and more convinced that the 'scientific-technical revolution' was going to decide international competition. The New Economic System of Planners and Leaders of 1963 was one mani-festation; the 1968 university reform with its manic application of cyberne-tics to all fields, appropriate or not, was another. From 1971–75 there was another upswing in the economy as Ulbricht was replaced and Honecker brought in new pragmatic blood. Innovative Party sociologists were now beginning to suggest that some differentiation and inequality within the work force was desirable, otherwise why would people bother to become more qualified? There is a large literature of sociological studies of the structure of the work force, and the levelling vs. differentiating – or equality vs. inequality – poles run throughout both the descriptive and the prescriptive studies. Thus there was a periodic debate – within this Party that did not even brook internal, let alone external controversy – about whether equality or inequality is a better strategy. The debate became open with Gorbachev's economic perestroika, but since the leadership was deathly afraid of social glasnost, they also repressed the debate.

To overgeneralize, then, the major group in the population was a politically and socially almost undifferentiated mass, their old communities of solidarity often disbanded to move the work force around to new priority projects as well as presumably to keep them from developing independent organizational forms. They were reluctant socialists, doing the work asked of them at first with great energy and (some of them) with some sense of altruistic purpose, then more and more passively and just for the material rewards – which never equalled those of the West. With a lot of fanfare and publicity, certain individual workers performed prodigious feats of surpassing the general norm; but far from being heroes to their fellow workers, with time they just became responsible for the justification of speedup.[9] And if they got a premium for their feat – or later, in the 'innovators movement' for their suggestion – the triumph of material over moral incentives once again turned morale into its opposite. 'We have a lot of suggestions here from below, and they are even applied, but in the end it's the worker who's the idiot [der Dußlige], because it's himself he's screwing. He makes a suggestion for improvement and maybe he even gets a one-time premium for it, but then he's got to keep producing more, and his colleagues too, who didn't get any premium.'[10]

When material incentives stagnate with economic slowdown, it is hard to hold the loyalty of workers. Ever since the workers' protests of June 17, 1953, they had been courted with concessions and a gradually increasing standard of living, but twenty years later the expansion of production slowed for good (starting, perhaps, with the energy crisis). It was less than twenty years afterward that they or their children voted, first with their feet and then with ballots, for the material benefits they had been promised as their reward all along. No one knows whether it would have been possible to develop values that would outweigh consumption; the temptation from the alleged rewards of capitalism may be too hard to withstand no matter what. But anyway, it wasn't tried. If nonalienated labour, free development of all the abilities of each individual, and self-determination are fundamental to socialism, then we simply lack any evidence to show it can't work. Or that it can. The GDR might have had the chance to come closest to that version of socialism, but it also started with two strikes against it: the proximity and consanguinity of the ruthlessly successful and actively anticommunist West Germany, and the mentalities left over from the Third Reich. Then the Party itself struck out, through its inflexible Leninist-Stalinist conception that it must always be organizing and controlling everything its people did. The dogma that 'the Party is always right', resulted in a drastic limitation of the diversity of ideas. Future, more detailed study of East German society, economy, and government will have to find out how to separate the mistakes of a paranoid leadership from the economic structures, in order to answer the question all socialists must ask: could the economy have worked?[11]

Intellectuals

When the 'Ulbricht group' were sent home to the Soviet Zone by the Russians in 1945, they were confronted not only with a general working populace that had supported Hitler, but also with a bourgeois and intellectual elite who had often not just supported but actively collaborated.[12] Furthermore, the leaders themselves tended to come from proletarian backgrounds, and their social context had been the autonomous worker culture of the Weimar period. For both legitimate and envy reasons then, they were deeply suspicious of intellectuals, and this anti-intellectualism continued right up until the end. It has long been part of Marxist tradition to consider intellectuals as untrustworthy allies, who when the going gets tough will start remembering their individual moral principles and back out, and who tend to think too much for themselves and too little 'parteilich', partisan, unclear on where their class loyalty lies.

However, because workers or 'the people' had been in their way just as untrustworthy as intellectuals, the communist leadership needed the intellectuals. They needed the 'technical intelligentsia' - mostly employed in industry – in the desperate attempt to make production efficient and innovative. A catchup with the West and sometimes the express intention of surpassing it were a constant pressure. These were the intellectuals who had direct contact with blue-collar workers, playing a constant mediating role between the official central plan and national goals on one hand vs. the norms, working conditions, and motivation of the manual labourers on the other. I do not know the extent they themselves identified up or down; that would be another interesting subject for research. The way the Party used them appears to have swung back and forth from a divide-and-rule tactic encouraging workers ('we' in Party language) to resent them and their minor privileges – which could even have been designed to cause resentment – and criticism of workers for not sufficiently educating and accepting the technicians. The ironies are rife here, for often the socialist consciousness (read Party loyalty) of the better-paid technicians was higher than the workers'; furthermore, the language used allegedly to draw them together would ipso facto result in further separation.

The social relations within a factory or combine were a microcosm of the roles in society as a whole. The workers correspond to 'the people', the scientists and technical employees to the 'class' or 'stratum' of intellectuals, and the local Party functionaries to the Politburo. The intellectuals we would be more likely to give that name to in the West – educators, artists and writers, scientists, social scientists, and philosophers – were needed to play a similar mediator role in society as a whole. In most of what follows the word 'intellectual' refers to that cultural section of the intelligentsia.

If scientists and technicians were needed to improve production, artists and especially writers were needed to create a climate of enthusiasm for the new values. It was their job to portray the 'new socialist person' as a flesh-and-blood real figure; 'party hacks' are aware they can't really persuade through their canned holiday speeches. This was not necessarily the writers' and scientists' own idea of their job descriptions, however. Not that they did not want to be useful; the emphasis on art for art's sake and damn the audience came about largely as a reaction to being *mis*used. Really, it is very gratifying to be useful, and people who work with ideas and images are generally delighted to see their suggestions have some effect on society. In fact, a number of GDR intellectuals chose to move to the fledgling socialist nation, from West Germany or exile, precisely because they wanted to be useful. But the rub is, they tend to think they can be most useful if they keep the gene pool of ideas rich and varied, doing science no matter where it leads, helping the leadership to see that life is more complex than it appears from their Party offices, providing a portrait of people as they are, not as ideal types, and keeping an ear open for dissatisfaction, problems, conflicts, even for tragedy. In doing this they genuinely believe they are being helpful, if only someone in authority would listen. It is for their Sisyphean attempts to use the existing channels to try to influence power rather than to discredit and overthrow it that they are now being widely branded as naive and collaborators. They tended to see themselves, however, as testing and expanding the borders of the permissible, and more embattled than coddled.

Since the workers' role is to produce wealth, they are not judged on the basis of their ideology. Since intellectuals' job however is to produce consciousness, every word they say is examined for its ideological content. The situation is really quite contradictory: on the one hand, the working-class standpoint is the correct one and the petty bourgeois intellectuals are urged to get with it; on the other hand, the intellectuals are needed to mediate the correct working-class standpoint to the workers. The workers' error, economism, is eventually permitted and even encouraged, anything to increase productivity. The intellectuals' error, open criticism and failure to understand the importance of unity, is not permitted. The first error only undermines the fundamental ethos of socialism; the second undermines power. Whenever the SED had a choice between weakening socialism and weakening itself, it chose power. It had to, given its vanguardist conviction that it was the only element not subject to false motivation.

Pity the Party: it was always fighting on two fronts. It was squeezed between aggressive anticommunism from the West and creeping liberalization from the East, including Eurocommunism and convergence theory. (Some interpreters think it saw the developments to its East as the greater danger; note also that there are commentators who think it was right to predict any loosening of the reins would mean total collapse of the communist world.) But also internally: it was fighting an uphill battle simultaneously against a lagging economy and against the false consciousness of the people. It was far too insecure to experiment.

Intellectuals in the West tend to periodize GDR history by the high points of repression – starting with 1953, against the workers' rebellion, and after that against the whole people or against intellectuals: 1961, the wall: 1965, the 11th Plenum that muzzled writers; 1968, Czechoslovakia; 1976, the expatriation of Biermann; 1979, expulsions from the writers' union; and throughout the eighties, increasing numbers of artists and thinkers leaving the country with the Party's blessing. (Take this visa – please.) Like knowing a city by its subway stops or freeway offramps, this is probably a distorted map of what the place felt like day to day. In between those nadirs there were some periods of 'liberalization', when the Party toyed with the idea of letting intellectuals do what they do best, depicting reality. But there was always a pendulum swing. It would turn out after a while that reality was not what the Party had decreed it to be. This dilemma – what counts as reality – trapped not only writers and broadcasters but also all the social scientists doing research on the people for the Academy of Sciences, all the teachers and professors, the filmmakers and plastic artists, the diplomats, the managers and engineers who had to assess and improve productive capacity, natural scientists assessing environmental damage . . . All were confronted daily with the fatal refusal of the Party to hear any messages from Cassandra.[13]

True, it was possible to send all sorts of critical letters internally to specific individuals in government: the archives of the various bureaus include astonishingly personal correspondences and attention by people in leadership to individual wrongs and slights. If you needed a better apartment in order to be able to write, you could beg for one with a letter, and you might well get it, even if you weren't particularly obsequious. But you couldn't go *public* with any complaints about significant, collective conditions (and the greatest crime was of course to go public in the West), and you couldn't get the leadership to take your concerns about the state of the nation seriously. This drove some people to share their concerns with the

Stasi, under the misimpression that its purpose was to gather accurate information on the mood of the public and transmit it to the administration, or even that it was the reform-minded organ of government.

Some just left: Ernst Bloch, Hans Mayer. A few became openly defiant: Robert Havemann, Rudolf Bahro. The sad part is, they got so little support. Today, people look back and feel very bad about not having supported them then. What most did was to try to find some way of combining their desire to serve a state which unfortunately claimed the right to define the truth, with their desire to portray the truth as they saw it. Some flourished, either because of their basic support for socialism or because political censorship is more fruitful conflict material for art than is the effective censorship of the market. Others went under, silent or imprisoned. A surprising number of creative artists took occasional work in manual labour in order to be able to write on their own what they wanted, rather than filling the slots foreseen for an intellectual elite. (There was actually a much broader palette of attitudes and life choices to support the habit of portraying the truth through art than I ever suspected.)

The intellectuals' or Westerners' periodization of GDR history has little to do with the workers', whose collective history was more even: a long period of gradual improvement, and then a long period of stagnation. Workers continued to get their theatre tickets through the union, and occasionally there was something unusual to see like *Die neuen Leiden des jungen W.* [The New Sorrows of Young W.], *Die Überganggesellschaft* [The Transitional Society], or the latest bold cabaret at the Distel, but especially for the younger generation the real action was in popular music, available on the airwaves. Although there were unusually high reader numbers among workers (books were sold cheap right at the workplace, which also had libraries and readings and writing classes with authors), it is questionable whether even the books that were most widely read and discussed, such as Neutsch's *Spur der Steine* [Trail of Stones] or Christa Wolf's *Geteilter Himmel* [Divided Heaven], really influenced consciousness as much as either the Party or the writers thought and hoped they did. It would be hard to do reception research because workers got premium points for cultural participation; they would probably have answered interviewers by saying Oh yes, they found those works very important.

Nevertheless, the army of intellectuals was called out to do damage control whenever there was a crisis of legitimacy. On the night of August 13, 1961, cultural establishments throughout the entire country were instructed to put on particularly enticing programmes nonstop, getting the people into dance halls with live bands, or into movie theatres showing the most popular movies, and they all had to report to Berlin daily on exactly what events they were organizing:[14] artists as preventers of popular protest. Many people hardly even were aware that the wall was being built, since they had been successfully enticed away from home where they might have heard the news from RIAS radio. There was almost no protest against the building of the wall, except for the people who made quick getaways. The mission, distraction, was accomplished. In August 1968 (why did these things always happen during the university vacation?) intellectuals and artists in every kind of institution were pressured to send letters and petitions of support for the 'action of the brother countries' in Czechoslovakia.[15] There are people who to this day are ashamed of nothing so much as signing those letters. The head of the Institute for Marxism-Leninism – about as high and ideological an intellectual position as you can get – was fired and demoted to factory work because his daughter protested the invasion and he refused to condemn her.[16] It is not clear what purpose all these testimonials were to serve; they apparently weren't published, but the Party was able to say it had received support from artists and professors all over the land, and be telling the truth. There was a certain kind of pedantic honour among thieves about wanting to be telling the literal truth even when on a deeper level it is clearly false. Most likely the real reason was to compromise the signers themselves in their own minds; many in the intellectual community had been fervent supporters of Dubcek.

The loyalty of intellectuals was, it seems to me, definitively lost as of 1968. They recognized some danger in Prague's opening to the West (and certainly, the CIA and Western business interests would have done better to stay away had they really wanted a reform socialism to succeed). But the reforms seemed like the answer to the long-pent-up dreams of all those who believed, fervently or passively, that socialism was intrinsically a better system than capitalism and had just been hijacked by power-hungry leaders who didn't trust the people. After all, this was not a rebellion against the Party as in 1953 or 1956; it was the leadership and the Communist Party itself in Czechoslovakia who, with pressure and participation from below, were making the democratic changes. There was no theoretical reason why the same couldn't happen at home. Dresden and Prague are only a few hours apart, and many people will tell you of the heady spring and summer days when they sat in cafes in Prague and saw the second revolution happening before their eyes. To learn that such a movement had no hope of surviving Russian repression, and that their own government and army helped crush it, put an end forever to many people's idealism and participation.

One finds again and again references to the break experienced in 1968. The writer Franz Fühmann sees that year as a liberation, i.e. the end of an illusion and his tendency to identify with finished ideologies. He speaks of the 'deep shock [Erschütterung] of August 1968', which produced the 'resolve: now I want to see "what is", as Rosa Luxemburg said. That's where the essential [das Eigentliche] begins'. And further, of the 'enormous impression the experience of August 1968 made, which gave me something like a last chance'.[17] For Christoph Hein, though, the end of illusion is negative: 'Loss of illusion for me is associated not with the year '89 but with '68: the invasion of Prague. Something definitively died for me then. Like most people in the GDR I was very enthusiastic about Gorbachev when he came. But I knew it was too late. 1968 would have been the last chance.'[18]

It is strange to note that each of the rebellions and resulting repressions involved *either* the workers *or* the intellectuals. Somehow they never seemed to coalesce. Where were the writers in 1953, where were the workers in 1968? (There were some protest movements within factories, but the Party worked hard to keep them isolated.[19]) We can assume that if (and only if) they *had* gotten together, they could have been powerful. This was a further dilemma for the Party: it wanted each group to teach the other 'correct' consciousness, but there was always the equal danger that each might teach the other false consciousness. This dilemma is at the root of the contradictoriness or halfheartedness of measures to bring them together.

Workers and Intellectuals Together

The common rhetorical formula was 'the workers and farmers and their allies, the intelligentsia'. Even before we get to intelligentsia, the formula is already problematic: what about the other 'Werktätige', or does 'workers' this time mean everyone who works, i.e. everyone? And in the case of farmers, who we have ignored in this study, there were also two kinds. Those who counted as part of the class were the 'Genossenschaftsbauern', who had joined the collective farms that were the rural equivalent of the big factory Kombinate. (Collectivization was carried out semi-voluntarily, unlike in the Soviet Union, but with almost irresistible incentives and disincentives.) Also, we have totally ignored here the ambiguous role of women's labour, including both their work outside the home (approximately 92% of women 'worked', they were nearly half the labour force, and enjoyed benefits unknown to women in almost any other country), and their work inside the home (which like everywhere, was uncounted, and the sexual division of labour there seldom even a topic of discussion).

The truth in the formula lies in significant and ambitious steps taken by the Party to break down the barriers, not just barriers between workers and intellectuals, but also barriers to advancement. Partly out of conviction, partly out of necessity (flight of the middle class to the West), people with little education were in the early years placed in all kinds of positions of responsibility and authority. A complaint heard throughout the 40 years was that people were assigned responsibility on the basis of loyalty (i.e. non-thinking) rather than qualification. (This complaint could be *partly* resentment by the middle class at its displacement.) This could be one source of the anti-intellectualism of Party officials: the fear that they might not be as competent as their critics or subordinates led to exaggerated measures to humiliate and control.

The educational opportunities for workers also contributed to their mobility. The statistics on university applications and acceptances are hard to interpret, partly because the 'Hochschulen' (universities) and 'Fach-schulen' (professional and trade schools) were lumped in together, also partly because the criteria for class membership got confused. In 1972, for instance, a report attempting to state the percentage of higher-education applicants from the intelligentsia broke them down into 1) 'intelligentsia due to their social position', 2) 'workers' and farmers' children, whose parents belong to the socialist intelligentsia because of their level of qualification', 3) 'children of employees, where one parental unit belongs to the intelligentsia by consideration of that parent's qualification level', 4) 'others, who have one parental unit who according to qualification belongs to the intelligentsia'![20] Nevertheless, in spite of this hopeless proliferation of definitionism, real progress was indeed made in opening opportunities to the 'lower' levels of society. In a sense the society was a meritocracy, with merit evaluated partly by adherence to the ideals of the society (to put positively what is often called dogmatism, loyalty, or opportunism).

There were, then, these two contradictory directions: the stasis of class origin, and the motion of qualification. Biographies tended to specify not only parentage but also whether people came up through the workers' and farmers' faculties and whether they had worked in production. People from working-class backgrounds probably tended to be steered into the technical branch of the intelligentsia, which came to be seen as a significant factor of production. From what I understand, there were good, fairly equal relationships between them and the production workers at the workplace. There were also opportunities for the workers themselves to delegate members of their brigade to study and advance themselves.

The estrangement between workers and the intellectuals outside the workplace however is a different matter. Thousands were employed by the Academy of Sciences to do pure research, and had little contact outside their own institutes. Teachers in elementary and secondary schools were resented because they – reluctantly or enthusiastically – had to teach the line, no matter how absurd, and far too many were petty authoritarian disciplinarians. Actors, movie stars, musicians at least provided entertain-ment, and the audiences were large due to extensive free ticket pro-grammes through the workplace, but they belonged to another world, full of the glamour of fashion and guest performances in the West.[21]

The most interesting love-hate relationship was between writers and workers – both in the narrow meaning of 'workers' and in the sense of writers and society. The role assigned to writers by the Party, and accepted partially by most, was also the role in which the people – the audience – saw them. That is, the writers were to portray and interpret the lived experience of the people, holding up a mirror and helping them to understand what meaning their lives might have: how they fit in society, whether their lives were significant, how to deal with their alienation, their problems with spouses and children and the collective institutions around them. But what was wanted above all went beyond the role foreseen by the Party: some recognition of those aspects of life about which there was official silence. This is not necessarily an oppositional attitude, or it wouldn't be if the Party hadn't defined it as such; it is just that human need to feel that one is not crazy, that there are others who share one's secret feelings. The Party could organize letter-writing campaigns by workers who protested any deviation from heroic depiction, but they were not expressing the true hunger that produced 'Leserland DDR', a nation of readers. That hunger for depiction and confirmation of unofficial reality was the source of the – to us – bizarre discussion of subjectivity in literature unleashed by Christa Wolf's *Nachdenken über Christa T* [Thinking about Christa T.]. It was, then, partly *audience* demand that made writers intermediaries between people and Party, with a foot in each world, explaining them to each other. Thus, writers may have delivered what the Party expected of them (a large number were in fact Party members), but to a greater extent the best of them delivered what the people *needed* of them.

This was not the purpose the government had in mind when it proclaimed the 'Bitterfelder Weg' or Bitterfeld Path in 1959. The ulterior motive behind the founding conference was the same old role for workers: get them to produce more. The 'Zirkel schreibender Arbeiter' or Workers Writing Groups (part of the truly impressive cultural offering at the workplace) were to focus on workplace issues, especially on uncovering inefficiencies in production. The organizers were especially interested in the chemical industry, centred in Bitterfeld (famous today as the site of pollution and unemployment). Besides encouraging the workers themselves in their brigade diaries and other writings to depict working conditions and bottlenecks, they would also encourage professional writers to 'change their life style' by coming to live and work in the big collective farms and factories, so they could write about the life of the people at the base with genuine knowledge of their life and their work. Though today it is often ridiculed, at the time enough of the best writers thought it was a good idea so that it became a real movement. But only for a while.

The analyses that say it was doomed because it was only an initiative from above, and that the writers found it too artificial,[22] overlook the wide participation by workers in their writing groups (though over the years the kind of 'workers' who participated tended to be more and more the non-manual type), and the enthusiasm that carried that activity right up until the end of the GDR. According to a leader of such a group in Bitterfeld itself, their writing activity is one of the few fond memories that the workers have of the former system[23] (apart from just plain being employed, which may also never happen again). Unfortunately it is difficult to find any materials on their participation and their response; brigade diaries have disappeared in the general mania to throw away everything from the GDR, and the records we have about the programme, like historical records generally, come from the writers not the workers. History is written by those who write. Indeed, after the initial phase of enthusiasm, professional writers started complaining about the Bitterfeld Path and the concept gradually disappeared from official rhetoric; this is the attitude to it that has come down to us from the literary historians as well.

However, it was not just the writers who were sceptical. It seems that in attempting to uncover inefficiencies and portray the real processes on the shop floor, worker-writers and professional writers alike found some 'antagonistic contradictions' among the 'non-antagonistic contradictions'. That is, the most serious problems turned out to be the result of stupidity or bullheaded rigidity on the part of Party representatives themselves. Asked to portray reality, the writers did the assignment all too well. Holding a mirror up to the workers is one thing; holding it up to the Party quite another. So there is reason to believe that the Party itself started to beat a retreat from the programme, using writers' complaints[24] as the excuse. It is hard to find evidence for this because in their documents and even in the protocols of their meetings, Party members seldom discuss failures for the record; the old approach is just allowed to lapse silently while the new one replacing it is trumpeted. The promising word 'problem' turns out just to mean 'topic'. (In reading archived Party documents one finds that the leaders seem to need to persuade themselves that there is only one possible correct line as much as they need to persuade the populace.)

One of the products of the Bitterfeld Path, the massive 1964 novel *Spur der Steine* (set at the construction site of a large factory) was promoted, feted, and discussed widely, but the film (directed by Frank Beyer) and the play (*Der Bau* [Construction] by Heiner Müller) based on it were both forbidden. The two latter works, being much shorter and more concentrated, brought out the conflict between the workers and the planners, and also the moral failure of the Party Secretary; and they did not end with the main character, superworker Balla, joining the Party. After portraying too much reality, Beyer was not permitted to make any more films set in contemporary socialist reality, although precisely that had been demanded before. ('I was trained as a movie director with the express mission of portraying themes of the present as the centrepiece of my future work.') Why? He came to realize, he says, that it was because he broke the taboo against showing division within the Party.[26]

Thus, even in its well-meaning and successful project to get workers and intellectuals together, the Party was caught on the dilemma that the reality that really existed was not the same as the reality it proclaimed. Since the portrayal of reality had the purpose not simply of portraying reality but of persuading people that reality was what was proclaimed, a project of bringing the portrayers in closer contact with the reality revealed itself to be a Trojan horse. For the worker-writers, this was not a serious problem. In the first place, except for the Brigade diaries the workplace was not their subject of choice anyway; and in the second place, what they wrote was never going to see a wide audience. The Party made clear that they were writing in order to express themselves locally and to increase their appreciation of real, professional writing, not in order to suppose they might ever themselves become professional writers. This impermeability of class frontiers probably originated, again, in the German and European separation of occupations growing out of the guild system: even writers, artists, and actors learn their trade by going through a professional training, and then that is their career. But directives warned the workers not to get their hopes up that their writing would ever make them 'writers'; they were told to restrict themselves to the smaller forms and to print them just for local consumption.[27] The insistence was a little strange, since they were also encouraged to move up the educational ladder and qualify for less manual, more mental jobs. Once again, a good programme that could have liberatory results was turned into its opposite by Party rigidity and fear.

Perhaps holding the worker-writers back was really intended as reassurance to the intellectuals, the 'real' writers, that there would not be too much competition. It would not be the first time that the Party perceived class struggle, or at least opposing interests, between the workers and the intellectuals. In 1953, for instance, the 'New Course' was announced with the admission that 'a series of mistakes' had been made, among them that 'the interests of such elements of the population as independent farmers, independent tradespeople, craftspeople, the intelligentsia were neglected'.[28] Stringency against these bourgeois, non-proletarian groups was loosened, while the higher production norms for workers were maintained, and this started the workers' rebellion of June 17. After that, concessions had to be made to the workers, which led to more flight by farmers, professionals, intellectuals, and craftspeople, which meant that they had to be catered for. So it went until the wall was built and loss of certain population groups was no longer a factor to consider. But the habit of thinking that these various groups are in competition with each other – for scarce resources and for honour, favours, and privileges – persisted. There seems to have been an acceptance (or even encouragement?) of the psychological need for educated people in a land of very little income differentiation to think of themselves as an elite, even while the working class was supposedly in the saddle.

Of course the situation was contradictory. On the one hand everyone was equal, distinctions had been erased to the point where autonomous political identification or action was impossible.[29] Whether this means socialist equality had been achieved is another question. On the other hand, there were certainly conflicts between the interests of different groups, exacerbated partly by the apostrophization of the working class and partly by perceived favours granted to intellectuals. The Party itself was caught in this double vision: sometimes the ethic was that each individual should melt into and contribute to the good of society as a whole (as opposed to the Western parliamentary model of interest groups); other times the practical and perhaps necessary path was to differentiate. The working class was, on the one hand, the 'universal class'; on the other hand, one group vying for favours among others. Whether the ideal of equality was subverted by a divide-and-rule strategy, or whether the attempt truly to raise the level of the labouring classes was subverted by the economic necessity of keeping the educated happy, or whether the naive belief in worker support was subverted by the absurd need to have the intellectuals tell the workers what the workers really think . . . regardless of how the contradiction is defined, what it really says is that any human society is far more complex than any official ideology can encompass.

Responsibility

It seems as though the number-one topic about the GDR in the press for the last four years has been the complicity of intellectuals with the repressive system. Not only are they attacked by the West, there are plenty of mea culpas coming from within as well.[30] Some are concluding that it's better to leave politics alone altogether, you only get in trouble for having anything to do with the system. But these accusations and confessions miss the point. It is time to stop thinking that the major failure was operating through the system to try to get what changes might be possible; everyone in any system would be remiss not to use what channels are available, encouraging the good and undermining the bad. *The real failing of the intellectuals was not their contact with the rulers, but their lack of contact with the ruled.*

Christa Wolf may be correct in her assessment that the intelligentsia was intentionally separated from the working class, but it was not a very reluctant separation. The artificiality of methods of contact and the discourse of difference were reinforced by the attitude of the intellectuals themselves. They made forays into the world of the workers like missionaries or anthropologists – with good intentions, but from a position of superiority. They wrote novels about the 17th of June[31] but where were they during the street action? They fought against censorship but where were they in the struggles over working conditions and production norms?

What about attempts to develop support for the 1968 Czech reforms among workers? Why was there little interest in Solidarnosz; could it be because that was largely a workers' movement? Some writers were genuinely interested in the world of work in the early sixties, but gradually the attitude won out that this was beneath the dignity of real writers. Franz Fühmann going to the mines in the late seventies stands out as a rare exception: by then it was no longer the Party line.

And ultimately it may be to this failure that the hopelessness of the intellectuals' dream of a third way in 1989 is due: they simply lost contact with the real concerns of the vast majority. Whose concerns were more legitimate, which approach would have actually served the interests of the working (now non-working) population better, is another question. Had the thinkers, the courageous protesters, the small oppositional groups, the writers, been working closely through the years with the population instead of giving up on them as materialistic and apolitical, there might have been a chance of developing a convincing alternative. Writers and intellectuals and churchpeople had prepared the way for 1989 in the many originally clandestine small groups. As they became more open and grew into social movements, the groups would welcome the few token workers who joined, but there was no large-scale strategic attempt to bridge the gap. When the people occupied the space the intellectuals had opened for them, somehow it came as a surprise that the first thing they would want to do would be to go shopping in West Berlin. (But what do any tourists do when they visit a foreign city?) And as soon as the reformers realized it, their experience of separation from the people returned. In the end, the oppositional intellectuals may have been as far from understanding – or liking – the people as the Party itself was.

And still today, the main concern of many East German intellectuals and the 'Bürgerbewegung' or citizens' movement seems to continue to be uncovering examples of collaboration and moral decay in their own ranks – or defending them – rather than applying their extensive skills to the epochal changes taking place for the majority. Where is the thinking about what a population used to working should do, now that it is in a state of permanent unemployment? What happened to the critiques of the work ethic? Surely now is the time to think about going beyond the production-and-consumption values of industrial society – since the people won't be employed in it anyway. But academics and intellectuals are busy defending their own jobs in the universities. Who is working with the alienated working-class youth who are fodder for ideologies of power and racism? The contempt for people continues: they voted CDU, we wash our hands of them, they sold us out. This harsh assessment leaves out the isolated examples of people who in fact are doing this work, in churches, job-creation projects, women's houses. But in the public discourse of 'Vergangenheitsbewältigung' or dealing with the past of the GDR period, concern for the fatal separation between workers and intellectuals hardly plays a role at all.

Intellectuals cooperated with power in the GDR because of the fabulous chance, or the temptation, to be able to shape a whole society according to their ideas, to put a rationally-thought-out social system into practice. For centuries writers and social philosophers have dreamed up utopian visions that correct the ills of the society they lived in. But it precisely this blueprint aspect of utopia, this voluntarism and starting-afresh, that is the problem. Utopia has fallen into disrepute with the fall of the 70-year-long experiment in deliberately forming society; if anything, it is now more fashionable to see utopian thinking as manipulative, totalitarian, and Stalinist. 'We children burned by the twentieth century' can now see that even the literary utopias are 'visions of horror . . . products [Ausgeburten] of a monstrous will to power . . . blueprints for concentration camps.'[32]

But the death of utopia brings a fatal resignation and cynical acceptance of the triumph of the status quo. Must we give up all hope of transforming class society in any fundamental way? Are socially responsible people doomed to fight rear guard actions against the excesses of unjust societies without ever hoping to change their basic structure? Are we caught forever between inadequate reforms of an ever-more unequal and repressive system, and imposing a system against the will of the people?

If there is a solution to the dilemma of the intellectual, it lies in those last four words.

NOTES

1. 'Es tut Weh zu wissen', *Wochenpost* November 24, 1989, reprinted in *Reden im Herbst*, Berlin and Weimar: Aufbau-Verlag 1990, p. 125.
2. Ehrhart Neubert, *Eine protestantische Revolution*, Osnabrück: Kontext-Verlag 1990, p. 23.
3. In his well-known poem 'Die Lösung', The Solution.
4. Cf. Michael Hofmann and Dieter Rink , 'Die Kohlearbeiter von Espenhain', in Rainer Geissler, ed., *Gesellschaftlicher Umbruch in Ostdeutschland*, Opladen 1993.
5. A recent example shows that this confusion between the worker and the Party/state continues since unification: in 1991, people who had been doormen and janitors in the Stasi building were fired from their new jobs in the Charité hospital because they had 'worked for the Stasi', making them ineligible for civil service jobs.
6. Sigrid Meuschel, *Legitimation und Parteiherrschaft in der DDR*, Frankfurt am Main: Suhrkamp 1992, p. 117.
7. 'Freiheit als Notwendigkeit,' 1975, in *Berliner Schriften*, Berlin: Verlag Europäische Ideen 1977, p. 57.
8. Cf. the interviews with workers now in their '60s to '80s in Lutz Niethammer, Alexander von Plato, and Dorothee Wierling, *Die volkseigene Erfahrung*, Berlin: Rowohlt 1991.
9. This is the theme of Heiner Müller's subversive play, *Der Lohndrücker* (1956).
10. 'Fragen an eine Brigade,' *Kursbuch* 38 (December 1974), p. 144.
11. Calling them paranoid is not to deny that 'just because you're paranoid doesn't mean you don't have enemies'.
12. For instance, over 70% of schoolteachers in the Soviet Occupation Zone had been in Nazi organizations. Friedrich Ebert-Stiftung, *Zur Bewältigung der NS-Zeit in der DDR: Defizite und Neubewertungen*, Bonn 1989, p. 40.

13. This tendency is of course not unknown among more open governments, cf. the US failure to believe it could be losing the Vietnam War.
14. SAPMO-BArch: ZPA [i.e. SED Central Party Archives], IV 2/906/102 – Abteilung Kultur.
15. E.g. in SAPMO -BArch: ZPA IV A/9.04/22 – Sektor Hoch – un Fachschulpolitik.
16. SAPMO-BArch: ZPA J IV 2/2/1201, p. 3 – Central Committee November 12, 1968.
17. 'Franz Fühmann im Gespräch mit Wilfried F. Schoeller', in Franz Fühmann, *Den Katzenartigen wollten wir verbrennen: Ein Lesebuch*, ed. Hans-Jürgen Schmitt, Hamburg: Hoffman und Campe Verlag 1983. Quoted in Fühmann exhibit, Akademie der Künste Berlin March–April 1993.
18. Interview in *Freitag* May 28, 1993. Incidentally, even 'superspy' Markus Wolf experienced a similar 'Einschnitt' or turning point in 1968, beginning his process of thinking things could not go on the way they were; his conclusion, however, was that the responsible position was to shore up power against the danger of total collapse. (TV interview May 9, 1993.)
19. For a treatment of worker protests against the invasion of Czechoslovakia, see Stefan Wolle, 'Die DDR-Bevölkerung und der Prager Frühling', *Politik und Zeitgeschichte* 1992: B36, 35–45.
20. SAPMO-BArch: ZPA IV B 2/9.04/124, Sektor Hoch- und Fachschulpolitik, document dated April 26, 1972.
21. I do not speak of salary levels here; I have heard so many contradictory reports about whether workers were better paid than intellectuals or vice versa that I don't feel competent to judge. Access to convertible currency from performing or publishing in the West was however a point of serious resentment, especially as the need for collecting this currency became acute for the state, causing it to expand the Intershop system. This produced a serious rift in society, and contributed to the rush to the D-Mark in 1989.
22. E.g. Ingeborg Gerlach, *Bitterfeld: Arbeiterliteratur und Literatur der Arbeitswelt in der DDR*, Kronberg: Scriptor Verlag 1974, p. 23.
23. Conversation June 1993 with Reiner Tetzner, who led a writing group in the Chemiekombinat Bitterfeld from 1975–90.
24. Collected in *In eigener Sache: Briefe von Künstlern und Schriftstellern*, ed. Erwin Kohn for Ministry of Culture, Halle 1964.
25. 'Offener Brief an den Generaldirektor des DEFA Studios für Spielfilme', September 25, 1977, SAPMO-BArch: ZPA IV 2/2.033/49 – Büro Lamberz.
26. Conversation with Frank Beyer May 1993.
27. Manfred Jäger, *Kultur und Politik in der DDR: Ein historischer Abriß*, Cologne: Verlag Wissenschaft und Politik 1982, pp. 95–8; cf. also the *Handbuch für schriebende Arbeiter*, ed. Ursula Steinhaußen, Dieter Faulseit and Jürgen Bonk, Berlin (East) 1967.
28. Hermann Weber, *Geschichte der DDR*, Munich: Deutscher Taschenbuch Verlag 1989, p. 235.
29. This is Sigrid Meuschel's main thesis, op. cit.
30. For two rather different examples, see Jens Reich, *Abschied von den Lebenslügen: Die Intelligenz und die Macht*, Berlin: Rowohlt 1992, and Jürgen Kuczynski, *Nicht ohne Einfluß: Macht und Ohnmacht der Intellektuellen*, Cologne: PapyRossa Verlag 1993.
31. Cf. Heinrich Mohr, 'Der 17. Juni als Thema der Literatur in der DDR', in *17. Juni 1953: Arbeiteraufstand in der DDR*, ed. Ilse Spittmann and Karl Wilhelm Fricke, Cologne 1982, and Johannes Pernkopf, *Der 17. Juni 1953 in der Literatur der beiden deutschen Staaten*. Stuttgart: Akademischer Verlag Hans-Dieter Heinz 1982.
32. Ruth Römer, 'Die Utopisten und das unordentliche Menschengeschlecht', *Deutschland Archiv* 24: 11 (November 1991), pp. 1202, 1206.

GERMANY'S PARTY OF DEMOCRATIC SOCIALISM

Eric Canepa

A great many people expected in 1989 that the break with the old East-bloc communist parties might lead to some strong forces for the renewal of socialism. Many people in the West were surprised at the time that there was so little expression of this. In the German Democratic Republic there was, in fact, a strong democratic socialist current in the demonstrations of the Fall of 1989. Although in the context of the abrupt unification with West Germany this current was smothered, it nevertheless re-emerged via the Party of Democratic Socialism (PDS). This is a development that bears very careful examination.

The following essay is an attempt to illuminate the PDS's potential as a socialist organisation. It is impossible to cover here the legal-political struggles between the PDS and the state as regards expropriation attempts, attempts to delegitimise or criminalise some of its leaders, etc., nor the mainstream media distortion of the PDS. The main purpose, rather, must be to describe and analyse this organisation's programme, its actual political practice, the character of its membership, its relationship to the rest of the left, and the attitudes of the population, principally in the East, towards it.

The Political Culture of GDR Intellectuals

To understand the PDS, it is necessary to begin by noting the rather special characteristics of the GDR intelligentsia which contained more critically-minded Marxists than that of any other East-bloc country. In the first weeks of the *Wende* (*Wende* = the 1989 "turning point" in the GDR) it was possible to hear expressions of socialist sentiment on the part of several of the citizen-movement leaders. And the overwhelmingly socialist slogans of the first demonstrations in the GDR were not a mirage simply because they were finally eclipsed by a pro-unification wave. There was indeed a sentiment for socialism in the GDR, most conspicuously among Berlin intellectuals and artists, and among other strata, especially in the central and northern regions.

312

Of all the countries later to be included in the East-bloc, the Eastern part of Germany had experienced the highest level of pre-war industrialisation, and had developed the largest indigenous socialist and communist intelligentsia and working class. No other East-bloc country was enriched by so many prestigious left and communist artists and intellectuals returning to it from war-time emigration in Western Europe or North and South America. The SED (Sozialistische Einheitspartei Deutschland = Socialist Unity Party, the GDR's ruling party that resulted from the KPD-SPD merger) was still in 1989 "in however deformed a way, the repository of the strong socialist and communist traditions in the parts of the former German Reich that now constitute the GDR. It has not suffered the traumatic splits and purges of its Hungarian, Polish and Czechoslovak counterparts since the 1950s, and its considerable reform-communist potential has not so far been displayed."[1] The SED was able to absorb and retain so many pre-war communists and socialists because the guilt of social-democrats, Christian activists and communists for having failed to avert or defeat Nazism led to a determination to hold out in the face of a repressive atmosphere and stay in the country, retaining their socialist ideals.[2] Moreover, the guilt at having inflicted suffering on the Soviet people was not only an official ideology; it was widely felt by left intellectuals outside the KPD. In this connection, even the merger of the KPD and SPD in 1946 was not entirely a manipulated sham; there was a genuine feeling in the Berlin SPD for it. The SPD even had a "pro-Russian" wing![3]

The repercussions of the purges of the 1950s were comparatively less devastating in the GDR than in Poland and Hungary, because the workers' and intellectuals' revolts of 1953 and 1956 respectively were separate and, therefore, less explosively dangerous. The SED leadership was able to "break" the intellectuals' revolt more surgically and selectively. In Poland, by contrast, there were still some notable, creative Marxists in the 1950s, but after the purges only a handful remained; in the GDR many more such people survived all purges. Although it was not allowed real public exposure, there was widespread debate and dissent in the GDR, but it took place much more within a Marxist orbit. (One factor that helped keep Marxism attractive for the intellectuals was the fact that, unlike in the libraries of the USSR, for example, it was possible to read Western Marxist literature in GDR libraries.)

The ranks of Marxist intellectuals were less devastated in the GDR because of the regime's policy of privileging them and applying a carrot-and-stick policy. It was often the older loyal intellectuals who exhibited the most consistently critical attitudes. Stefan Hermlin (a Spanish Civil-War veteran, now in the PDS) had organised daring symposia and written courageous position papers on artistic freedom, which were then followed by rebukes and punishments but which still left him enough freedom to publish and be widely read. Not all dissidents were as lucky, but nevertheless Hermlin's career, and those of Stefan Heym and Christa Wolf are typical enough of a representative group of dissidents to illustrate the distinct character of the GDR intelligentsia.

In the context of the current backlash of the Eastern populations which are experiencing a wave of nostalgia and defensiveness vis-à-vis their specifically Eastern ethnic or national identities, the case of the East German population, especially the intellectuals, again stands out from the rest. The exceptional situation of two countries, the GDR and the FRG, sharing the same language and basic culture, but with two different social systems, has, now as before, left GDR citizens with less of a national, ethnic, basis for any local pride and identity and has forced that identity to be much more centred around the idea of a social system than is the case in other Eastern European countries. Thus even people who would not directly profess socialist beliefs are able, when their pride is wounded, to identify with the social system in which they had grown up. This is not contradicted by the fact that there is now a dangerous minority that supports xenophobic attacks against immigrant workers. Those who were most militant in accepting a new "Germanness" opposed to the communist past in 1990 were forced to suppress their "Easternness". And when the same people were suddenly beset with the current specifically Eastern problems they could only blame non-Germans. But racist explanations for social pressures are still new to GDR culture, as is greater-German nationalism, and polls consistently show negligible electoral support for such nationalist projects as well as for the extreme right-Republikaner in the East. There is now, moreover, a swing away from the right towards the SPD and PDS. It is important, also, that this GDR specificum should not be lost amidst a common-sense assumption, based on the Nazi experience, of a given and immutable German racism more virulent than e.g. Polish or French racism.

The PDS

The rebellion within the SED in November–December 1989 was the accomplishment of the rank-and-file; it was never initiated at the top. The Central Committee building was besieged several times in those months (when both a CC plenum and a Special Party Congress were held) by the rank-and-file groups of the Berlin party organisation. Even the normally hostile *tageszeitung* (*taz*), Germany's principal pro-Green Party daily, reported as moving and sincere the expressions of radical democratic positions *and* allegiance to communist traditions coming from the rank-and-filers. "Tens of thousands of SED members from the 'rank-and-file' on November 8th in front of the CC building. It was a spontaneous demo called by word of mouth in the city. They were even more bitter than others in the society because what was done wrong or criminally was done in the name of socialism. . . . 'We want finally to play a role, even if not a leading one!' The SED rank-and-file protested against years-long tutelage. A locksmith's introduction was typical: 'I am a powerless comrade.' Almost every speaker demanded democratization, delegation from bottom to top, a special party congress. . . . A woman asked whether the movement was passing the women by. She demanded quotas in all Party structures. . . . A female tractor driver, a fireman, etc. spoke. 'The self-righteousness of the leadership is unbearable . . .' The SED rank-and-file concluded by singing defiantly, desperately and movingly the Internationale. Many waved their Party card in their hands or held up their fists."[4] There were similar actions in Halle and Neubrandenburg, where the party rank-and-file threatened strikes. At the November CC meeting, compromises were made, some reformers were added and almost all of the old leadership were dropped, but the rank-and-file wanted a Special Party Congress to enact more radical changes.

By December 3rd the whole CC resigned; Gregor Gysi was given the role of investigating corruption and preventing the destruction of evidence; delegates for the upcoming December 8th Special Party Congress were coming forward with demands from their constituents for what amounted to the foundation of a new socialist party. During that week about 500,000 members, including entire district leaderships, left the party.

In the December 8th Special Party Congress, where the SED was turned into the SED-PDS, the 2,700 delegates voted 95% for Gregor Gysi, the lawyer who had defended Rudolf Bahro, Robert Havemann, Bärbel Bohley and New Forum, as new chair. They unanimously rejected liquidation of the party and elected 101 national Vorstand (directorate) members to replace the old 300-member Central Committee. (By the Feb 24th 1990 Electoral Party Congress 33 of these had left the Vorstand.) Gysi warned that the overcoming of the 40-year Stalinist tradition was still before them. Immediately, there was the expression of the wish not to have a single line, that the members should "not wait for the new line" but should "struggle over the Party's path." Unity from now on was not to mean closed ranks within the Party but rather "openness vis-à-vis all democratic movements and people." Gysi's speech named the progressive lines of the communist, social-democratic and antifascist and pacifist traditions which should be absorbed into the Party's platform. This was the beginning of the party's struggle to absorb and go beyond communist, social-democratic and social-movement traditions. As Gysi said, "What we're trying out here doesn't yet exist in the world." He called for the dissolution of the Betriebskampfgruppen (factory-based militia) and the abolition of the Ministry of State Security (MfS or "Stasi").

Although the initial changes were driven by rank-and-file pressures, nevertheless in that first congress the voting was still passive, with delegates approving everything the new young leadership proposed. It was only later, starting in 1991, but largely in 1992, that radical democratic rank-and-file processes become more firmly rooted.

In the first few months of the party's existence in its new form, the continuity with part of the old apparatus still made many people uneasy. (The apparatus before the reform included 44,000 people.) Lothar Bisky, now chair of the PDS, recalls how, "as the PDS was founded, everyday it was a decisive question if one was falsely informed by the apparatus. Who's representing what interests? One didn't know."[5]

The first major problem was the Treptow Monument rally in January 1990 which illustrated the difficulty of calling for defence of the GDR against neo-fascists as a way to rally people behind the party, with the Stasi and party apparatus essentially still present. The party called a mass anti-fascist rally at the Soviet memorial in Treptow Park, Berlin on January 3rd, 1990. Using the neo-Nazi defacements and graffiti that had recently appeared in Berlin, including on the Treptow monument, the SED-PDS planned a show of force to rally the party and its allies and boost morale. 250,000 people came, and although the demo did on the surface accomplish its immediate goals, calling upon the anti-fascist traditions of the country, the damage it caused was longer-lasting. Vestiges of Stalinist anti-fascist rhetoric from some speakers conveyed an image of continuity with the SED tradition of using such rhetoric to eclipse other problems. As Gysi later realised, it was clearly ill-considered to demand a new security force without having thoroughly dismantled the old one and just after Prime Minister Modrow's regime had called for a new security force. Those among the organisers with whom I spoke were happy with the morale and spirit but had a sinking feeling observing types in the crowd who merely yelled slogans calling for a security force. Any GDR citizen could have recognised them as MfS (State Security Ministry) plainclothesmen. The leadership was embarrassed. Intra-party conflicts resulted, the citizens movements were even more alienated, and the Western press made much of it.

During the second half of January 1990 criticism within the Party reached a peak. There was increasing external pressure on members, yet demands for dissolving the party came mostly from its own ranks. Thousands of members left daily, and the infrastructure crumbled rapidly. It was at this point (Jan 21st) that Dresden mayor and party vice-chair Wolfgang Berghofer quit and joined the SPD. He favoured quick economic and currency union with the West. Up to that time the SED-PDS's internal debates were driven by a series of legal – and, indeed, encouraged – factions or "platforms" e.g. the Social-Democratic Platform, "Third-Way" Platform, PDS Initiative Platform, Communist Platform (KPF). The departure of Berghofer and other leading Dresden party officials triggered another wave of resignations, principally of social-democratically oriented members, careerists, economic functionaries and apparatus members, the Volkspolizei and officer corps. But, as Gysi pointed out,[6] there were also some who left simply out of fear of blacklisting on their jobs. They were reacting to the climate of increased anti-SED hostility in January (as a result of more revelations of SED leadership corruption and the Treptow demonstration).

On January 18th, all party factions (except the KPF) were calling for the dissolution of the SED-PDS.[7] At this point there was a counter-movement, which itself was a continuation of the spontaneous rank-and-file demos during the CC meeting in November '89: young people, especially women, demanded thorough-going renewal instead of liquidation. On the 20th, the Vorstand passed a resolution for a rapid and consistent renewal of the party to be laid out in detailed steps. This would include the further reduction of the apparatus, the quickest possible separation from discredited party members, and the consistent continuation of rehabilitation proceedings.

After the Berghofer withdrawal, a second rank-and-file impulse turned into a movement with an amazing constructive capacity for the rescue of the party. It caught almost everybody by surprise.[8] An example was the spontaneous meeting, on the same evening as Berghofer's resignation announcement on TV, of young members of the Dresden district directorate to form a presidium capable of getting to work immediately. The dissolution decision of the Saalfeld directorate brought more than 100 rank-and-filers out of their houses during the night to elect immediately a new local directorate. Thus at several crucial stages, from November 1989 on, it was not old functionaries, but rank-and-file movements of largely young members who kept the PDS alive and, moreover, gave some reality to the leadership's conception of the party as a movement.[9]

On January 26th, the Party directorate met with the district and local leaderships, and as a result Gysi announced that there would be no dissolution of the party.[10]

Out of these spontaneous grassroots reform actions came the so-called "initiative groups".[11] These groups often took over local party organisations. By January/February a series of task forces ("AG"s) (gays and lesbians, feminists, ecology, artists, and others) were formally established. Among these, the AG Junge GenossInnen (Young Comrades) played an increasingly crucial role. Their credibility with non-party young people did much to render the PDS more attractive to progressive youth, and they brought radical grassroots conceptions and ways of working into the party. The Young Comrades developed structures throughout the ex-GDR and have played a prominent role in the initiation or challenging of the party's programmes and statute. Although these AGs and initiative groups led the way to the now generally accepted political culture of the party, it has to be borne in mind that they alienated many working-class members who saw the SED-PDS as a "party of intellectuals and platforms."

It became clear in January that the GDR would be absorbed into the FRG. This alone ensured that the PDS, if it could survive, would be radically different from any other Eastern reformed ruling party. It could have no hope of being a party of government, and no career could be made in it. It was forced to be an inevitably persecuted left opposition, and did not even have the option of being social-democratic, there being no room for a second SPD in Germany. This realisation set in during January, and the Berghofer withdrawal of January 21st sealed it. From this moment on, the party was destined to diverge ever more sharply from the patterns of Eastern-European social-democratised communist parties. At this time, part of the membership published a critical statement in *Neues Deutschland* – the daily newspaper which had been the SED organ and by 1991, although very close to the PDS, had gained considerable editorial independence from it – on the policies emerging from the GDR's new regime headed by party-member Hans Modrow. There is no evidence of an unequivocal official party position sanctioning the regime's policies on reunification and on market economy[12] at that time. Indeed, harsh debate and resignations took place in reaction to those policies.

In February 1990 there was a kind of truce between the intra-party factions in view of the upcoming elections (to the GDR's first democratically elected Volkskammer). This was also the period of the PDS's "comeback" (on February 3rd–4th "SED" was dropped from the name "SED-PDS") in which many of those afraid of the consequences of unification and many progressive youths seeking "a strong left opposition" (as I often heard during my polling-place interviews on March 18th, 1990) considered voting for the PDS. During the Volkskammer election campaign, Gysi showed himself to be the most sympathetic, entertaining and agile politician in Germany, in the opinion of much of the mainstream media, in this way contributing greatly to the self-esteem and optimism of PDS members and of many other GDR citizens as well.

The Electoral Party Congress of 24th–25th February 1990 elected a new presidium consisting of 13 men and 14 women, and among the 595 delegates there were many young people. In all, about 200,000 had left the party in January. Gysi spoke of "650,000 to 700,000 members" (2.3 million before November 1989), and he mentioned an interesting point: women had left the party in much smaller numbers than men, so that the proportion of women in the PDS had risen. The staff of the national party directorate consisted of 360 people (42% of the size of the former CC staff), with a lot of new young members among them. The district directorates had been reduced to 10–20% of the size of the SED ones; the local directorates had from 5 to 15 paid staff. This was a time in which many young people joined the party.

The mass exodus from the party in the second half of January had included most of the apparatus. By the end of 1990 only a thin layer of them remained. The new leadership wavered between keeping secrets from some of the remaining "apparatchiki" and relying on their often considerable expertise. It appeared too extreme, based on mere suspicion and feeling, to get rid of all loyal staffers who had a connection to the old way of doing things. But the continued presence of such elements in the PDS inevitably left many problems in store. In October 1990, those responsible for managing the PDS's assets, Wolfgang Pohl and Wolfgang Langnitschke, carried out an absurd plan of stashing away some of the old SED assets in a fictitious Moscow firm. West-German intelligence had been on to it from the start and waited for the kickoff of the Bundestag electoral campaign in October 1990 to make it public.

"Inevitable Social-Democratization" and Market-Economy Naiveté

After its first programmatic utterances (December 8th, 1989 and February 24th, 1990), the PDS was placed in a long series of crisis situations which delayed programme discussion. Summary dismissals of the PDS's politics and potential based solely on the programmatic statements of those months, treating the party, outside of its real context, like a newly-founded Western party, prevent a serious examination of a complex new reality. The surrounding context of the PDS and the dynamics of the social-political situation in which the party found itself differed from those of other East-bloc CPs or of West-European parties with greater incentives to social-democratisation. Considerable sensitivity to the chronology and context of the programmatic utterances and politics of the PDS is needed. The party's electoral programme of February 1990 was predicated on the idea of a GDR that was, to some degree, independent. Therefore, demands like co-determination and democratisation within factories, addition of more market to the state economy, etc., could have been portrayed as conventionally social-democratic if the PDS had been proposing these demands within West Germany, but they were trying to rescue and democratise an already existing highly centralised state-run economy and then, increasingly, to cushion the inevitable capitalisation and re-unification process.

By June 1990, however, Modrow declared the PDS to be "a left socialist force in fundamental opposition to the capitalist conception of the solution of global problems of humanity."[13] And, facing the full reality of the triumph of capitalism in the GDR, Gysi said at the same time: "The party needs a new programmatic, a new identity. We have to think differently vis-à-vis capitalism than was thought in January/February, a time when we were still figuring out what could be taken over that would be good for the GDR's own [separate] society. New also is the PDS's position on social democracy which indeed has in principle made peace with capital. That

peace we cannot make."[14] Nevertheless, the leadership still was determined to try to co-operate with the SPD on some issues, and to stress the
"many commonalities" between itself and the (left) SPDers and Greens.
As the PDS's Press Secretary said: "These naive things ['capital-
dominated society,' 'social market economy,' 'the civilizing achievements
of capitalism'] went away quite quickly during 1991. It's hard to pin it
down, but at one point it was seen that one could not get a majority in the
party any more for such dreamy concepts."[15]

Finances

On May 31st, 1990 the creation of a Volkskammer commission concerned
with the assets of GDR parties and mass organisations was the start of
expropriation procedures against the PDS. The commission's executive
arm became the Treuhand (state trusteeship for the privatisation and
rehabilitation of factories, etc. and management of assets).

Although the PDS had voluntarily given away 75-80% of the SED assets
in early 1990 (consisting of 2.6 billion GDR marks worth of factories,
vacation homes and guest houses, five publishing firms, 3 billion in reserve
funds, etc. totalling 3 billion DM) to the health system, universities, etc.,
they resolved, after the Pohl/Langnitschke affair at the end of 1990, to give
up most of what still remained. And although the real apparatchiks had left
the party long before, there was a decision to cut down the number of full-
time employees still more drastically and ensure extreme transparency in
all affairs, especially financial. The party wanted to give most of its assets
to the state and municipalities for public works. By that time the PDS was
willing to defend its right only to the legally unassailable property confis-
cated by the Nazis from the pre-war KPD and returned by the Soviet
Occupation Authority.[16]

As of January 1st, 1992 the PDS became an organisation supported
exclusively by membership dues. With 147,000 dues-paying members this
has been possible. The only usable real estate is the Karl-Liebknecht Haus
in Berlin (federal headquarters) and a small restaurant property. This
means that the PDS is now the poorest party in the Bundestag, poorer than
the Greens who get support for their educational foundation. The PDS, as
of now, does not even have election funds granted them, because the
Treuhand says it still has to decide the assets question.[17]

The Volkskammer Elections and After

The PDS's partial recovery from its image as a Stalinist party occurred as
early as February-March 1990. On March 18th it received 16.33% of the
vote. This reflected considerable popular enthusiasm – especially among
the youth – for Gysi, as well as the immense popularity of Hans Modrow

(in February 1990 a poll showed him to be by far the most popular political figure in the GDR).

The difference between the SED and the PDS could be seen reflected in the PDS's electorate: polls showed that three quarters of the PDS's 1.9 million voters on March 18th, 1990 had never belonged to the SED. That also meant that the majority of former SED members did not vote for the PDS.

The youth vote of the PDS was 16% (SPD: 20%; Bü90: 5%).[18] (Bü90 = Bündnis 90, the March 1990 citizens-movement electoral alliance bringing together the three main organisations, and now, since the December 1990 Bundestag elections, joined together with the Green Party as Grüne/Bü '90). Very striking were the preferences of those still in school: 23% of them voted for the PDS (SPD: 23%; Bü90: 7%). But blue-collar workers punished the SED by giving the PDS only 10% (11.9% MFW), especially in the south, while workers in some northern industrial centres gave the party over 20%. Geographically the PDS did much better in the northern areas, with top results in East Berlin (almost 30% MFW).

Meanwhile, PDS leadership bodies were being reduced in size, and formal membership was shrinking (down to 460,000 by April 18th 1990 with only 320,000 applying for new cards). The proportion of women was 40%, but those under 30 made up only 10–11%. However, de facto youth participation, then as now, is greater than membership figures would indicate.[19] Significantly, the vast majority of rank-and-file organisations had "moved" from factories to residential areas.

Due to prosecution, fear of job loss, the "finance scandal" and, for some, the inadequate pace of renewal, the PDS lost about 60,000 members between June '90 and January '91. Middle-aged members in particular – naturally most concerned about career and advancement – left in disproportionate numbers. A high proportion of state and economic functionaries and members of the armed forces had characterised SED membership, comprising about one-third of the former party. The PDS lost this character, but, of course, not all functionaries left the PDS.[20]

A comparison with Russia is useful. In the Ex-GDR there is no "red-brown" coalition, and moderate or extreme nationalists and opportunists can only find a place in Western parties. And unlike in Bulgaria, for example, those who choose to channel their former *nomenklatura* careers in a social-democratic direction do not do so within the successor organisation of the former ruling party. Other channels are available to them. Moreover, the former high functionaries, military and *nomenklatura* careerists either resent the PDS or cannot be integrated into its new culture.

Right after the Volkskammer elections it became clear that the citizens movements would generally interpret any vote for the PDS as a conservative vote. There are two variants of this argument: 1) the people, above all the working class, are conservative by definition, and therefore the party for whom they vote is conservative; 2) the PDS is conservative (because most of its members did not fundamentally reject the SED or had something to do with the state), and therefore the people who vote for it are displaying conservative thinking. But by 1992 the PDS had acquired the identity of a left opposition party, and yet, after the stunning victory for the PDS in the May Berlin municipal elections, Uwe Lehmann, a West-Berlin Green, put forward the theory that the PDS and the CDU draw from the same electorate-group, i.e. that the same people periodically swing back and forth between PDS and CDU.[21] But all available studies and polls show only a current swing from the CDU to the SPD or PDS. There is no evidence of a voter migration from the PDS to the CDU from 1990 to the present (February 1994).[22]

Is the Old Berlin Apparatus the PDS's Only Electorate?

The Berlin electorate tends to get singled out by anti-PDS analysts when trying to cope with PDS electoral successes. They point to the high concentration of employees and high functionaries of the former state apparatus, who, it is assumed, will vote for the PDS and account for most of that vote.

In a *tageszeitung* (GDR edition) (April 10th, 1990) interview, the SPD candidate for the Berlin mayoralty, Tino Schwierzina, accounted for the PDS's success in Berlin on March 18th by pointing to Berlin as the stronghold of the administration and the Stasi. "These people voted for the PDS, because they believed that it best represented their interests; for example, secure pensions. That's one reason." But then he admits: "On the other hand an astoundingly large number of young people voted for the PDS, either out of an oppositional stance or to give us a light boxing on the ear in the first elections." The interviewer, Walter Süss, intervened: "I know many people who a year ago opposed the SED state but who then on March 18th voted for the PDS. In the reunification of the two German states they did not wish to be overrun and apparently trusted the PDS more than the SPD to attend to matters of social security. If the GDR-countrywide SPD now enters a coalition with the CDU [which it did] and its right arm the DSU, won't its possibilities of winning these young people to the SPD be even less than it is now?"

The discomfort with the Berlin electorate on the part of the social-democratic establishment is best illustrated by a study of East-European free elections commissioned by the Swedish Social-Democratic Party. First there is the familiar accusation that old functionaries comprise the Berlin PDS electorate. Next comes the admission that many young, typically "alternative" left-inclined people vote for the party. To cast the latter in a negative light it is then said that these people have been rendered lazy by too many benefits from the former state-socialist regime and hope for more such. And so the young left vote is turned into something negative as well.

My own interviews of 47 voters in East Berlin on March 18th 1990 in Pankow, Mitte and Friedrichshain showed more than 85% who gave as their reason for voting PDS the need for "a strong left opposition." Most of this group seemed to be under 40, and to represent the typical left or "alternative scene." There was another frequently recurring type, though, who admitted to voting PDS. This consisted of young people rather of a traditional working-class type with young children. Their reason was almost always a concern for social security, but even a few of them mentioned "left opposition."

Furthermore, the "old apparatus" theory of the PDS electorate does not fit well with present PDS popularity in the youthful Berlin districts of Hellersdorf and Prenzlauerberg.

In any case, the terms "apparatchik," "functionary" and "bureaucrat" are thrown around all too easily to convey any sort of realistic picture of the texture of life in state socialist societies. Without a more nuanced and differentiated understanding of those terms it is possible to dismiss many whom might otherwise be regarded as modern progressive people.

Statute and Process

The PDS's Second Party Congress, second session, in June 1991 approved what is clearly the most modern party statute in Germany. In it, the PDS is defined as a voluntary association of independent individuals. All membership-candidacy procedures are abolished. A 50% minimum quota for women is established, also affecting parliamentary groups. Non-member sympathisers are granted voting rights in various bodies, except in financial and statutory matters, and the various smaller subdivisions of the PDS are empowered to grant membership rights to sympathisers to the extent they wish. The statute even permits double membership in other parties (which the SPD statute does not). By mid-September 1991 97% of the entire membership approved it, making this the first time in German history that a statute was decided on directly by the rank and file of a party.

In counting the votes on the statute the party was able to get some grasp on card-holding membership: official membership totalled 180,000 in September 1991. However, the looseness of the party structure, the ability of non-members to be active in it, even before this statute, and the blacklisting that attends PDS membership, all tend to reduce the incentive to acquire official membership. There are significant numbers of young PDS activists who have never requested membership.

In any preparation for a congress or meeting in which programme or major political decisions have to be voted on there are endless motions for changing drafts, declarations, etc. The party's various publications are, as required by the statute, open to all rank-and-file groups to express their opinions, and party literature bears abundant witness to this. The considerable transactional costs of democracy are accepted in the PDS, making procedures far less efficient than in establishment parties. The charge contained in a study on the PDS commissioned by the FDP (Free Democratic Party)[23] that the radical left task forces have no influence on the federal directorate is directly contradicted by the fact that the current 18-member directorate is made up of members mostly drawn from these very task forces, e.g. the anti-racist, media, legal, feminist, Western PDS task forces, as well as the Communist Platform. So the left debates are brought right into the highest body of the party, with no other party entity able to subdue them in the interests of efficiency or pragmatism.

The party now has only 150 staff in all Germany to its 147,000 members, and half are only part-timers on contract. The staff of the Liebknecht Haus (the federal headquarters) is only 30 people. People with important positions have to do night duty at the switchboard. In a normal SED Kreisleitung (district leadership) there were 30 to 50 staff – now a Kreisvorstand consists of some 4 volunteers in total. A normal Landesvorstand (regional directorate) has 8–10 staff. Of the 147,000 members there are 30,000 to 40,000 activist volunteers who do most of the work in the 3,000 odd rank-and-file organisations. All meetings of all party and parliamentary groups and bodies of the PDS are, by statute, open to the public.[24]

Composition and Attitudes of the PDS Membership From 1991

A study conducted by a group of sociologists (Institut für Sozialdatenanalyse (ISDA)) in May/June 1991[25] showed that between June '90 and May '91 worker membership went up: in 1990 the worker share in membership was 20%, in 1991 it was 26% (some were pensioners or forced-retirees). The PDS's share of still-employed workers in 1990 was 12% and in 1991 19%. Their membership share rose because, due to the liquidation of the GDR's social and cultural infrastructure and the consequent blacklisting and intimidation of academics and employees, the latter resigned in greater numbers from June '90–May '91 than did blue-collar workers, especially pensioned workers. In June '91 workers, farmers, and craftspeople made up 30% of PDS membership, while the still-employed members in this category made up 22.5%.

In May 1991 ISDA's inquiry could no longer perceive top SED functionaries and military in the party as a group. But unemployed or pensioned former middle- or lower-level state and economic functionaries do form a sizeable portion of party membership.

Diverging from the East-German average PDS youth membership (10–11%), 30% of the Neubrandenburg PDS membership was under 30.

Anhalt-Saxony shows a similar divergence with an 18% youth member-ship. In any case, German unification tends to bring Eastern workers, students and intelligentsia together, because all three groups suffer from the unemployment caused by recent societal changes.

The political character of the PDS rank-and-file is often the object of careless remarks tending to dismiss it as conservative, elderly, incapable of new thinking and oppositional activism. The rank-and-file is certainly problematic in its tilt to the higher age groups and the presence of people who cannot go far beyond GDR nostalgia. But the ISDA study on membership motivations gives a more differentiated picture. The study was done in June 1991, and since that time the development has been in the direction of more participation and acceptance of the culture of debate. Moreover, half of the 300,000 members at the time of ISDA's study have since left, removing many who could not understand the party's new oppositional activism and culture.

The result of ISDA's cluster analysis is the establishment of five types of PDS members by motivation:

1) 13.8% of the members are emancipatory socialists (i.e. their political-programmatic thinking is democratic socialist and anti-capitalist).

2) 45% of the members' principal motivation is their feeling that the party is their home. They would feel socially isolated without it.

3) 17% are members out of pride and stubbornness: "I am an anti-capitalist, and I am not a *Wendehälse*." (*Wendehälse* = turncoat, an expression used during the Wende for those who were able to do an opportunistic about-face and deny their past.)

4) 14.4% are motivated by the idea that the party represents their interests. This group is divided into those who say a) the PDS represents the interests of the working class, and b) the PDS represents the interests of citizens living in the East.

5) 9.1% are motivated by their conscious theoretical Weltanschauung, specifically by their identification with Marxism, or their hope of renewing Marxism.

The study could not find a correlation of these motivation groups to social/class categories. There is, however, a slight correlation to age. The younger members are overrepresented in groups 1 and 5; the older in 1, 3 and 4. Essentially all groups show a very mixed age profile. Further, there is about the same proportion of activists to inactive people in each group. These even spreads, in the opinion of the report, were related to the lack of a political crystallisation point in the party at the time the study was done in 1991. But the political practice, if not the programme, of the party has since acquired more focus.

The East-German Electorate in 1993–1994

Starting with a detailed study done by ISDA in June 1993 it has become clear that "the established ruling parties now have . . . a relatively small and shrinking following in the East."[26]

The 1993 ISDA study confirms the earlier established popularity of the PDS among academics. 22.5% of them said in 1993 they would vote for the PDS (Bü90: 11%; SPD: 12.2%), and 40.4% of graduates of institutions of higher learning favoured the PDS. Southern blue-collar workers were still shying away from the PDS.

It is obviously possible to establish a more stable political behaviour and preference profile for the Western electoral abstainees than for the potential Eastern non-voters who are still recovering from the shock of a new political system and the invasion of their political landscape by Western parties. What is, therefore, most interesting in the Eastern electorate is the large group who say they will vote for no party or who do not want to say anything (50% of ISDA's respondents). On the basis of their responses to political and ideological questions it is possible to say that this potential-voter block has a more left profile than those of their Western counterparts,[27] so that if they come to the polls it is the SPD and PDS who are likely to be favoured. Furthermore, it is certain that the reason many did not state their preference is the fear of answering "PDS" in public, while no fear of blacklisting attaches itself to the SPD.

The ISDA study's basic object is the political, social and ideological profile of the people according to the party they declared they would vote for, and this profile without relation to party in the case of the potential non-voters. The study is important, therefore, also because it is one of the few sociological studies of the GDR population concerning matters relevant to socialist politics. ISDA's observations of the potential left voters show twice as many women as men, a high proportion of potential left voters in *rural* areas because of the fear of expressing risky opinions in close-knit communities.

But cutting across all groups within the potential voters are a set of political demands which are identified with the PDS: the desire for a change in Treuhand policies to favour factory rehabilitation, the wish for higher taxing of higher earners, and the unconditional abolition of 218 (the clause of the Federal Republic's Basic Law restricting abortion).[28] It was also found that "a demand for a differentiated evaluation of life in the GDR is not the singular plaint of a disadvantaged sect [the PDS], but the concern of broad circles of the electorate of all parties," and this is also a concern primarily represented by the PDS.[29]

Programme

One cannot evaluate the PDS's programme apart from the context and dynamics of the situation the party finds itself in. Two prominent PDS activists from the Trotskyist tradition, federal-directorate member Jakob Moneta (who had edited IG Metall's newspaper in the 60s and 70s) and Berlin city deputy Harald Wolf (one of the young city deputies of the Red-Green Coalition of the 80s) feel that the party's actual anti-capitalist politics so overshadows in importance the ever-evolving and tentative programmatic utterances that a narrow concentration on the imperfect programme is one way the Western left has avoided dealing with the PDS on a political level.[30]

In the debates leading to the final programme Gysi and André Brie (the national election campaign manager and head of the programme commission) decided it was time to wage a more aggressive struggle, on behalf of their vision of a synthesis of left traditions, against three groups: a) the "biography-protectors," i.e. those incapable of criticising the Stalinist past, b) those social-movement members excessively hostile to working-class-based politics, and c) those social-democrats incapable of understanding radical oppositional politics.

A central debate has been "right to jobs/full employment" vs. "more employment would be anti-ecological/ask only for basic income for the population," the latter influenced by ideas of André Gorz. It is obvious that the second position, as a programme for the here and now of East Germany, with its massive unemployment, and the need for labour to get some leverage over the labour market, could not be adopted, but the programme excerpted below shows clear signs of harmonising the two positions.

The summer of 1991 saw the beginning of the end of certain conservative or naive attitudes left over from the party's period of birth. The Second Party Congress, which met that summer, was marked by harsh clashes. By the Third Congress in January 1993 most of the criticisms were absorbed and implemented in the present programme. In the Second Congress Sonja Kemnitz, a factory-council activist, along with the "Young Comrades," had attacked the tendency in the regional PDS organisations and parliamentary groups to concentrate on paper proposals while slighting extra-parliamentary action. Also criticised was an inadequate emphasis among some members on the importance of becoming active in other mass organisations of the left.[31] (Gysi had made this point as well.) But the 1993 programme makes parliamentary clearly dependent on extra-parliamentary work.

And Roswitha Steinbrenner, a member of the *Strömung* group which also fought to heighten the level of extra-parliamentary struggle in the first three years of the PDS, affirms that a shift in this direction has taken place in the regional parliamentary groups.[32] Finally, the activism of PDSers in the struggles of Belfa, MFAG and Bischofferode (see below) reflect the implementation of Kemnitz's other point.[33]

The drafting of the 1993 programme was an exhausting process characterised by raging debates, endless revisions and compromises.[34] It was clearly the result of compromises between left social-democratic, left-wing Marxist and social-movement views. But the fundamental condition influencing a pluralistic programme is the fact that the PDS is forced to address a constituency that no Western left group, especially in West Germany, must address. That is, it must project its politics to an Eastern population which, although it has largely internalised socialist, anti-capitalist morality, is nevertheless partly hostile to Marxist language and much of what was socialist practice, and yet expects help from the party. But one has also to ask whether in West Germany the present social individualisation and the essentially complete disarray and collapse of the left does not likewise make a socialist party with a programmatic unity containing nothing other than direct class politics inappropriate.

Also evident from the programme (and from the PDS's practice) is the PDS's resistance to the populism of which many in the Western left accuse it. The PDS risks many potentially unpopular positions (although the abolition of the restrictive abortion clause does have majority support in the East because the GDR's population was long accustomed, in this case, to a progressive policy) and has shown that it is possible to move the population towards some very advanced positions. Some of the positions on feminisation of society are very daring, and the PDS's well-known total opposition to any softening of the right to asylum meets with only 50% approval among the socially oppositional group established by the ISDA electoral study (see above). The PDS has up to now taken seriously the challenge to "try to bridge the gap between social struggles in Germany and global problems" (e.g. holding the metropolitan countries responsible for underdevelopment and political repression in the Third World).[35]

The following is a selection from the programme of passages relevant to the controversy over the party's social democratic features:

On the self-conception of the party: The programme sees a modern socialist party as a necessary component of a larger group of self-initiated grassroots movements.[36] "The PDS regards itself as an alliance of differing left forces. Its commitment to democratic socialism is not tied to any defined philosophical outlook, ideology or religion." It welcomes both people who totally reject capitalist society and those who "combine their opposition with the desire to change these relationships positively and overcome them step by step . . . The PDS believes that extra-parliamentary struggle is decisive for social changes . . . Like other parliamentary activities, local government activities can only be agents of social change if they are propelled by diverse extra-parliamentary actions." The PDS wants to see "the emergence of broad left movements . . . Critically aware of the legacy of Marx and Engels," the party wants to develop a highly pluralistic inner-party culture . . .

Critique of capitalism: "Together we hold the opinion that it is the capitalist character of modern society that is causally responsible for endangering human civilisation and culture, for the militarised character of international relations, for the crisis of the world ecosystem and for the indescribable misery to be found above all in the southern hemisphere . . . We are of one mind that the rule of capital must be overcome. Humankind must in an historically brief period find a way out of its hitherto destructive developmental logic . . . The root causes of these global problems [new world order, military intervention] are the capitalist mode of production, distribution and consumption as practised in the power centres of the world economy, together with the supremacy of patriarchy."

But then there is a formulation reflecting a strong reaction in the PDS, beginning in 1989, against official SED positions negating everything that has occurred under capitalism: "How to overcome this social structure by democratic means, while preserving and expanding its ability to be open to development and its civilising achievements – this is the most important contemporary challenge."

On socialism: "Beyond all differences of opinion we share the primary standpoint that the dominance of private capitalist property has to be ended. A range of property forms – private, cooperative, municipal and nationalised – are to be placed at the service of human requirements and the natural and social foundations of our lives. There are differing views as to whether real socialisation of property is best achieved by socialisation of control over [private] property or if conversion into common property, especially into property of the whole society, must play the decisive part."

Politics for the present: "democratising society": Here the programme presents a variety of general goals proposed apparently more or less to be realised at some point on the road to a socialist society involving radical democratic control of local institutions. It goes on to speak of rights of sexual orientation and other civil rights, expansion of constitutional rights, etc. The programme's preliminary measures and demands leading to socialist transformation are the kinds of proposals which draw the accusation of "social-democratic accommodationism," and, if an underlying drive to overcome capitalism is not maintained, could indeed deserve that accusation: The proposals for reorientation of the economy include various measures to set up radically democratic controls over the existing economic order and active government employment policies. It includes proposals to assist medium-size and small business, enlarge public municipal property, and "to put an end to the disadvantages of small shareholders, boost staff funds and give employees more stake in productive capital." The programme's proposals for agriculture include "the special promotion of cooperative property."

Regarding the full-employment controversy the programme demands "an economic policy aiming at full employment; just distribution of paid work; reduction of weekly and lifelong working time," etc. And it advocates "an increasing decoupling of social services from individually performed paid work." "We fight for a basic insurance oriented to people's needs for all age groups, calculated on average social income." And on East Germany specifically: "We stand for an elected East German Board, which can actively represent the interests of East Germans in partnership with Government and Parliament, and thus offer resistance to the erosion of the Reunification Treaty."

There are, further, interesting proposals for democratic control of academia and for the third world (debt forgiveness, redistribution of wealth, and overcoming of monocultures).

Internal criticism

The PDS has carried on a remarkable programme of self-searching, rather ruthless confrontation with the history of the SED, of the communist movement as a whole, and of self-analysis of the psychology and individual responsibility of everyone who had been a GDR citizen and especially a party member. No bi-weekly meeting of the 18-member federal directorate is allowed to go by without at least some of this analysis and discussion. It is also required in all the rank-and-file party organisations throughout the country. Even the liberal weekly *Die Zeit* said of the published papers of a recent PDS conference: "How many people, how many parties, will, on October 3rd, after three years of German unity, look back on the role they played before the *Wende*? The PDS does it in a noteworthily self-critical way. . . . Such a calling of oneself to account one could only wish for among the former Eastern CDU and the Eastern Liberals."[37]

From afar the statement of PDS-member Michail Nelken (a serious political thinker deeply concerned about the PDS) that the PDS will always be an old party because "the PDS represents the greatest concentration of the stratum of those who formerly exercised power in the GDR"[38] [i.e., it carries within it the leading layers of GDR society] sounds as if he is characterising the PDS as a party of the rulers of the GDR. In reality, since there is no question of the latter, he is reaching much deeper and calling for a self-criticism of the whole critically minded SED-intelligentsia, including himself, for having internalised, even if indirectly and subtly, the vanguardism of the SED's tradition.

Nelken declared in 1991 that the "renewal of the PDS has failed."[39] When I spoke with him in November 1993 he did not disown that statement although he acknowledged that the PDS had absorbed and put into practice radical-democratic ideas – in the composition of its leadership, and in its adoption of the most innovatingly democratic statute in Germany, largely drafted by himself! He pointed rather to the continuing need for self-analysis of the kind of subtle, internalised elitism almost inherent in the left by definition, including sincerely democratic leftists.

In 1993 Nelken referred to "the failure of the demands for an open approach to history in the PDS."[40] Yet Roswitha Steinbrenner, a member of the same loose tendency in the PDS, the *Strömung*,[41] to which Nelken belongs, acknowledges the PDS's extraordinary advances in this area and feels that Nelken's demands for this kind of self-criticism have largely been met. Since the PDS collectively bends over backwards to accommodate and publish such criticism it becomes particularly visible. One has the impression that most of the Strömung's demands have in fact been met. Rainer Börner, a former PDS member, said, on hearing of the results of the 1993 Berlin State Congress: "the Strömung has really won after all."[42] In 1993 Steinbrenner could say: "We have up until last year, still as the Strömung, achieved substantively quite a lot. Thus, we've gotten the history debate to go in a direction that really is near to our positions, that is, a thoroughly critical evaluation of the GDR past and one's own actions in that past."

One of the tendencies in the PDS against which the Strömung – and Kemnitz – fought was, in their opinion, an orientation to parliamentarism as primary and an insufficient appreciation of extra-parliamentary work. Steinbrenner said in 1993 that this has changed. "And I think, however, that state associations increasingly are also distancing themselves from parliamentary activity or from what is put forward as oppositional politics. Thus, . . . the Berlin state association clearly defined . . . what it understands by oppositional politics: clear anti-capitalist politics, . . . to make alternative media effective, together with non-parliamentary groups the organizing of self-representation . . ."

The 1994 Elections and Beyond

The 1990 and the 1994 federal elections in Germany have two qualitatively completely different meanings for the PDS, and two qualitatively different meanings for the West German left, such as it is. In 1990 it was still possible for leftists to interpret the PDS entry into the Bundestag as a one-time occurrence due to the special provisions made for two separate national electoral areas, i.e. one only needed to make the 5% hurdle in either the East or the West alone in order to be seated in the Bundestag. Further, the left theorised that the PDS was running on the last vestiges of its 1989–90 impulse, that it was a "discontinued model". But the PDS has increased its strength dramatically in the 1992 Berlin elections and the 1993 Brandenburg municipal elections. Recent polls show that it is possible that the PDS will get 5% nationwide.[43] But it does not need that to re-enter the Bundestag, for with the second vote each citizen has – for a person, not a party – the PDS can conceivably get 6–10 such direct mandates in several districts, and it only needs three of them to override the 5% hurdle. A likely victory in 1994 with the handicap of a single electoral area has a completely different meaning for the viability of the PDS than the 1990 elections did. The Green Party, moreover, will have a more left-liberal, less radical, profile in the next Bundestag than it did when last represented there. Obviously then, elements of the Western left will view the PDS somewhat differently.

INFAS (Institut für angewandte Sozialforschung, Bonn-Bad Godesberg), published an *East-Germany Report: Image of the PDS* in the ninth week of 1993. This indicated that a spectacular change of opinion had occurred in the previous months. The East-Germans selected responded as follows: To the question "should the PDS be equated with the former SED" (this is hammered into the population incessantly by the media) only 8% said "totally and completely" and 25% said "for the most part yes"; but 39% answered "for the most part no" and 17% said "not at all." INFAS asked East Germans their opinions on the PDS presence in the Bundestag. 21% had no opinion about the work PDS deputies were doing there; 39% felt they were "not doing good work"; but 40% said they were performing "good work." 29% thought the PDS should not be represented in the next Bundestag; but 58% said they should (28% had no opinion). Thus "a clear majority of the East Germans would be happy if the PDS were represented in the next Bundestag." People were asked whether "the PDS represented their interests as East Germans." 9% said "not at all", 27% said "not so strongly"; but 42% answered "strongly" and 10% said "very strongly." Thus about half look upon the PDS favourably in this regard. To the question whether the "PDS has a lasting place in the party system" 46% said no and 42% said yes (12% had no opinion).

The results of the Brandenburg municipal elections of December 1993 seem to have confirmed the findings of the INFAS poll.[44] There the PDS surpassed the CDU with 22% of the vote. The top results (45%) obtained by the PDS's mayoral candidate in Potsdam, moreover, was widely interpreted as demonstrating that campaigns designed to discredit individuals as Stasi collaborators no longer have an impact on the public.[45]

One of the reasons for the change in the climate of opinion regarding the PDS is that, for the consciously left constituency, it has become difficult to categorise the other principal non-establishment Eastern political grouping, Bü90, as a left force, and for the general population Bü90 shows too little interest in social issues. The politicised left constituency, cannot, for example, accept the Brandenburg Bü90's call for the extension of the activities of the West-German domestic intelligence agency into that state (each state legislature must formally approve the introduction of this agency into their territories), nor can it accept Konrad Weiss's (Bü90) suggestion of a possible coalition of Bü90 with the Saxon CDU. This constituency also has problems with Bü90's Bundestag group's hesitation in condemning the US invasion during the Gulf war, and the UN operations in Somalia, their ambivalence about the participation of German troops in UN actions, etc. Bü90's obsession with no-longer existing communist repression, the Stasi, etc. no longer strikes a sympathetic chord in the general population. This and their lack of participation in social struggles, with the exception of the Bischofferode hunger strike, has marginalised them as far as the general population is concerned.[46]

The other reason for the increased favour the PDS has begun to enjoy in the last two years in the East is its work among the population. The party is now generally perceived as playing the leading role in the East-German tenants organisation and in anti-Treuhand mobilisations. In the Bundestag it is seen as the strongest voice against weakening of the asylum law, for the total abolition of the West-German abortion clause, and is by far the strongest in opposing any involvement of the Bundeswehr abroad. In 1993 the party made spectacular advances in a series of trade-union struggles, most notably in the potassium miners strike in the Thuringian town of Bischofferode (which had voted heavily for the CDU in 1990). The sustained nature of PDS participation led to demonstrations of appreciation for the PDS there and to the miners asking Gysi to be their legal representative in Bonn.[47] Similar spectacular changes towards greater acceptance of the party took place during the labour struggles in Märkische Faser AG in Brandenberg and Belfa in Berlin. Even in the West, at the 17th Congress of the German Postal Workers Union, held in October 1993 the PDS got many more congress delegates to come to their event than did the SPD, something no one could have expected.[48]

The West-German Left's Reception of the PDS

a) The non-socialist Greens

After the West-German social movements, from which the Green Party drew its meaning and strength in the early 1980s, had waned, the politics of the Realo wing increasingly moved the party away from the socialist politics of the Hamburg Marxists who had exercised a strong influence within the Greens. By 1990 a group of Realos were exaggerating the interest shown by some Left Greens in the PDS, depicting it as a wish to merge the Greens with the latter. The rumour of a desired merger was used to scare people into passing an incompatibility declaration against not only the PDS but also against the GDR's United Left (VL) and against the GDR's Autonomous Women's Federation (UFV). It all came to a head at the April 1990 conference in Hagen. The motion proposed the exclusion of any cooperation with VL and PDS reformers no matter how the party evolved, along with an assertion of the incompatibility of the socialist tradition and Green politics.[49] The majority rejected it as too extreme.[50] But attempts to drive out the Left Greens continued, and it was inevitable that the latter should either join a broad electoral alliance with the PDS or the PDS itself, or go into other formations, such as the Radikale Linke. Rainer Trampert and Thomas Ebermann joined the latter, while Verena Krieger and Jürgen Reents, for example, joined the former. And the whole process accelerated the disintegration of the Greens as the main force on the left. By the December 1990 Bundestag elections the Green Party no longer could make the 5% electoral hurdle, and at present Green Party members are only in parliament via their electoral alliance with the Eastern citizen's groups and Eastern Greens.

The anti-communism of this part of the left has hindered any rational assessment of the PDS, and media close to the Greens have maintained an eerie silence on the PDS after the initial attacks. Michael Sontheimer, the new editor-in-chief of the *tageszeitung* (*taz*), the principal pro-Green daily, is trying to improve his newspaper's coverage of the PDS.[51]

b) West-German Left Marxist Groups

Less well-known than the anti-communism of the Greens and citizens movements are the set of attitudes found among some of West-Germany's most sophisticated Marxist intellectuals (in *Konkret* for example), specifically their allergy to "populism," which they define extraordinarily broadly, and their German self-hatred.

The extreme anti-nationalism leads to a type of cynical, symbolic non-politics. Demands had been raised in 1989 among the anti-nationalist group of Hamburg's Communist League[52] that the West-German left must be "anti-German,"[53] and the politics they proposed to express this was an international alliance which would have to "unquestionably comprehend even bourgeois, indeed even conservative opponents of the 'Fourth Reich'"; "The profile of the campaign would accordingly be rather anti-German than anti-imperialist."[54] And this thinking characterised a part of the Radikale Linke which was formed at the time the Left Greens withdrew from the Green Party in Winter-Spring 1990. This is summed up in the hope expressed that "the Germans perhaps will still catch up to the punishment which they have deserved for 45 years."[55] Thus, the Radikale Linke's politics amounted to saying "no" to a greater Germany after it obviously was an irreversible reality, and it consequently condemned any attempts to accept unification and try to improve the people's lot within it as shabby populism and nationalism. Such an outlook can only express itself in demonstrations and rallies having a merely symbolic purpose and devoid of any attempt to engage the population.

Even while predicting its potential rootedness in the population, the West-German left has nevertheless been able to dismiss the PDS on the grounds of its East-German regional character – as if the addition of a strongly rooted socialist force anywhere within the FRG's boundaries were not to be greeted, and as if this force could not, given time, have some impact on a Western socialist movement.[56] (It has been claimed that some Western PDS members, desperate for a political job, were at first extremely impatient with the PDS's eastern character and pushed for an unrealistically speedy assimilation to Western left conditions and views.)

The population is always essentially suspect in this milieu. First of all, the population's populism is associated only with right-wing varieties, e.g. Nazism, and secondly the core working-class is considered hopelessly in the arms of the SPD. If the population votes for the PDS that is proof that the PDS and the population is conservative. Any attempt to reach them is "opportunistic shit," any attempt to do something for the people in the here and now is "social-democratic," any wavering from purist positions aimed at the ultimate socialist goals will lead to one's joining the SPD. There is a natural law operating by which every attempt to wage politics ends in social-democracy. If the PDS petitions for observer status in the SI this is proof of their hopeless and inexorable slide into "social-democratic opportunism," and there is no need to examine their programme or politics in any detail at all.[57] Michael Mäde, anti-Stalinist victim of SED persecution and VL member who sees his role as a left gadfly to the PDS, chided the Western left for the excuses it finds to not deal with the PDS: "And then there is the accusation, on the part of radical-left circles, of social-democratization. And the Federal Republic's left, which itself shows a certain closeness to social democracy, is, when the PDS theme is brought up, always given to pulling out a magnifying glass: and guess what! they also find a little Stalinism there, if you please!"[58]

The PDS: Dilemma and Opportunity

The dilemma of the PDS then has essentially to do with its closeness to the Eastern population. This is both a problem for the party and an obvious advantage. The problem is that many in the population, which often displays an unconscious closeness to the PDS, a love-hate relationship, want a traditionally "Eastern" political force to paternalistically protect them. This tends to pull especially the regional PDS in a pragmatic and populist direction. On the other hand, the party strives to be radical. The party has, for example, been asked by the Eastern Lutheran organisation to represent its interests as against what they consider the encroachments of the Western Lutheran association. In Gysi's words: "we are a left party, but we are also an East party." This is reflected in the style and appearance of the party at rallies and congresses, where a young, radical-looking leadership, and other young activists, contrasts with a more conservatively dressed and mannered base. But the "normal" population itself may become more oppositional through the West's imposition of "Stalinist-textbook capitalism."

One thinks of a dilemma also in connection with party property: on the one hand, the initial extensive assets the party inherited from the Weimar KPD and the GDR SED engendered distrust and resentment from the citizens movements and much of the Eastern population (although less so from the Western left), and the consequent expropriation-harassment distracted the party from political work. (To be sure, it is doubtful whether the party could have avoided harassment in general by re-founding itself.) On the other hand, most of those who favoured a new foundation in 1989–90 (which would have meant renunciation of assets) now feel the party could not have done as well as it did in the early elections and have carried out the public activities and rallies that it did without the financial assets of its incipient phase and the consequent ability to do effective publicity work.[59] I found near unanimity among these people by the end of 1993 that a new foundation would have caused most of the present older rank-and-file members to leave and that the present party, totally self-financed out of their dues which support a radical young leadership and its ideas, would probably not exist. The irony is that some of the party's severest critics, including those who have called for it to give up all of its assets, hope that the party will get back into the Bundestag in 1994, a possibility that probably would not exist if the party had earlier done what they demanded. There was another reason not to re-found, and this must be taken seriously: the importance of *keeping* continuity with the SED in order to give people an "address" where they can deal with the problems of the GDR and SED past, and where responsibility, including legal responsibilities in certain matters, can rest, and also where one can confront the history of ruling parties in states like the GDR. It is thus beginning to look as though the decision to keep some of the infrastructure and assets was a sound one. Additionally, if the PDS had immediately given up the publishing firm ZENTRAG, it is doubtful whether *Neues Deutschland*, the largest supra-national Eastern paper of the left or right (which was rescued from extinction by a campaign involving a variety of non-sectarian leftists, including people very critical of the PDS), could have weathered the period. The association with SED assets has proven also not to be an eternal burden, as witnessed by the fact that it has not prevented the PDS, after four years, from getting creditable electoral results, as well as the more general credibility the INFAS "Image of the PDS" poll revealed.

Finally, on the party's relationship to the population, Roswitha Steinbrenner conveys something of the essence of the PDS project, which differentiates it from the citizens movements and most West-German left groups in its tolerance for the normal conservative or apolitical citizen. The fear the progressive German intelligentsia has of populism, for obvious historical reasons, has worked to distance much of the German left from broader layers of the population. It is particularly significant that Steinbrenner, a radical feminist, anti-populist, social-movement activist

and member of the Strömung, the group most critical of conservative or
nostalgic tendencies in party members, displays an appreciation of the
decency and progressive potential of much of the population and of the
older PDS rank-and-file so often dismissed by social-movement critics:

I also get the objection from the Autonomous Women's Federation (UFV) that the party
has a great program, but the members don't stand behind it. And then I say: perhaps they
haven't fully understood or read it, but as long as they tolerate it it's okay. There really is a
tolerance there on the part of the members for this statute and for this program. Because
otherwise people would withdraw. And what is productive in this membership mix is that
one is forced to permanently question positions that one has developed, that one remains
continually in discussion . . . I think that, in contrast to the majority of former GDR
citizens, they question their own actions and their own past critically . . . They are shy
about bringing all this self-criticism before the public, but the thinking is already a new one,
and also their actions. I can't change people's consciousness if I only act for myself and if I
deal with all others as per se conservative and incapable of movement, because that's not
the way people are. People act on their own concerns, and I think the Greens in the 60s and
80s in the old FRG have shown us, with ecological consciousness, how one can really
change people's behaviour . . . But we've also experienced this capacity for change in the
GDR. In 1945 the level of consciousness of people in the East and the West was not
different. And I think that such human values that did exist in the GDR, such as the sense
of responsibility for others and for society as a whole, for example, a social way of thinking,
that is, to let no one fall through the net . . . or the sensitivity to violence in families – there
was significantly less violence in families, because they were publicly criticized and because
the neighbors, for example, involved themselves when children were beaten or if women
were beaten – that didn't happen over night. A social debate on such problems was
initiated, and it changed consciousness, possibly not deeply enough, otherwise many East
Germans wouldn't be living as they are now living, that is, using their elbows again. But it
did exist. Those who are today again using their elbows and who grew up in this country, in
the GDR, are doing it with a bad conscience. Who does it in the West with a bad
conscience? So, I think these are examples showing that it is worth carrying out a social
debate on alternatives regardless of alleged human nature.
    It makes no sense constantly to block people with verbal radicalism and insult them,
rather than really to go to them and ask "where does your problem lie, and where do you
see the causes for your problem, and can you imagine that the causes you see may not at all
be the causes?" But that has to be done carefully, and it has to be done steadily, with
participation, with visible action . . . you have to meet people where they are, you can't
curse that they are where they are. Because somehow they got there, and it's also your own
failing that they're there. The East German population is indeed very contradictory in its
actions, and it is, to a great extent, our fault, the fault of the PDS as successor to the
SED . . . It's also important for those of us remaining from the Strömung to understand
that you can't get victories overnight.[60]

Perhaps the PDS is *the* hope for German socialism or perhaps it will help
rekindle a left movement and disappear into it. Perhaps it will not even
have that measure of success. But the present essay makes clear that the
PDS has weathered the storms thus far, defying earlier predictions of its
imminent demise, and has by now politically turned a decisive corner. It
appears to be an electorally viable socialist organisation and could be the
first large political force to the left of social-democracy in central Europe
since the Weimar Republic, with large implications for the world socialist
movement. Whether it survives the next couple of decades or not, it is
novel and important enough finally to be the object of more energetic
interest and investigation on the part of the international left.

NOTES

1. Günter Minnerup, "Freedom in East Germany: Opening up a New Europe?", *The Nation*, December 4, 1989, p. 673.
2. The last reflection of this was the slogan of the citizens movements during the *Wende*: "Bleibe im Land und wehre dich täglich!" (Stay in the country and defend yourself daily).
3. Jonathan Steele, *Inside East Germany: The State that Came in from the Cold*. New York: Urizen, c1977, p. 46; and Wolfgang Leonhard, *Child of the Revolution*. New York: Gateway, 1967, pp. 446–447.
4. Klaus Hartung, "SED-BASIS auf der Strasse: Grundorganisationen vor dem ZK-Gebäude fordern Parteitag," *taz*, Nov 10, 1990, p. 94.
5. Conversation with Lothar Bisky, November 17, 1993.
6. *Neues Deutschland*, February 1, 1990.
7. *Ibid.*, January 20/21, 1990; and Heinrich Bortfeldt, *Von der SED zur PDS – Aufbruch zu neuen Ufern? controvers. Diskussionsangebot der PDS* Berlin 1990, p. 28.
8. Ibid p. 30.
9. *Ibid.*, p. 30.
10. *Neues Deutschland*, January 27/28, 1990.
11. Among the earliest intra-party factions, the Social-Democratic Platform essentially disappeared at the time of the "Berghofer Syndrome." The "Third-Way" Platform was also dissolved, though some of its members have become prominent in the PDS now. Today only the Communist Platform continues to exist. The latter cannot be dismissed as Stalinist, although it certainly includes such people. Its processes are highly democratic; it played a major role in the early history of PDS reform; and it stressed gay/lesbian and feminist liberation, etc.
12. A respectable case can be made, however, to show that the Modrow regime's policies constituted the last attempt to inject positive features into what was by then an inevitable German unification.
13. *Neues Deutschland* June 18, 1990, cited in Knut Mellenthin, "PDS: Kein Frieden mit dem Kapital," *arbeiterkampf* 320 (June 25, 1990), p. 6.
14. *Ibid.*
15. Conversation with Hanno Harnisch, PDS Press Secretary, Berlin, November 22, 1993.
16. In June 1991 the trusteeship moved to confiscate even current membership dues! This was done while much of the left was on vacation to avoid protests, and its illegality was quite unambiguous.
17. In answer to fantasies about "foreign SED millions" the PDS Press-Secretary, Hanno Harnisch, said in a conversation in Berlin on November 22, 1993: "Then as now there could be a firm in Switzerland, even now, some journalists say. But if such firms exist then they haven't the slightest connection to the PDS. The proof is that we really gave over notarially to the Federal Republic all claims on old assets abroad. So that even if a firm should still be there, about which we do not know, and which is still doing business, they don't do it to the benefit of our bank account, and then the owner would be either the manager there or the Federal Republic. The party has no knowledge of and no claims on such firms. And no access, and it doesn't want access."
18. Unless otherwise indicated all figures from: *INFAS-Report DDR 1990. Wahl der Volkskammer der DDR am 18. März 1990. Analysen und Dokumente*. Bonn-Bad Godesberg, March 1990 (which includes INFAS Deutschland-Politogramm 6-7/1990 (Wahltagbefragung am 18. März 1990)); and from a study by the AG "Analyse," cited by Bortfeldt, *op. cit.*, (fn. 38): *Meinungsforschung zur Volkskammerwahl* (Manuscript) Berlin, March 26, 1990. MFS = Mannheimer Forschungsgruppe Wahlen. These figures are quoted in Knut Mellenthin, "PDS der DDR – eine Herausforderung für die BRD-Linke," *arbeiterkampf* 318, (April 30, 1990), p. 12.
19. The youthful appearance of the PDS's major electoral rallies, etc. indicates the reluctance of such young people formally to join this, or any, party. On the difficulties all German parties face regarding youth recruitment see Ingo Preusker, "Vom Gängelband befreit: Die PDS hat anderen Parteien eins voraus: den Mut zur Verjüngung," *Wochenpost*, January 13, 1994.

20. Bortfeldt, *op. cit.*, p. 39.
21. Interview with Uwe Lehmann and Petra Pau (PDS), *Freitag*, June 5, 1992, p. 4.
22. On the December 1993 Brandenburg municipal elections see INFAS poll summarized in *Sächsische Zeitung*, December 7, 1993; and Michael Müller, "Weniger Testwahl, dafür vielleicht Signal für Systemkritik," *Neues Deutschland*, December 7, 1993. On voter migration in May 1992 in Berlin see *tageszeitung*, May 26, 1992.
23. Armin Pfahl-Traughaber, "Wo steht die PDS? Versuch einer extremismusorientierten Einschätung," *liberal* March 1993, pp. 6–8. (*liberal* is the party journal of the FDP.). This and Patrick Moreau's book are apparently the only non-left studies on the PDS. Moreau is close to French foreign intelligence circles and writes on terrorism and intelligence. See Patrick Moreau, *PDS: Anatomie einer postkommunistischen Partei*. Bonn: Bouvier, 1992 (Schriftenreihe Extremismus und Demokratie, Vol. 3). Moreau equates the PDS with the SED and believes it would effect the same policies if it came to power.
24. Occasionally, however, the national directorate makes an exception and discusses a problem in closed session, and always attracts party criticism for this.
25. ISDA – Institut für Sozialdatenanalyse, *Forschungsbericht: Strukturen, politische Aktivitäten und Motivationen in der PDS. Mitgliederbefragung der PDS 1991*. Berlin, June 1991. This East-Berlin-based institute occasionally collaborates with the West-German EMNID polling organization on "Sonntagsfragen."
26. *ISDA-Studie Nr. 11. Im Blick: Wahlen '94. Soziologische Zielgruppenanalyse*. Berlin, June 1993, p. 4. See also *Der Spiegel*, February 21, 1994, p. 39, 42–43.
27. Michael Sontheimer ("Der Osten wählt rot," *taz* December 7, 1993) claims that the 1990 CDU vote was a one-time exception to a structural left (including the SPD) electorate in the East.
28. *ISDA Im Blick: Wahlen '94*, p. 28.
29. *Ibid.*, p. 31–32.
30. A somewhat myopic attention to programme has had this effect on the only two substantial articles on the PDS in English: Gus Fagan, "The Party of Democratic Socialism," *Labour Focus on Eastern Europe* 41/1 (1992), pp. 30ff.; and John Rosenthal, "On the Long Road to the Third Way? The Second Party Congress of the PDS," *Socialism and Democracy*, 13 (May 1991), pp. 7ff. Although neither article displays the emotionally-charged abhorrence of the PDS typical of much of the West-German left, both end by dismissing the PDS as reformist or accommodationist, or as probably developing in that direction.
31. *PDS-Pressedienst* 1991, No. 26 (June 28), p. 9–10.
32. Conversation with Roswitha Steinbrenner, November 24, 1993.
33. Kemnitz still criticizes an excessive respect for legality in PDS trade-union work. (private communication, January 12, 1994).
34. See André Brie's history of this process in *Disput* 3/4 (Sonderausgabe) 1993, pp. 32ff.
35. *Im Blick: Wahlen '94*, (see fn 34), p. 41.
36. *Programme of the Party of Democratic Socialism*, Berlin, 1993, p. 30. (Translation occasionally corrected by the author from original in *Disput* 3/4 (February 1993), pp. 36ff). All citations, in what follows, are taken from this publication.
37. "Bonner Bühne: Wo bleibt der Mensch?," *Die Zeit*, August 27, 1993.
38. From Dieter Reichelt's summary of the history debate of the first session of the third party congress on 26/27 June 1993 in *Disput* 13/14, 1993, p. 54.
39. See Wolfgang Sabath, "Immer wieder Gehversuche: Vom 2. Parteitag der PDS," *Freitag* June 28, 1991, p. 4.
40. Reichelt, *op. cit.* Again, this is Reichelt's paraphrase. Nelken announced his intention to publish a reply to Michael Schumann's paper on the subject.
41. The Strömung [="tendency"] was a loose conglomeration of critics in the PDS. Politically it ranges from people with less of a class-based social-movement politics to people with more of a feel for class politics, but certain left critics who are especially worried by "abandonment of class politics," like Thomas Kuczynski and Sonja Kemnitz, were never in the Strömung. Strömung figures still in the PDS include Nelken, Steinbrenner, Thomas Nord and Judith Delheim.
42. Conversation with Roswitha Steinbrenner, Berlin November 24, 1993. All citations from Steinbrenner are from this conversation.

43. Starting in September 93 the PDS got its first 5% result from polls taken of Western and Eastern citizens regarding their party choice for the 1994 Bundestag elections. By January 1994 5% results became more frequent, the range being from 3% to 5.3% in January–February 1994. Polls in the West alone show a rise from ca. 0.3% to 2%.

44. Before the major electoral breakthrough for the PDS in December 1993 in Brandenburg (see below) the May 24, 1992 municipal elections in Berlin represented the first turning point. The PDS got 29.7% of the East Berlin vote. (from INFAS's preliminary results published in *Frankfurter Rundschau*, May 26, 1992). But, with still higher percentages, the PDS became the strongest party in five East-Berlin districts. (Lichtenberg (35.5%), Marzahn (34.9%), Hellersdorf (30.9%), Hohenschönhausen (35.5%), Mitte (35.8%). (From preliminary official results, *Berliner Zeitung*, May 26, 1992).

45. Further statistics contradict the theory that the PDS got only protest votes. Michael Müller, in *Neues Deutschland*, refers to an INFAS poll (more fully covered i the *Sächsische Zeitung*, December 7, 1993) in Brandenburg according to which 28% of the unemployed voted for the PDS (SPD: 34%). He points out that protest votes always come overwhelmingly from people in relatively secure situations. Michael Müller, "Weniger Testwahl, dafür vielleicht Signal für Systemkritik," *Neues Deutschland*, December 7, 1993. And the ISDA study on the 1994 elections shows that the unemployed, when they do vote at all, vote fearfully and pragmatically. Konrad Weiss, a leading figure of Democracy Now and Bü90, issued a call on December 6 to deny the PDS any cooperation "as a matter of political hygiene."

46. Gr/Bü90's lack of concern with social issues is reflected in the opinions of their electorate, half of which, according to ISDA's study, think the workers should bear *more* burdens. (ISDA: *Im Blick: Wahlen '94.*, p. 33.)

47. See Hannah Behrend, "Social Struggles After Unification," *New Politics* IV, 4 (Winter 1994), pp. 119–121.

48. There were ca. 600 delegates. One evening of such congresses is customarily set aside as a *party evening*. Parties have always regarded these as important barometers, especially in pre-election periods. The organisers of the congress themselves noted during the preparation for the congress that the PDS Party Evening was stimulating "an extraordinary interest." Only 250 seats were optimistically prepared, but 380 came, and they were without exception congress delegates. In contrast to this, the SPD got about 250 congress delegates, but they directed their invitations strongly towards the local party prominence, invited their whole rank and file and hired a dance band and famous performers, so that 800 people in all came. The Gr/Bü90 evening attracted 30 people, that of the CDU 60. (The FDP did not participate.) The delegates attending the PDS evening included a striking proportion of young and female colleagues. The evening was much more characterised by direct, engaged substantive political discussion than the SPD evening was. (Gerd Graw, "17. Kongress der Deutschen Postgewerkschaft: Konflikt zwischen Arbeit und Kapital," *betrieb & gewerkschaft* 9 (November 1993) [bulletin of the PDS Task Force on Factories and Unions], p. 23ff.)

49. Ralf Fücks, a representative of this part of the Realo wing, admitted in a *Volkszeitung* interview (March 30, 1990) that cooperation with the PDS could be very positive for a socialist project: with "16% for the rennovated PDS, a simpatico media star like Gysi, an honourable figure like Modrow, a professional apparatus, several hundred thousand members – doesn't that open new pan-German perspectives for the left? The potential is there, also in the Federal Republic – left social-democrats, purged DKP members, oppositional trade-unionists, homeless 68ers. Whether such an alliance could survive does not concern us. Perhaps it is historically necessary in the sense of one last attempt to save the socialist project. He who wants to do so should – but please not with the Greens. Ecological politics is a new beginning opposed to traditional directions and goals, not a continuation of socialist politics by other means. A political alliance with the PDS would be the end of the Green Party."

50. After a majority of the delegates refused to so categorically limit future alliance possibilities to the Greens, New Forum and the UFV, a left resolution succeeded in being adopted with the support of critical Realos which stated that the Greens do not wish "to ignore the originally radical-democratic and humanistic content of the socialist world of ideas," despite its discrediting through SED rule.

51. Conversation with Michael Sontheimer, December, 1993.
52. A part of the now defunct Kommunistischer Bund played an important role in the growth of the Green Party, and its still surviving monthly journal, *arbeiterkampf* (*ak*) is a forum of debate and analysis on a level much higher than its name ("workers' struggle") would lead English-speaking readers familiar with the names of sectarian periodicals to expect. An article by Knut Mellenthin appears in *ak* 318 (April 30, 1990): "PDS der DDR – eine Herausforderung für die BRD-Linke," (pp. 12ff). It remains the most penetrating treatment of the underlying resistance of West-German Marxists to the PDS and the most sober consideration of the PDS, especially remarkable for its time. I have drawn heavily on it in this section on the Western Marxists' relation to the PDS.
53. Jürgen, "Weshalb die Linke anti-deutsch sein muss," *ak* 315 (February 5, 1990), pp. 32ff.
54. Jürgen, "Mit Schönhuber gegen die Alliierten," *ak* 314 (January 8, 1990), pp. 17ff.
55. Wolfgang Pohrt, "Spiel mit verteilten Rollen," *konkret* (April 1990), pp. 69ff. Or see Detlef zum Winkel's wish that Germany itself might finally be destroyed: "Ceterum censeo," (*konkret* (January 1990), pp. 21ff.
56. See Gus Fagan, "The Party of Democratic Socialism," *Labour Focus on Eastern Europe* 41/1 (1992), p. 36.
57. Declaration of withdrawal of the Hamburg Eco-socialists and Linksradikaler from the GAL, April 6, 1990: "Wir verlassen die Grüne Partei," (*konkret* May 1990), p. 22; and Georg Fülberth (Ex-DKP) and Siggi Fries (Bundestag deputy of the Greens), "Auf Honecker einen Noske?," (*konkret* May 1990), pp. 24ff. In their article they even fleetingly count the votes of the PDS and the SPD together for the election of March 18, 1990.
58. Mäde in *ak* 319 (28. Mai 1990), p. 21.
59. Interviews conducted by the author in November 1993 in Berlin.
60. Conversation with Roswitha Steinbrenner, Berlin November 24, 1993.